DIRT, GREED, & SEX

DIRT, GREED, & SEX

Sexual Ethics in the New Testament
and Their Implications for Today

REVISED EDITION

L. WILLIAM COUNTRYMAN

FORTRESS PRESS

MINNEAPOLIS

DIRT, GREED, & SEX
Sexual Ethics in the New Testament and Their Implications for Today

Cover design: Kevin van der Leek
Book design: Danielle Carnito

Library of Congress Cataloging-in-Publication Data

Countryman, Louis William, 1941-
  Dirt, greed, and sex : sexual ethics in the New Testament and their implications for today / L. William Countryman.—Rev. ed.
    p. cm.
  Includes bibliographical references and index.
  ISBN-13: 978-0-8006-6224-0 (alk. paper)
  ISBN-13: 978-0-8006-3848-1 (alk. paper)
  1. Sex in the Bible. 2. Sexual ethics—History. 3. Sex customs—History.
4. Bible. N.T.—Criticism, interpretation, etc. I. Title.
  BS2545.S36C68 2007b
  241'.6609015—dc22

                                                                    2007026478

The paper used in this publication meets the minimum requirements of American National Standard for Information Sciences — Permanence of Paper for Printed Library Materials, ANSI Z329.48-1984.

Manufactured in the U.S.A.

11   10   09   08   07   1   2   3   4   5   6   7   8   9   10

IN MEMORIAM

Frederick Arthur Countryman

CONTENTS

PREFACE

TO THE

SECOND EDITION

The first edition of *Dirt, Greed, and Sex* has played a continuing role in discussions of human sexuality over the past eighteen years in both the academy and Christian communities of faith. I am gratified that it found audiences in both venues because I aimed to write in a way that would be clear for academic audiences (and therefore open to argument, refutation, or even perhaps verification) and also accessible to the wider audience that is deeply involved and concerned with these complex and controversial topics.

I hoped that the book would contribute to encouraging discussion of sexuality between biblical scholars and ethicists, something that has indeed been happening. In practice, the link I offered to Christian ethicists proved somewhat difficult for them to respond to because their own conversations, at that point, had moved away from discussion of the goodness or badness of specific acts (which is the way the scriptural material tends to be framed) and toward issues of character or virtue ethics. It is a problem endemic to interdisciplinary work to find that the disciplines one is trying to connect are themselves moving in unrelated directions, but such work is not the less necessary for that. And I have been told by many ethicists that it did not deprive the book of value for them.

My hope that the book might also serve as an opportunity for discussion between "liberals" and "conservatives" in the Christian communities has been largely disappointed. I have never been at home with either label. I am, I suppose, a "conservative" by principle whose devotion to scripture has more than once led me in directions considered "liberal" by others. I would like to see both definitions dissolve so that we could discuss difficult topics on their merits rather than as members of partisan groups that push one another into becoming sworn enemies. "Liberals," however, sometimes found *Dirt, Greed, and Sex* perplexing; they could not figure out why anyone would spend that much energy on what the Bible says about sex. And the more partisan sorts of "conservatives" immediately dismissed the book's conclusions because they did not square with their predetermined reading of the Bible. The few scholars who have responded to the book from conservative evangelical perspectives have tended to ignore or sidestep its principal arguments.

Alongside this disappointment, however, I have made the positive discovery of how many people in the Christian churches and the academy found that the work opened up new prospects of reading scripture. Christians can still read scripture in the expectation that God will surprise us with good news, even through texts we have read so often that we thought their potential for meaning was exhausted. The dialogue for which I hoped has indeed emerged in ways I could not have predicted.

The present edition of *Dirt, Greed, and Sex* does not represent a radical change in my conclusions. But it benefits from work done by many scholars since it first appeared. It includes aspects of the subject that I omitted from the original work because they seemed to me much less central in determining scriptural approaches to sexual ethics than the two central concerns for purity and property. I am now persuaded that they deserve more specific treatment, partly by reason of their importance to the overall scriptural narrative and partly because they have been significant in modern controversies. I could perhaps expand the title to accommodate their addition: *Dirt, Greed, Other Things, and Sex*. But I remain convinced that purity and property are the central considerations behind the ancient sexual ethics inherited and reshaped by the New Testament writers.

I could willingly have allowed the original edition of *Dirt, Greed, and Sex* to remain an artifact of its own time—perhaps even a "classic," as one reissue kindly christened it. My own propensity as a scholar has typically been to move on to another topic of interest once I have completed a book. I am perhaps more of an explorer by temperament than an archeologist, more interested in pursuing other connections than in settling down on one topic to learn everything I possibly can about it.

Two reasons, however, prompt me to return to this book for the purpose of revision. One is the ongoing importance of sexual ethics in the Christian communities. The level of anger and venom in these conflicts has actually grown with the passing years. If there is any way to reinforce the embattled prospects of reasonable discourse about scripture and sexuality, it seems incumbent upon anyone who hopes to be found a good citizen of the church (and, God willing, of the age to come) to make some contribution to that cause.

Second, while many have written valuable contributions to the study of these topics over the intervening years, no one has apparently found the vocation (or perhaps the temerity) to attempt a comparable overview of sexual ethics in scripture. We find broad treatments of "New Testament ethics," with chapters on sexual issues, or more narrowly focused treatments of "the Bible and homosexuality." I doubt that there is any constructive way to talk about the latter topic without broadening the field of vision to sexual ethics in general. But when sexual ethics becomes a subheading of New Testament ethics generally, there is seldom the time or space to look at them as closely as we need to.

For me as a scholar, a teacher, a priest, and a person of faith, this is not the central project of my life or even of my scholarship, but it is probably the one by which I have been most widely known. For a person who is anything but fond of conflict, this has sometimes been problematic. But God, it seems, conveys the message of the gospel by whatever means catch people's attention in a given era. In this regard, I am thankful that this work has not only prompted thought but has also proved a source of new life, faith, and hope for many. The Spirit does things her own way. I am also grateful for the way in which the initial writing of the work pushed me into interdisciplinary ways of working and thinking, habits that have stuck with me and made my life as a scholar more interesting and productive. Perhaps the creation of this second edition is as much a way of expressing gratitude as anything else.

In addition to the acknowledgments expressed in the preface to the first edition of this work, I wish to add my thanks to the innumerable partners in conversation who have kept me thinking and rethinking issues of sexual ethics and spirituality over the intervening years—a group too numerous to name. The long and sometimes tedious work of revision would have been impossible without the excellent resources of the Flora Lamson Hewlett Library at the Graduate Theological Union and the generous granting of sabbaticals by the Board of the Church Divinity School of the Pacific in 2004 and 2006. I thank Neil Elliott of Fortress Press for getting the project back on track when it had almost lapsed. I thank the Rev. Thomas Schultz, OHC, for ongoing encouragement and the clergy and people of Good Shepherd Episcopal Church in Berkeley for their shared love of the gospel. I particularly thank my partner Jon for the life together that sustains me in all my work.

PREFACE

TO THE

FIRST EDITION

It was very far from my mind to write a book on sexual ethics until the autumn of 1985, when I was asked to give some lectures on the topic. It has been, of course, very much in the air for some time both in the churches and among the larger public, and one frequently hears claims that the Bible says this or that about sexual ethics. I had reason to suspect that some of those claims needed re-examining, for I had begun to wrestle in my own mind with the question of early Christian attitudes toward sexual property a good many years ago, largely as a result of my study of the rich in early Christianity. I had also begun to include discussion of New Testament teachings on sex in my courses, but I did not immediately recognize that the various insights I had garnered actually formed a coherent picture.

The picture that emerged was of a twofold sexual ethic inherited and transformed by the New Testament authors. One part of it was a property ethic; its cardinal sin was greed, leading one to trespass on one's neighbor's property. The other part was a purity ethic, against which the fundamental offense was—well, it is difficult to say in modern English. We are accustomed to refer to it in academic language as "impurity" or "uncleanness." Yet these terms, indispensable as they are, have an air of academic remoteness about them; they do not convey a sense of the visceral impact, the repugnance felt toward those things a given society has defined as "dirty." Hence, I have written somewhat indiscriminately here of "impurity," "uncleanness," and "dirt"— varying manifestations of the same phenomenon. Modern American definitions of what is "dirty" lack the precision or coherence of those still to be found in Leviticus, but only by using the common term can we form some impression—even a pallid one—of the emotional force of ancient purity codes.

The present book owes a great deal to the opportunity I was given of putting my reflections in order when I was asked to lecture on the subject, first to the college chaplains of Province VIII (the Pacific province) of the Episcopal Church at San Francisco in January 1986, and then to the national convention of Integrity, the gay-lesbian caucus of the Episcopal Church, in Minneapolis the following summer. Thanks to a sabbatical leave from the Church Divinity School of the Pacific, I was able to devote the fall semester of 1986 to writing the first draft of this book. I owe great thanks to the school and its trustees for that opportunity. I owe thanks also to all those in Austin, Texas, who made me welcome there during that time, including the rector and people of All Saints parish and the faculty and staff of the Episcopal Theological Seminary of the Southwest, particularly those connected with its library and the library of Christ Seminary Seminex, sojourning there. Without the encouragement and support of these groups, I could not have proceeded so rapidly to completion of this project.

I also owe a great debt of thanks to the friends and colleagues who read all or parts of the manuscript and whose critiques have improved it substantially: Linda Clader, Howard Miller, Donn Morgan, Paul Strid, and Penelope Warren. Their varied expertise and careful reading have saved me from pitfalls I was unprepared to see and, I hope, ensured that the book will be intelligible to an audience including but spreading beyond the New Testament scholarly community. I must also thank John A. Hollar of Fortress Press and those who read portions of the manuscript for the press, Jacob Neusner as well as the other, anonymous readers. They all gave both encouragement and many helpful suggestions about clarifying the book's scope and argument. Finally, I owe an incalculable debt to many partners in dialogue over the years whom I could not even begin to name, who have challenged me to explore and clarify the matters discussed here. Needless to say, only I can be held responsible for whatever faults the reader may still find in my treatment of the subject. My responsibility extends to the translations of biblical texts, as well, which are my own except where otherwise indicated.

My great goal throughout has been to present a faithful reading of the pertinent biblical texts, even if that should at times prove uncongenial to one or another group today—or quite different from what I myself expected. If I have succeeded in that, I believe that I shall have offered a useful addition to the ongoing discussion of sexual ethics in our time. If not, I trust that I shall at least have stimulated the kind of careful and dispassionate study by others that will carry the investigation further.

L. William Countryman
The Church Divinity School of the Pacific
Graduate Theological Union
Berkeley, California
12th Sunday after Pentecost, 1987

Disputes about gender and sex are rife in our world, and the Bible has often been an important factor in them. Some voices invoke it as an authority; others attack it as a baleful influence. Some hold that it prescribes a clear-cut sexual ethic; others hear in it a multiplicity of sometimes conflicting messages. The one thing we can be sure of is that those who study scripture do not all agree with one another and that people can invoke the Bible on behalf of a variety of contemporary positions. Such a situation calls for fresh and careful reading of the scriptures. We should read *afresh*, in the sense of not assuming that we know in advance everything the text has to say. We also should read *carefully*, in the sense of attending closely to the details of the text, particularly those that seem odd or alien in terms of our presuppositions.

The present book first arose out of my efforts, in the early 1980s, to do just this. I did, inevitably, bring some presuppositions to the reading. One was that the New Testament authors regarded the subject of sexuality as peripheral and were unlikely to offer more than scattered and uncoordinated moral pronouncements on sexual issues. Another was that the biblical authors as a whole were negative toward sex and regarded it, as do many post-biblical Christian writers, as something to be avoided or, at most, permitted only under narrowly defined circumstances. In both cases, I found that close study of these texts modified my understanding of the matter sharply and in directions that I could not have predicted.

Two things were particularly responsible for this outcome. The first was that I made every effort to read the texts as literally as possible. If a text seemed to be expressing a familiar idea in a clumsy or awkward way, I began to consider whether the seeming awkwardness might in fact express some unfamiliar idea that only close attention to the language could reveal. In many cases, this process forced me to reevaluate familiar passages in unexpected ways. The second was that, in studying a variety of texts from different biblical authors, I found a certain shared stock of language, presuppositions, and concerns significantly different from those that usually frame modern discussions of these same topics. Where we are likely to think of sexual ethics in terms of personal relationships, power differentials, fidelity, and so forth, the biblical writers think primarily in terms of purity and of property.

The result of this kind of study was to direct attention to neglected features of individual texts and also to place the whole topic in a different historical, religious, and cultural context—one more familiar to the times in which the biblical documents were written. This last element has proven difficult for some readers. Contemporary people in general, given the ease of travel in our time and the increasingly multiethnic makeup of most nation-states, are used to the idea that human cultures vary significantly from one another; but that does not always mean that it is easy for us to shift into another cultural perspective. And we are used to thinking of the biblical texts as part of our own culture, forgetting that they emerged in a very different world two thousand and more years ago. Insofar as Christians look to the scriptures for a timeless message, we are sometimes reluctant to admit that there is also a very time-bound element in them.

There is no easy way, of course, to get inside the perspective of another culture; and the problem is even more difficult when the culture in question has no living exemplars to whom we might address questions. The documentation left to us from antiquity is often meager and unrepresentative. For the Mediterranean world of Late Antiquity (roughly 300 B.C.E. to 300 C.E.), almost all our written documents come from males of high social and educational status. The New Testament writers are less elite than others, but still male.[1] The writings we have naturally deal with the sorts of things that interested such persons, omitting much else. They also assume plenty of practical knowledge of the culture—a knowledge we must now try to reconstruct largely by reading between the lines of texts, with occasional help from archeology. What we cannot presume, as we begin this study, is that human sexuality will have been precisely the same thing for people in the first century as it is for us.[2] We have to remain open to surprise.

What I write here is in the tradition of biblical theology, and because this imposes a certain character (and accompanying limitations) on this book, it will be helpful to say a few words in explanation. To begin, let me distinguish it in a very rough way from some other ways of doing theology. Systematic theology begins with issues and questions contemporary with the theologian and justifies its answers in terms of the theologian's philosophical presuppositions and of their continuity with the Christian tradition. Dogmatic theology begins with various schemata of Christian orthodoxy enunciated from the second century onward and tends to claim authenticity primarily from its coherence with those authoritative statements. Biblical theology, on the other hand, begins with the biblical texts themselves. Because these antedate the clarification of Christian dogma that began with the Gnostic controversies of the second century and have little interest in philosophical coherence, they reflect on the faith and experience of their ancient religious communities. Biblical theology seeks to understand how the biblical authors expressed themselves in terms of both their inherited religious tradition and the world in which they lived and worked. Biblical theology thus differs from systematics and dogmatics in seeking not a final answer to theological questions but rather the historical foundations of theological discourse.[3]

This is a historical study, but it is likely to differ from such study in terms of its method and scope and in terms of its implications. Biblical theology, for example, gives preference to the specifically Israelite and Jewish background of the New Testament writings. This does not mean that we ignore the influence of Greco-Roman culture, which provided the context in which the writings arose, but it does imply a particular interest in the continuities within scripture itself. Biblical theology also tends to focus on the scriptures as acknowledged by various Christian traditions. A purely historical approach might be equally interested in delving behind the texts, for example, in the interest of rediscovering the historical Jesus. While the texts themselves often bear witness to the complexity of their own historical development and may even be unintelligible if we do not take it into account, Biblical theology, as I understand it, focuses primarily on the writings as we have them. The present book, accordingly, concentrates on the ways in which the New Testament authors have responded to and developed the themes of sexual ethics that we find witnessed in the scriptures of Israel and maintained and developed in the Judaism of their time.[4]

If biblical theology is, in this sense, narrower than history in its scope and method, it may be broader than history in its implications. It is a function of history to show us the "differentness and irretrievability of the past."[5] This in itself is a worthy goal in that it helps free us from merely imposing our own perception of reality on other people, places, and times. Biblical theology, however, has the further goal of showing how the inevitably alien past that formed the context of the works canonized in the Bible can break in on our present presuppositions and help us discover new opportunities of faithfulness in the future—a future that will inevitably be different both from our present and from the past of the scriptures.[6] This means that the task of the biblical theologian is not done when one has elucidated the world of the biblical texts and called attention to its distance from our own; it is also important to reflect on what the scriptures imply for human life in the future.

This is not to say that biblical theologians can settle such issues on their own. Immediate, practical authority for Christian life and belief is located in the ongoing Christian community rather than the Bible— even in those Christian traditions that insist that they are doing the opposite![7] Biblical theology offers a questioning, even disruptive intervention in the self-assurance of the present to call Christians to new faithfulness and new understanding of what faithfulness means. It helps stir up new reflection. It does not, by itself, determine the results of this reflection, but it makes an important contribution by identifying the assumptions of the biblical authors and by describing the distance between their world and the present. The final chapter of this book represents a particular effort to further such reflection.

The main body of this book is divided into two parts, one on purity ethics ("Dirt"), the other on property ethics ("Greed"). My study of the New Testament has convinced me that most of the texts dealing with sexual morality are expressions of these two principles. Each part begins with discussion of the nature of the ethic in question and its role in the scriptures of Israel and the practice of first-century Judaism. The remaining chapters then trace the New Testament writers' treatment of the ethical principle in relation to sexual issues—mostly in the familiar canonical order of Gospels-Paul-other writings. My choice of this order (over, for example, one based on the relative age of the New Testament documents) arises from a theological conviction that the traditions about Jesus and his teaching are the central texts of Christianity and that other authors are best understood with reference to them. After "Greed," a further chapter deals with other possible ethical elements in the New Testament's treatment of sexuality, including the influence of ancient Stoicism and the modern proposal by conservative evangelicals of a "creation" ethic for sexuality.

The study treats a great variety of issues in sexual ethics. It thus differs from works on broader aspects of New Testament or biblical ethics, which deal with sexual ethics as one element. Again, it differs from books more narrowly focused, such as the numerous recent volumes on homosexuality. The particular focus of this study allows a more detailed reflection on sexual issues than the broader sort of book and, I believe, a more measured one than most of the books on narrower issues. If we try to treat one current "hot" topic in isolation, it adds to the danger of distorting the study and allowing modern anxieties to overwhelm the biblical text.

The readers of this book will come to it with varied backgrounds. The book itself aims to offer a scholarly presentation of a particular way of understanding the sexual ethics of biblical, particularly New Testament, writers. The normal course of events in biblical scholarship is that such ideas should first be threshed out and criticized by experts and only then be presented in a form more accessible to nonspecialist readers— whether those who, like the seminary educated, have some background in biblical scholarship or those who may have little or no formal preparation. In view of the widespread public interest in the topic of the present work, however, my aim is to write in a way intelligible to educated readers generally and to confine topics of more specialized concern to the notes. The nonspecialist reader will still have to reckon, however, with the fact that the book involves close reading of biblical texts and that it could not make its points in any other way. I assume that the reader who is not already familiar with the texts in question will read this book with a Bible translation at hand—preferably a relatively literal translation such as the Revised Standard Version.

There is a temptation, I realize, for the reader to jump to the last chapter—perhaps before reading this paragraph! Indeed, many people did exactly that with the first edition, with the result that some completely misunderstood that chapter and sometimes the rest of the book as well. If you have persevered this far, I urge you to read the argument in its full development. The final chapter is in no way intended to stand on its own. Indeed, it may seem bizarre to the reader who has not absorbed the argument about New Testament sexual ethics on which it is based.

Finally, let me clarify the way I use two key elements in the vocabulary of this book, the terms *morality* and *ethics* and their related adjectives. By "morality" (or "morals" or "mores"), I mean "significant norms of behavior accepted in a given community, society, or culture." They tell a person how to behave to be thought a respectable and worthy person in that particular context. These rules may be miscellaneous in character; they are authoritative not so much because they express any particular principle as because they are accepted custom. They may vary widely from culture to culture; for example, in one society it is perfectly moral for a woman to have several husbands and she would never be criticized for it, while in another it is proof of depravity.

By "ethics," on the other hand, I mean a coherent presentation of morals—either the actual morals of a particular society or an idealized set of morals—showing their internal coherence. Whereas morals are a set of rules, ethics involves specifying principles that explain why these rules are valid, even beyond or apart from the fact that a given society prescribes them. If a particular set of morals is closely tied together by dependence on a single principle, one can then begin to speak of them as an "ethic"; for example, a purity ethic is a set of morals depending on and expressing the principle of purity. Other important ethical principles include justice, love, equality, property, privacy. A justice ethic would not necessarily ground or give rise to the same moral rules as a purity ethic or a love ethic.

An illustration may help make the basic terms clearer: Suppose that a family spends a large percentage of its food budget on fresh produce and feels that it has done something irregular or unsettling if it does the same on meat. This is a "morality," a rule to which the group feels itself committed. Several possible "ethics" might explain or ground this morality. The family might, for example, be vegetarian; an ethic of meat avoidance (which in turn might be the expression of various other ethical principles such as concern for the poor or planetary ecology or reverence for life) would here find expression in its purchasing morality. On the other hand, if the family lives in an area where produce is plentiful and cheap, its moral rule of buying produce might be an expression of convictions about responsible use of income—an ethic concerned with stewardship of funds. There are other possibilities, too, of course, but these may suffice for illustration.

Moral rules by themselves are not self-explanatory because the same action can arise from diverse ethics. On the other hand, the phrasing of a moral rule will often reveal an ethical principle on which it is based, and the associations of moral rules with one another or the ways they change in new circumstances will often do the same. The vegetarian family, for example, will also have a rule against eating fast-food hamburgers, whereas the frugal family may seek them out as an inexpensive way to eat away from home. Again, if our vegetarian family were to move to a region where produce is expensive, its ethic would demand that the family increase its food budget rather than buy meat, while the other family might eat more meat instead. Possibly we could have identified the two families' different ethics even before their move: the vegetarian family would tend to express its moral rule by saying, "We don't eat meat," the frugal family by saying, "We don't buy meat."

In studying the biblical documents, we are often dealing with morality, with what is permitted or forbidden; the biblical authors, like all people, conducted much of the business of ethics on the level of mores. But we must also ask of these texts, "Why?" The *why* is critical, for it alone will enable us to understand the precise language of the texts, to perceive the reasons for changes in biblical morality, and to interpret the sexual ethics of the New Testament in ways that can enter into conversion with our own very different world. Without looking for an ethical "why," we can say little more than "Well, when they were writing, that's what they thought people should do."

Finally, note that the focus on rules and principles implied in the preceding is not a complete picture of Christian life and behavior. Because Christianity is focused around the good news (gospel) preached and embodied by Jesus of Nazareth—a message that gave rise to conversion and transformation among those who truly heard it—we have to admit that Christian ethics or moral theology are not limited to prescribing acceptable behavior in the church community. They have to do with conversation and transformation. They have a part in the process of growth in faith, hope, and love that is the real purpose of Jesus' work among us. Ethics must feed into what is increasingly referred to as "spirituality." Without that, it has not yet become fully Christian. The present book cannot, among all its other tasks, take the discussion very far in this direction, but it will at least try to remind the reader of its importance.

PART I

DIRT

CHAPTER 1

WHAT IS PURITY?

One dominant theme in biblical treatments of sexual morality is purity—avoidance of what is deemed dirty. This principle of avoidance is a common theme of morality in many cultures, perhaps most. Rules that govern the boundaries of the human body, even those that have other reasons behind them, tend at least to be presented as purity rules: *Don't eat that; it's dirty. Don't do that; it's dirty.* Everything that touches us carries with it the potential of rendering us dirty, and all human societies are concerned, albeit in varying degrees, to keep dirt at bay. All regulations dealing with human sexual activity, then, are related to a purity ethic because they deal with the body's boundaries. Not all originate, however, from that source. Some sexual rules are simply and solely purity rules while others, even when they take the form of purity rules, represent other ethics as well. To take an example from modern Western culture, we are likely to feel revulsion toward rape as dirty and defiling, but our more serious objection to it is that it violates its victim's freedom, dignity, and integrity.

We begin our study with purity precisely because it is so pervasive, both in the biblical world and in our own, and also because its particular affinity for sexual rules can sometimes confuse us as we think about other aspects of sexual ethics. The human concern about dirt, moreover, can actually take many different forms. Even if the concern to avoid what is dirty is more or less universal, different cultures define what is dirty in quite different ways. Yet we still tend to think of the definitions of clean and dirty we grew up with as self-evident. Thus, it is useful to begin with the purity side of sexual ethics, partly for its intrinsic importance and partly, too, as a necessary first step in disentangling considerations of purity from other ethical principles that have been at work.

It may surprise some readers to hear that modern Western society has purity rules. We are more apt to think of them as an anthropological category or as a concern of specific religious groups such as Orthodox Jews or Hindus. While our society does not, in fact, have a highly sophisticated, coherent, or articulated system of purity rules or display a consistently high level of concern about purity issues, it does inculcate in its children a sense of what is "dirty." This is in part a matter of practical hygiene, as when children are warned against putting coins in their mouths; it is also, in part, something quite different, as when children are warned not to masturbate, even though it has long been recognized that this is not harmful to health. What is this "dirt," which children are told to avoid, but which is neither literal, physical dirt nor anything threatening to health?

Because anthropologists are used to examining such questions in a cross-cultural way, an anthropologist is probably the best person to help us gain perspective on it in our own culture. Such help is necessary because it is of the nature of "dirt" in any culture that we do not ask what makes it dirty. We simply know what is dirty and what is not, having learned it so early in life that we were not yet asking "Why?" Afterwards, we forget, in effect, that it was something we learned rather than a purely instinctual response. In other words, we have little perspective or objectivity in relation to it; we cannot readily step back from it far enough to see what it is.

Mary Douglas, the cultural anthropologist, has argued that dirt can be understood only in relation to a system that excludes it. "As we know it," she says, "dirt is essentially disorder"; she also invokes "the old definition of dirt as matter out of place."[1] We might add (what is implied in her treatment of the subject) that dirt is matter out of place in relation to human beings. It is generally meaningless to ask whether animals in the wild behave in ways that are clean or unclean; the distinction matters only insofar as they come in touch or are analogized with human beings. A system that divides clean from dirty is a way of understanding and defining what it is to be human—or, more precisely, what it is to belong to a particular human group that defines purity in this particular way. Purity is basically a system with the human being at or near its center. Dirt is what lies outside the system, what is perceived as not belonging in association with people of this particular society, whether as unfamiliar, irregular, unhealthy, or otherwise objectionable.

The enormous differences in purity systems from one culture to another show that people do not automatically attach the labels *clean* and *dirty* to the same objects or actions. What is clean in one culture is dirty in another. Ancient Israel forbade the eating of pork (Lev. 11:7), which was common enough among its neighbors. This was not merely a matter of greater fastidiousness on the part of Israelite culture because it could accept other foods that some pork-eating cultures would reject as dirty or disgusting (e.g., grasshoppers, Lev. 11:22). What is consistent from one culture to another is not a single set of purity rules but the fact that such rules relate to the boundaries of the human body, especially to its orifices. Whatever passes these boundaries can figure as part of purity law: foods, waste products, shed blood, menstrual blood, sexual emissions, sexual acts, birth, death. On these topics purity rules issue their directives, but always in terms of the specific definitions accepted in the local culture and shaped by the history of their development.

Every culture's purity law must be understood as expressing that culture's uniqueness as well as our common human interest in purity.[2] Western presuppositions will not, by and large, be a useful key to understanding the purity rules of ancient Israel, any more than they would be with those of Hinduism or of the Zuni people. This means that we should become aware, in a preliminary way, of some of the main outlines of purity as manifest in modern Western culture and also of ways in which our practice of purity differs from that of ancient Israel. I hope that the reader whose background is not Western will be able to use these comparisons to help identify the distinctive character of her or his own cultural definitions as well.

It is difficult to give a simple, coherent account of purity in the modern West. For one thing, purity is not of preeminent importance in our culture. Cultures vary widely in the importance they ascribe to it, and Western culture has perhaps never numbered among those most concerned with it. Rather than thinking of purity as a single, coherent system, we split it among a variety of headings, such as hygiene and aesthetics, as well as religion. And given the increasingly multicultural character of Western cities today, there is no single tradition universally in use. There can also be substantial variation along class lines, with people of the middle class traditionally assumed to be more concerned about purity than those of the upper class or the working class.

Perhaps it is easiest to see our purity rules at work in connection with food. "Dirt is matter out of place." Thus, the coffee in the cup is clean but, when spilled on a pair of pants, it renders them dirty. The infant has no sense of food on clothes as constituting dirt. Strained peas are fine in the bowl, on the spoon, in the hair, wherever. The parent or other caregiver teaches the purity distinctions among these locations. Even the preverbal infant may pick them up from the observed example of others or the facial expressions of the person wielding the spoon of peas.

Distinctions between clean and unclean foods are inculcated early on through this kind of direct instruction—and also through a kind of exclusionary presumption suggesting that what is unfamiliar in our particular cultural setting is likely to be unacceptable. Most Americans, for example, grow up without encountering snails as an item of human food and are apt to feel some repugnance toward them on first encounter. New food items, unless they are easily approximated to familiar ones, are likely to evoke some discomfort, and the act of eating unusual cuisine for the first time was often, for Americans of my generation, a kind of door into adult sophistication. What changed in that process, however, was our particular list of clean and unclean foods, not the distinction itself, which remained in force. Those who have passed the threshold represented by their first plate of escargot will probably still gag at the thought of eating that snail's near relative, the garden slug. This is not an issue of abstract edibility; we do not even inquire whether slugs might or might not be edible. It is a revulsion dictated by scarcely conscious laws of clean and unclean foods.[3]

What is "clean" is apt to seem as self-evident to the average American or European as what is dirty. The Gentile who is repelled by the notion of eating dogs or cats or slugs may find it bizarre that orthodox Jews will not eat pork or lobster. As a result, if we try to read the dietary laws of Leviticus, they may appear pointless and inexplicable, although they are simply food taboos like our own and are more coherent and reasoned than the ones commonly accepted in the United States.[4]

The relative lack of coherence in Western culture's treatment of purity also implies that food purity seems to us unrelated to other kinds of purity. Although slugs and pornography can both be described as "dirty," we do not at first think of the two judgments as belonging to the same world of discourse. Other possible areas of purity law (e.g., birth, death, and menstruation) are less clearly articulated than food and sex, leaving us without a coherent, overall purity system. Of the two areas where rules are relatively well articulated, we generally consign food to the purely secular realm—eating slugs is disgusting, but not a moral offense. "Dirty" sex, on the other hand, we may see as a moral or religious offense. In the process, we lose the sense of continuity among all areas of purity that is evident in some other cultures, including that of ancient Israel.

In the area of sexual activity, American purity law is a powerful force, yet it is, if anything, more fragmented than in the matter of foods. American society became more tolerant in sexual matters during the 1960s and 1970s. Much of that tolerance survives, despite concerted efforts to turn the culture in a more restrictive direction in recent decades. Throughout the last five or six decades, there has been intense conflict over such issues as divorce, reproductive issues (such as birth control and abortion), gender equality, and sexual orientation. Perhaps the most important shift that has taken place is simply the transition from relative unanimity in the 1950s to the present multiplicity of voices.

In the 1950s, churches held to a highly restrictive code for the young. Almost no physical contact between the sexes was approved before marriage. Young couples who were engaged might be allowed some forms of physical contact short of sexual intercourse, but some churches forbade even kissing to couples who were not yet engaged. All sexual intercourse outside marriage was condemned, as were all nonvaginal forms of intercourse, even within marriage. This purity code was not just that of the churches in the United States of the 1950s; it was the officially acknowledged code of the society as a whole, however often it may have been ignored in practice.

The change in American sexual codes since then has been the result of many factors: shifts in intellectual leadership; changes in popular culture; a change in women's control of their fertility with the invention of more reliable methods of birth control; the rise of movements demanding equality for women and for gay and lesbian people; increasing diversity of ethnic traditions, combined with an increasing respect for such diversity; and, perhaps most important, a vast demographic change that greatly increased the number of "singles" who are now a major population element of every American city. The code of sexual purity has become individualized. There is a widespread sense at present that people have some right to individual opinions in the matter, provided that no harm is done to another person. As in the matter of food, however, this is not so much an abolition of purity considerations as a change in the way they are expressed. Instead of standards universal to the entire culture, there is the assumption that everyone has to identify personal limits. "Morality"—meaning, in this case, one's definitions of sexual purity—came to be treated as a matter of private determination.

Purity codes are still very much alive among us, and some groups actively advocate universal imposition of their particular codes. At the same time, local and state governments have been more reluctant than in the past to "legislate morality"—or, in the language of the present study, "legislate purity." This is most evident in the legal treatment of homosexuality, perhaps the greatest purity bugbear of the 1950s. The effort, as I write, to ban same-sex marriage may succeed in many places, but there is little significant success in rolling back the greater degree of freedom for gay and lesbian people gained since the 1960s. There has been increasing reluctance to impose a single purity code in the matter—not because legislators regard same-gender sexual acts as "pure" or entirely acceptable, but because purity alone, without other clear evidence of harm, no longer seems a sufficient basis for legislation. It appears that purity does not deserve a major expenditure of public attention.

The current American situation is still in flux and has not reached consensus. Some segments of the culture have declared a "culture war" intended to restore a stricter purity code. Even on the religious right, however, there are also signs, such as marital manuals emphasizing the pleasures of sex, that the purity code will not return to exactly the form of the 1950s, when sexual pleasure was virtually unmentionable. In the population at large, the substantial percentage of adults who are single, whether as never married or as widowed or divorced, means that it would be hard to impose a purity code that forbids all sexual activity outside marriage. Finally, women in general and gay and lesbian people will presumably not surrender their new freedoms easily.

In any case, it would be a mistake to imagine a society totally dedicated to purity, whatever its definition, for purity is never an unambiguous value. If the purity code is a manifestation of order and coherence, the "dirt" that lies outside it is both a residue and also a reservoir of power, whether destructive or creative.[5] The long-standing assumption in Western culture that artists are more indifferent than the public at large to sexual purity shows our culture's awareness of the creative value

of dirt. Dirt also represents the individual's liberation from the sometimes oppressive control of society: children making a deliberate mess
of their plates, using dirty words, "grossing" each other out; adults eating suspicious foods such as snails (or slugs!) or watching "dirty" mov-
ies. Consequently, one cannot readily predict whether purity or dirt will
be symbolically more significant in the near future—only that each is
bound up with the other. A living society never comes to a final resolution of the issue, for perfect purity would create a deathlike immobility
and complete dirtiness would be equivalent to catastrophic chaos. The
life of a society depends on finding a sustainable balance.

It is likely, then, that the average Western reader of this work will
acknowledge some purity rules in the area of sex, probably derived from
the culture of one's childhood and possibly modified by exposure to
the purity codes of others, whether more conservative or more liberal.
In some cases, the reader will not have learned to distinguish between
purity ethics and other kinds of sexual ethics, but will simply think of all
sexual wrongs as "dirty." It may not be easy, at first, for such a reader
to separate purity from other considerations. For present purposes, it
is enough to say that what marks particular sexual acts as violations of
purity—rather than of some other ethic—is that the acts are deemed
repellent in and of themselves, like snails or slugs on a dinner plate. One
rejects them because they seem self-evidently unacceptable, not because
of any identifiable, concrete harm that they threaten to a society or to a
person involved in them. Although one may think an act both dirty and
harmful, it should be possible to analyze the various ethical principles at
work in such cases, even where the distinction is blurred to begin with.

Because of the complexity and incoherence of modern Western
purity values, the reader of this book has to perform several difficult
tasks to understand the topic at hand. One is to discover that what has
long seemed self-evident with regard to sexual ethics—namely, that certain acts are right or wrong in and of themselves—reflects learned purity
values specific to our culture. The equivalent values of other cultures will
often be significantly different. Another is to accept that purity systems
change and that we cannot assume that ours is identical with that of our
ancestral cultures, Israel or Greece, or even with the West of a few centuries ago. Yet another task is to see that purity systems differ not only in
detail from culture to culture but also in the coherence with which they
are organized and the intensity with which they are held. Some cultures

(e.g., ancient Israel) simply take the whole matter more seriously than others.

Purity and impurity (or "dirt" as we usually call it) are culturally and emotionally powerful for us. They can also be difficult topics to grasp and understand, all the more so for the fact that we first assimilated them in childhood as things self-evident, permanent, and largely beyond question. As we turn now to examine the role of purity considerations in the sexual ethics of the Christian scriptures, we shall find it important both to understand the official purity system of ancient Israel and also to see how it was actually being appropriated among Jewish groups in the first century of the Common Era. Only then can we begin to comprehend the significance of purity in the New Testament.

C H A P T E R   2

ISRAEL'S BASIC PURITY LAW

THE DISTINCTIVENESS OF ISRAEL

Christianity first emerged as a sect[1] within the Judaism of the Roman Empire—a Judaism that placed a very high value on the distinctive practices that set it apart from the Nations (or, as we usually say in English, the Gentiles). There were many such practices: the rejection of images in worship, insistence on one God only, observance of a weekly day of rest, concern for food purity, circumcision, and a reluctance to intermarry with Gentiles—to name those most obvious to outsiders. To be sure, every nation of the time had its distinctive traditions, but Israel stood out by the degree to which it kept itself separate from other ethnic groups and perpetuated its identity over time. Most ethnic groups in the Eastern Mediterranean world became heavily Hellenized during the last few centuries B.C.E., identifying their gods with those of the Greeks and, often, adopting Greek as their principal language, at least among the elite. While Jews also took much from Hellenistic culture, they kept their distance from it in matters of religious practice in a way virtually unparalleled at the time.

For the foundations of their distinctive faith and culture, Jews referred to their sacred writings. They had no "Bible" in the later sense of a single compendium; ancient book technology could not encompass that much in a single volume. Consequently, the exact boundaries of scripture were not as clear as they seem to us today, and different groups might have slightly different canons (official lists of scriptural writings). The works they referred to included not only those known to later Christians as the Old Testament and the Apocrypha (or deutero-canonical books), but also other writings now lost or accorded little authority.[2] Whatever differences there might be, however, one group of books was fundamental for all Jews: the first five books of modern Bibles, called *Torah* or "Instruction." In English, they are traditionally called "The Law"; although this is not an ideal translation of *torah*, it does acknowledge the fact that these writings included, among other things, the written law of ancient Israel— criminal, civil, and religious.

In antiquity, religion was not easily separable from other forms of public life. One's worship was dictated mainly by the social units to which one belonged (e.g., family, nation, city-state). The household, including slaves as well as the kin group, honored the God or gods of its tradition. The great holidays of any ancient city were religious festivals, celebrated with rites, feasting, and various entertainments. In the Roman Empire, religious respect was also paid to the *divine spirit* of the ruling city and of the emperor who embodied its rule.

In addition to household or state-sponsored cults,[3] there were unofficial ones as well, which could function a bit more like the modern notion of a personal religion. Some were brought by resident aliens from their home country, and these might offer initiation to interested individuals from outside the immigrant community. Philosophical groups, too, sometimes organized themselves as voluntary communities of worship, as did social clubs. Even so, for most people, religion remained first and foremost a part of their familial, ethnic, or political identity. Because the individual as such had little significance in society (a topic this study explores further in part 2), one scarcely thought of changing one's worship except insofar as one's larger social units might do so.

To be a Jew, then, did not mean primarily to confess a certain faith, but rather to belong to a certain people. As a consequence of that identity, one participated fully in the nation's life, including its faith and worship. To abandon your community, in most cases, was to become a nonperson. One could not convert to another "denomination" or become a "secular" person while still retaining one's full association with the group, and there was little possibility of entertaining such an idea. The modern reader who thinks of the Torah, then, strictly in terms of a religious document is apt to have a misconception of its importance in Late Antiquity. It was a religious document, but it also embodied the basic laws and customs of Israel in all areas of life, no distinction being made between religious and nonreligious elements.

PURITY CODES IN THE TORAH

Because the present study treats the Bible in terms of the Christian canon of scripture, the Torah plays the role here primarily of background for understanding how the early Christians dealt with issues of purity. This chapter will endeavor to read the relevant materials as a single, more or less coherent document, as was the dominant practice among ancient Jews and Christians. Most scholars of the Torah, however, will readily acknowledge that there are various layers and strands of tradition within these five books and that they are not all in perfect agreement with one another. We will look briefly at some aspects of this historical development at the end of this chapter because it will shed light on certain inconsistencies.

The reader of the Torah can scarcely miss its intense concern with purity, and this concern was one of the principal forces keeping Israel distinct from the Nations. I have already noted that food purity and the reluctance of Israel to intermarry with Gentiles were important distinctions of the people. Such purity rules were familiar from their constant use within the day-to-day life of the society. But the Torah, already hundreds of years old by the first century C.E., contained their written codification. To study the Torah has always been a high vocation in Jewish culture (e.g., Ps. 119; Sir. 39); and even those who could not read it themselves could hear it read and expounded in the synagogue. The Torah contains a great deal besides purity rules, but these do bulk large among its contents.

Although individual purity rules are scattered through most of the five books, the two most substantial collections of purity laws appear in Leviticus (chaps. 11–16 and 17–26). These two codes form the best place for us to begin because they provide broad enough surveys, presented with sufficiently consistent perspectives, to give an overall impression of the content and nature of Israel's purity law. To be sure, the two have significantly different interests. The first is a priestly code concerned primarily with those aspects of uncleanness that called for rites of purification and, often, priestly involvement; the second, usually called the "Holiness Code," is concerned rather with the historical consequences of uncleanness for the land of Canaan and the people of Israel resident there.[4]

Thus, the priestly code gives directions about discerning when uncleanness exists and about the kinds of purification required. It concludes with a full description of the rites for the Day of Atonement, when the high priest makes "atonement for the holy place, because of the uncleannesses of the people of Israel, and because of their transgressions, all their sins" (Lev. 16:16 RSV). (Note that uncleanness is included here in the category of sins, but forms a recognizably distinct category of it.) The Holiness Code, on the other hand, is characterized by the frequent reiteration of God's claim on the people (e.g., "I am the Lord your God, who brought you out of the land of Egypt"; "You shall be holy; for I the Lord your God am holy") and by its assertion that sins of uncleanness had caused the land of Canaan to "vomit out" its former inhabitants and may do the same with the Israelites. The Holiness Code has little interest in the cleansing of individuals, but calls on the nation as a whole to cleanse itself by the removal of offenders. If Israel disregards these demands and becomes polluted, God will punish the nation with exile (26:21–39), yet their repentance will be enough to restore them to God's favor, without explicit reference to cleansing rites (26:40–45).

The difference between the two codes appears clearly in the few instances where they handle the same topics. In dealing with clean and unclean animals, for example, the first code carefully defines what is clean and unclean and provides means for the purification of people and vessels defiled by contact with unclean animals or their carcasses (chap. 11). The Holiness Code simply emphasizes the importance of the distinction and prohibits violations (20:25–26). Again, in the matter of intercourse during the menstrual period, the first code defines how long the man becomes impure (seven days) and how contagious his impurity is (he communicates it to any bed on which he lies) (15:24). The Holiness Code, on the other hand, simply prohibits a man from having intercourse with a menstruating woman (18:19) and provides that the two offenders shall be "cut off from among their people" (20:18).[5] The first code is relatively pragmatic; it recognizes dirt as an inevitable aspect of daily existence, however much the society may seek to avoid it, and offers remedies to restore those polluted by it to the normal state of cleanness.[6] The Holiness Code holds up the ideal of an absolute separation between Israel and all that is unclean and utters a "no" to uncleanness so absolute that it may be enforced through the execution or the "cutting off" of the polluted.

A SURVEY OF TORAH PURITY

Despite their significant differences, the two codes have broadly consistent understandings of pure and impure. Purity concerns applied to the full range of social life, as a brief sketch of the contents of the two codes in Leviticus makes clear. Their contents include, in order: clean and unclean animals (chap. 11); a woman's impurity after giving birth (12); leprosy of persons, houses, and textiles or skins (13–14); genital discharges, including menstruation (15); slaughter of animals and disposition of blood (17); incest and other prohibited sexual acts (18); idolatry, errors in consuming sacrifices, oppression, injustice, hatred, mixture of "kinds," the "foreskin" of fruit trees, blood, haircuts, etc. (19); sacrifice of "seed,"[7] wizardry, adultery, incest, and other sexual acts (20); defilement of priests and of members of their households and unsuitability of sacrificial animals (21–22); the festival calendar (23); obligations of resident aliens to observe the Torah (24); Sabbath years and jubilees (25); idolatry and Sabbath-keeping, along with blessings and curses related to the keeping of the laws (26).

The multifarious nature of this "table of contents" (which represents some simplification of the materials) illustrates the breadth of the purity system as a way of shaping life. And it also reminds us that it is concerned, at times, with issues other than physical bodily purity. As Mary Douglas has noted, there is a tendency for purity law, strictly so-called, to attract to itself regulations that may have other origins or rationales. Pollution rules, while they do not often correspond closely to other kinds of ethical principles, may be used to reinforce other rules as a kind of "highlighting."[8] In the Holiness Code, one finds a number of such instances—for example, "You shall love your neighbor as yourself" or "You shall do no wrong in judgment, in measures of length or weight or quantity" (Lev. 19:18, 35 RSV). These are not purity rules themselves, but are set in this context to reinforce them through association with purity rules, taking advantage of the almost automatic distaste or disgust that dirt evokes. Deuteronomy also uses purity associations in this way: "You shall not have in your bag two kinds of weights, a large and a small. . . . A full and just weight you shall have, a full and just measure you shall have. . . . For all who do such things, all who act dishonestly, are an abomination to the Lord your God" (25:13–16 RSV). Jeremiah and Ezekiel often apply purity language to other kinds of offenses, and Proverbs almost routinely describes liars, scoffers, and other wicked persons as objects of revulsion ("abominations"). This does not mean that the purity system was being "spiritualized" or "moralized" but that it was a ready source of emotional reinforcement for other kinds of moral or ethical concerns.[9]

In matters of sexual ethics, then, we cannot assume that an act treated in the purity codes is simply and solely a purity concern. I shall show, in part 2, that rules about adultery, prostitution, and incest had about them an important element of property law as well. However, because sexual acts are of concern in almost any purity system, all sexual offenses are likely to be *felt* to some degree as purity offenses, and we shall need to pay close attention to distinguish between rules prompted entirely by purity considerations and those where other concerns are at work, too. The language of purity in English translations of scripture includes such terms as "clean/pure," "dirty/unclean/impure/common/polluted," and "abomination" (the last a translation of Hebrew and Greek terms denoting something that called forth revulsion in the spectator). The appearance of such language in a text is a first indicator that we are dealing with purity rules. Then we must also look for indicators that other principles may be at work, such as references to "justice/righteousness," to the rights of other persons being violated, and so forth. In what follows, we take a closer look at the specifically sexual elements of purity in the Torah.

SEXUAL PURITY
Emissions from the sexual organs

One prominent concern is the menstruating woman. During her menstrual period, she is unclean for seven days, and her uncleanness is so contagious that it can affect others indirectly if they touch any furniture on which she has lain or sat. This uncleanness also extends to any woman who has a hemorrhage and thus appears to be in a kind of ongoing menstrual state. A man is forbidden to have sexual intercourse with such women, no grounds being given for this other than concern for purity. A man's emission of semen also defiles—both himself and also the woman, if it occurs in intercourse—but only for one day. If, however, a man has an unusual, continuing discharge (perhaps gonorrhea, as the Old Greek translation calls it), it is more nearly equivalent to the woman's menstrual or quasi-menstrual impurity. The importance attached to discharges from the sexual organs is evident not only from the chapter devoted to it in Leviticus (15), but also from isolated individual laws elsewhere that prohibit intercourse with a menstruating woman (Lev. 18:19; 20:18) and prescribe the correct treatment of a man who has an ongoing discharge (Num. 5:1) or a wet dream (Deut. 23:11–12, ET 10–11).[10]

Even apart from menstruation, female impurity appears to be more contagious than male. For example, a new mother's purification time after the birth of a daughter is twice as long as after that of a son (eighty days as opposed to forty) (Lev. 12). At Mount Sinai, "the people" (i.e., the adult males) are told to consecrate themselves for the great epiphany and not to "go near a woman" (Exod. 19:10–15). No doubt the fear is primarily that the men will have intercourse with women and thus pollute themselves, yet the text speaks as if the danger lay in the women. Priests, who must take special pains to avoid impurity, are forbidden to marry women who have had intercourse with other men: harlots or women who are "defiled," divorced, or widowed (Lev. 21:7, 14). What is more, any woman who is divorced from her husband and then married to another becomes "defiled" in relation to the previous husband; should she become free again, through divorce or widowhood, it would be an abomination for him to remarry her (Deut. 24:1–4). A priest's daughter who commits prostitution is condemned to be burnt—an unusual, perhaps sacral mode of execution (Lev. 21:9). And all foreign women are automatically suspected of trying to introduce foreign cults, so that Deuteronomy requires the slaughtering of all women and children taken captive from nearby enemies (and thus still in or near their home cultures), although it allows Israelite men to have sex with those captured at a greater distance (20:10–18; cf. 21:10–14 for sexual use of captives). It is not too much to suggest that the texts demonstrate a broad anxiety about the polluting potential of women.

Cross-dressing and male-male intercourse

There is also anxiety, though much less commonly expressed, about gender confusions, including cross-dressing (Deut. 22:5) and one same-gender sexual act between men (Lev. 18:22; 20:13). Both of these confuse the purer male with the more unclean female.[11] In fact, the prohibition of male-male sexual intercourse is phrased in a way that suggests that this was the central concern—in literal translation, "lying with a male the lyings of a woman." What precisely was being prohibited? Most scholars suggest anal intercourse—an interpretation accepted in what follows.[12] The common practice of treating the text as a blanket prohibition of all sexual interaction between males or even between females goes far beyond what it actually says.[13]

These two prohibitions appear as isolated rules, with the violations being described as "abominations"—that is, "disgusting things." This language does not mean that they are exceptionally horrid in terms of the purity system. The Hebrew term *toebah* and its synonym *shiqquts*, both usually translated *bdelygma* in ancient Greek[14] and "abomination" in English, apply, in the Torah, to things as diverse as unclean foods (Lev. 11:10, 11, 12, etc.; Deut. 14:3), the sacrifice of a blemished animal (Deut. 17:1), remarriage to a former wife (Deut. 24:4), and idols (Deut. 29:16, ET 17). Because the prohibition of cross-dressing occurs only once, in Deuteronomy, and the prohibition of anal intercourse only in the Holiness Code, these, unlike the food laws or the regulations about menstruation, seem to form a relatively peripheral aspect of the overall purity system, which concerned itself primarily with the everyday life of the ordinary household.

Were there also principles other than purity at work here in relation to male-male sexual intercourse? Beginning from the first century C.E., some have argued that this was an expression of a broader condemnation of all nonprocreative sex.[15] There is no explicit reference, however, to such a motive; at most, one can base such an argument on the context and organization of the materials. The Torah begins with a creation account emphasizing procreation (Gen. 1:26–28) and shows an ongoing interest in the topic, particularly as it leads from the first humans to the numerous descendants of Jacob/Israel. The narrower context of Leviticus 18, which combines regulations about incest with prohibitions of intercourse with a menstruating woman, child sacrifice, male-male anal intercourse, and intercourse with an animal, can then be read as expressing a overall concern for legitimate offspring. We shall return to this topic in chapter 12, but we should note at this point that the argument depends not on the explicit language of the text in question but on a possible interpretation of the Torah's larger principles of organization. And the fact that the prohibition requires the death of both participants, with no allowance for extenuating factors such as age or rape, tends to confirm that the concern is one of physical purity that can only be purged by execution.[16]

From the Middle Ages onward, theologians have attached the term *sodomy* to male-male sexual acts;[17] and there is a long tradition of interpreting the account of the angels' visit to Sodom (Gen. 19:1–11)—and sometimes the similar story of the Levite and his concubine at Gibeah (Judg. 19)—as implying a condemnation of same-gender sexual acts. Both stories tell of male visitors who receive threatening treatment from the men of a town where they seek lodging. The only person willing to take them in is a resident alien, unrelated to the townspeople and lacking influence. At night, the townsmen gather outside and demand to "know" the wayfarers, and the host seeks to appease them by offering one or more women to be raped instead. In the Sodom story, the wayfarers are actually angels, who blind their would-be attackers and, after sending their host and his family away, destroy the city. In the Gibeah story, the traveler is a Levite. The appalling sacrifice of his concubine saves his life, but he stirs up a civil war in retaliation for the outrage done him.

Neither story, as it stands in scripture, condemns same-gender sexual intercourse as such; violence against strangers is the point. Genesis does not specify the original complaint that drew down God's judgment on Sodom. The demand of the townsmen there and at Gibeah to "know" the strangers is itself ambiguous. While it may well include a component of rape, what is beyond question is that the mob, in each case, intends violence. In the Gibeah story, the Levite interprets the demand as meaning that "They meant to kill me" (Judg. 20:5). Condemnation of violence, even where it seems to include homosexual rape, can hardly be equated with a universal condemnation of all same-gender sexual acts. If one asks whether the punishment visited on Sodom or on Gibeah was occasioned by impurity or by violence against strangers, only the latter answer is persuasive.[18] The Holiness Code's prohibition of male-male anal intercourse, by contrast, is based on considerations of purity.[19]

Elsewhere, the scriptures of Israel often refer to Sodom's ruins as an example of desolation and of divine judgment—usually without specifying exactly what sins led to this judgment. Isaiah, however, comparing Jerusalem with Sodom, suggests that the sin was oppression (1:10–17) or partiality (3:9 RSV; the Hebrew is of uncertain meaning). Jeremiah accuses Sodom of adultery, lies, and the encouragement of the wicked (23:14). Ezekiel says that, although Sodom had pride and abundance, it refused to help the poor and committed abominations (16:49–50). The word *abominations* here might conceivably echo Leviticus 18:22;[20] but, as we have seen, the word's meaning was sufficiently broad that, in the absence of more explicit indications, we cannot be sure. When Zephaniah threatens Moab and Ammon with the fate of Sodom, he is denouncing their taunting of Israel and their paganism (2:8–11).[21] Whether we look to Leviticus, then, or to the tradition about Sodom, we must conclude that the issue of same-gender sexual acts in ancient Israel was much less central than the one it occupies in certain modern purity systems.

If the Holiness Code invokes the death penalty for anal intercourse between two males (Lev. 20:13), this is of a piece with its generally Draconian style, which reflects the peculiar purpose of the work. The death penalty is not a rarity in this code, being invoked also for sacrifice of "seed" to Molech (20:1), cursing one's father or mother (20:9), adultery (20:10), incest with one's father's wife or one's daughter-in-law (20:11–12), marriage to both daughter and mother (20:14), intercourse with an animal (20:15–16), prostitution by the daughter of a priest (21:9), blasphemy (24:10), and manslaughter (24:18). As we have already noted, the author of the Holiness Code threatens that if the people of Israel fail to keep themselves pure, their land will become defiled, God will punish the land, and the land will vomit them out (18:24–30). But what if some individuals do not heed these warnings? Must the whole people suffer for the transgressions of a few? The Code allows for the people as a whole to purge itself of responsibility for the offenses of the few by separating itself decisively from the offenders. Thus, Leviticus 20 largely repeats the list of unclean acts in chapter 18, this time not to prohibit them, but to call for the eradication of offenders from Israel, demanding the execution of some and threatening those who have committed other offenses, such as intercourse with a menstruating woman and certain types of incest, with "cutting off."

Intercourse with an animal and cult prostitution

The Holiness Code places intercourse with an animal (18:23; 20:15–16) in fairly close proximity to its prohibition of male-male anal intercourse, but makes no explicit linkage between them.[22] The latter is categorized as an abomination, the former as "confusion." Both may well have been relatively rare or unusual violations of purity in contrast to more everyday issues such as those occasioned by menstruation. Some, however, have suggested that they shared an association with idolatry. Such a link with bestiality seems likely in Exodus, which places its prohibition of bestiality in just such a context: "You shall not permit a sorceress to live. Whoever lies with a beast shall be put to death. Whoever sacrifices to any God save to the Lord only, shall be utterly destroyed" (Exod. 22:18–20 RSV). In this short, isolated purity code, the theme that links the three elements is their association with non-Israelite cultus, which was often lumped with "sorcery" (e.g., Isa. 8:19).

We do know that cult prostitutes existed in Israel itself (e.g., 1 Kings 14:24) as well as the broader Ancient Near East. Deuteronomy forbids Israel to allow its children, female or male, to serve as cult prostitutes (literally, "holy people") or to use the wages of such prostitution in payment of vows (23:18–19, ET 17–18). While we do not know much about male cult prostitutes in Israel or even the larger Ancient Near Eastern milieu, it is possible that they engaged in intercourse with other men.[23] Such a cultic connection would have made the prohibition of certain male-male sexual acts seem more urgent to the authors of the Holiness Code.[24] It remains true, however, that their express reasoning is based solely on purity considerations. The most one can say is that the chapters in the Holiness Code that condemn male-male anal intercourse and intercourse with animals also prohibit cultic acts, namely sacrifice of seed to Molech (possibly child sacrifice) (Lev. 18:21; 20:1–5) and sorcery (20:6). While the chapters are too miscellaneous to be quite clear on the point, the author may have regarded both male-male anal intercourse and intercourse with an animal as tainted with idolatry.[25]

Masturbation

Though later religious authorities regarded masturbation as unclean, the Torah contains no prohibition of it. The death of Onan (Gen. 38:1–10) was at one time taken as expressing a judgment on masturbators, but this interpretation is unlikely at best. Onan was obligated by the tradition of levirate marriage (cf. Deut. 25:5–10) to beget children for his deceased elder brother with the brother's widow. Because any male child born of this union might then take precedence over Onan as heir of his father Judah, he sought to avoid conception. The narrative suggests that he practiced coitus interruptus, not masturbation. Elsewhere, spilled semen is treated merely as a source of temporary uncleanness (Lev. 15:16–17). Onan's sin was his refusal to fulfill his obligation to his dead brother.[26] Masturbation to orgasm would have occasioned temporary uncleanness for a man, but does not otherwise seem to have been an issue for the purity system. Female masturbation would not have violated the purity code at all; as with female-female sexual acts, it could hardly come within the law's purview. As with the Torah generally, the purity code placed the adult male at the center of the human picture and was interested in other beings only as they impinged on him.[27]

Incest

By contrast with the rather incidental handling of same-gender sexual acts or intercourse with an animal, the detailed treatment of incest found in the Holiness Code and elsewhere suggests it was a familiar and substantial problem for ancient Israelite society. Incest is a difficult topic to discuss in any dispassionate way. We, too, have the revulsion toward it that marks it as a purity issue for us, and we also argue that it should be prohibited on other grounds, usually those of genetics (since inbreeding is likely to make disorders dependent on recessive genes more prevalent) or of justice and family order (on the grounds that incest involving a child is a form of child abuse). We thus apply a variety of ethical principles to incest, but the revulsion that is part of our purity response can make it difficult for us to look patiently at another culture's rules where they differ from our own.

The circumstances of family life in ancient Israel and the related rules about incest were substantially different from ours. Whereas we define incest primarily as intercourse between two persons too closely related in terms of their shared genetic endowment, ancient Israel defined it more in terms of the social obligations owed by a male (or, rarely, a female) to close kin. A son must not act disrespectfully toward male kindred of his own or a prior generation: father, father's brother, or own brother. This principle demanded that he not approach their wives sexually, for a man's wife was an aspect of himself. The language of the Holiness Code is specific and makes the point clear: "You shall not uncover the nakedness of your father's wife; it is your father's nakedness" (Lev. 18:8 RSV). The gravity of the affront implied in "uncovering your father's nakedness" is evident from the account of the drunkenness of Noah, when Ham saw his father naked and was cursed for it (Gen. 9:20–27).[28] The sacredness of the patriarch's genitals was such that, in patriarchal narratives, one even swore oaths on them (Gen. 24:2–3, Abraham; 47:29–31, Israel), suggesting that any failure of respect toward one's physical progenitor or the head of one's household was sure to be visited with swift retribution.[29] Thus, it is the man's father whom he violates in incest, even though the physical act takes place with the father's wife.[30]

The wife in question is not the mother of the perpetrator of incest. (That case is handled separately and in terms of the man's relationship to his own mother, 18:7.) The majority of people in ancient Israel may well have lived in small family or household units. But since polygyny was common among the elite, a man of importance was likely to have more than one wife in his household at the same time; the incest regulations in the Holiness Code are framed to deal with such circumstances. The grown son could readily become interested in a wife who was not his mother. No "blood" kinship would be transgressed, yet the offense was not the less serious. There are narrative instances of such incest in scripture, with predictably disastrous consequences. Reuben had a liaison with his father's concubine, for which he lost his rights as firstborn (Gen. 35:22; cf. 49:4); and when Adonijah requested the hand of David's concubine, Abishag the Shunammite, after David's death, Solomon took it as a claim to succeed their father as head of the household and had him executed (1 Kings 2:13–25). The primary concern that shaped the Torah incest code was violation of family hierarchies. I treat it here under the heading of purity law partly because there was clearly a purity element in it, but also to show that we can best understand the specific rules in terms of the property ethic, interpreted as hierarchy.

Adultery and prostitution

A similar mixture of ethical concerns shapes the handling of two other sexual offenses, the last items of sexual impurity we investigate here: adultery and prostitution. In the Torah, adultery is understood as a man's having intercourse with a woman married or betrothed to another man. The male who commits adultery does not violate his own marriage, but that of the woman and her husband.[31] The Holiness Code treats adultery as defiling (Lev. 18:20) and calls for the execution of both the man and the woman (20:10). As noted above in the discussion of male-male anal intercourse, such executions are a way of purging the people as a whole of uncleanness so that the land will not vomit them out. There are signs, however, even in the Holiness Code, to show that adultery was not solely, or even primarily, a purity offense.

If adultery were entirely an issue of purity, we could not explain the unusual rule about the slave woman who has been designated as another man's concubine or wife but not yet ransomed and emancipated for the purpose (Lev. 19:20–22). The woman appears to be at least approximately in the state of betrothal, and elsewhere this is held to mean that any violation of her is equivalent to adultery (Deut. 22:25–27). Nonetheless, if a man other than her betrothed has intercourse with her, the Holiness Code specifically provides that the two shall *not* be put to death "because she had not been emancipated." The law demands either an "inquest" or "damages"[32] and instructs the man to offer a ram as a guilt offering.

The passage is difficult until we recognize that in this case an exception is being made to the purity system itself. Because uncleanness is defiling in and of itself, the objective of the Holiness Code is to purge it from the people and thus prevent it from working its inevitable destruction. In cases of intercourse with an animal, for example, the animal is killed as well as the human being, because both have become centers of impurity. In ordinary cases of adultery, the Holiness Code does not even make an exception to the death penalty for women who may have been raped, as Deuteronomy 22:23–27 does. The object is to expunge the uncleanness as such. In this particular case, however, Leviticus rejects the death penalty for both partners on the grounds that the woman had not been emancipated.

Because the ordinance gives her slave status as the reason why they are not to be executed, it may mean simply that slave women are incapable of adultery—that is, adultery is by definition an offense that can be committed only with a free woman. This, in itself, would make it clear that adultery is a property-related matter. Another explanation, however, would suggest that her slave status is what links the two offenders; in other words, the man who has had intercourse with the slave woman is her master. Hence the difficulty in this particular case: the relationship between the slave woman and her intended has been violated, but by a man who also had some rights over her because a master could make sexual use of his female slaves. The act is a violation of the purity system and therefore demands an act of atonement, but the author of the Holiness Code refrains from invoking the full severity of the system to avoid diminishing the rights of sexual property. Because two men's rights were involved, they are then rebalanced by requiring the woman's master to pay damages to her intended.[33]

The inclusion of adultery within the Holiness Code exemplifies the tendency for all sexual rules to be assimilated to the purity ethic, whatever their true ethical origins. Outside Leviticus, we find little to suggest that adultery was a purity violation. The rite of the water of bitterness, used to determine whether a woman accused of adultery was in fact guilty, may be the only clear instance (Num. 5:11–31). There was also, presumably, a sense that the perfect woman was to receive only the semen of her husband and that reception of other semen defiled her in relation to that husband. The priest, as the male who must avoid uncleanness most rigorously, was forbidden to contract marriage with a nonvirgin (Lev. 21:7–15), and it was a "disgusting thing" (abomination) for a man to remarry his divorced wife if she had been married to another in the interim (Deut. 24:1–4, affirmed in Jer. 3:1).[34] Adultery was a breach of purity in this sense, but it was just as significantly a violation of property rights, a topic we explore further in part 2.

As with adultery, ordinary noncultic prostitution was treated as both a property and a purity offense. The purity element tends to link prostitution in general with foreign cults, a link made easy by the existence of cult prostitutes. These persons, whose sexual activities played some role in the worship of the gods, existed within Israel itself before the exile. They were present, for example, in the reigns of Rehoboam (1 Kings 14:24) and Asa (22:46), despite the latter's efforts to abolish them (15:12); and Josiah found chambers set aside for them in the Temple at Jerusalem, which he destroyed in his reform (2 Kings 23:7).[35]

Deuteronomy bans cult prostitutes, male and female, and prohibits use of their wages in payment of vows, as a "disgusting thing" (23:18–19, ET 17–18). An equivalent prohibition in Leviticus (19:29) refers only to women and uses different language, which could include secular as well as sacred prostitutes, yet it occurs in the context of a series of prohibitions on various cultic acts, from eating blood to tattooing to the consulting of mediums and wizards. Both passages prohibit Israelite men from prostituting their children; the danger envisioned was probably the dedication of children to such cultic use—not very different, in principle, from sacrificing seed to Molech (Lev. 20:1–5). Strictly speaking, condemnation falls upon the parent who prostituted the child rather than the prostitutes themselves.

It remained possible, to be sure, that a child might exercise his or her own volition in choosing a life of prostitution. Such a child would disgrace the parent. (We know that cult prostitutes, at least, were considered the dregs of society, Job 36:14.) But the Torah has nothing to say about this except where a female prostitute might compromise the holiness of a priest. A priest may not marry a prostitute (Lev. 21:7), and if his daughter becomes a prostitute, she is to be burned because her action has profaned her father (21:9). The daughter of a priest, before she married or if she returned to him as a divorcee or a childless widow, was reckoned a part of his family and given the right to eat of the sacred dues he received for the part he played in sacrifices (22:10–13); hence her purity was more critical than that of other Israelite women.

The Torah does not explicitly condemn men who visit prostitutes. In the story of Tamar, Judah is furious when he thinks that his daughter-in-law has prostituted herself, but he exhibits no particular shame about his own behavior in having intercourse with her when he thought she was a wayside prostitute (Gen. 38). A critical perspective was certainly implied in the way Israelite participation in foreign cults was described with the metaphor of prostitution. Some of the prophets make this connection explicit. Hosea, for example, says that God will not punish Israel's daughters for prostitution or their wives for adultery, since the men themselves, in their pursuit of idolatrous rites, visit prostitutes and sacrifice with "holy women" (4:12–14). "Playing the harlot," as English translations classically put it, became a common idiom for worshiping other gods, both in the Torah (e.g., Exod. 34:16) and in prophetic literature, so that both sacred and secular prostitution were under a religious cloud.

Summary

We can summarize the purity code of the Torah as it touches on sexual matters thus: All sexual and quasi-sexual emissions defile, and the rules that govern these matters belong entirely to the sphere of purity concerns. The prohibitions against male-male anal intercourse, cross-dressing, and intercourse with an animal also belong entirely to the sphere of purity ethics, no other rationale being offered for them. Prostitution is a purity offense insofar as it is an aspect of rejected cults. What is particularly condemned under this heading is the dedication of one's children to cult prostitution or anything that might bring prostitutes into close association with the Israelite priesthood. Males do not otherwise appear to be defiled by associating with noncultic prostitutes. Incest, which Israel defined differently from the modern West, is partly a purity offense, but also involves aspects of household hierarchy that we must consider more fully in part 2 of this book. Adultery is primarily an offense against sexual property, but there is a certain purity element in the Torah's treatment of it, partly because the purity system has a certain affinity for sexual rules as such and partly because adultery breaches the ideal woman's complete dedication to her husband's seed. This code was the scriptural basis of the purity system in force among Jews at the time of the origins of Christianity where sexual matters are concerned.

PURITY AND THE GENTILES

The Torah does not treat this purity system as a universal law, applicable to all of humanity; it was a gift specifically to Israel, affirming its separation from other nations and its unique relationship to God.[36] Other nations might have purity rules, too, and the Torah acknowledges that these might be sharply at variance with those of Israel. We are told that Egyptians thought it an abomination to eat with Hebrews (Gen. 43:32) and that they abominated shepherds (46:34) and the kinds of sacrifices that the Israelites offered to their God (Exod. 8:22, ET 26). Israel, in turn, must avoid doing "as they do in the land of Egypt where you dwelt" and "as they do in the land of Canaan, to which I am bringing you" (Lev. 18:3 RSV). Gentiles who lived among the people of Israel in Canaan were required to keep a certain level of purity according to the Israelite concept (e.g., Lev. 18:26). Yet, even in Canaan, the carrion which Israelites must not eat because of its impurity was permissible for resident aliens (Deut. 14:21). In other words, the Torah understands purity systems to be specific to each nation.[37]

The Torah's standards of purity belong not only to the specific nation of Israel, but also to a certain stage in its life, beginning at Sinai. Even the earlier patriarchs of Israel were free of them. Thus, two of the patriarchs were guilty of incest: Abraham by reason of having married his half-sister (Gen. 20:12; cf. Lev. 18:11) and Jacob because his two principal wives were sisters (Gen. 29:21–30; cf. Lev. 18:18). Even Amram, the father of Moses and Aaron, married his father's sister (Exod. 6:20; cf. Lev. 18:12). If this were held against them, there would have been no need to report the information in the first place; at the very least, some apology would have been needed. But the Sinai covenant and its purity rules did not apply to those who were outside it because they antedated it.[38] Nor did it apply to non-Israelites, with the exception of the pre-Israelite inhabitants of Canaan. The Holiness Code maintains that their uncleanness caused the land to vomit them out (e.g., Lev. 18:24–30). But this is a special case because Canaan is a special case. It is the Lord's own land, which he will give to his own people. No other land is pure— and therefore capable of defilement—in the same sense. The purity system, therefore, is simply not relevant to the Gentile world at large.[39]

Although the Gentiles are not required—nor even, for the most part, given the opportunity—to embrace the purity system of the Torah, they are not reckoned as "clean."[40] Just the contrary—because they neither know how dirty they are nor have means of cleansing available to them, they are irremediably filthy. Even Gentiles who have the status of resident aliens in Israel and are therefore expected to abide by certain Israelite purity laws (Lev. 18:26) are only partial exceptions.[41] Numbers 9:14, for example, might appear to grant all resident aliens the right to participate in the Passover, but Exodus 12:43–49 makes this right dependent on their males' receiving circumcision. Ultimately, circumcision formed the decisive boundary.

It was an apt boundary marker. For one thing, the practice distinguished ancient Israel from many of its neighbors, the Egyptians, it seems, being the major exception. For another, the foreskin seems to have symbolized, for Israel, excess and closure. To be pure, a man had to surrender it. Gentiles, accordingly, were not fit marriage partners (Gen. 34:14)—not even their women because they were committed to their ancestral culture (Exod. 34:16). The decisiveness of this contrast between Israel and the uncircumcised lost nothing with time. Ezekiel regarded it as an abomination for a Gentile to enter the Temple (44:6–7). During the exile, the second Isaiah promised that Zion, once revived, would be forever free of "the uncircumcised and the unclean" (Isa. 52:1). After the return from exile, Nehemiah found that Tobiah the Ammonite actually had a suite of rooms in the Temple, and he expelled him and cleansed the chambers (Neh. 13:4–9). Nehemiah and Ezra both acted to halt mixed marriages and dissolve those already contracted (Neh. 13:23–31; Ezra 9:1–10:44).

Biblical writings from the Hellenistic period make the same points.[42] In the Additions to Esther that are found in the Old Greek version of that book, but not in the Hebrew, Esther gives vent to her loathing for "the marriage bed of uncircumcised men and of every foreigner" and declares that even the crown on her head (a sign, of course, of her marriage to the Gentile king) is as disgusting to her as "a rag used during menstruation" (Ad. Est. 14:15–16 = Est. 4:17u-w LXX). The author of 3 Maccabees speaks, as a matter of course, of the "abominable lawless Gentiles" (6:9). Gentiles, in turn, perceived circumcision, along with the observance of Sabbath and the refusal to eat pork, as principal distinctive signs of Jewishness.[43] Over the long history of Jewish-Gentile relations in antiquity, the degree of animosity varied with the degree of provocation on either side;[44] but Jews seem to have retained, on the whole, a sense that the uncircumcised represent the opposite of all that is pure.

So clear was the symbolic value of circumcision that it could be used in ways that are sometimes surprising to the modern reader. The Holiness Code directs that the fruit of a newly planted tree be treated as its "foreskin" for three years. The fruit of the fourth year is holy to God, rather like the act of circumcision, and only in the fifth year does the fruit become available for human use (Lev. 19:23–25). In another context, Moses speaks of himself as a man of "uncircumcised lips," meaning that he is a poor public speaker and incompetent to represent God (Exod. 6:12, 30). Again, authors who wish to reproach Israel itself may refer to the people as being uncircumcised of heart (Lev. 26:41; Deut. 10:16; Jer. 4:4; 9:25–26) or ears (Jer. 6:10), implying that they are, to that extent, not fully Israel. Israel may become unclean by falling short of what the purity system demands, but Gentiles are unclean because they are entirely outside the purity system. Circumcision is the boundary that separates them.[45]

PRINCIPLES OF TORAH PURITY

Purity codes, once assimilated, function in ways that are largely visceral and almost automatic. But as we have noted, even if the sense of purity and impurity may be more or less universal to humanity, the specific details are not. This relatively inarticulate quality of purity ethics can lead to a certain dissatisfaction with them, particularly on the part of people who have inherited their code from a somewhat different cultural context. Even if they are committed to the keeping of an existing purity code, they may want to be able to "make sense" of it in terms of principles more broadly recognized in their own specific circumstances. The Torah itself sometimes relates its purity rules to concerns for property or intra-family hierarchy or authentically Israelite worship; at other times, purity rules simply stand on their own: Purity is purity is purity. . . . How, then, is one to understand them or explain them to others if they have come to seem less than obvious or inevitable?

From antiquity onward, interpreters of the Torah have endeavored to do this. Some read the rules about food purity as allegories of other ethical principles. Certain birds were held to be prohibited as unclean because they were raptors and therefore represented a way of life that human beings should shun. At least as far back as the Middle Ages, students of the Torah began to argue that the prohibition of pork was based on considerations of health. In neither case does the Torah itself support such explanations. That, of course, does not mean that they are definitively wrong, but there is no way to demonstrate that the writers of the Torah had these principles in mind. They remain, at the most, possibilities.[46]

The need to identify principles of purity goes back even to the time of the writing of the documents. The Holiness Code itself relates impurity to non-Israelite practices, perhaps especially cultic ones: "Do not defile yourselves by any of these things, for by all these the nations I am casting out before you defiled themselves; and the land became defiled, so that I punished its iniquity, and the land vomited out its inhabitants" (Lev. 18:24–25 RSV). This, however, was not a disinterested scholarly analysis of the purity code's origins. Rather, it is a particular theological interpretation of purity related to the contemporary situation. Exile was a real threat: the Assyrians exiled many from the Kingdom of Israel in the late eighth century B.C.E., and the Neo-Babylonian Empire deported the elite of the Kingdom of Judah in the early sixth. It was easy to notice a parallel between the destruction of these kingdoms and the Israelites' own conquest of Canaan as narrated in the book of Joshua.

Some of the behavior condemned by the Holiness Code was indeed related to cults shared by Israelites and their Gentile neighbors—cults that could therefore be condemned as less than truly Israelite. Still, reaction to pagan cults cannot explain the whole of the purity code. Take, for example, the matter of clean and unclean animals: the use of the pig in Canaanite sacrificial rituals may help explain its rejection in Leviticus; but the ox, which is reckoned clean, was at least equally important to the Canaanites[47] and the dove, likewise clean, was sacred to the fertility goddess of the region.[48] It thus appears that, even though rejection of alien cultic practices probably helped shape the Israelite purity system, this is not a full explanation of it.

Modern students of the topic have sometimes been still more ambitious in their efforts to explain the system as a coherent whole. Mary Douglas stimulated renewed scholarly study of the topic by bringing an anthropological perspective to it.[49] She noted that the texts themselves treat purity as related to holiness; in other words, purity is a property of the sanctuary and of the worshipers who approach God there. She then went on to explain "holiness" as defined by wholeness and completeness, both in God and in God's creation. This idea, too, is found in the codes. A priest, for example, even though duly entitled to the priesthood by descent, may not officiate in that capacity if he suffers from any "blemish": "a man blind or lame, or one who has a mutilated face or a limb too long, or a man who has an injured foot or an injured hand, or a hunchback, or a dwarf, or a man with a defect in his sight or an itching disease or scabs or crushed testicles" (Lev. 21:18–20 RSV). Again, there is an ideal for the category "land animal"—that it should be a ruminant with cloven hooves—and if it does not match up with the ideal, it is unclean. Thus, the ox, sheep, and goat are clean while the pig and camel are not (Lev. 11:3–8).[50]

According to Douglas's analysis, "wholeness" in this system demands two things: first, that every individual should be a complete and self-contained specimen of its kind (hence the rejection of "blemished" animals for sacrifice, Lev. 3:1, 6) and, second, that there should be no mixing of kinds. Hence, human beings must not have sexual intercourse with animals because it is "confusion" (Lev. 18:23).[51] But, equally, one must not mate different species of domestic animals (for example, to produce mules), or sow a field with two different kinds of seed, or weave a fabric out of two kinds of fibers (19:19)—no doubt for the same reason: unrelated "kinds" must not be allowed to join in sexual or quasi-sexual unions.[52] Similarly, no one person must combine mutually exclusive qualities. Douglas explains the prohibition of a man's lying "with a male the lyings of a woman" (18:22; 20:13) on the grounds that the male who fulfills the "female" role is a combination of kinds and therefore unclean, like a cloth composed of both linen and wool; the act that renders him unclean is the joint responsibility of both partners.

Douglas seems to have identified some principles that influenced the writers of the Torah, but not everything fits her analysis. There are indeed general definitions of what constitutes a clean domestic animal or a clean water animal, but when the writers of Leviticus tackle the question of flying animals, they can only offer lists, suggesting that, at this point, they could only pass on traditional information (11:13–19). The purity code, as we have it in Leviticus, has been brought up to a certain level of clarity and coherence, but its roots lay in preexisting, unsystematic usage rather than in the working out of abstract principles. To a great extent, what was clean was simply whatever the culture regarded clean.

Among recent writers, Jacob Milgrom has been particularly thorough and creative in his study of the subject. He argues that the key issue for the Torah codes is death, which they are concerned to keep at a distance from the Israelite cultus. There can be no doubt that the single most contagiously unclean thing in the codes is a human corpse (Num. 19:14–20); Milgrom brings other issues into that same orbit by associating with death whatever other practices might militate against procreation and life.[53] Helpful as this perception is in some areas, however, there are others (e.g., food purity) where it seems to have little or no bearing.

The Torah's purity code is not entirely coherent or systematic. The writers of the two principal codes in Leviticus moved in this direction, but they did not operate in a vacuum or derive a complete body of legislation from an a priori theoretical system. They did not have the power to do so had they wished. They worked, rather, with a basic practice of purity that was already in place, emphasizing certain aspects of it and perhaps adding others, but hardly creating it from scratch. Walter Houston has shown, for example, that the contents and shape of the code in regard to clean and unclean animals were influenced by multiple factors, ranging from climate and topography in the land of Canaan to widespread social usage in the Ancient Near East to concern over idolatry and the writers' desire to offer a clear and cogent statement of the subject.[54] What held the purity code together was not so much a unifying theory as the power of living custom, which the writers attempted to present in a coherent way and no doubt modified in accord with their own purposes.

THE HISTORY OF PURITY IN THE TORAH

Whatever coherence we may manage to discern in the Torah's purity code, it was never a seamless web. What is more, different parts of the Torah disagree. For example, the Holiness Code forbade the slaughtering of domestic animals for food without a presentation of their blood at the sanctuary of the Lord (Lev. 17:3–6), but Deuteronomy specifically commanded that animals could be slaughtered, with certain safeguards, in a nonsacrificial manner (12:20–28). In this case, the provisions of Deuteronomy won out. Again, individual rules might or might not be honored, even after they were committed to writing and the writings themselves achieved scriptural status. Thus, the author of Judith, who was punctilious in most matters of purity, makes the conversion of Achior the Ammonite one of the crowning points of the story (Jdt. 14:10) despite the fact that Deuteronomy absolutely forbids an Ammonite to "enter the assembly" (23:3). By contrast, Nehemiah expelled an Ammonite from the Temple and purified the chambers where he had lived (Neh. 13:4–9).

Because the Torah presents itself as the work of Moses, it implies that it contains a single, consistent point of view. Ancient readers did not, on the whole, question the basic unity of the text. Where contradictions appeared, they tended to place the divergent passages in conversation with each other and with the practice of their own day and to work out harmonizations or other ways of resolving differences. Modern readers, on the other hand, are likely to see such contradictions as evidence for a process of historical development behind the text as we have it. This is a useful corrective to my emphasis thus far on the coherence of the system. Although broadly coherent, the system enshrined more than one perspective.[55]

The two purity codes in Leviticus are difficult to date, but were almost certainly written out prior to their incorporation into the Torah as we now have it. The first of them is commonly associated with the "Priestly Source" that appears elsewhere in the Torah, while the Holiness Code stands more on its own. Many scholars would date their written form to the period around the Babylonian Exile (587 B.C.E.).[56] They may have been written down at least partly to reformulate Israelite traditions for rebuilding the Temple after the exile. In addition, the Holiness Code sought to lay blame for the catastrophe of exile at the door of those who had been indifferent, by the standards of the writers, to the demands of purity in the preceding era (Lev. 18:24–30).

Jacob Milgrom has argued for an earlier date for both sources, no later than the late eighth century.[57] Here, too, the desire to lay blame for exile (that of the Northern Kingdom) is active. But he also sees the Holiness

Code as the work of "young Turks" among the priestly establishment who wanted to extend the purview of purity. The authors of the Priestly Source (which Milgrom sees as earlier) were concerned largely with the sanctuary and the way in which the accumulation of impurities might defile it and render it unusable as a point of contact between God and the people. Accordingly, they were also particularly interested in the way the Day of Atonement served to purify the sanctuary anew. The Holiness Code, on the other hand, extends its concerns from the sanctuary to the land as a whole. Rites alone cannot maintain the connection of God to an impure people. Only the expunging of those tainted by grave impurities can do this—hence this source's predilection for executing or "cutting off" offenders. This created some confusion in the sacred texts with which subsequent readers and commentators would need to interpret.

On either dating, the written purity codes post-date much of the biblical history narrated in Joshua–2 Kings. We have already noted that the Torah implies a certain freedom from the demands of purity for those who lived before the giving of the Torah at Mt. Sinai. For example, both Abraham and Jacob violated the law of incest in their marriages, but they are not reproached for this failure. For those Israelites living later, however, the structure of the Torah as a written code given to or penned by Moses implies that knowledge of the purity codes was fully available thereafter. Because there is reason not to take the mosaic authorship and early dating of the text at face value, we can look to other records to see whether or to what degree the legal prescriptions in the Torah seem to have been in force at any given time.

We have already made some comparisons with narrative sources clarifying the social context of the incest code. It is unlikely, in fact, that an incest code precisely like that of Leviticus 18 existed yet at the time of David, but his intra-family problems help us to understand the forces that shaped it. The rape of Tamar is a case in point. Tamar protests Amnon's violence as a thing "not done in Israel." But it seems to be the violence rather than the incest that concerns her because she goes on to say that, if he asked for her, David would certainly give her to him (2 Sam. 13:12–13). The rape then becomes grounds for a vendetta by Tamar's full brother Absalom against their half-brother Amnon, resulting in Amnon's death and Absalom's flight into exile (2 Sam. 13:33–39). One could not ask for a more vivid illustration of the kind of troubles that the incest code was designed to prevent.

Another case in point is that of David and Jonathan. Their story presents them as intimates. Indeed, the lament for Jonathan ascribed to David includes a passage that, in any other cultural context, would probably be taken as evidence for some kind of sexual expression of their relationship:

> I am distressed for you, my brother Jonathan;
> greatly beloved were you to me;
> your love to me was wonderful,
> passing the love of women. [2 Sam. 2:26, NRSV]

Saul, in fact, denounces his son Jonathan for preferring David's house to his own, describing this as shameful and rebellious behavior that will end in Jonathan's loss of his kingdom (1 Sam. 20:30–31). Apart from this outburst by Saul, however, the narrative does not treat the relationship negatively. And it nowhere raises the issue of purity.

Leviticus assumes that anal intercourse between two males was already prohibited long before the time of David and Jonathan, and later readers have often broadened that prohibition to apply to all kinds of sexual intercourse between people of the same gender. The narrative of David and Jonathan, however, seems to know nothing of such ideas. Its author or authors, had they known them, might well have intentionally excluded an erotic interpretation. The only reason today for *not* reading their story as expressing an erotic attachment is the assumption that such a male-male attachment was impossible in their time and place. Given a modern awareness aware of the pervasiveness of such attachments in later history, even at times when they were not supposed to exist, much less appear in public discourse, this is not a persuasive argument.[58]

Because the Holiness Code represents a particular formulation of purity at a particular time, we are ill advised to assume that it was the decisive word through the history of ancient Israel. In matters of sexual purity, as in other legal issues, one must be prepared for the possibility of greater diversity within ancient Israelite ethics than is countenanced by the Torah, particularly by its most restrictive components. While we cannot say exactly what kind of relationship existed between David and Jonathan or what sexual practices might have been a part of it, we also cannot exclude a priori the possibility that it had a sexual component.

We must, instead, read the story in its own terms. We cannot even take it for granted that such a relationship was prohibited by the purity practices of the time.

PURITY AND SOCIAL BOUNDARIES

The heart of the purity system in ancient Israel lay in the holy place and its sacrificial cultus. Such a cultus, with its attendant phenomena of blood and offal, of stench and smoke, might not exemplify modern Western notions of cleanness, but this reminds us that purity is not defined in the same way in every culture. The great importance of sacrificial worship was that it afforded humanity's nearest approach to God. Human worshipers, therefore, needed to be in the most fitting state possible when they made this approach. Everything unclean had to be kept at a distance from the sanctuary. The Priestly Source demanded a particularly high level of purity from the priestly officiants. The Holiness Code moved toward extending high purity demands to the whole population of the land of Israel.

But the demand for purity bore on different groups differently. We have already noted that it established a boundary between Israel and the Gentiles. Gentiles were not, by and large, expected to observe it (although the Holiness Code did lay certain obligations on resident aliens in Israel). The impurity of Gentiles would come to be a more pressing issue when the Jewish people found themselves a scattered minority in Gentile territory, where they felt an ongoing obligation to keep themselves distinct from others. And in a world of empires where Gentile authorities might visit Jerusalem, Jews also had an obligation to keep Gentiles at an appropriate distance from the Temple and its rites.[59]

But purity also constructed certain differences of status within Israel. Gender was one important issue. Women were not only socially inferior to men but also more likely to become impure. And their impurity was more contagious. Behaviors that confused the gender boundary, such as crossdressing and male-male sexual intercourse, were also potently impure.[60] "Lepers" (those suffering from a variety of skin diseases) were categorically impure. The poor were probably more likely to be or remain impure than others because they would not necessarily be able to afford the rites that signified the conclusion of one's impurity—a particular problem once the sacrificial cultus was restricted to the one Temple in Jerusalem, with the result that purification might demand a pilgrimage as well as a rite. Purity thus shaped the society as a whole in pervasive ways and sometimes reflected elements of domination and subordination within it.

The purity code was not simply a veiled equivalent to gender, ethnic, or class distinctions within society. It was related to these, but not identical to them. Any person was liable to experience uncleanness in various ways and was obliged to observe the appropriate means for cleansing. In many cases, these were not onerous. And even a powerful person might become unclean in a radical, ongoing sense, as in the case of King Uzziah, who was a "leper." The purity code required that he be expelled from the "camp" and made to wear rags and warn other people away from him (Lev. 13:45–46). One may doubt exactly how far this went in practice, but we are told that he lived in a separate house after the condition became apparent, while his son Jotham took over the palace and the government (2 Kings 15:5; 2 Chron. 26:21). The Chronicler even claims that he was buried separately from the other kings of Judah, though apparently not far off (2 Chron. 26:23).

Purity and other forms of social status interacted with each other, sometimes reinforcing each other, sometimes conflicting. Purity was never simply equivalent to social status nor was impurity simply another way of speaking about violations of social status or property. Where the language of purity and that of property interact with each other in our texts (e.g., in the incest code), the language of property must be taken seriously in its own right—something we will do in a later chapter. At the same time, we can see that purity was not completely independent of social status.

UNITY OF THE PURITY SYSTEM

Perhaps the most difficult thing for the modern Westerner to grasp is that the ancient purity system of Israel was more or less of a single piece. The casual reader, beginning with modern presuppositions about the subject, is apt to separate different aspects of the system, discarding those that have no real equivalent in our experience, such as the food laws and the laws about menstruation, and retaining those that seem more familiar—usually a selection of other sexual rules. The former seem "self-evidently" unimportant, while the latter seem "self-evidently" relevant.[61] The "self-evident" quality of such responses lies chiefly in the eye of the reader, not in the texts being read.

In making this separation, we often invoke a venerable distinction between "ritual" and "moral" law.[62] We then categorize food purity as "ritual" and sexual purity as "moral"—perhaps with a few exceptions for such things as impurity during menstruation or after childbirth.[63] While one can certainly make such distinctions, there is no foundation for them in the Torah itself, which simply does not have separate categories of "ritual" as opposed to "moral" offenses. This is a distinction imposed from the outside by a later Christian culture with a different set of interests. In adopting and arguing from it, one is no longer basing one's argument on scripture itself.

Jonathan Klawans, to be sure, has sought to distinguish two types of purity in the Torah—a "ritual" purity dealt with by Leviticus 11–16, which is morally neutral unless a worshiper approaches the sanctuary in an unclean state, and a "moral" purity in the Holiness Code. The former can be removed by rites of purification; the latter cannot be purified and must be punished by death or "cutting off." To some extent, this simply recognizes the different interests of the two codes in Leviticus—something we have already noted. And it builds on distinctions made in a less drastic fashion by Jacob Milgrom.[64]

Klawans's choice of terms, however, is misleading. Purity is a moral or ethical principle in its own right, even if not one that most philosophical ethicists find helpful. Moreover, as its terminology indicates, it originates in a sense of literal, physical dirtiness that is given cultural and religious significance. It would be more accurate to say that the Holiness Code is not introducing a different kind of purity but that it is raising the stakes of the purity system as such and sometimes also extending its scope to reinforce other ethical principles.[65] Whether increasing the penalty for a familiar purity violation (e.g., sex with a menstruating woman, Lev. 20:18) or reframing some other type of offense as a purity violation (e.g., adultery, Lev. 20:10), the Holiness Code continues to use the same purity language as the earlier code in Leviticus 11–16. Rather than introducing a separate category of purity, the Holiness Code is extending the existing category metaphorically to cover its own somewhat distinct interests.[66]

The Torah, in principle, stood or fell as a whole; ancient Israel did not ascribe greater authority to one class of laws or another. Even though one could distinguish between purity offenses and other transgressions (as in the law for the Day of Atonement, Lev. 16:16), both were of great weight and were prohibited by the same Torah. Anyone who doubts the seriousness with which the food laws were regarded need only read 4 Maccabees, an oration in celebration of some martyrs of the second century B.C.E. In a dramatic exchange, the Greek emperor Antiochus challenges the Jewish sage Eleazar to show his moderation and good sense by taking a single small bite of pork and thus saving his life. Eleazar refuses, saying, "Do not suppose that it is a small sin if we should eat what is polluted, for to transgress the laws in small matters or in great comes to the same thing, since either way the Law is still being scorned" (4 Macc. 5:19–21). The language here borrows heavily from Greco-Roman Stoicism, but the substance is an authentic expression of Israelite purity ethics.[67]

The reverse of Eleazar's position was also possible. If eating a single bite of pork was equivalent to idolatry, idolatry might in some sense seem equivalent to eating a bite of pork. When a faction of the Jewish elite in Jerusalem decided, early in the second century B.C.E., to assimilate more closely to their Gentile environment, they did not adopt a policy of trimming at the edges, as if food laws were less critical than prohibitions of idolatry. Their program seems to have included the building of a gymnasium (which implied nude athletic exercises in the Greek fashion),[68] surgery to reproduce the appearance of a foreskin, violation of the Sabbath, introduction of sacred images with their altars and cultus, sacrifice of unclean animals such as pigs, and prohibition of circumcision (1 Macc. 1:14–15, 44–49). It is not clear that these "reformers" thought that they were abandoning the worship of the Lord or their own identity as Jews. They may have seen themselves simply as "modernizing." For them, however, as for Eleazar, the purity law was a single coherent set of demands. There was no reason to retain one bit of it and ignore another. The significance of the purity law for the New Testament will become clear only if we keep this point firmly in mind. It functioned as a whole and was not open to being dismembered to retain what one wished and discard other parts.

CHAPTER 3

PURITY IN
FIRST-CENTURY JUDAISM

The purity code of Israel had prob-
ably reached its written form by the fifth century B.C.E., while the New
Testament documents date from half a millennium later. We cannot
expect that any societal code will remain absolutely unchanged over so
long a time. Changes of political and social circumstances can easily
make "ancient good uncouth" and, even where ancient customs are preserved, people may do so without full understanding of their original
meaning. In antiquity as today, there was an ongoing process of reap-
propriating the past for contemporary use. For this reason, the student
of the New Testament needs to ask not only "What did the scriptures of
Israel say about a given subject?" but also "How was their witness being
understood and put into practice at the time of Jesus and his disciples?"
The latter question is the more difficult of the two to answer, for Jewish
life and thought at the turn of the eras were rich and complex—and not
always well documented.

The reader who is not familiar with early Judaism will need to know
a few basic points by way of introduction. Membership in the nation
of Israel was primarily by birth (although some Gentiles became full
converts to Judaism). The center of national life lay in the territories of
Judaea and Galilee, which were subject to the Roman Empire, but the
majority of Jews lived elsewhere, in what was called the Diaspora ("Scat-
tering"). Some of these Jews lived in Mesopotamia, east of the Roman
Empire; others lived to the west and north in large, Greek-speaking cities
of the Empire. At the turn of the eras, the Jewish people had been politically subject to others for the better part of the preceding six centuries;
for the last century and a half of this period, the Jewish community in

Palestine had been through a bewildering period of historical flux, taking it from near-dissolution to revived independence and then into new subjugation.

During this difficult period, particularly devout people began to band together into like-minded groups whose way of practicing the national religion distinguished them from one another and from their less devout compatriots. There were four such groups or "sects" of particular importance in the years before the destruction of the Temple in 70 c.e.: Sadducees, Essenes, Pharisees, and what one ancient writer called the "Fourth Philosophy." The first two were mainly priestly groups. But where the Sadducees were rich and powerful because of their control of the Jerusalem Temple, the Essenes were dispossessed, alienated from the Temple, and leading a life apart from the mainstream. The Pharisees were mainly laymen committed to a very high standard in observing the Torah and highly regarded by the populace as legal experts. The Fourth Philosophy was an assortment of revolutionary groups, including the Zealots, that aimed to restore the independence of Israel. In due course, Jewish Christians became a fifth sect.

Of these sects, we know very little about the Sadducees except that they were literalists and strict constructionists in the interpretation of the Torah. Probably, their attitude toward purity was still close to that of the Torah itself. There was one law for all of Israel, but it bore on them, the Sadducees, with particular stringency—not because they were Sadducees, but because they were priests. Because priestly families received special portions from the sacrifices, which had to be eaten in cleanness, they were compelled to keep a higher standard than others.

ESSENES

By an archaeological accident, we have come to know the Essenes much better. The discovery of the Dead Sea Scrolls, beginning in the late 1940s, revealed something of the life of a Jewish group that lived, between about 150 B.C.E. and 68 C.E., at a place in the Judean desert called Qumran.[1] The writings have not been easy to interpret, but there is broad agreement that they come from the group described by several ancient writers under the name "Essenes." This sect thus became the only first-century Jewish sect other than Christians for which we have contemporary documentation in the form of their own writings. The works in their library came from a long period of time and not all were uniquely theirs, for they included fragments of almost all the scriptures of Israel and of the many quasi-biblical documents that we call "Pseudepigrapha." There were also books more particular to their sect, however, ranging in time of origin from the *Temple Scroll*, which may reflect a time before the sect reached its classic form,[2] to the *Commentary on Habakkuk*, which can hardly be earlier than the reign of Augustus (27 B.C.E.–14 C.E.).[3]

The sect probably included two distinct levels of adherents. A plausible reconstruction holds that the majority of the members lived in the towns and villages of Judaea, but kept themselves rather apart from their neighbors. These people married, had children, held private property, and worked at ordinary occupations. The inner circle of the group, on the other hand, lived at Qumran itself, were celibate, held their property communally, worked the land surrounding their settlement, and devoted a significant amount of time to studying scripture. In all the life of the community, priests took the lead, and one of them was probably the head of the whole group.[4]

The complex organization thus established drew its sense of unity and significance from conceiving itself as the only true Israel or as the real Temple (in contrast to the building in Jerusalem). To the Essenes, the rest of the Jewish people had forsaken the right way, and the Sadducean priests who had been in command of the Jerusalem Temple since the mid-second century B.C.E. had defiled it and made it useless. In place of chosen Israel, then, was the membership of the sect, and in place of the Temple with its sacrificial worship were the "men of perfect holiness," who made atonement for sins through prayer and "perfection of way" (*CR* VIII, 20–IX, 6).[5]

The sect's writings treat the issue of purity in a highly consistent way. Its central importance to the Essenes is clear from the process of initiation into the inner circle: only after instruction, examination, and a year's probation did the initiate gain the right to "touch the purity of the many." This purity has been variously interpreted. Most probably, it signified the solid foods served as part of the group's common meal. (The new initiate had to wait another year before sharing in the community's drink because liquids, as Leviticus 11:29–38 specifies, are more liable to pollution.)[6] More broadly, the purity may have included other common property of the community that could receive or transmit impurity and had therefore to be guarded from the careless or uninformed.[7] Purity thus lay at the center of the meaning of the inner group or Council of the Community.[8]

Very likely, this meaning was connected with the sect's conception of this group as equivalent to the Temple. Just as the sanctuary and priesthood, according to Leviticus, had to be kept pure of the people's uncleanness, so, too, must the Council remain undefiled, even more than the members of lower rank. Thus the men of the Council were severely admonished against any display of nakedness (*CR* VII,14), just as the priestly rules in the Torah forbade steps at God's altar so that there would be no exposure of the priests' genitals (Exod. 20:26) and required the priests always to wear underwear when officiating (28:42–43). No equivalent rule survives for the ordinary Essene, but purity was surely important for them, too.

The purity system of the Torah was fully binding on the community, but in accordance with the Essenes' own particular interpretation of it. In the specific area of sexual purity, the *Damascus Rule* (which included rules for ordinary Essenes) reaffirms the Torah's rules on incest (V), but extends them by asserting that the rules are the same for women as for men; thus a woman may not marry her uncle any more than a man his aunt (V,7–11). The *Temple Scroll*, an idealized picture of the perfect Temple and its environs, also "rationalizes" the incest rules in a similar way (66.12–17).[9] The *Damascus Rule* also forbids "fornication" and defines it to mean polygyny. Because many of the Torah rules assume that a man may have more than one wife, it was necessary to explain such a claim and ground it in terms of Torah. The Essenes constructed such a grounding by reading into the creation narrative and other passages a requirement of monogamy (IV,19–V,6). Similarly, the *Temple Scroll* forbids polygyny, although apparently only in the case of the king (56.18–19).

The Essenes also added some purity rules of their own, following a general pattern of restricting sexuality further than the Torah did. One program for an ideal community life forbade a man to have intercourse with a woman before he was 20 (*MR* I,9–11). The *Damascus Rule* forbade all sexual intercourse in "the city of the sanctuary" on the grounds that it would defile the city (XII,1–2). The *Temple Scroll* may have assumed the same kind of rule because it forbade a man who is unclean because he has ejaculated during intercourse with his wife to enter the "city of the sanctuary" for three days (45:11–12). For the *Temple Scroll*, the "city" in question was Jerusalem, but for the practical purposes of the *Damascus Rule*, it may perhaps have been the settlement at Qumran, which was, in many ways, the Essenes' equivalent.[10]

The Essene sect thus saw itself as committed to a level of purity far above that required of ordinary Israelites in the Torah, a purity, in fact, more suitable to priest and sanctuary. In Leviticus (21:16–24), there is a list of deformities that disqualify a priest from officiating in the Temple. In the Qumran documents, we find similar lists of people who are excluded from membership in the sect: the mad, the simple, the blind, the maimed, the lame, the deaf, those with a visible blemish, minors, the old and tottery (*DR* XV,15ff.; *MR* II,3–9; *WR* VII,3–6). The community was to incorporate a consummate purity understood as perfection.[11] (Even more than with the Torah itself, this perfection is assumed to be male; women are alluded to only as dependents of the members of the sect's lower order.)

Some scholars have suggested that this focus on purity is not to be understood as a true purity system and that the Qumran community had, in fact, little interest in or conception of physical purity as a distinct quality. "It is inappropriate," says one scholar, "to put any weight on the distinction between 'moral' and 'ritual' purity at Qumran. If one slanders one's brother or touches a corpse, one has transgressed and is unclean, one's sin pollutes the community, and means have to be taken to cleanse the community and prevent further contamination."[12] This statement is undoubtedly correct in the sense that the Essenes, as with Jeremiah, Ezekiel, and the Book of Proverbs, spoke of all kinds of sin as uncleanness (see above, p. 35). Indeed, they went further and required rites of purification from sins originally unrelated to the purity system.[13]

It would be a mistake, however, to assume that all kinds of uncleanness were equated with deliberate sin or that one could not distinguish at all, in the context of Qumran, between purity issues and other kinds of ethical concerns. The *Temple Scroll*, for example, distinguishes between the man who has had a wet dream and is therefore excluded from the sanctuary for three days and the man who has ejaculated during intercourse with a woman and is therefore excluded from the whole city of the sanctuary for the same time (45.7–12). The distinction here is whether the defilement was deliberately incurred. Impurity deliberately courted apparently seemed more defiling, although not, in this case, more sinful. If one also refused to restrict one's activities while impure (thus spreading impurity to others through contagion) and failed to undertake the prescribed methods of purification, no doubt one's impurity crossed over into the realm of sin. The community of the scrolls, however, could not have maintained its existence at all if it had regarded all impurity as ipso facto sinful.[14]

It was impossible, even from the Essene perspective, for life in flesh to be entirely free of impurity. Humanity is a thing kneaded of dust and water, originating in the nakedness of the sexual act, and only God's grace renders one righteous (*H* XIII,14–17). Still, the Essenes saw themselves as unique in Israel in terms of their correct understanding of and commitment to the purity system, and this led to a significant redefinition of the boundaries marked and defended by that system. The Qumran sect still regarded the Gentiles as the ultimate outsiders and foes. The sectarians were to avoid them as much as possible, not spending Sabbath near them (*DR* XI,14–15), not selling them any clean animal, any grain or wine, or any slave who had become a member of the sect (XII,8-11). In the last days, the members of the sect would participate in a great messianic war, which would lead to the defeat and enslavement of the Gentiles (*MR* I,21; *WR* passim, esp. XII,14–15) and would set them permanently at a distance from the "sanctuary of men" —that is, the Qumran Community itself (*Midrash on the Last Days* I,3–7).

Gentiles were not, however, the primary threat to the Qumran sectarians during most of their existence. Their enemies, particularly in their formative period, were to be found rather in the priestly establishment and other Jewish sects. The Wicked Priest who persecuted the Essenes' Teacher of Righteousness was a high priest of the Jerusalem Temple and their subsequent opponents included Sadducees and Pharisees.[15] Because the Essenes made a point of their own devotion to purity, it is not surprising that they accused their opponents of a comparable contempt for it, particularly of having "committed pollution" (*MA* 27) and defiled the Temple (*CHab* XII,7–9). One specific complaint against them was that they condoned (and perhaps committed) intercourse with menstruating women (*DR* V,6–7).

Because they perceived these Jewish opponents as indifferent to the requirements of purity and to pollution of the Temple, the Essenes spoke of them in terms borrowed from traditional language about Gentiles. The author of the *Hymns* describes them as having chosen "uncircumcision of lip" and a foreign tongue (II,18–19; cf. IV,16). The *Commentary on*

Psalm 37 links together "the violent [of the Gentiles and] the wicked of Israel" as the people who are to be "cut off" (III,12–13).[16] The *Commentary on Habakkuk* declares that the Wicked Priest "did not circumcise the foreskin of his heart" (XI,13). The Qumran sect, in other words, understood Jews outside its ranks as quasi-Gentiles. Perhaps they saw a poetic justice in the death of the Wicked Priest at Gentile hands (*CPs37* IV,9–10) and in predicting a similar fate for their other enemies (*CNah* II,4–5).

So strong was their sense of the outside world as "uncircumcised" that the Essenes even spoke of themselves as having been, figuratively, Gentiles before they became members of the sect. The author of the *Hymns*, speaking of how one recognized the truth of the sect's teaching, described it as a grace granted to the uncircumcised mouth (II,7) and ear (XVIII,20), and every member was exhorted to "circumcise in the Community the foreskin of evil inclination and of stiffness of neck" (*CR* V,5). What is more, they were to shun other Jews as unclean and to avoid sharing anything with them, except through commercial transactions (*CR* V,10–20), also allowed with Gentiles. Figurative use of the language of circumcision was not, of course, new; we noted its biblical occurrence earlier (p. 48). What is new here is the use of the purity system to draw a line not only between Israel and the Gentiles but also between one small group of pious people and the great mass of Israelites, including other pious groups who were at odds with the Essenes. The sect represented "the way of [holiness] where no man goes who is uncircumcised or unclean or violent " (*H* VI,20-21).[17] Gentiles and quasi-Gentiles occupied the outside world. Neither had any part in the true Israel; to become part of the elect, either kind of outsider must undergo a conversion. The boundary function of purity rules had now given rise to a new, intra-Jewish border.

PHARISEES

Turning to the sect of the Pharisees, we find a related picture, but the lines here are less sharp because of the nature of the sources and the historical problems they present. Our knowledge of the Pharisees is based on three groups of writings: the New Testament, the works of the first-century Jewish historian Josephus, and the Mishnah. Of these, the first two are close in time to the historical Pharisees, but Josephus stood in an ambiguous political relationship to them and the New Testament authors treat them only incidentally and usually in a hostile fashion. None of these authors viewed them with detachment. The Mishnah, on the other hand, includes many traditions about the Pharisees handed down through their own disciples; but since the material was not reduced to writing until about 200 C.E., the choice of what was preserved and the way in which it was recorded and edited must necessarily reflect the interests of later generations. The result is that students of the Pharisees, evaluating the data in different ways, can sometimes produce surprisingly divergent descriptions of the group.[18]

In what follows, I take my cue from what appears to me to be the dominant view, which holds that the Pharisees went through several distinct phases in their existence over a period of centuries. For our present purposes, it will be enough to think of these as three phases. First, from their origins in the second century B.C.E. to the time of Herod the Great in the late first, they were primarily a political party, competing with the Sadducees for influence at the Jewish royal court. By the time of Herod, they had lost this contest and, under their great leader Hillel, entered a second phase in their self-understanding. Withdrawing from the political arena, they became an association of men committed to the precise observance of the Torah, which, for them, meant not only the written Torah acknowledged by all Jews, but also the unwritten traditions of their own sect, the "oral Torah," to which they accorded an authority at least equal to that of its written counterpart. This phase of their community life lasted until the First Jewish War (66–70 C.E.), after which, in the social and political disarray that followed defeat and the burning of the Temple, they reemerged, in a third phase, as a significant political power, gradually becoming the dominant Jewish authorities. The writing down of their oral traditions at the very end of the second century C.E. signified the completion of this process, and the Rabbinic Judaism of the Mishnah is their enduring legacy.[19]

The second and third of these periods overlap with the writing of the New Testament, and the second (or sectarian) phase is of particular interest because it is also the time of Jesus and Paul. During this time, the Pharisees seem to have concentrated their attention on issues of table fellowship. They undertook to eat their ordinary meals in the high state of purity that Leviticus demanded only of the priestly families who ate the special sacrificial portions reserved to them. This commitment required

constant vigilance against contracting uncleanness or, if one had contracted it, against communicating it to utensils and foodstuffs. In this
regard, the concerns of the Pharisees were not markedly different from
those of the Sadducees, who were obliged to maintain a high degree of
purity because most of them were Temple priests, or of the Essenes, who
undertook a similar obligation when they identified their desert community as a substitute for the Temple and its sacrifices. The working out of
these concerns, however, had to be quite different, for where the Sadducees and Essenes were surrounded by institutions (the Temple, the desert
community) that kept the ignorant and careless at a suitable distance, the
Pharisees lived among the general population and sought to maintain
purity household by household.

The oral Torah that the Pharisees generated and handed on seems
to have been concerned with exactly the issues that would be involved in
ensuring such a result. They were interested in the correct tithing of produce because untithed food, although not precisely impure, was nonetheless beyond the bounds of the priestly table. They were also interested
in those types of uncleanness considered particularly contagious, which
might therefore pollute food. Among these, menstruation was particularly important because women did most preparing of food. Alongside
menstruation, of course, went other forms of genital discharge: hemor-
rhages in women and gonorrhea in men. Corpses were also sources of
contagion and particularly virulent, since they could transmit uncleanness through "overshadowing," that is, by being under the same cover
(tent, roof, etc.) as a person or object susceptible to being made unclean.
By contrast, purity issues raised by the written Torah but having no relation to the issue of table purity received little attention; examples would
be wizardry, incest, emissions of semen, same-gender sexual intercourse,
or intercourse with an animal, which were not considered to generate
contagion.[20]

In the great corpus of Mishnaic law, it is difficult to disentangle the
earliest elements, coming from the first or second phase of the history of
the Pharisees, from the overlay of later interpretation and elaboration (in
its literal sense of the detailed "working out" of principles). Jacob Neusner
has argued, however, in his massive work on "Purities" (the sixth major
division of the Mishnah) that the authorities of what I have called the
third phase were interested not only in exploring principles and making
details explicit, but also in understanding the theme of personal respon-

sibility and, therefore, the role of human intention in matters of purity. The purity code of the written Torah had no great interest in intention. Purity and impurity were simply facts: Play with mud and you will get dirty. The later Mishnaic authorities, however, saw in the purity system a grand interchange between nature and human purpose that took it out of the realm of the merely factual.[21]

Whether this theological and anthropological interest existed in the first or second phase is far from clear. It has been argued that the rabbis as a whole "felt" violations of purity as guilt rather than as a quasi-physical contamination—that is, they saw purity and impurity in terms of virtue and vice rather than as simple facts of existence.[22] We have already seen that purity and virtue get mixed up with one another in a variety of ways: feelings associated with purity are used to reinforce virtue, and violations of virtue may be regarded as communicating impurity. Certainly, the earlier Pharisees must have seen their decision to maintain Levitical purity at their own tables as something more than mere fastidiousness. They, like the Essenes, probably intended a direct reference to the Temple and its altar, although, unlike the Essenes, they wished not to replace that altar but only to claim a related and comparable sacredness for their own life of piety. This does not mean that, for them, purity was subsumed under virtue or that it became a "mere" theological gesture; it still maintained its distinct reality and importance, which interpenetrated with the other aspects of their religious concern.[23]

The Pharisees of the early first century C.E., then, had a strong interest in maintaining a high degree of purity at their own tables.[24] In the absence of geographic boundaries around their community, they had to devise ways to make this possible. In all probability, they did so by creating a network of "associates" who understood the sect's standards and were pledged to maintain them rigorously. Any Pharisee could eat with confidence what was set before him by a fellow-associate, but, conversely, he had to be suspicious of food prepared by other Jews. The Pharisee who bought produce from an outsider, even if the seller claimed to have paid tithe, tithed it anew to be sure that all obligations had been met. In matters of food preparation, too, those who were not members of Pharisee households were at least suspect. While one should not overplay the division between Pharisees and *am ha-arets* ("people of the land"; ordinary, nonsectarian Jews), turning it into some sort of deep-rooted and invariable antipathy, it remains true that the Pharisees' interest in purity imposed a barrier between them and less rigorous Jews—a barrier that gave a particular identity to the Pharisees and, at the same time, characterized outsiders as habitually unclean.[25]

The Pharisees did not retreat to the desert or behind the walls of the Temple, yet they did separate themselves decisively from other Jews by a barrier of purity. If the original purpose of that barrier was to associate their meals with the sanctuary, the inevitable effect of it, nonetheless, was to set them apart. As long as the Pharisees continued primarily as a sect within Judaism, this would have given impetus to the elaboration of purity laws, for these laws, in effect, defined them as a group. By the late second century C.E., however, the spiritual descendants of the Pharisees were no longer a sect, with the task of keeping themselves distinct, but the acknowledged guides of the whole people. One may guess that this carefully elaborated system then ceased to be useful. In fact, as Neusner has observed, it fell out of use just as it approximated perfection of form and completeness of substance.[26]

The Pharisees, then, used purity for purposes similar to those of the Essenes, although without desiring or producing the drastic measure of separation that Qumran represents.[27] If we accept Josephus's claim (*Antiquities* 18.23) that the advocates of the Fourth Philosophy—Zealots and other revolutionaries—differed from the Pharisees not at all except in their uncompromising devotion to the independence of Israel, then we can say that, of all the first-century Jewish sects known to us, every one made some use of purity as a device to mark itself off from other Jews, whether adherents of rival sects or ordinary "people of the land." This use of purity marks the situation of the first century as radically different from that envisioned in Leviticus. The older presupposition was a single people adhering to a single law of purity, with a higher degree of purity incumbent upon priestly families. The purity law did draw boundaries, but they were primarily boundaries between Israel and the uncircumcised. In the first century C.E., however, purity law was increasingly important for the way it could draw boundaries between Jew and Jew.[28] The sects identified themselves in terms of the interpretation of the law to which they adhered and the structures they created to support them in their practice of it. Outside the boundaries of the sects, the ordinary "people of the land," whether by explicit judgment or only by clear implication, were unclean, removed from holiness.[29]

THE DIASPORA AMONG THE GREEKS

The picture I have drawn thus far applies primarily to Judea and Galilee. Many Jews, as noted earlier, lived elsewhere; those who lived in the great Hellenistic cities of the Roman world are particularly important to any study of the New Testament because it was among them and through their synagogues that Christianity first spread most widely. These Jews spoke Greek as their principal or, in most cases, only language. They read their scriptures in the Old Greek Version, often called the Septuagint. They interacted with the Gentile culture that surrounded them to a degree nearly unimaginable in Palestine itself. The circumstances of their lives made the issue of purity somewhat different for them from what it was to their Palestinian coreligionists.

For one thing, the Jews of the Diaspora do not seem to have given rise to a rich growth of sects. The only one that we know of was a contemplative group called the Therapeutae. Like the Essenes, they retreated into a kind of monastery in the desert, although, in their case, it was near Alexandria rather than the Dead Sea. They seem to have had only this one center. Philo, our sole source of information about them, describes them as ascetics who devoted themselves to the study of scripture and held periodic common meals marked by teaching, singing, and sacred dance. He says nothing of specialized purity rules surrounding their life together, although it is not impossible that such existed.[30]

The heart of the purity issue, however, for Hellenistic Jews lay not in the self-definition of sects but in that of Israel itself. Surrounded as they were by Gentiles who spoke the same language as they and with whom they dealt constantly in matters of trade and politics, the issue of their distinct ethnic identity came to the fore. Jew and Gentile alike were conscious of the purity laws (and the parallel issue of Sabbath observance) as things that separated Jews and Gentiles from one another. Some Gentiles even accused Jews of disliking humanity in general because of what they perceived as standoffish behavior. It was important for Jews to respond to this kind of critique, both for their own sake and also to present a more amiable account of themselves to their neighbors.[31]

We find such an account in the *Letter of Aristeas*, an Alexandrian Jewish work of perhaps the second century B.C.E. that tells a legendary tale of the origins of the Septuagint.[32] A long speech by the high priest (128–71) explains that the food laws were given to Israel precisely to keep them separate from other peoples. This separation preserved them from being tempted into idolatry and left them free to focus entirely on the wonderful wisdom that God gave them in the Torah. Even the contents of these laws are not merely arbitrary, but are designed to set before the people, as they practice them, an ongoing allegory of just living. The weasel, for example, is forbidden as food because it conceives through the ear and gives birth through the mouth, thereby serving as an allegory of the informer, whose unjust way of life is to be rejected. Here, we see a Jewish apologist accepting the fact that purity laws have an exclusionary effect and seeking to make a virtue of it.

Not all Hellenistic Jews were content with this answer. Some, in fact, wished to abolish the purity laws or at least let them drop out of use. In Jerusalem itself, in the early second century B.C.E., Greek-speaking Jews who had drawn close, politically and culturally, to their Gentile neighbors sought to reform Judaism by eliminating the distinctive purity laws, probably in the name of a return to a more primitive and universal form of their ancestral faith.[33] In the Diaspora, some Jews argued that the allegorical meaning of the purity laws, their hidden teaching about the just life, was in fact their whole significance and that the person who understood this meaning and lived by it need not obey the commands in their literal sense.[34] While the dominant tradition within Judaism insisted on retaining the purity code, Jews were not completely united in the matter. The code itself, therefore, had to be explicated and defended in terms that would make it intelligible both to Gentile outsiders and to those insiders who had come to regard it as an imposition.

Several apologetic tacks were possible. One was to say, "We are just like you Gentiles only better." This approach would emphasize the areas of overlap between Jewish and Greek morality without making a point of Jewish particularity except where it could be related to some theme in Gentile ethics. Because Greeks and Jews alike typically disapproved of sexual promiscuity, however defined, this could provide the rubric for a presentation of common themes.[35] The *Testaments of the Twelve Patriarchs*, accordingly, presents a series of moral exhortations, in a context redolent of biblical history that would nonetheless have been generally intelligible to Gentiles, too.[36]

A similar approach appears in the work of a first-century Jewish writer posing as the ancient Greek poet Phocylides. He warns his audience against most transgressions of the Mosaic laws of sexual purity: adultery (3), prostitution (177–78), incest (179–83), intercourse with animals (188), same-gender sexual acts (3, 190–92), and perhaps even intercourse with a menstruating woman, though the language is unclear (189). Yet he does all this "in character" as Phocylides and therefore never mentions the Torah as an authority. He also forbids a couple of acts not mentioned in Torah, but sufficiently familiar in Greek culture that they served as convenient indexes of the differences between Jews and Greeks: abortion (184–85) and castration of youths (187). He reproves sensuality, even in a man's sexual relations with his wife (193–94). The whole work offers a sexual morality more Jewish than Greek, yet it is presented without reference to its sources and in a thoroughly Greek manner.

The most thorough presentation of the Israelite purity ethic in the context of the Diaspora comes from one of the great minds of Late Antiquity—Philo of Alexandria, a contemporary of Paul. He seems to have addressed a significant portion of his massive literary achievement to Gentiles with a positive regard for Judaism, but he nonetheless found the particularity of Israel, as manifested in its purity code, a barrier to full identification with it.[37] Philo takes a somewhat different apologetic tack from pseudo-Phocylides or the author of *Testaments of the Twelve Patriarchs*. Where they were content to make Judaism speak in the accents of Greek ethics ("We are like you, only better"), Philo prefers to say, "We are intelligible in terms of the best of your own thinking, but we have things to tell you that you could never have arrived at on your own." He thus balances efforts to make Judaism speak Greek with efforts to emphasize its distinctiveness.

The clearest examples of his method come from the third book of the *Special Laws*, an exposition of the Torah under headings provided by the Ten Commandments. In discussing the prohibition against intercourse with a menstruating woman, he seeks to show the rationality of this commandment in terms meaningful to any ancient reader, based on a common ancient understanding of conception. Because there was no specific knowledge of the mammalian ovum until the seventeenth century, one ancient theory of conception held that the male's semen constituted the entire germ of the new being; the mother provided only a place for it to grow and essential nourishment while it was in the womb. This made the ejaculation of semen into the womb precisely analogous to the planting of seed in a field.

Philo agreed with some Greco-Roman philosophers of the time who taught that the only "natural" purpose of sexual intercourse was the begetting of children.[38] To sow seed in a menstruating woman was therefore wrong for the same reason that sowing barley in a swamp would be (3.32–33). The same analogy explains for Philo why the Torah condemns male-male sexual intercourse; it is equivalent to sowing seed in a desert (3.39–40).[39] The analogy, however, has implications that go beyond the laws of Moses. If it is wrong to sow seed in a male because it cannot grow, it must be equally wrong to do so in a woman known to be barren, which the Torah does not in fact forbid. Philo allows some excuse for the man who stays married to a wife he married as a virgin and who has turned out to be barren, for their "long love will have been impressed on their souls by the length of their life together." The man who deliberately contracts a fruitless marriage, however, is acting under the sway of pleasure alone (3.34–36).

Philo has thus shifted the focus and scope of the Torah purity code in the process of making it intelligible to his Gentile contemporaries. Having made the begetting of children the only justification for sexual intercourse and categorized all other indulgence in it as hedonistic and animalistic (3.113), he finds that this newly imported principle makes marital intercourse with a barren woman as wrong as intercourse with a man. Accordingly, he must then add to the Torah's commandments to accommodate this new principle. In this way, Philo accommodates the Torah more than he may have recognized to the contemporary Stoic ethic, which regarded pleasure and passion as the great moral evils to be avoided and therefore exalted self-control and orderliness.[40] In his treatise *The Contemplative Life*, he exalts self-control (*enkrateia*) as the basis of all the virtues (34); in *Special Laws* 3.8–10, he argues, like pseudo-Phocylides (193–94), that even intercourse with a lawful spouse deserves blame if one indulges in it immoderately and insatiably. In the process of defending the Torah by Hellenistic standards, Philo has actually recreated it in a new form.

The Jews of the Hellenistic Diaspora thus found themselves interpreting their particularity in terms of a thought-world that bore no original relationship to it. The particularity of Israel was sometimes a burden to them in relationships with Gentiles, but it was also essential to their own sense of national and religious identity. Without it, they could not survive as a people. Yet they could not survive with it, either, unless they were prepared to explain and defend it in terms intelligible to the larger world, and the very process of explanation and defense tended to alter the character of the thing being explained.

This is most vividly apparent in regard to a subject that comes up repeatedly in Hellenistic Jewish writings: same-gender sexual acts. In the earlier history of Israel, as we have already noted, the Holiness Code forbade male-male anal intercourse; otherwise, the scriptures paid little attention to the subject. Even the traditions about Sodom were focused on violence, not sameness of gender. The prohibition of such acts was one aspect of the purity code as a whole, but it was hardly a central theme for Jews in the pre-Hellenistic world. Jews of the Hellenistic Diaspora, however, lived in the context of a dominant culture that accepted certain kinds of same-gender sexual relationships, mainly of a pederastic type, as quite usual.[42] From being a largely theoretical dimension of the purity code, disapproval of same-gender sexual acts thus became a day-to-day defining characteristic of Jewish culture. From the standpoint of apologetics, such ethnic distinctiveness was both a problem and an opportunity. It was a problem because it made Jews odd, an opportunity because they could claim it as a point of ethical superiority in terms that at least some Gentiles might acknowledge as valid.

Hellenistic Jewish authors, accordingly, made same-gender sexual acts a perennial theme of their ethical discourse and borrowed motifs from certain streams of Greek philosophical thought that had become critical of them. For their purpose, the contemporary Stoic doctrine that sexual intercourse was legitimate only when it aimed at begetting children, with its attendant rejection of all nonprocreative sexual intercourse, was ideally suited.[43] Because the Stoics often described what is morally right as "according to nature," Jewish authors could also appeal to "nature," rather vaguely defined, as a universal criterion that would justify their culture's traditional antagonism toward same-gender sexual acts.

The language here is specific to late Stoicism, with its intense concern for the overcoming of passion. In defining procreation as the only "natural" end of sexual acts, the Stoic ethicist was setting it in specific opposition to sexual acts undertaken for the satisfaction of desire. Any sexual intercourse in which procreation is not a possibility—as for example, during menstruation or after menopause—was therefore "unnatural" in this sense.[44] And the "unnaturalness" of same-gender sexual acts is a recurrent theme of Hellenistic Jewish literature. Pseudo-Phocylides condemned both male-male and female-female sexual acts in these terms (190–92). And several of the Jewish authors whose works are collected in the *Sibylline Oracles* attacked pederasty as a characteristically Roman offense.[45]

Philo attacked male-male sexual intercourse and those who engage in it not only in *Special Laws*, as we have seen, but also in *The Contemplative Life* 59–62 and *Abraham* 133–41. In all three contexts, he attacked pederasty for depopulating cities and wasting semen—and also for what he claimed it did to the characters of the partners. Boys were feminized by it—a grave matter to both Jews and Greeks of the period because both groups regarded women as intrinsically inferior to men;[46] the men involved were responsible not only for the corruption of the boys, but also for their own financial and physical ruin as they chased after them. In *Special Laws* 3.41–42, Philo went on (more for rhetorical reasons, it seems, than logical ones) to associate males who practiced same-gender sexual intercourse with the unpopular eunuchs who filled offices in the imperial bureaucracy and even claimed, wrongly, that Moses required the execution of eunuchs.

In Philo and other Diaspora authors, the usefulness of the subject of homosexuality for both distinguishing and defending Jewish culture gave it a certain prominence. One should not overread the evidence, however, as if all Jewish authors were preoccupied with the subject. Some texts that have been instanced as condemnations of same-gender sexuality seem dubious. In *Wisdom of Solomon* 14:26, one finds the Greek phrase *geneseōs enallagē*, which David Winston translates "interchange of sex roles."[47] As Winston notes, however, the language is odd, and one would expect *genous* rather than *geneseōs*. A more literal translation would be "alteration of generation," or "of procreation," which would designate the whole range of nonprocreative sexual activities rather than same-gender sexual acts specifically.

Another such passage, *Testament of Naphtali* 3:4, warns against becoming "like Sodom, which altered the order of its nature." While this sounds, from a modern perspective, very much like a warning against homosexuality, the discussion of Sodom in chapter 2 suggests that one should not leap to such a conclusion in regard to an ancient text without examining the context. In this case, what leads into the statement quoted is a warning against idolatrous practices; a knowledge of God as Creator will serve to keep Naphtali's descendants from becoming like Sodom. And there follows immediately an admonitory reference to the wickedness of the Watchers in Genesis 6, "who altered the order of their nature" and thereby brought on the flood. The fault of the Watchers was not same-gender sexual acts or nonprocreative sex of any kind, but procreative intercourse between angels (usually conceived as male) and human women. For this author, "becoming like Sodom" may mean indulging in any kind of prohibited sex; this hypothesis is confirmed by the reference to Sodom in *Testament of Benjamin* 9:1, where it serves as a warning against sensual indulgence with women.

The overall picture that emerges of the Hellenistic Diaspora is that of a minority community with a strong need to defend its particularity in terms of the dominant culture. The purity laws that preserved Israel's distinct identity also served to characterize it among outsiders, often in an unflattering way. It was necessary to try to explain these laws in terms intelligible to Gentiles while, at the same time, not allowing Israel to dissolve into the larger culture. The food rules were difficult to handle in this regard; it was easier to stress the sexual side of the Mosaic purity code because one could link it with those strands of contemporary Greek philosophical thought that were suspicious of passion and of pleasure and held that sexual intercourse could be justified only for procreation. Philo, by arguments of this kind, may have expected to win sympathetic Gentiles to full conversion. Other writers, too, looked forward to a time when Gentiles would come under the Law of Moses, though they may have thought of that prospect more as a remote and miraculous result of divine intervention in history.[48] In the meantime, the role of Israel was to serve as an island of purity in the midst of the unclean Gentiles.

CONCLUSION

Although the life and faith of all Jews, whether in Palestine or in the Diaspora, rested on the common foundation of the Torah, there were significant differences among them in the matter of purity. For the Hellenistic Jews of the Diaspora, purity continued to function almost entirely as a way of distinguishing Jew from Gentile. The social pressures of being a minority group in an alien culture, however, demanded that Jews attempt to justify their separateness and particularity in terms intelligible to the larger culture. The apologetics by which they did so had the effect of skewing the Torah's purity concerns to accommodate them to developments in Greek philosophical ethics. Yet this shift was the price of preserving the purity code under the circumstances.

In Galilee and Judea, by contrast, the purity code was, to a great extent, simply the way of life of the dominant population group. It served, although not to the same degree as in the Diaspora, as a daily reminder of Israelite identity. At the same time, however, particular interpretations of the purity code, especially those of the Essenes and Pharisees, became ways of distinguishing one Jew from another, both in terms of their interpretation of the code and in terms of their devotion to the keeping of it. In both cases, the code was still serving the function of establishing and keeping boundaries; the boundaries thus guarded, however—ethnic in the one case; sectarian in the other—were significantly different.

CHAPTER 4

PURITY AND CHRISTIANITY

A FIRST-CENTURY HISTORIAN'S INTERPRETATION

Given the pervasive importance of purity in their world, any Jewish group of the first century C.E. had to define its position on the issue. The early Christians were no exception to this rule. Indeed, we would expect purity to be a critical subject for them to deal with. They originated as a sect among the predominantly Aramaic-speaking people of Palestine, where their founder came into conflict, according to the Gospels, with Pharisees and Sadducees. They soon expanded to include Greek-speaking Jews of Palestine and the Diaspora and eventually even Gentiles. In the course of this development, they encountered the purity code in both its boundary roles: distinguishing one Jewish sect from another or from the people of the land and separating the Jewish people from their Gentile neighbors.

The business of this chapter is to discover and lay out the basic principles by which Christians (at least, that stream of Christianity that produced the New Testament writings) dealt with these boundary issues—with the purity law of Israel and its effects on their mission. I begin this exploration with Acts of the Apostles, a choice that calls for some explanation. Acts is not the oldest work in the New Testament, nor does it deal with Christianity's first origins in the teaching of Jesus. Moreover, there are ongoing debates about Luke's accuracy and reliability as a historian. The usefulness of Acts to this inquiry, however, lies in the fact that it contains a contemporary observer's interpretation of the single most critical passage in the early Christians' struggle with the issue of purity, the decision to admit Gentiles into their community without requiring circumcision of the males among them.

Whether Luke, in writing Acts, recorded the historical data accurately is not of primary importance for this study.[1] My purpose is not to trace the actual historical developments, but to see how Luke interpreted events in relation to the inherited, biblical motif of purity. Luke has given us, in Acts, an exceptionally clear and sustained treatment of the issues. After taking a close look at what he tells us, we shall be in a better position to look afresh at the more fragmentary and uncertain evidence we find in the other New Testament writings. Although we cannot assume that the other writers necessarily agreed with Luke, we shall have the advantage, when we turn to their works, of having heard one first-century voice speak explicitly to the matter at hand.

ACTS

How, then, from the point of view of Luke, did purity figure in the origins of Christianity? We find an emphatic answer to that question—one made emphatic by Luke himself—in the vision of Peter, narrated first in Acts 10. It is a double vision, actually, with each part confirming the other. The first vision was granted not to Peter, but to a Gentile, a centurion in the Roman army named Cornelius. This man was earnest in giving alms and prayed faithfully to the God of Israel, his household joining him in this, but he had not become a proselyte, that is, a full convert to Judaism. He remained uncircumcised and unclean. An angel appeared to him at the time of the evening sacrifice in the Temple,[2] telling him that his prayers and alms had won him a hearing with God and that he should send for one Simon Peter to bring him an important message.

Peter's half of the double vision was timed so that it just preceded the arrival of Cornelius's messengers. He was hungry and was waiting for lunch to be brought when he saw an enormous sheet being let down from the sky, containing all sorts of animals, many if not all of them unclean. A heavenly voice said, "Get up, Peter, slaughter and eat." Peter, perhaps thinking this a test of some kind, answered, "Certainly not, Lord, for I've never eaten anything common and unclean." To this the voice responded, "What God has pronounced clean, you are not to regard as common." This conversation was repeated three times and then the sheet was drawn up into heaven.

According to Luke, Peter did not know what to make of this (10:17). Matthew and Mark represent Jesus as having dismissed the issue of food purity during his ministry (Matt. 15:1–20; Mark 7:1–23), but Luke did not include this tradition or anything quite equivalent to it in his Gospel. To the contrary, Luke represented the early Christians as keeping to a very high standard of purity, manifest in the fact that, from the time of Jesus' ascension onward, they spent much of their time in the Temple (Luke 24:53). At times, they even went daily (Acts 2:46; 5:42). Because worshipers were expected to be pure when entering the Temple, the implication is that the Christians maintained themselves in a state of constant purity.[3]

In Luke's narrative, then, it would not occur to Peter that he, as a Jew and a disciple of Jesus, might take his vision literally as a simple canceling of the laws of food purity. His reflections were interrupted, however, by the arrival of the messengers from Cornelius and by the voice of the Spirit, commanding him to go with the men without hesitation. At this point in Luke's narrative, be it noted, there was not a single Gentile in the Christian community. There were other people marginal to Israel, a large number of Samaritan converts, and a eunuch who served the Queen of Ethiopia, all noted in Acts 8, but no full-fledged Gentiles.[4]

Peter goes to Cornelius, taking several other believers with him, and arriving there, he tells the story of his own vision and explains its significance—a significance that is only now clear to him. "You know," he says, "how unlawful it is for a Jewish man to associate with or visit a foreigner; and to me God has shown that one is to call no human being common or unclean" (10:28). Peter preaches to the assembled group, as requested, but in the midst of his speech, the Holy Spirit falls upon this audience of Gentiles. The Jewish Christians accompanying Peter are astonished, but there is no denying the event because they hear them speaking in tongues and glorifying God. Peter then says, "Can anyone forbid the water and keep these people from being baptized?" This question serves to show that Peter acted with the consent of the other faithful present, so that this was not an individual decision on his part. Hearing no objection, he orders the baptisms to proceed (10:44–48).[5]

Others did object, however, to the idea that Gentiles could be Christians. More exactly, they objected to the fact that Peter had even visited and shared food with such persons (11:1–3); the sharing of food was a basic way of expressing membership in the Christian community, as

Luke made clear earlier (2:46). Many Christians, as with the Essenes or Pharisees, will have been sharing their food in a state of purity, for they were in daily attendance at the Temple. Some Christians were also Pharisees (15:5). Thus, the addition of true Gentiles to the community created a serious problem about the relationship of believers to one another in terms of the purity of their food. Luke acknowledged the seriousness of this issue by having Peter repeat the whole story in full detail for his Jerusalem colleagues in chapter 11, thus also ensuring that the audience of Acts would hear it twice. Because Luke normally did not use repetition in his narrative style, his choice of this solemn device shows not only that he wished to be sure his audience heard and absorbed all the details of the incident, but also that he wanted to clothe the telling of it in an aura of divine authority. (His own book, of course, was not regarded as scripture instantly upon publication; it had to acquire that status over generations.)

For Luke, the baptism of Cornelius was pivotal to an understanding of the development of the church. When it happened, it appeared to be an isolated incident. God had specifically chosen one particular Gentile, with his household and friends—one distinguished for his almsgiving and devotion to prayer; it was not taken as precedent for a deliberate mission to Gentiles. That mission began separately, at Antioch, under the auspices of Greek-speaking Jews who had fled Jerusalem because of a persecution a short while earlier (8:1–3; 11:19–21).[6] The leaders in this new departure were Christians in sympathy with Stephen, who had been stoned for suggesting that the Temple at Jerusalem and its sacrifices had no true religious value (6:8–8:1). The skepticism these "Hellenists" felt toward the Temple probably implied a certain lack of interest in purity as well, which in turn made it relatively easy for them to accept Gentiles into their Christian community. Their initiative and the success that attended it, however, caused misgivings in Jerusalem; the church there sent Barnabas, one of its trusted members, to inspect (11:22–24). His approval was apparently enough to quiet critics for the moment, but in due course the matter had to be dealt with at the highest levels.

This is the significance of the apostolic council in Acts 15. Some visitors from Judea had told the Gentile Christians at Antioch, "Unless you get circumcised according to the Mosaic custom, you cannot be saved" (15:1). This teaching divided the community there, which sent Paul and Barnabas to Jerusalem to consult with the authorities. At the ensuing council, Peter now claimed his experience with Cornelius as giving divine sanction for the Gentile mission. God, he said, "made no distinction at all between us and them, having pronounced their hearts clean by faith" (15:9). In other words, the church could not require circumcision of Gentile converts, nor could it treat them as unclean. Peter went on to say, "So why are you now putting God to the test by laying on the disciples' necks a yoke that neither our fathers nor we have been strong enough to bear?" (15:10).

Of what yoke was Peter speaking? It seems unlikely that he—or Luke—would have thought of circumcision, in and of itself, as an impossible yoke.[7] Greeks frowned on it as an act of personal mutilation, but it did not constitute a true disadvantage for most Jewish men, certainly not for one who, like Peter, lived in a predominantly Jewish environment. The "yoke" was rather all that went with circumcision—the special relationship of Israel with God expressed both in Israel's unique status as the Chosen and in the Torah. This suggests that the Judeans who started the controversy at Antioch were demanding of Gentile converts not only circumcision, but also observance of the whole Torah.[8] This was by no means an irrational or narrowly partisan demand on their part. No one had any idea exactly how clean Jews and unclean Gentiles were to coexist in a single community and share the same table. The problem was both genuine and serious. If the Gentiles were not going to accept responsibility for keeping the whole purity system, those Jewish Christians who were faithful in their observance of it would inevitably be compromised.

At the council, the arguments that won the day, according to Luke, were based on revelation and miracle. Peter recounted his vision and experience with Cornelius, and Barnabas and Paul told of the "signs and wonders that God had done among the Gentiles through them" (15:12). The weight of the evidence and its evident effect on the assembly allowed James, the Lord's brother, as president of the council to sum up its consensus, which was "not to cause trouble for those of the Gentiles who are turning to God" (15:19). This did not in itself, however, resolve the outstanding question, which was how Jewish Christians who took purity seriously were to coexist with Gentile Christians. James suggested that a compromise could be reached, by which the Gentile Christians would be strongly urged to practice a modified purity code, involving abstinence from "pollutions of idols and harlotry and what has been strangled and blood" (15:20).[9]

What, specifically, did these rules entail? Like many compromises, they are not particularly clear. "Pollutions of idols" is a vague expression that could be interpreted various ways, but it probably had to do specifically with food.[10] At a minimum, avoidance of these would exclude direct and immediate participation in such meals as were part of Gentile worship. Questions, however, would arise about just where to draw the line. Could one supply the sacrificial animal, if one took no part in the sacrifice? (The Essenes forbade all trade in animals with Gentiles, lest they use what they bought for sacrifice to their gods.)[11] Could one eat, in a nonsacrificial context, meat from an animal that had been sacrificed? (This would become a difficult problem for Paul.)[12] Nothing in James's language settles such issues.

The other provisions about food purity are somewhat clearer. The prohibition of eating blood (and therefore strangled meats, from which the blood had not been drained) is one of the very few purity laws in the Torah to which a theological rationale is attached: "For the life of the flesh is in the blood; and I have given it for you upon the altar to make atonement for your souls; for it is the blood that makes atonement, by reason of the life" (Lev. 17:11 RSV). What is more, the Torah presents the prohibition of eating blood as a law given to all humanity through Noah at the time when God first authorized the eating of meat (Gen. 9:1–7), so that Jewish Christians could argue that this was a universal law, equally applicable to Gentiles. Finally, Leviticus itself directs that this prohibition be equally applicable both to native Israelites and to resident aliens living among them (17:10–13).

Thus, a variety of reasons might have inspired the adoption of such a rule; compromises being what they are, the variety of reasons may have been exactly what recommended it. Different parties within the church could understand it in different ways. Those who were most insistent that Gentile Christians did not have to become in any sense Jewish were free to see it as a command given to Noah or to derive it from the theological principle that blood is for the altar. Even if they were uninterested in the altar at Jerusalem, they might agree with the author of Hebrews that Christians "have an altar from which those who minister in the Tabernacle cannot eat" (13:10) and might therefore avoid animal blood because of its symbolic relationship to the blood of Jesus. Yet those who wanted Gentile Christians to accept circumcision and become full proselytes could draw encouragement from the fact that Leviticus 17 lays this law specifically on resident aliens and that the Septuagint called these people *prosēlytoi*. The council's decision thus, in some ways, represented a postponement of any final solution to the problem. It expressed an interest in having Gentile Christians observe a limited degree of purity in relation to foods, but left the nature and extent of that interest vague.

In this context, we must ask about sexual purity. What did the council mean by its rule against "harlotry"? That question proves very difficult to answer. Even a suitable translation of the Greek word in question (*porneia*) is problematic.[13] I have chosen the archaic "harlotry" because it both incorporates the basic meaning of the Greek term, which is "prostitution," and also has other overtones drawn from nonliteral usages commonly found in the Bible. In the scriptures of Israel, *porneia* (or its Hebrew equivalent, *zenuth*) is sometimes used in an expanded sense to include sexual offenses other than literal prostitution; it also frequently serves as metaphor for Israel's unfaithfulness in abandoning its own God to worship others. Perhaps the existence of sacred prostitution in the environment of ancient Israel contributed to the ease with which this metaphorical shift was made. Elsewhere in the New Testament, *porneia* usually appears in contexts, such as lists, which give us little help in defining it. When Paul gives specific content to it, he includes incest (1 Cor. 5:1) as well as literal prostitution (6:12–17). But because it occurs nowhere in Luke's works except in passages associated with the decision of the Jerusalem council, we cannot be certain what he would have understood by it.[14]

In James's speech to the council, the term *porneia* appears sandwiched between "pollutions of idols" and "what has been strangled and blood" (Acts 15:20). Given that order of words, we might readily understand "harlotry" as metaphorical for worship of other gods. Interestingly, this same usage is found in the very chapter of Leviticus discussed above in relation to the eating of blood, which describes the people as "playing the harlot" after rural fertility deities ("satyrs," 17:7 RSV). Leviticus, in fact, uses "harlotry" only in the literal sense of prostitution (19:29; 21:7, 9, 14) or in the metaphorical sense of practicing alien cults (20:4–6), not in the expanded sense of "fornication." If the Leviticus reference is dominating James's choice of words, then "harlotry" in the context of the Jerusalem council has no direct reference to sexual ethics, but refers to participation in Gentile cults. It thus supplements the rule against "pollutions of idols" by including other kinds of worship along with the eating of sacrificial foods. It would, for example, rule out magical practices; note that Luke does tell a story about how Gentile Christians gave these up in Ephesus (Acts 19:11–20).[15]

On the other hand, in the actual letter of the council (and in James's later reference to it), the order of the rules is different: they are to abstain from "things sacrificed to idols and blood and things strangled and harlotry" (15:29; cf. 21:25). This arrangement of the list might suggest that the council was following not so much the language as the order of Leviticus 17–18, which begins with regulations about sacrifice, goes on to the prohibition of eating blood and carrion,[16] and then proceeds to a list of sexual offenses, including incest, intercourse with a menstruating woman, adultery, giving "seed" to Molech, male-male anal intercourse, and intercourse with an animal. These sexual rules, as with the prohibition of blood, are said to be binding on both native Israelite and resident alien or proselyte (Lev. 18:26). On this analysis, "harlotry" might include this entire range of sexual offenses,[17] and the Jerusalem council would have been reenacting the whole of Leviticus 17–18 as a kind of abbreviated purity law for Gentile converts.

If one wished, however, to maintain that the council was specifically reaffirming those two chapters of Leviticus as binding on all Christians, one would be forced to admit that no one paid much attention to its key provision. Among the sexual concerns of Leviticus 18, one stands foremost among all the rest in terms of its relationship to table fellowship and was a key issue for both Essenes and Pharisees. It is the contagious uncleanness of the menstruating woman; there is no evidence either in the New Testament or in other early Christian literature that Christians retained any concern about this matter. To anyone familiar with the Mishnah, this will seem an inexplicable oversight, unless Gentile Christians regarded themselves as completely free of that concern. That, in turn, implies that they saw themselves as under no obligation to Leviticus 18.[18]

On balance, we can be certain only that the council concerned itself with two matters: idolatry, whether in the form of sacrificial meals or of other rites, and the eating of blood. By the exclusion of these, the Christian leaders hoped to ensure that Jews and Gentiles in the church could continue to enjoy table fellowship with one another without "causing trouble" for the Gentile converts or outraging Jews concerned about purity.

Note that Luke did not represent the council as having laid down conditions for Gentile membership. Both James's speech and the council's letter are carefully worded to avoid that impression. James says only that they should "write to them to abstain," not "command them" to do so. The letter is more strongly worded, but not in a way that violates what James had suggested: "It has seemed good to the Holy Spirit and to us to lay on you no heavier weight than these necessary things: to abstain from things sacrificed to idols and from blood and from things strangled and from harlotry. If you keep yourselves from these things, you will do well" (Acts 15:28–29). The letter brings strong pressure to bear in such phrases as "these necessary things." (Necessary to what end? To the preservation of table fellowship.) Yet it stops short of saying "You shall" or "You shall not," and, in the end, says only, "If you do this, you will do well." One might paraphrase these expressions as saying, "This is a matter of greatest importance in which we need your cooperation. Do not fail us."[19]

Peter provided the theological reason for the council's caution at the beginning of its deliberations, when he said, "Why are you now putting God to the test by laying on the disciples' necks a yoke that neither our fathers nor we have been strong enough to bear? But through the grace of the Lord Jesus we believe that we are saved in just the same way as they" (15:10–11).[20] Because Luke presents Peter elsewhere as abiding faithfully and uncomplainingly by the Torah, presumably he does not mean him to say here that no one can keep the Torah or that Jews (or Jewish Christians) ought to give it up. He means rather that the history of Israel as a whole turns out to be a history of failures in this respect—a teaching with a venerable ancestry in scripture itself. God gives salvation, accordingly, by grace, not waiting for the perfect fulfillment of the Torah, and this is why salvation is available now to Gentiles in the same free way as to Jews. If any further condition were applied to them, whether circumcision or even abstinence from blood, it would imply that the grace of the Lord Jesus was not sufficient by itself. The council is free to urge certain kinds of purity upon Gentile converts for the sake of unity in the church, but not to set them as conditions of baptism.[21]

The rest of Luke-Acts bears out the interpretation of the apostolic council offered here. The opening of the church to the Gentiles and its problems in adjusting to their impure presence form the main themes of Acts. The work moves from a strong emphasis on the pure Judaism of the earliest Christians, as manifested by their frequent presence in the Temple, to Paul's unsatisfactory interview with leaders of the Jewish community at Rome and his final turning to the Gentiles: "Let it be known to you, then, that this salvation from God has been sent to the Gentiles. And they will listen" (Acts 28:28). Luke presents the turn to the Gentiles as being the result of divine guidance, not human planning. This is nowhere more obvious than in the two great visions that Luke recites or refers to repeatedly in the book—that granted to Peter, which we have looked at in some detail, and that granted to Paul, which, in every recital, concludes by saying that he will become God's messenger to the Gentiles (9:1–19; 22:6–21; 26:12–18).

At the same time, Acts does not suggest that the gospel abolishes the Torah with respect to Jewish Christians. Quite the contrary, all the Jewish representatives of Christianity are represented as being fully law abiding. Paul, for example, circumcises Timothy before including him in his ministry (16:1–3). As son of a Jewish mother and Greek father, Timothy's ethnicity was ambiguous, and the Jewish communities where Paul worked would take his resolution of that ambiguity as a sign of his commitment to the faith and identity of Israel. Paul also fulfills his own vows (18:18) and assists others in doing so (21:20-26). Wherever possible, he begins his missionary work in the local synagogue. He calls attention to his Pharisaic training and his lifelong faithfulness (22:3; 23:6; 25:8; 26:4–5; 28:17). Luke presents him as more law abiding than the high priest (23:1–5). Others claimed that Paul had brought a Gentile into the Temple (21:27–29), but Luke insists that this was a false charge. And James, in his speech to the council, does not propose to dismiss or devalue the concern for purity but rather to leave its propagation to the existing network of synagogues (15:21).[22]

For Luke, the major Jewish Christian leaders were distinguished by their zeal for the whole Law. He also acknowledges that there were others, such as Stephen, who were pivotal figures in the original opening toward the Gentiles and were perhaps less committed to the Temple and its sacrifices. Perhaps Luke has made less of these persons than they in fact merited, but our task here is not so much to reconstruct the actual events as to understand how Luke presents them. For him, the earliest Christian church was composed of Jews who were personally committed to the Torah in all respects, including its purity requirements—such people as Peter, who had never eaten anything common and unclean, and Paul, who practiced their people's faith with great strictness. Only the insistence of the Spirit could lead such people to break the ultimate boundary of purity and accept unclean Gentiles into their community. Yet they did so, under the conviction that any other course of action would violate the fundamental reality of God's grace.

LUKE

Luke leaves the story of Gentile integration into the church to Acts, but his Gospel provides an appropriate introduction to it. The Gospel begins and ends in the Temple—with the annunciation to Zechariah and with the rejoicing of the disciples after the Ascension. In between, we meet a Jesus who is, in some respects, a model of purity. He was circumcised on the eighth day (2:21) and his parents took him to the Temple for his mother's purification and the redemption of the firstborn, obeying, as Luke specifies, the dictates of the Torah (2:24, 27). There he was greeted by Anna, an aged woman so pure as to be virtually a permanent resident of the Temple (2:36–38). Jesus went on to exorcise "unclean spirits" (4:31–37; 9:37–43a). When he healed lepers, he commanded them to do everything the law required (5:12–14; 17:11–14). And, although he allowed a woman with a hemorrhage to touch him and himself voluntarily touched a corpse and a corpse's bier (7:11–17; 8:40–56), the results, which were healing and resurrection, perhaps justified his recklessness.[23]

Still, Jesus foreshadows the church's future openness to the unclean in important ways. His own disciples are not all gathered from among the most law-abiding Jews (5:27–28). He is repeatedly shown as associating, of his own volition, with tax collectors and sinners (5:29–32; 7:29–30; 15:1–2; 19:1–10). He rejects the Pharisees' concern for cleanliness of hands and the tithing of herbs, which were aspects of their concern for table purity (11:37–42), and he flouts their concern for such purity by accepting the ministrations of a "sinful" woman at one Pharisee's own table (7:36–50). He even goes on the attack, comparing the Pharisees to concealed tombs that render people unclean without their knowing it (11:44) and telling a parable in which a Pharisee's prayer is unfavorably contrasted with that of a tax collector. All in all, the Jesus of Luke's Gospel seems rather less concerned about purity than Peter is at the time of his vision in Acts.[24]

Luke's Jesus also shows an interest in and concern for Gentiles, even though his experience of them is minimal. In his first sermon, a programmatic piece that Luke places at Nazareth, he reminds his hearers of how, at a time when there were many widows in Israel, Elijah was sent only to one who was a Gentile and, at a time when there were many lepers in Israel, Elisha only healed one who was a Gentile (4:24–30). Jesus heals the slave of a centurion and says of this Gentile soldier, "I tell you, not even in Israel have I found so much faith" (7:1–10). It is even possible that the slave in question is actually the centurion's *eromenos* (male beloved); if the story appeared in a purely Roman cultural setting, this would be the obvious conclusion.[25] Jesus also forbids his disciples to attack a village of quasi-Gentile Samaritans who had refused to receive him (9:51–56). He says more than once that Gentiles will fare better in the judgment than will Israel (10:12–13; 11:29–32), and he himself commands the Gentile mission after his resurrection (24:47).

Luke was not romantic about Gentiles. He was well aware that it was Gentiles who killed Jesus (Luke 18:31–34) and destroyed Jerusalem (21:24). He also included them among the antagonists of Paul on his missionary tours (e.g., in Ephesus; Acts 19:23–41). The point about the opening of the church to Gentiles was not that Gentiles were somehow better than Jews or more favored of God or even readier converts; Luke's history did not extend far enough for him to have to deal with a time when Gentiles were the dominant group within Christianity. The point rather is the sufficiency of grace. "Through the grace of the Lord Jesus we believe that we are saved in just the same way as they" (Acts 15:11). For Christians to make such a claim, purity law had to be relativized. For Israel, before 70 C.E., purity gave access to the Temple and the Temple to God. For Christians a different understanding of the dynamics of the holy now took precedence—one saying that grace gives access to Jesus and Jesus to God. By the inclusion of Gentiles, the Spirit forced a choice, according to Luke, and the church responded as it should have. Jewish Christians would continue to keep the Torah's purity rules, while Gentile converts were urged to avoid blood and the kinds of idol-connected foods and rites that would render their table fellowship obnoxious to Jews.[26] Even this reduced purity code, however, was not a condition for their being baptized or remaining in the fellowship of the community; other aspects of purity law were simply irrelevant to them. Salvation itself could come only by the grace of Jesus.

CHAPTER 5

PURITY IN THE GOSPELS

The teachings of Jesus were the fountainhead of Christianity, but Jesus' followers did not begin writing them down until some decades after his death and resurrection. At first, they were preserved through oral tradition by trusted teachers, who repeated them and, as one second-century source tells us, adapted them to the needs of the moment.[1] Only during the second half of the first century, it seems, did people begin committing the traditions to writing, eventually producing the four New Testament Gospels.

Jesus' teachings were preserved not from historical interest alone, but also because they were part of the very fabric of Christian faith. Teachers repeated them, as well as applied them, interpreted them, perhaps even added to them. The evangelists (as we call the authors of written Gospels) probably continued this tradition. Their books report the traditions about what Jesus did and said and also present them as coherent aspects of their four different portraits of Jesus. It is never easy to identify, on the basis of what the evangelists tell us, exactly what Jesus actually said; from the perspective of biblical theology, it is not of primary importance.[2] We shall be looking here not so much for the Jesus of history as for the Jesus to whom the four evangelists point in their distinctive ways. Each evangelist's portrait of him treats purity differently, but all four are of interest and share some deep-lying principles in common.

LUKE

We have already noted how Luke presented the life and teachings of Jesus as a prelude to vital decisions the church subsequently made about the role of physical purity in determining its community boundaries. While he portrayed Jesus' parents and, to a degree, Jesus himself as remaining within the prescribed limits of purity, he also showed him as foreshadowing later developments by his open treatment of Gentiles and of the impure within Israel itself. A closer look at an important text will help us see how Luke understood this opening to the impure in ethical terms.

The text is an encounter between Jesus and a Pharisee that turns on the issue of table purity and the kind of legal care that Pharisees took in relation to it:

> As he was talking, a Pharisee asked him to eat with him, and he came in and sat down. And the Pharisee was astonished when he saw that he did not wash first before the meal. But the Lord said to him, "Now you Pharisees cleanse the outside of the cup and the plate, but what's inside of you is full of rapacity and evil. Fools, didn't the one who made the outside make the inside, too? Only give the contents for alms and, behold, all things are clean for you. But woe to you Pharisees, because you tithe mint and rue and every herb and bypass judgment and God's love. You should have done the latter and not omitted the former." (Luke 11:37-42)

This discussion of inside and outside is not immediately clear, for the terms are being used in a condensed metaphorical way that is hard to unravel. The simplest sense would be that the Pharisees cleaned the outside surface of hollow containers, but not the hollow interior. Because this is unlikely,[3] one must see this not as a factual claim, but as an attention-getting riddle. A second sense would be to take the "outside" as meaning "all surfaces," while the "inside" would mean the body or the fabric from which the vessel was made—clay, for example. This makes little sense in relation to a literal vessel, but becomes intelligible in terms of its application to people, who are thus described as externally pure, but inwardly rapacious and evil. In a third and final twist, the terms come to refer to the container as the "outside" and its contents as the "inside," so that if the contents are given as alms, both contents and container are assured of being pure.

The point of this curiously compressed saying is to subordinate physical purity radically to another kind of purity subsisting on the level of intention and its expression in life. Physical purity has a certain facticity about it; when one touches a corpse, one is rendered impure, regardless of whether one intended to touch it or even knew that one had touched it. Luke's Jesus, however, subordinates that kind of purity concern to another, metaphorical kind of purity or impurity, consisting of the intent to do good or to do harm. Thus, the care one takes to ensure the physical purity of hands or of containers is, for Jesus, wasted if one is impure at the level of intent—not intent to contract or to avoid impurity, but intent to do good or to do harm. Rapacity—that is, the intent to do harm— renders everything in a person's life unclean; conversely, the intent to benefit another, as expressed, for example, in almsgiving, makes everything clean. We are suddenly far removed from the automatic cleanness or dirtiness of objects and acts in a true purity ethic. This is a radical shift in the understanding of purity, one that we shall see expressed in other accounts of Jesus' teaching as well.[4]

Luke is not saying that the sense of physical purity is obliterated for Christians or that it is now illegitimate for Christians to practice purity as an aspect of their religious life. That is clear from what Jesus says about tithing mint and rue. While exactitude in tithing was not strictly a purity issue, it was an aspect of the Pharisees' carefulness about table fellowship, so that they may have tithed, as in the present instance, even those forms of produce that the Torah had not specified as subject to the tithe.[5] What Jesus faults, in this situation, is not care about tithing, but failure to be equally attentive to the claims of justice and love. The externals of religion, whether purity law or tithing or public recognition (11:43), have a tendency to displace the demands of justice and love. When this happens, external, physical purity may actually be an evil, if it disguises internal "uncleanness" of intent. Hence, Jesus goes on to say to the Pharisees, "Woe to you, because you are like concealed tombs, and people do not know they are walking over them" (11:44). Inner rapacity and evil are only concealed by outer attention to purity; they do not lose their power to defile.

The practical consequences of such teaching appear in the story of Zacchaeus, a rich tax collector with whom Jesus stayed in Jericho

(19:1–10). The Mishnah suggests that tax collectors were under suspicion of being impure in such a way as to transfer their impurity to whatever they touched (*Tohoroth* 7.6).[6] When Zacchaeus, however, becomes a follower of Jesus, not a word is said about the purity issue. He promises rather to give half of all that he owns to the poor and to compensate anyone he has defrauded four times over. Jesus' response is that "Today there has come to be salvation for this household, for he, too, is a son of Abraham" (19:9). This resolution to the story is perfectly in tune with the principle Jesus had previously enunciated: "Give the contents for alms and, behold, all things are clean for you" (11:41).

Luke, then, suggests that Jesus, well in advance of the conflicts in Acts, had already raised a fundamental objection to the ethic of physical purity. The problem of such an ethic is that conformity to it is a matter of externals. Because it takes no account of motive, it is possible for persons to be pure for the worst of reasons and to combine a high level of physical purity with vicious attitudes and behavior in other respects. Similar themes are found in Matthew and Mark, where they are developed more fully.

MARK

Mark is perhaps the most radical of all the Gospel writers on the general subject of purity; he has Jesus dismiss physical purity as a matter of religious concern and replace it with the kind of metaphorical purity of intent that we have already seen hinted at in Luke's Gospel. As in Luke, the occasion was a disagreement with the Pharisees and "certain of the scribes" about washing before eating. Mark stresses the importance of the matter for contemporary Jews: "[coming] from the marketplace,[7] unless they wash they do not eat; and there are many other things that they have accepted as traditional to keep: washings of cups and jugs and bronze pots and couches" (7:4). Questions have been raised about the accuracy of Mark's report here,[8] but in any case, it shows us what he regarded as being at stake in Jesus' confrontation with his critics. The conversation itself is complex, because there are really two topics under discussion. One topic is tradition: because the specific regulations about washing were part of the oral rather than the written law, the authority of the oral law is at issue, and Jesus rejects it (7:5–13). The other topic, more important to us here, is purity itself, and Mark goes out of his way to mark this part of Jesus' response as of great importance.

Mark has Jesus summon "the crowd," thus making his response to the other religious leaders part of his public teaching. Jesus says to the crowd, in his most solemn style, "Listen to me, all of you, and understand. There is nothing outside the human being that, by entering into him, can render him unclean, but the things that come out from a human being are what render the person unclean" (7:14–15). Then, after this public pronouncement, Jesus explains what he said privately to his disciples, while Mark provides a crucial element of interpretation in his own voice (7:17–23). This further explanation is necessary because Jesus' public declaration admits of more than one interpretation. We could understand it entirely in physical terms, meaning that one is rendered impure only by what leaves one's body, not by what enters it. In this case, to choose a sexual example, an ejaculation of semen during intercourse would render the ejaculator unclean, but not the other person involved. This, of course, would represent a substantial revision of the written Torah, but it would not negate the principle of physical purity.[9] In his private explanation, however, Jesus speaks quite differently: "Whatever enters into the human being from without cannot render him common because it does not enter into his heart, but into his belly, and passes out into the latrine." By this, Mark adds, Jesus was "declaring all the foods clean" (7:18–19).

At this point, a certain discrepancy has appeared between the original statement and the elucidation of it. The original statement said that nothing from without could render one unclean, and, as we have seen, it was easy enough to find a sexual example that would correspond to that language. Does Mark, then, mean to limit the applicability of the saying to food and exclude its being applied to sexual uncleanness? We need not think so. Mark's language represents not a restriction of the original subject under discussion, but an expansion of it. The original issue was whether one must wash before eating, and Jesus' response could be heard as applying only to that one matter, namely the incidental ingestion of unclean matter adhering to the hands.[10] Mark asserts instead, in his authorial aside, that Jesus set aside not only the purity concerns related to washing, but also the whole category of food purity and impurity. He thus rejected a provision of the oral Torah and even the plain distinction between clean and unclean animals in Leviticus itself. Mark's aside, then, should be understood not as restricting the saying's applicability to foods, but rather as underlining that it prevails even against the explicit purity rules of the written Torah.[11]

Jesus' statement that things from without do not "enter into the heart, but into the belly" implies a certain understanding of the human being that makes the digestive tract peripheral and emphasizes instead the organ of thinking and planning (as the heart was then understood to be). The force of this shift is clarified in another statement: "He went on to say, 'What comes out of the human being—that's what renders the person unclean. For out from within, from the human heart, come evil designs, harlotries, thefts, murders, adulteries, acts of greed, evils, deceit, license, evil eye, blasphemy, arrogance, foolishness. All these evil things come out from within and render the human being unclean'" (7:20–23).[12]

It is always difficult to interpret such lists of vices (or the corresponding lists of virtues). The words lack the kind of context in usage that would help us understand what about them particularly concerns the maker of the list. The best we can do is to look for continuities within the list: What holds it together? What common themes might it be developing? This particular list of what renders impure does contain some words associated with sexual acts, but they are not of a sort to suggest that the old purity code is being reinstituted under a new rubric. After a general heading ("evil designs"), the next five items seem to constitute a short list drawn from the Ten Commandments.[13] "Harlotries" thus has its metaphorical sense of "idolatrous worship" rather than literal prostitution. "Adulteries" are primarily a matter of property rather than purity law, and we will return to that issue in part 2. The remainder of the list seems miscellaneous. It includes "license," which may include sexual libertinism, but signifies any kind of behavior lacking restraint.[14] The term describes a character trait rather than a physical impurity. Finally, "foolishness" sometimes refers specifically to sexual offenses (e.g., Deut. 22:21; 2 Sam. 13:12), but that is by no means its invariable sense. Its place as the last item in Mark's list makes it more likely that it is here serving as a general summary: all sin is "foolishness," the opposite of true wisdom.[15] Mark, then, presents Jesus as having set the whole issue of physical purity aside in favor of the metaphorical purity of the "heart."[16] Because purity is not a matter of automatic physical contagion, the physical purity or impurity of sexual acts is no longer critical—any more than that of foods. Intent to harm, however, renders a sexual act impure in the metaphorical sense.

Like Luke, Mark shows Jesus as behaving in a way consistent with this understanding of purity: associating with tax collectors and sinners (2:14–17), touching a leper (1:41) or a corpse (5:41), being touched by a woman with a hemorrhage (5:25–34).[17] Jesus has no fear of contamination, but rather dominates uncleanness through his own power. Mark calls the demons whom Jesus exorcises "unclean spirits." Jesus again and again exerts control over them, even on behalf of people who, as Gentiles, are themselves unclean and therefore, in some sense, congruent with such spirits. One of these, the man with the Legion, Jesus heals on his own initiative; when the man asks to become a disciple, Jesus gives him the first commission to proclaim him openly, even though he does not admit him to the group that accompanies him (5:1-20). The other is a Syrophoenician woman whom Jesus at first scorns as a "dog," but he heals her daughter after admitting that she has bested him in argument (7:24–30).

The uncleanness of these spirits is closely linked to the uncleanness of the heart that Jesus substitutes for physical uncleanness. The spirits delight in doing harm—even, in the story of Legion, to animals (5:12–13); beyond that, they are also a test for purity of the heart in human beings. When some of Jesus' opponents claimed that he did his exorcisms by cooperating with the demons, Jesus replied, "Amen, I say to you that all things will be forgiven the children of humanity—all the sins and the blasphemies that they commit; but whoever blasphemes against the Holy Spirit never has forgiveness but is liable for an eternal sin." He said this, Mark explains, "because they were saying, 'He has an unclean spirit'" (3:28–30). In other words, if one credits an act of loving kindness to evil intent, this in itself is so complete a violation of the purity of the heart as to place one beyond the scope of forgiveness. The new purity thus draws as sharp a boundary as the old, but it is of a very different order. It reveals itself not in observable avoidance of the sources of impurity but in the motives that inspire action, the intentions with which action is undertaken, and the way in which one assesses the motives and intentions of others.

Mark does not reject all observance of the purity code by Christians. He shows Jesus ordering the leper he has cleansed to go show himself to the priest and make the prescribed offering (1:44). He also seems to approve of John the Baptist's denunciation of Herod Antipas for marrying his brother's wife (incest according to Leviticus) (6:17–18), but, then, incest is not an issue of purity alone. Still, Mark is more radical than Luke in this matter, having little use for purity rules. His Jesus leaves scant motivation for continued observance of them. Accordingly, it is not surprising that Mark has Jesus himself authorize the mission to Gentiles, both by sending the man delivered from the Legion of demons to preach to his own people (5:18–20) and by predicting that, before the end of the world, "the gospel must first be preached to all the Gentiles" (13:10). From Mark's point of view, Jesus had already cleared away the barrier of purity law.[18]

MATTHEW

The presentation of purity in Matthew's Gospel represents a complex balancing of both traditionalist and radical tendencies. On the traditionalist side, Matthew's Jesus is by no means indifferent to the purity code. Except for touching a leper or a corpse in the performing of miracles (8:1–4; 9:18–26), he does not deliberately come into contact with uncleanness any more than any devout Jew of the time would have done. What is more, Matthew's Jesus reaffirms the Torah in the strongest terms: "till heaven and earth pass away not the least letter or fragment of a letter will pass away from the law until all things take place" (5:17–20). He even tells his followers to heed the teachings of the scribes and Pharisees, though not their example (23:1–4). He warns his hearers not to love or pray or be anxious like the tax collectors and Gentiles (5:46–48; 6:7, 32), and he confines the ministry of the Twelve to Jews, excluding even the Samaritans (10:5–6, 23). At one point, he tries to limit his own ministry in a similar way, and only the great faith of a Canaanite woman—the irony cannot be less than deliberate—prompts him to relent (15:21–28).

One side of Matthew's Jesus, then, appears to be at least moderately traditionalist on purity issues. Another side, however, is quite different. It comes out in Jesus' preference for the company of tax collectors and sinners. Matthew makes it plain that he consorted with such people on a casual basis and even included one of them in the Twelve (9:9; 10:3). When challenged about his eating with such people, Jesus replies, "I have not come to call righteous people, but sinners";[19] and he justifies such action by quoting a scriptural text: "I want mercy and not sacrifice" (Hos. 6:6), thus setting the sacrificial cult, the focus of the purity system, over against another kind of ethical demand (9:10–13).[20]

This more radical Jesus even places the tax collectors and prostitutes ahead of the acknowledged religious leadership:

> [Jesus says,] "What do you think? A person had two children. He came and said to the first, 'Child, go work in the vineyard today.' He replied, 'I won't do it'; but later, he changed his mind and went. And he went to the second and said the same thing. He replied, 'I'm going, sir,' and did not go. Which of these two did what the father wanted?" They say, "The first." Jesus says to them, "Amen, I say to you that the tax collectors and the prostitutes are entering the reign of God ahead of you. For John came to you people with a way of righteousness and you didn't believe him, but the tax collectors and the prostitutes believed him. And you—even though you saw, you didn't change your minds afterward so as to believe him." [21:28–32]

Jesus here contrasts a kind of religion that gives formal assent but not real obedience with a kind that does not give formal assent and yet does obey.

Matthew gives us little direct help in sorting out exactly what, practically, is meant in either case.[21] In part, he may simply be accusing the authorities of hypocrisy, as he has Jesus do a little further on: "They say and they do not" (23:3); they make rules which they themselves do not obey. There is also an element, however, of the contrast between purity and other ethical norms. As in Luke, Matthew's Jesus accuses the Pharisees of tithing minor herbs while neglecting the weightier aspects of the Torah, among which Matthew specifically includes "judgment and mercy and faith" (23:23). A prostitute, then, who observes "judgment, mercy, and faith" may enter the reign of God ahead of one who is meticulous about purity but neglects these. The formal, observable nature of purity practices makes them a ready basis for judging the comparative religious worth of individuals, but Matthew's Jesus finds such comparisons misleading. The scribes and Pharisees, indeed, are like "whitewashed tombs, which look beautiful from the outside but on the inside are full of bones of the dead and all uncleanness." The religious leaders, too, "look righteous to people from the outside, but inside are full of hypocrisy and lawlessness" (23:27–28).[22]

The same Jesus who takes the part of unclean Israelites against the righteous also looks forward to a future time when his mission will broaden to include impure Gentiles. In Jesus' own ministry, the Gentile mission is prefigured in his praise of a centurion's faith (8:5-13), his exorcising of Gentile demoniacs (8:28–34), and his encounter with a Canaanite woman of great faith (15:21–28). He also makes certain predictions about Gentiles and how they will fare in the last judgment: many will have seats at the eschatological banquet, while "the sons of the kingdom" are shut out (8:11–12); it will be more tolerable then for Sodom and Gomorrah than for the Israelite towns that reject the ministry of the Twelve (10:15); Tyre, Sidon, and Sodom would repent more readily (11:20–24), and the men of Nineveh and the Queen of the South will be found more righteous (12:41–42). The Gentiles, indeed, will be judged not by the Torah at all but simply by their acts of loving-kindness (25:31–46).

The apparent contradiction between the Jesus who upholds the Torah in Matthew and the Jesus who vindicates those who fall short of its standards or live outside its scope is not easy to resolve. Yet it belongs to Matthew's basic conception of the person and work of Christ. We might be tempted to suppose that Matthew has simply incorporated divergent strands of oral tradition without attempting to make them agree. Even Matthew's most distinctive contributions to his own work, however, show the same tension. His Gospel opens with a genealogy of Jesus, patterned on models in the Torah itself (1:1–17). In one sense, it is a traditionalist piece, documenting Jesus' descent from Abraham, who received the promise, from Jacob, the ancestor of all Israel, and from David, the founder of the royal line. Yet it is also radical in its inclusion of four women who share with one another two disreputable qualities: at least three and possibly all four were Gentiles and all four were involved in some kind of violation of the sexual codes.

The first, Tamar, was a Canaanite woman who acted the part of a prostitute in order to trick her father-in-law, Judah, into having intercourse with her (Gen. 38). To be sure, Judah was in the wrong, for he had failed in his obligations to her. He ought to have married her to his surviving son, Shelah, to beget a child in the name of Er, the deceased son who had been her original husband; when he evaded this responsibility, she simply claimed what was in some sense hers by right. Judah himself admitted that "she is more righteous than I" (38:26). Yet she had committed what appeared to be an act of prostitution and could be understood as having violated the incest rules.[23]

The second woman in Matthew's list is Rahab, the Canaanite prostitute of Jericho who rescued Israelite spies from her fellow townsfolk (Josh. 2). She was rewarded by being spared, along with "her father's household and all who belonged to her" from the otherwise complete massacre of the city's population (6:22-25). The third, Ruth, belonged to the nation of Moab, which was forever excluded by the Torah itself from membership in the assembly of Israel (Deut. 23:3). Moreover, she initiated sexual relations with Boaz by uncovering his "feet" (euphemistic for genitals) at the harvest celebration, well before she could be understood properly to belong to him (Ruth 3).

The fourth was "the wife of Uriah." By referring to her in this way and not as Bathsheba, Matthew underlines the act of adultery by which David first took her and the treachery by which he killed her husband and made her his own wife (2 Sam. 11). Since her husband was a Hittite, one may guess that she, too, was a Gentile. In legal terms, she would have to be reckoned as having consented to the adultery, however difficult it might have been, in practice, to refuse an absolute monarch; she was therefore as guilty in the matter as David.[24]

Thus, at the very beginning of his Gospel, Matthew presents us with a genealogy of Jesus that calls attention both to his impeccable Israelite descent and to the foreign and scandalous elements in it. The genealogy also, of course, includes a fifth woman, Mary. Matthew notes that Jesus' mother was under suspicion of adultery and was saved from divorce only by the intervention of an angel (1:18–25). In addition, he says that the first to pay homage to the infant Jesus were a group of *magoi*, Gentile priests of the god Mithras (2:1–12).

Despite his insistence on the inclusion of the impure and the foreign, Matthew does not appear to have been antagonistic toward the observance of purity law as such. It is not the observance of such rules that Matthew's Jesus condemned, but the tendency to substitute them for "the weightier matters" of judgment and mercy and faith. A comparison of Matthew's version of the controversy about hand washing with that of Mark is instructive. Mark, as we have seen, used the passage to declare all foods clean and to substitute, in a quite unambiguous way, the purity of the heart for that of the body. Matthew narrates the matter somewhat differently. His Jesus does, to be sure, reject the Pharisees' reliance on tradition (15:1–9), but rather than declaring all foods clean, he applies his argument only to the tradition of washing the hands before eating (15:20).[25] Still, the basic principle is the same as in Mark: a new purity, that of the heart, is now decisive (15:15–20).[26]

The same underlying principle is at work in the Sermon on the Mount, when Jesus declares that "everyone who looks at a woman to desire her has already committed adultery with her in his heart" (5:28). Such a claim excludes any understanding of adultery in terms of physical purity, for no physical contamination has yet taken place. Purity of intention, the purity of "the heart," is the only purity that counts.

Matthew's treatment of the purity issue is thus more traditionalist than that of Luke and Mark in appearance, but it is equally radical in its implications. Matthew's Gospel pictures Jesus as a companion of tax collectors and sinners and preserves the teaching that purity of the heart, not physical purity, is central. It also portrays Gentiles and sinfully impure women as full and significant participants in God's work of salvation. It suggests that even though Matthew's church was probably predominantly Jewish, it adhered to the purity law as, at most, an expression of its membership in Israel. It was warned against making it a point of pride in comparison to other Jews or demanding its observance of Gentile converts.

Matthew saw the church as fully open to Gentiles—and not on the condition of their becoming Jews through circumcision of males. At the end of his Gospel, he has Jesus inaugurate a new era of salvation by directing his followers to begin converting Gentiles (28:19–20): "Go make disciples of all the Gentiles, baptizing them in the name of the Father and of the Son and of the Holy Spirit, teaching them to keep all the things that I have commanded you." The Gentile mission thus takes as its primary "text" not the Torah, but the commands of Jesus. It knows nothing of a mandatory requirement of physical purity.

JOHN

The Gospel of John is quite different from those we have already discussed. Indeed, on the subject of purity, it has almost no traditions in common with the three Synoptic evangelists. John notes that purification was a point of contention among Jewish groups in the time of Jesus' ministry (3:25). Yet he has no teaching about "purity of heart" and he says not a word about associating with tax collectors. Alone of the New Testament writers, he portrays Jesus himself as administering purification rites, consisting of baptism (3:22; 4:1–2) and foot washing (13:1–17).

These differences must be seen as results of John's very individual aims in writing, which make the Fourth Gospel unique in almost all respects.[27] They do not, however, represent a radically different understanding of the purity issue, as becomes clear in other ways. If John tells of no dinners with "tax collectors and sinners," he does narrate a long private conversation with a Samaritan woman who has a less than ideal marital history (4:4–26).[28] As with the man with the Legion in Mark's Gospel, this foreigner becomes an effective bearer of Jesus' gospel, indeed the first truly successful missionary (4:27–30, 39–42). An independent tradition, often attached to John's Gospel, also presents him as the champion of a woman taken in the act of adultery (7:53–8:11).

The most striking element, however, in John's handling of the matter is the surprising way he uses things impure as vehicles of the Gospel. For example, in his conversation with Nicodemus (3:1–15), Jesus says that entry into the Reign of God is conditional on being born *anōthen*, a term which can mean either "again" or "from above." I have argued elsewhere that this rebirth takes place in Christian baptism,[29] but however we interpret the saying, it is playing off the purity code in the Torah. Giving birth, according to Leviticus, renders a woman unclean, yet John can even speak of God as giving birth to the chosen (1:13). The waters of baptism, for John, are waters of birth, comparable to the amniotic fluid; they convey not impurity but intimate association with God.[30]

The other great Christian rite, the Eucharist, is even more intriguing to John in this respect. In the long Eucharistic discourse of chapter 6, he presents the rite in precisely the way most offensive to purity. Jesus starts by talking about bread from heaven (6:26–33) and then makes the startling claim, "I am the bread of life" (6:35). His audience does not take this claim literally (6:41–42) until he goes on to say, "The bread that I shall give is my flesh for the life of the world" (6:51). When this, too, seems impossible to the audience, Jesus repeats it and adds to it the doubly offensive notion of drinking his blood: "Amen, amen, I say to you, unless you eat the flesh of the son of humanity and drink his blood, you do not have life in yourselves" (6:53).[31] Finally, he even switches from the ordinary word for "eat" to the more graphic "chew": "The one that chews my flesh and drinks my blood has eternal life" (6:54). The choice of motifs obnoxious to purity law and the careful and steady escalation of uncleanness throughout the discourse show that John is deliberately emphasizing the symbolic impurity of the Christian rites. It is by impure foods that one is saved.[32]

John, then, is less attached to physical purity than any of the other evangelists. Indeed, for him, impure things have become, for Christians, the means of approach to God. There is no reason to see this as an exaltation of impurity for its own sake. The enormous tension between the Jewish-Christian communities in which John lived and wrote and the contemporary Jewish authorities has long been recognized as a major influence on the Fourth Gospel. Such a context might easily encourage flaunting whatever in one's own tradition was most apt to be obnoxious to one's opponents. We can find the same point, however, being made in a less polemical context in the story of the first miracle at Cana (2:1–11). There, Jesus commandeers large jars intended for Jewish purification rites, has them filled with water, and then transforms it into wine of the finest quality to help celebrate a wedding. The miracle announces that a new means of relationship with God is here to replace the approach by way of physical purity.

CONCLUSION

The four New Testament evangelists have rather different ways of presenting the subject of purity. It would be a mistake to try to reduce their varied witness to a single synthesis, yet there is at least one point on which they all agree: for Christians, physical purity is no longer a determinative element in their relationship with God. This does not mean that they abolished the categories of pure and impure. Even the Johannine community continued to be aware of a distinction between clean and unclean, which gave their distinctive use of the impure its particular power. What Christians rejected was the age-old link between physical purity and access to God.[33]

Some New Testament Christians, like John, celebrated this repudiation of the purity law by speaking of even their most central and treasured rites in impure images. Others, like Mark, Luke, and Matthew, saw physical purity as giving way to an emphasis on "purity of the heart," which defined true uncleanness as consisting in the intention to do harm. One did not have to break with the old law of physical purity to embrace the new purity of the heart. Luke almost certainly assumed that Jewish Christians would continue to practice the whole of the Torah as an aspect of their Jewish identity, and Matthew's Gospel is by no means inconsistent with such an assumption. What every Christian, Jew or Gentile, must reject was rather the insistence on physical purity, which the evangelists ascribed to the historical Pharisees.

Modern readers of the Gospels should not make the mistake of supposing that it was only or even primarily the historical Pharisees who were being attacked in these texts. The issues, according to Acts, were primarily intra-Christian. The evangelists were attacking any kind of religion that rates people according to externally verifiable scales—among which physical purity will always be popular.[34] Such puritanism is a generic phenomenon, as common among Christians as anywhere. As Matthew saw, such religion, even if its original purpose may have been to encourage zeal in a good cause, tends to become a means to compliment oneself by criticizing others. That, in turn, leads to hypocrisy, for the goal of such religion eventually comes to be no more than the maintenance of a certain reputation within one's social milieu. To suppose that all the historical Pharisees turned their practice of purity into such a caricature of faith is absurd; to suppose that Christianity has been free of the same tendency is even more so. The practice of purity was not in itself wrong, in any case, but lent itself to the exaltation of one's own religious excellence at the expense of others. Christianity's way of dealing with this danger was to make physical purity entirely optional, related to (and perhaps normal for) Israelite identity, but irrelevant to salvation or to membership in the church.

The Gospels, to be sure, do not say much about sexual issues; the ones on which they are clearest—divorce, remarriage, family, adultery—belong to part 2 of this study. If we compare our earlier discussion of purity law, however, both in its written form in the Torah and in terms of first-century Jewish practice, with the Gospel texts we have now examined, we see that the Gospels dismiss purity, not selectively, but across the board. They do not isolate some one aspect of it (food laws) for repudiation while tacitly retaining other aspects (leprosy, say, or circumcision, or sex). It is physical purity as such, in all its ramifications, that they set aside.

CHAPTER 6

PAUL AND PURITY

It would be difficult to overstate the importance of Paul for the topic of purity in the New Testament—or the importance of this topic both for Paul's mission and for his understanding of Christian faith. He had been a Pharisee (Phil. 3:5), and we have seen that this variety of ancient Judaism was particularly interested in the practice of purity. Because purity gave access to the holiness of the sanctuary, the teaching of the Pharisees was a way of affirming the whole of Israel as holy and inviting all into a practice that honored that holiness. Whatever else Paul may have been, he was expert in the law of purity and had long been committed to the strict practice of it.

This was not the most obvious background for a man who would later become the principal figure in the Christian mission to Gentiles. In fact, he must have experienced a high level of cognitive dissonance when the Risen Jesus accosted him and commissioned him to take his message to the Nations. Exactly how was he, a strictly observant Jew of the Pharisaic persuasion, supposed to interact with unclean Gentiles in a way that would make the message of Jesus intelligible to them? Because purity, more than any other one thing, kept Jews apart from Gentiles, Paul was brought to the point of actively crossing this borderline and living among people excluded by it.

Paul's letters, written before Acts or any of the Gospels, testify to his involvement in the resulting tensions.[1] He insisted that Gentiles were welcome to become members of the church without becoming Jews. Male Gentile converts did not need to get circumcised; indeed, Paul feared that doing so would imply some doubt as to whether their connection with God through Jesus was sufficient (Gal. 5:1–6). If Paul had been willing either to encourage full conversion to Judaism on the part of his Gentile converts or to accept the existence of two separate networks of congregations, one Jewish, one Gentile, the problems about purity would have been easier to work out. But Paul insisted that both groups join together in what had become the usual social manifestation of Christian identity: the church's gathering over dinner. This, of course, brought issues of food purity into play.

How, then, did Paul deal with sexual purity, given that Jewish and Greco-Roman standards were significantly different in this area, too? This will be the primary question for the present chapter. On the one hand, Paul probably saw all purity issues as related. We have already seen that the Torah itself does not put purity into different boxes according to the specific area of life to which it applies. Leviticus freely mingles areas that seem distinct to us: food, menstruation, ejaculation, leprosy, hybridization of animals, textiles woven of mixed fibers, incest, adultery, foreign worship, male-male anal intercourse, sexual intercourse with an animal, and so forth. It treats them all under the rubric of purity (while also offering additional reasons for some of its prohibitions).

Paul, to be sure, came to the problem not out of an interest in abstract ethical reasoning, but as a practicing missionary who found that he could not pursue his vocation at all without trying to resolve the tensions between Jews and Gentiles over precisely these issues. These were the things that kept them from settling readily into a common life together. When Jewish and Gentile practice coincided, Paul saw no problem and was not interested in discussion. At Corinth, for example, it was enough for Paul that the man who "had" his father's wife had violated not just Jewish incest law but the usual Greek assumptions as well (1 Cor. 5:1–5).[2] There was no drive to work out further ethical analysis. Only actual conflicts provoked Paul to deal with such issues.

Paul wrote no treatise on purity. In fact, his primary mode of communication was clearly preaching rather than writing. Accordingly, we can only try to reconstruct some sense of how he was thinking about sexual purity by close examination and comparison of the letters.

PURITY AND THE GENTILE MISSION

One thing, at least, is clear: Paul's vehement opposition to any requirement of circumcision for male Gentile converts compelled him to articulate a stance on the relationship of Gospel to law, of grace to works, of circumcision to observance of the Torah, and of purity to salvation. It is hardly surprising that this would constitute one basic foundation of his thinking. Another important influence is less commonly remarked— his strong concern for the unity of the local congregation. The spread of the gospel seems to have unleashed an extraordinary (and, to Paul, sometimes unwelcome) creativity among converts. The new ideas and practices thus engendered combined with the social competitiveness endemic to Greek culture to cause strong centrifugal tendencies within his churches. Paul (and, indeed, other New Testament letter writers) devoted a great deal of energy to combating such divisivenes and, as we shall see, often employed purity language metaphorically as a weapon against it.[3]

In Galatians, Paul wrote about some of the same events that Luke presents as connected with the Jerusalem council (Acts 15). Attempting to counteract a move by some of his churches in Galatia toward accepting circumcision as a requirement for membership, Paul wrote an angry defense of his mission. In it, he insisted that the church leadership at Jerusalem had acknowledged his mission to Gentiles as inspired and empowered by God and had required nothing of him except to "remember the poor" (Gal. 2:1–10). There is nothing here about the council's decree—about avoiding meat sacrificed to idols, harlotry, blood, or things that have been strangled. If Luke's history of the council is accurate, this calls for explanation. Perhaps Paul's rejection of purity law was more radical than that of Luke, and he refused to convey the decree to his converts. Or again, Paul may simply have found the council's compromise irrelevant in places like Galatia, where the churches seem to have been composed almost entirely of Gentiles and there were few occasions for intra-church conflict over table purity.

In Antioch, however, the church was mixed, and Paul told of the kind of troubles that could arise in such a situation:

> When Cephas [i.e., Peter] came to Antioch, I resisted him
> to his face, since he stood condemned. For before certain
> people came from James, he was eating with the Gentiles;
> but when they came, he drew back and separated himself,
> fearing those of the circumcision. And the other Jews joined
> him in his hypocrisy, with the result that even Barnabas was

carried away into their hypocrisy. But when I saw that they were not keeping to the straight path as regards the truth of the gospel, I said to Cephas in the presence of them all, "If you, Jew though you are, live in the Gentile and not the Jewish way, how can you compel the Gentiles to live as Jews?" (Gal. 2:11–14)

Despite the extreme compression of this narrative, its drift is clear enough: Jewish Christians at Antioch had so far relaxed their concern for purity as to eat with Gentile Christians, but pressure from stricter Jewish Christians associated with Jerusalem induced them to draw back and reestablish the purity boundaries. Paul saw their behavior as proceeding not from conviction, but from political expediency. He not only objected to its inconsistency with their past practice, but went on to insult Peter by claiming that he was not a very observant Jew under the best of circumstances.

It is easy to see the Paul of this incident as continuous with the Paul who described himself as a devout Jew of the strictest persuasion: "circumcised on the eighth day, of the nation of Israel and the tribe of Benjamin, a Hebrew of Hebrews, as to the law a Pharisee, as to jealousy [for the law] a persecutor of the church, as to righteousness by law one who had become blameless" (Phil. 3:5–6). Clearly, Paul had undergone a major change in becoming a missionary of Christ to Gentiles, but it was still the Paul who could say of himself that he had "become blameless" in terms of "righteousness by law" who could also say of a certain Galilean fisherman that, Jew though he was, he lived like a Gentile. Peter was, from the point of view of the Pharisee party, an *am ha'arets*, a Jew relatively indifferent to and ignorant of the finer points of the Torah.

Paul's encounter with the Risen Jesus did not entail a rejection of his Jewish identity or of the Torah, but rather a reevaluation of the place these held in what he now saw as the larger scheme of God's purpose for salvation. What had formerly been central now became peripheral: "All the things that were profit to me, these things on account of Christ I counted as loss . . . so that I might gain Christ and be found in him, having as my righteousness not the righteousness that comes from the law, but the one that comes through Christ's faithfulness [or, faith in Christ],[4] the righteousness from God conditional upon faith" (Phil. 3:7–9).

The great issue of conversion for Paul, then, was not primarily whether to *keep* the Law, but whether to *rely* on it. Once he had become convinced that he must rely on another source of righteousness, he was no longer tied to the Law, but could use it or not in accordance with the "righteousness that comes through Christ's faith." For example, he could subordinate his practice of the Torah to the requirements of missionary strategy:

> For though I am free from all, I have made myself slave to all, in order to gain the majority. I have become to the Jews as a Jew to gain Jews, to those under law as one under law (though I am not in fact under law) to gain those under law, to those without law as one without law (though I am not without God's law, but within Christ's law) to gain those without law. I have become, to the weak, weak to gain the weak. To all people I have become all things, in order at all events to save some. But I do all things on account of the gospel, so that I might become one who shares in it. (1 Cor. 9:19–23)

Only the proclamation of the Gospel and one's final sharing in it were of ultimate importance; all else, including all that separated Jew from Gentile, was instrumental.[5]

All this indicates that, while Paul did not consider it wrong to adhere to purity law, neither did he see it as an obligation—at least not where it might impede his work among non-Jews. Because he envisaged a church equally open to both Jews and Gentiles, he probably assumed that Jews would continue to observe their traditions except where it caused problems within the church, just as he assumed that Gentiles would remain Gentiles. To some degree, his own ability to move back and forth between both groups was specific to his divinely ordained mission. Others were to remain in the state in which they were called (1 Cor. 7:1–20).

Paul did not advocate a kind of synthesis of the more appealing bits of the two identities. With those Galatians who considered accepting circumcision, he was vehement: "Look, I Paul am telling you that if you get circumcised, Christ will do you no good. And I am testifying again to every person who gets circumcised that he is obligated to keep the whole law" (Gal. 5:2–3). The assertion that "Christ will do you no good" here is probably linked to the order of events; for a Gentile to be circumcised *after* conversion to the Gospel implied lack of faith in Christ and a fear that something more was necessary. The second assertion, however—that whoever is circumcised is obligated to keep the whole Law—was simply Paul's firmly held belief about the nature of Jewish identity. Israel is the chosen people; circumcision is the gateway into it for males; responsibility to observe the Torah is entailed in that status except insofar as "the righteousness from God" might demand some concession. We need not suppose that Paul excused himself from the full practice of the Torah except to the extent that his missionary responsibilities required it; he was always strongly conscious of the value of his Israelite heritage and its claim on him (2 Cor. 11:22; Rom. 2:25–3:2; 11:1–2).

TABLE FELLOWSHIP

The most common way in which Gentiles and Jews interacted in the church was through table fellowship. The blessing of bread and wine had not yet been separated from the church's common meal so as to constitute the Christian Eucharist in its classic form (1 Cor. 11:17–34); instead, the common meal itself, with its *anamnesis* (remembrance) of Jesus, was the focus of Christian community life. Hence the particular importance of food in early Christian disputes about purity. Even though Paul never mentions the decree that Luke attributes to the Jerusalem council (Acts 15:29), he shared at least one of its concerns—that with regard to food sacrificed to idols.[6] He left two extensive discussions of this issue (1 Cor. 8–10; Rom. 14:1–15:6), both of which aimed to persuade the "Strong" (those whose consciences were not perturbed by eating such foods) to modify their practices so as not to cause difficulty for the "Weak," who objected to them. The Strong, in other words, were those whose tolerance for physical impurity was high, the Weak those whose tolerance was low. The former group will probably have consisted mainly of Gentile, the latter of Jewish Christians, though we should allow for individual Christians associating themselves with one or the other group purely on principle. Paul, after all, identified himself as one of the Strong (Rom. 15:1).[7]

The earlier of these discussions is the one in 1 Corinthians 8–10. The passage is complex, for Paul employs four distinct and even contradictory arguments—a practice permitted by the rhetorical teachers of the day—to achieve his goal of changing his hearers' behavior.[8] In the first argument, Paul concedes to the Strong their basic theological claims:

that idols are nothing at all and that there is no god but the One (8:4).[9] Yet however correct the principles of the Strong may be, knowledge is less important than love (8:1–3), and they should pay attention to the effect their actions have on the Weak (8:9–13). Paul calls attention to his own manner of life, whereby he constantly declines acknowledged apostolic rights (e.g., the right to have a "sister wife" with him on his travels) "so as not to put any hindrance in the way of Christ's gospel" (9:1–18). Beyond that, Paul even "enslaves" himself to the expectations of others to communicate the good news (9:19–23). This is worthwhile to him if he gains even a few converts, and Paul wants the Strong to see this as analogous to the deprivations athletes voluntarily undergo in training and to join him in a kind of competition to save others (9:24–27). In sum, Paul's first argument grants the Strong their theological premise: foods sacrificed to idols mean nothing and the issue of physical purity is irrelevant. Yet he rejects their conclusion. One does not therefore eat such foods if doing so will cause a Weak Christian to stumble.

The second argument in 1 Corinthians is an admonition to the Strong not to be too sure of themselves. They should remember how the Exodus generation lost God's favor—precisely by indulging in foreign cults (idolatry and "harlotry") and by putting God and God's servants to the test (10:1–11). "If you think you are standing," says Paul, "watch out that you don't fall," but then he reassures his audience that God is not about to abandon them (10:12–13). This argument warns the Strong not to be too self-confident. But it adds nothing to the ethical analysis of the situation, for it does not deal with how one discerns the right course of action.

Paul follows this with a third argument, fundamentally at odds with the first: even if an idol is nothing at all and there is no god but God, there are still demons, and idolatrous sacrifices really do involve one in their worship (10:19–20). Christians are sharers in the Lord's table; to be sharers in the tables of demons may provoke God to jealousy (10:14–18, 21–22).

Finally, however, Paul returns to his first position. There is nothing inherently wrong in what the Strong are doing, but it is not expedient: "All things are permitted but not all things are beneficial; all things are permitted but not all things are constructive. Let no one seek one's own good, but that of the other person" (10:23–24). From these principles flow certain practical consequences: you may eat anything put before you unless someone specifically informs you that it has been sacrificed to an idol; in that case, you are to abstain "not for your own conscience, but for the other person's" (10:25–30). This conclusion implies that what is to be feared in relation to idolatrous cults is not any intrinsic, physical impurity associated with demons or with alien worship, but rather the possibility that the Strong may lead the Weak to act contrary to their conscience.

Note that Paul does not use purity language here except in saying, "Some, through being accustomed to the idol in the past, eat as if the food really were sacrificed to an idol, and their conscience, being weak, is polluted" (8:7).[10] This principle assumes a clearer and more developed form in Romans: "All things are pure, but it is wrong for the person who eats by way of stumbling. . . . The one who is uncertain is condemned if he eats, because it is not from faith and everything that is not from faith is sin. But we who are strong have an obligation to bear the weaknesses of those who are not and not to please ourselves" (Rom. 14:20, 23–15:1). In this way, Paul's treatment of the subject in Romans avoids the metaphysical uncertainties and conflicting arguments of 1 Corinthians. The point is simply that Christians are to accept the existence of both Strong and Weak and to avoid conflict between the two groups. (Paul's ongoing concern for unity within Christian congregations is prominent here.) The Strong are not to debate with the Weak or to despise them (14:13–15:3); the Weak are not to judge the Strong (14:1–12). The essential consideration, however, is a direct reflection of the basic principle: "I know and am persuaded in the Lord Jesus that nothing is unclean in and of itself, except that for the person who regards anything as unclean it is" (14:14).[11] There can be no question here of the classic conception of impurity as a physical contagion, which communicates itself automatically. Paul's principle is that one must not do what is contrary to one's own *conscience/consciousness* of purity.[12] If, by faith, that consciousness is altered, what was formerly impure would cease to be so. But if in following the example of others one transgresses one's own conscience/consciousness of purity, that action is not only impure but sinful. The only thing that is impure for you is what you yourself regard as impure.[13]

SEXUAL PURITY

Did Paul apply the same principles to sexual purity as to food purity? He was certainly capable of drawing a sharp distinction between food and sex:

> All things are permitted me, but not all are beneficial. All
> things are permitted me, but I will not be dominated by any.
> The foods are for the belly and the belly for the foods—and
> God will destroy both the one and the others. The body,
> however, is not for *porneia*, but for the Lord, and the Lord
> for the body; and God both raised the Lord and will raise us
> through his power. (1 Cor. 6:12–14)

Here, Paul rejects an exact correspondence between arguments
about food and those about sex. Although acknowledging that "all things
are permitted," he still asserts that there are reasons to avoid certain
sexual acts. Does this mean that he retained purity as an ethical principle
in the sexual sphere? That does not appear to be the case. He dismisses
both "belly" and "foods" as something purely physical. The sexual, however, he sees as going beyond the physical and connecting one more intimately with God.[14]

The particular sexual act in question in this passage is *porneia*. We
have already seen that this term is difficult to pin down in the New Testament writings; we shall discuss below some of its range of meaning for
Paul. The context, however, makes its meaning clear in the quotation
above: *porneia* refers here to literal prostitution, for some males in the
Corinthian church were visiting prostitutes (6:12–20). Because prostitution was as much an issue of property ethics as of purity, we will return
to this passage in part 2. At this point, note that Paul uses property language in the present context, not purity language. Repudiation of purity
requirements for Gentiles did not place all sexual acts outside the range
of ethical concern. There were no ethical principles forbidding specific
foods except for the purity system itself; set it aside and there was no
food law left. But in the area of sex, even if one did set aside the purity
law, other ethical principles still applied.[15] Prostitution, in any case, was
scarcely an issue in the purity system of the Torah and only when it was
connected with foreign cults.

Some, however, see this passage as suggesting that Paul was constructing a new, specifically Christian purity system around sex, with baptism
as the new dividing line.[16] Christians, he says, have been "washed," "hallowed," and "justified" in the name of Jesus and in the Spirit (1 Cor.
6:11). The belly may be for foods and foods for the belly, "but the body is

not for *porneia* but for the Lord, and the Lord for the body" (6:13)—and this body will be raised (6:14). We are already members of the body of Christ. It is unthinkable, then, to take the members of Christ and make them members of a prostitute. Paul seems to say that a sexual act on the part of a believer automatically implicates Christ. The man who "cleaves to" (has sexual intercourse with) a prostitute is "one body" with her; the person who "cleaves to the Lord" is "one spirit" with Jesus.

As the preceding translation brings out, Paul reaches back to Genesis 2 to borrow the language of "The two will become one flesh." What does he understand by this choice of quotation? Unlike Jesus, Paul is not speaking of a marital relationship between the man and the prostitute he visits.[17] Rather, he is stressing the word *flesh*, which he then reinterprets as "body." When Paul speaks of "one flesh," he appears to be thinking of the sexual act itself. But he contrasts "flesh" or "body," understood as an inferior state of being, with "spirit" as a superior one.[18] One's status as a member of Christ's body is also one's entree into the spiritual body of the resurrection (1 Cor. 15:44). Therefore it is important that sexual intercourse remain within the realm of Christ's body, the church.

There is another indication that Paul thinks of the church as a kind of realm of purity in regard to sexual relationships. Christian widows, he declares, are to remarry, if at all, "only in the Lord" (1 Cor. 7:39). On the other hand, existing marriages to people outside the church do not necessarily violate this realm of purity. Paul *allows* their dissolution, but recommends against it on the grounds that such marriages extend a kind of holy status even to the unbelieving partner and to the children of the union, who would otherwise be "unclean" (7:12–16). This is surprising, for the usual pattern of purity rules is that impurity drives out purity and inhibits access to the holy. In this case, however, Paul makes the same unexpected point made by certain of Jesus' miracles. Rather than being rendered unclean by touching a dead body, a leper, or a woman with a hemorrhage, Jesus actually raises, cleanses, and heals these sources of impurity. Here, too, Paul suggests that, in the context of the Christian community, holiness and purity are more powerful than the powers of defilement.

Why, then, does Paul object to Christian men visiting prostitutes? Paul's basic standard for intra-church marriages is that they are indissoluble (1 Cor. 7:10–11). He prefers that even marriages with unbelievers should continue, although he allows their dissolution. The relationship with a prostitute, however, constitutes the opposite case to marriage because it is casual and temporary. It is therefore inadequate as a channel for the hallowing of the sexual partner and will hardly create the long-term possibility of conversion that Paul hopes to find in marriage with an outsider. There is no element of "spirit" in the relationship—and no possibility of one. The man and the prostitute become one body, not one spirit. To be one spirit is possible only in the body of Christ and the context of the church.

1 Corinthians 6 does, then, represent a kind of purity code, but not in the sense of being a revival of the Torah codes. We must bear three points in mind. First, this not at all the same as the purity code of ancient Israel, where prostitution was not primarily a purity offense but, as we shall see in part 2, an offense against property. (Paul turns here, at the end of the passage, to the language of property: "you are not your own; you've been bought at a price" [6:19–20].) Second, this is an unusual purity code in terms of its relative balancing of pure and impure. As we have noted already, impurity is usually conceived as highly contagious and capable of driving out purity. Paul does not say that visiting the prostitute will destroy the Christian community—in the way that the Holiness Code feared that impurities committed by Israel compromised the purity of the land of Canaan—but simply that it brings together two incompatible things; it regresses from spirit to flesh. Third, the focus of holiness for Paul is not the Temple, but the body of Christ. The man who visits a prostitute "sins against" his own body, that is the body of Christ, to whom he now belongs and of which he is now a part. For sexual relationships to be compatible with membership in the body of Christ, for Paul, they must be long-term and, if newly contracted, with another believer.

LISTS—AND THEIR PROBLEMS

Unfortunately, any effort to sort out Paul's approach to sexual purity is severely hampered by the fact that there are few passage as detailed and explicit as 1 Corinthians 6. Most of Paul's discussion of sexual ethics resides clearly in the realm of property ethics, and we will turn to those passages in part 2. The principal exception is Romans 1, which brings its own set of problems and to which we shall turn shortly. Apart from it, most references that seem to combine sex and purity occur in lists of vices. As we have noted before, lists often give us little help in determining the precise meaning of their terms. Nowhere is this problem greater than with terms such as *akatharsia* ("uncleanness") and *porneia* (variously translated "prostitution, harlotry, fornication"). That *porneia* is used literally in 1 Corinthians 6 is clear from the context. Elsewhere, however, one is often at a loss for clear indications about the term's reference. If it is not literally a reference to prostitution, is it a metaphorical reference to idolatrous practices, as we have seen elsewhere? Or should it be read as a broad term for a variety of sexual offenses, like the English "fornication"? Moreover, if it does mean something like "fornication," precisely what does it cover? In the United States of the 1950s, masturbation fell under the heading of "fornication," but that is seldom true now. "Fornication" is itself, an ill-defined and shifting category. Again, when Paul does use the language of purity, does he mean to invoke some piece of the purity code of ancient Israel? Or is he using the terms metaphorically to speak of what we might call the "purity of the heart"? In simple lists, this is most often impossible to determine with any certainty.

We may get a little help from a passage where Paul uses both terms in a way that provides more context than a list can:

> This is God's will, your sanctification—for you to keep away from *porneia*, for each of you to know how to possess his own vessel in holiness and honor, not in a passion of desire like the Gentiles who do not know God, for each of you not to overreach his brother in the business and take what belongs to him, for the Lord is avenger in all these matters, just as we have also told you before and borne witness. For God has not called us for uncleanness (*akatharsia*), but in sanctification. So, then, the person who treats [another] as of no account is despising not a human being but the God who has put his Holy Spirit into you. (1 Thess. 4:3–8)

The first part of the passage, as far as "the Gentiles who do not know God," could be read as a generalized exhortation to observe sexual morality, reinforced by a Hellenistic suspicion of passion. In the following phrase, however, Paul specifies the particular offense that concerns him here. At first, it sounds as if it has to do with a business matter and the modern reader may well wonder what this has to do with *porneia*. But the issue turns out to be adultery, which means (as we shall see in part 2) one man's overreaching another by taking what is rightfully his—his wife. What Paul, then, goes on to call "uncleanness" in this case is not a simple violation of the purity code but the property offense wrought against a "brother" (i.e., the woman's husband). Each man is to "possess his own vessel[19] in holiness and honor" and not to infringe on the wife of another man. For Paul, as for the Torah, the evil of adultery is that one man is treating another man "as of no account." Worse yet, this offense, when directed against a fellow Christian, is really directed against "the God who has put his Holy Spirit into you."[20]

Is "impurity" functioning here as an independent ethical principle for condemning adultery? Or is it reinforcing an objection to adultery as a property violation? Or is a property violation here being interpreted metaphorically as an "uncleanness of the heart"? There is no way to be completely certain. Yet Paul devotes most of his argument here to the property ethic as providing reasons against adultery, which suggests that the property considerations are central. If Paul did intend to introduce physical purity as an independent principle here, he does not say so clearly. The simplest explanation is to take the reference to purity as metaphorical. Overreaching a fellow-Christian is "uncleanness." This is an interpretation that works in other passages as well.

If we return to Paul's lists, we find that he did speak of "impurity" fairly often. While some argue that he used this term in the broad sense of "fornication" and even retained the full Torah purity code,[21] such an assertion is far from self-evident. We have seen him reject the literal, physical purity of foods as decisive. His references to "impurity" in 1 Corinthians and 1 Thessalonians, where we have more context to help us, do not treat the Torah's rules of physical purity as the foundation of a sexual ethic. As we try to interpret Paul's lists of vices, the most helpful thing we can do is to note how the lists are organized; the grouping of words within lists is frequently our best—or even our only—clue to the meaning of individual items.[22]

Perhaps the most extensive list is the one in Galatians enumerating "the works of the flesh"—that is, of the whole human being in opposition to God (5:19–21).[23] The list includes "*porneia, akatharsia,* license, idolatry, sorcery, enmities, strife, jealousy, rages, selfish ambitions, dissensions, divisions, envies, drunkennesses, carousings, and things like these." Some of the list's component subgroups stand out clearly. The last two categories (drunkenness and carousing) are examples of excess, with public loss of control. The long central section of the list (from "enmities" through "envies") is composed of offenses against the internal peace of a community. At the beginning of the list, "idolatry" and "sorcery" are two words for the same thing—non-Israelite rites. The question, then, is how "*porneia, akatharsia,* and license" fit into the list. Do they go with "idolatry and sorcery" to form a single group referring to the cults of foreign gods? We are already familiar with both *porneia* and *akatharsia* in this sense, and Paul noted elsewhere that the idolatry of the people in the wilderness included licentious behavior (1 Cor. 10:7). Or do the first three terms form a separate group by themselves? And, if so, do they refer to sexual practices? And, if so, how were those sexual practices defined?

The same three terms appear together in another passage, where Paul is reproving the Corinthian church and threatening them with an unpleasant visit from him:

> I am afraid that somehow when I come I will not find you what I want and that you will find me not what you want; that somehow there will be strife, jealousy, rages, selfish ambitions, denunciations, gossipings, conceits, disorders; that when I come again my God will humiliate me in your presence and I will grieve over many of those who sinned before and have not repented for the *akatharsia* and *porneia* and license that they committed. (2 Cor. 12:20–21)

Some commentators have seen *porneia* here as a reference to the man who "had his father's wife" (1 Cor. 5:1). Paul did refer to that act as a case of *porneia,* and he could be speaking of the same or similar problems here. On the other hand, the dangers Paul explicitly cites in 2 Corinthians have nothing to do with sexual impurity and everything to do with the internal peace of the community. Does he make a shift in focus between the two parts of this list? Or do the latter offenses sum up the earlier part of the list?

The list is, as such lists go, surprisingly coherent; to read it as making a sudden and unprepared shift of subjects from social turmoil to sexual impurity has seemed difficult to interpreters.[24] It would be easiest to conclude that what Paul meant here by "uncleanness and harlotry and license" was in continuity with "strife, jealousy, rages, selfish ambitions," and so forth. The desire of partisans to seize control of the local community—a problem abundantly documented throughout Paul's Corinthian correspondence—would certainly qualify as impurity of the heart. We know that Paul did see license of all sorts as one of the typical causes of discord in the community. In Romans, he contrasted the love that is the "fullness of the law" with "carousings and drinking bouts, acts of sexual intercourse and license, strife and jealousy" (13:8–14). What he feared would humble him at Corinth was the "unclean" disunity and jockeying for advantage to be found there.

If we return to the list in Galatians, then, we have three possible ways of analyzing it. One way would be to read the list as composed of three basic categories: idolatry (including "uncleanness, harlotry, and license"), internal divisions, and acts of excess. The other two approaches would make four categories in the list by separating the first three items, but they would differ as to whether the first category should be understood as sexual impurity or as the desire to place oneself first in the community. Of these three options, the one that emphasizes sexual purity is least likely. There is little, if anything, elsewhere in Paul's writings to suggest that he maintained sexual purity, in the physical sense, as a leading Christian virtue, but there is a great deal to suggest that humility and peaceableness within the community were central for him. In the parallel list from 2 Corinthians, he used this same language for the offenses that threatened them.

If this interpretation seems odd to the modern reader, that is largely because we read Paul's letters now as part of a larger book (the Bible) that includes Leviticus and through the lens of a new, Christian purity code centered on virginity that arose in the second century.[25] "Uncleanness," to our mind, does not readily translate to "social greed."[26] Yet we have already noted Paul's identification of greed with uncleanness in 1 Thessalonians. And further evidence that this usage was familiar among his followers comes from two letters of uncertain authorship that are closely associated with Paul, Colossians, and Ephesians.

In each of these letters, references to uncleanness always link up with references to greed. This greed (*pleonexia*) is not merely the private vice of lust, the desire to have something for oneself, but rather the social one of covetousness, the desire to have more than another or to have what rightfully belongs to another. In Ephesians, the author warns the audience not to behave like the Gentiles, who, "having grown callous, surrendered themselves to license for working all uncleanness in greed" (4:19). License, uncleanness, and greed all work together here; for the abandonment of restraint and of concern for the rights of others is precisely what produces impurity of heart. The same point is echoed elsewhere in Ephesians: "Let harlotry and all uncleanness or greed [*pleonexia*] not even be named among you . . . for know this: that a person given to harlotry or an unclean or a greedy person [*pleonektēs*], that is, an idolater, has no inheritance in the reign of Christ and God" (5:3, 5). For the author of Ephesians, uncleanness, harlotry, and even idolatry seem to be synonyms of *pleonexia*.

Colossians takes a similar but more complex approach. Having admonished his audience to respect their baptism, in which they have died to this world and been raised with Christ, the author continues: "Put to death, then, the members that are on the earth, harlotry, uncleanness, passion, evil desire, and the greed [*pleonexia*] which is idolatry, on account of which things the wrath of God is coming upon the children of disobedience" (3:5–6). Here, one can certainly detect an association of harlotry and uncleanness with sexual acts because of their association with passion and evil desire (about as close as New Testament Greek comes to an unambiguous designation of "lust"). This need not mean, however, that the author is resurrecting the idea of physical uncleanness; it is more likely that the preeminent example of *pleonexia* here, as in 1 Thessalonians, is the desire to possess another person's sexual property through adultery. This understanding of the passage provides an easier transition to the following list of specific vices that the author wants Christian folk to reject: anger, rage, badness, blasphemy, shameless conversation, and lying (3:8–9). Issues of social disruption are dominant here, and the list barely even alludes to sexual activities. The corresponding list of virtues that concludes the passage (3:12–15) is concerned entirely with the peace of the community.

Paul and the early Pauline tradition, then, appear from the evidence discussed thus far to have little, if any, concern for sexual purity in the physical sense of the Torah purity code. Impurity, for them, consists above all in trying to get the better of someone else; impurity of the heart manifests itself in competitive greed—mainly for dominance in the community or for illicit possession of another's sexual property. Paul is in broad agreement with the Gospel traditions. He is familiar with the purity code of the Torah and with that of Pharisaism, and he does not object to their continued observance. The purity that counts, however, is that of the heart, which Paul identifies as the opposite of *pleonexia*. In comparison with the Gospels, Paul is unique, it seems, in two respects only: he expands the definition of purity of the heart so that physical purity becomes an aspect of it for those who believe it to be necessary (Rom. 14:14), and he begins the process of drawing a kind of purity boundary around the Christian community that makes marriage with outsiders problematic.

In what we have seen thus far, Paul never invokes the purity code of the Torah as the foundation for his discussions of sexual ethics. The most that can be said is that he may reinforce a property ethic with the language of purity. The few passages that *may* go beyond this are all in lists and impossible to interpret with full confidence. Accordingly, it is difficult to claim Paul on behalf of a physical purity ethic for sexuality.[27] Insofar as he did teach such an ethic, it was not that of the Torah, but a new one, based on the idea that Christians are members of Christ's body and taking the perimeters of the new Christian community as a kind of purity boundary. Interestingly, his proposal, in this regard, seems to have been something of a historical dead end. When a distinctively Christian purity code for sexuality did emerge in the second century, it was not based on these ideas of Paul, but on the exaltation of virginity as the supreme sexual value.

PURITY, SAME-GENDER SEXUAL ACTS, AND SIN

There remains one other passage of great importance to our discussion—the only passage in which Paul freely and repeatedly used the language of impurity in its physical sense with reference to sex: the discussion of same-gender sexual acts in Romans 1:18–32. Conventional interpretation of this passage has taken Paul as saying that God, as a punishment for the sin of idolatry, has abandoned some Gentiles to yet another sin—that of same-gender sexual acts (vv. 18–25). As punishment for this "error" (the sexual acts), God has also inflicted on the male offenders some further, unspecified "recompense" (vv. 26–27). Furthermore, same-gender sexual acts are part of a larger group of characteristically Gentile sins, all of which deserve death (vv. 28–32). This understanding of the passage has a long history, but, as far as I am aware, no one has identified its exact age or origins. If it is an accurate reading, it means that, in Romans 1, Paul took a very different stance toward purity from the one he took elsewhere in his writings, especially Romans 14.

A closer examination of the passage, however, shows that this common interpretation actually represents a careless reading of the text. The idea that Paul means to categorize same-gender sexual acts here as sinful is a presupposition brought to the text rather than being explicitly stated there. Paul did have a rich stock of words for sin: sin (*hamartia, hamartēma*), lawlessness or transgression (*anomia*), unrighteousness (*adikia*), impiety (*asebeia*). He does not apply them to same-gender sexual acts in this passage. This might, of course, be an oversight on his part. And yet, the language of sin does appear twice in the passage: once at the beginning, where it refers to idolatry (*asebeia, adikia*, 1:18), and again near the end (*adikia*, 1:29), where it forms the heading for a whole list of wrongs—a list which includes *pleonexia* and many other offenses against social peace, but nothing sexual (vv. 29–31). What is more, as we shall see, this list of sins is separate from the references to same-gender sexual acts—something that modern translations tend to overlook or obscure. If one wants to maintain that Paul was labeling same-gender sexual acts as sinful, one can do so only by showing that he used the language we do find here with an equivalent meaning. That turns out to be a difficult challenge.

Paul's basic argument, on closer reading, runs thus: Idolatry was the root sin of the Gentiles. The creation offers ample evidence of God's goodness, power, and divinity, so that any people should have known enough to worship and give thanks to God alone. The Gentiles, in the stupidity of their hearts, chose instead to worship "a likeness of an image of a perishable human being and of birds and beasts and vermin" (1:23). This was a voluntary act, committed in full knowledge of its meaning, and it is the reason why "God surrendered them in the desires of their hearts to uncleanness" (v. 24). Paul did not, of course, mean that every Gentile invented idolatry individually or that each began to experience homosexual desire as a result. He was writing in terms of Gentile culture as a whole, not of individuals: the original forebears of the Gentiles committed the sin of idolatry, in which their descendants, in the normal course of events, have followed them; and this is why God has decreed that certain unclean practices are to be characteristic of their culture.

Did Paul understand these practices as being sinful as well as unclean? This is not inconceivable; the religious tradition of Israel and of Christianity could at least entertain the notion that God might punish one sin by causing the sinner to commit another.[28] To determine whether that is Paul's meaning here, however, we must look carefully at his vocabulary in discussing homosexual acts. Unfortunately, the existing English translations, having been made with the presupposition that Paul regarded these acts as sinful, tend to predetermine the conclusions of those using them. For readers who cannot consult the Greek text directly, there is need for a more neutral translation, which I shall supply as we proceed.

Paul wrote:

> For this reason [idolatry], God surrendered them in the desires (*epithymia*) of their hearts to uncleanness so that they would dishonor (*atimazō*) their bodies among themselves— these people who exchanged the truth of God for the lie and revered and worshipped the creation instead of the Creator, who is blessed for ever, amen. [1:24–25]

English versions of this passage usually translate *epithymia* as "lust." But the Greek term is not always pejorative and, if we do not intend to prejudge Paul's meaning here, the more neutral "desire" is more appropriate. Paul often uses *epithymia* in a negative sense—sometimes, following the usage of the Septuagint in the Tenth Commandment, as meaning "covetousness" (Rom. 7:7; cf. Exod. 20:17 LXX). But he could also use it positively, as when he wrote to the Thessalonian church, "We, brethren, having been bereft of you for some time in face, though not in heart, have been all the more eager to see your face with much *epithymia*" (1 Thess. 2:17), where the term requires some positive translation, such as "eagerness." Here in Romans, a neutral translation will help us avoid prejudging its meaning. Paul says, then, that God dealt with the desires of Gentiles in such a way as to hand them over to uncleanness. Paul took the relative acceptability of same-gender sexual acts in Gentile culture as evidence that Gentile desire was different from that of Jews and interpreted this as an act of God, who had "surrendered" them to this state.[29]

Along with the uncleanness of these acts goes an element of social disgrace, which Paul describes as the "dishonoring" of bodies. Paul was by no means the first to link uncleanness and dishonor, a combination of motifs that one finds already in the scriptures of Israel. The sons of Jacob, for example, regard it as dishonorable for one of their women to be given in marriage to an uncircumcised man (Gen. 34:14). Ezekiel uses the phrase "death of the uncircumcised" as equivalent to "disgraceful death" (28:10) and says that the man who has intercourse with a menstruating woman has shamed her (22:10, cf. 18:6). Job refers to cult prostitutes as the lowest of the low in society (36:14). The incidental way in which biblical writers identify uncleanness as a source of disgrace or dishonor shows that this was a familiar fact of life in their world: those at the bottom of the social scale were assumed to be habitually unclean, and those who were chronically unclean (e.g., lepers) were often shifted to the margins or the bottom of society. Paul moves easily, in the present passage, between the language of purity and that of social honor or dishonor.

Paul continues the discussion by reiterating his original point and making it more explicit:

> On account of this [i.e., their sin of idolatry], God surrendered them to passions (*pathos*) of dishonor (*atimia*), for their females exchanged the natural use for that over against nature (*para physin*) and in the same way the males, too, having left the natural use of the female, burned with their desire (*orexis*) for one another, males accomplishing shamelessness (*aschemosyne)* with males and receiving the due recompense (*antimisthia*) of their error (*plane*) among themselves. (Rom. 1:26–27)

As in the preceding verses, we find terms for desire (*pathos, orexis*) that could carry either positive or negative connotations. Insofar as Paul regarded desire as something for the mature person to avoid or subdue, he is no doubt looking askance at it here. This is the same Paul, however, who wrote to the Corinthians that, even though he preferred for single persons not to marry, "it is better to marry than to burn" (1 Cor. 7:7). In other words, Paul was willing, albeit reluctantly, to accept the legitimacy of sexual desire and its appropriate satisfaction when a person did not have the gift of rising above it.

We again find, in these verses, the language of social dishonor, including the term "shamelessness" (*aschēmosynē*), which Paul applies to sexual acts between males.[30] This would have been intelligible to both Jewish and Gentile audiences because it was considered dishonorable for any free, adult male to assume the "female" role by being penetrated sexually. In the ancient world generally, the most important social imperative was to maintain or improve the standing of one's family, whether positively by increasing its public honor or negatively by avoiding anything that might shame the family. "Shamelessness" meant being deficient in concern for the latter. It was a synonym for dishonor, not a term denoting sinful behavior. King James's translators found a suitable equivalent in the English of their day: "that which is unseemly." Paul's choice of this particular term in Greek echoes the purity tradition of the Torah, for the Septuagint uses the term to denote (among other things) sexual violations of purity, genitalia, and human excrement.[31] All this language is pejorative. Paul clearly affirms that what the Gentiles do is contrary to the Israelite code of purity and abhorrent from a Jewish perspective—and also that it produces shameful, disgraceful consequences. This still does not settle, however, the question whether Paul considered these unclean acts to be *sinful*. Not every act that is described negatively is also sinful; to collapse all pejorative language into one category is, at best, ethically inept.[32]

Paul introduces a new element in verses 26–27 by saying that same-gender sexual intercourse is an abandonment of "natural use" for what is "over against nature." This terminology is not easy to interpret because the terms "nature" and "natural" can mean a great many different things, particularly in the context of ethical discourse.[33] Paul's own use of the term "nature" elsewhere offers us some important help in avoiding misinterpretations of it. In most instances, he uses the term to refer to the continuity of an organism with its past: thus, he distinguishes branches that are still attached to their original tree (*kata physin*, according to nature) from those that have been grafted into a tree of another species (*para physin*, over against nature) (Rom. 11:24), or he speaks of those who "by nature" are without law (Rom. 2:14) or are uncircumcised (2:27) or are Jewish, though today we might consider these "cultural" rather than "natural" distinctions (Gal. 2:15).[34] If this stress on continuity is what Paul has in mind in Romans 1:26-27, he is reiterating an idea he has already hinted at—that Gentiles experienced only heterosexual desire before God visited uncleanness on them and that they have therefore changed their "nature"—that is, lost a certain continuity with their remoter past.

In another context, Paul uses "nature" in what at first appears to be a completely different sense. In an effort to convince the Corinthians that women must cover their heads when they prophesy in the church gathering, he adduces a number of independent arguments, among them the following: "Judge among yourselves: is it proper for a woman to pray to God uncovered? Does not nature [*physis*] itself teach you that if a man wears his hair long it is a dishonor [*atimia*] to him but if a woman wears her hair long it is her glory? Because the hair has been given her in place of a covering" (1 Cor. 11:13–14). Here, "nature" seems to mean something like "widespread social usage." Paul draws an argument by analogy from such usage: just as women in his world were expected to wear their hair long and men short, so, too, women ought to wear something on their heads when leading worship while men should not. This sense of "nature," however, would seem odd in Romans because "widespread social usage" in the Greek world in fact accepted same-gender sexual intercourse. There is an element of coherence, however, in that both uses of "nature" imply that it reflects or even consists in a certain continuity of usage.[35]

Paul does not derive his use of the language of "nature" from the scriptures of Israel. It is not found at all in those works written originally in Hebrew or Aramaic.[36] But it does appear in the literature of Greek-speaking Judaism in Paul's time, with some indebtedness to contemporary Stoicism, where it played a significant role in ethical reasoning. Paul may have picked the terminology up indirectly from Stoic usage, but his own usage is not Stoic. If it were, he could scarcely write of God as acting "over against nature," as he does in Romans 11:24. Some Stoics did indeed regard same-gender sexual intercourse as "over against nature," which would seem to accord with Paul's use of the term in this context. This had to do with the Stoic theory that sexual intercourse existed for a single purpose: procreation. All intercourse for other purposes was "over against nature." Same-gender sexual intercourse was not unique in this regard. The Stoic Emperor Marcus Aurelius, for example, gave thanks "that I didn't touch Benedicta or Theodotus, but that even later on when I found myself in the midst of erotic passions I was restored to health."[37] He does not characterize sexual relations with the male Theodotus as being worse than or even different from having them with the female Benedicta. The wrong in either case, from the Stoic perspective, would have been to indulge in sexual intercourse purely for the sake of satisfying desire.[38]

Even if, for a Stoic philosopher, the phrase *para physin* would have had a force not unlike "sin," given Paul's other uses of the phrase itself and his other references to "nature," this is too heavy-handed in his case. What he means by it, rather, is that there has been a notable discontinuity from what would previously have been expected. The way Gentile culture is now is not the way it was originally—that is, one presumes, from the time it took shape in the aftermath of the Tower of Babel and the multiplication of languages. If we take the phrase *para physin* here as equivalent to "sinful," it makes Paul's reuse of it, later in Romans, in the image of God grafting Gentiles *para physin* into the olive tree of Israel intolerably strange.

It remains to ask, with regard to the verses above, what Paul meant by saying that Gentile males were "receiving the due recompense of their error among themselves." The common interpretation of this statement takes the "error" as same-gender sexual intercourse and the "recompense" as some evil punishing it. The RSV goes so far as to speak of a "penalty" that they suffered "in their own persons," although "among themselves" is a more likely translation of *en heautois*. Two difficulties attend this interpretation. First, no one has yet given a satisfactory explanation of what this "penalty" might have been. Hemorrhoids and sexually transmitted disease have been suggested, but neither is suitable because neither is confined either to homosexual males or to Gentiles.[39] The common interpretation thus makes nonsense of the text itself at this point. The second problem lies in supposing that Paul used the term *planē* (error) with reference to sexual acts. This term and its near relatives appear a good many times in Paul's undoubted writings, but always with reference to wrong belief rather than wrong action. Even in 1 Thessalonians, where "error" appears alongside "uncleanness" and "deceit" (2:3), a perusal of the whole passage will show that Paul refers to a kind of false teaching framed with a view to deceiving the audience and enriching the teacher (2:5–6). To take *planē* in Romans 1:27, then, as referring to same-gender sexual acts is to suggest that Paul departed from his normal usage for no apparent reason.

If the common interpretation is impossible to maintain, then how can this phrase be interpreted with greater fidelity to the text and to Paul's normal usage? The simplest solution would be to take the "error" as idolatry and the "recompense" as the uncleanness of Gentile culture. In other words, Paul is reiterating once again, at the end of verse 27, the point he had made previously in verses 24 and 26: because the progenitors of the Gentiles forsook the true God to worship idols, God visited on them and on their progeny a characteristic kind of uncleanness and disgrace, namely the desire for and practice of same-gender sexual relations. This is not a matter of individual idolaters receiving a recompense for their errors; it is a cultural characteristic. The Gentiles receive "*among themselves the due recompense* [unclean, disgraceful sexual practice] *of their error* [idolatry]."

Finally, Paul concludes this passage by saying that God's visiting of this uncleanness upon the Gentiles was justified by their idolatry and by other sins that they also accepted and practiced:

> And just as they did not agree to keep God in recognition, God surrendered them to a disagreeable mind, to do things that are not proper [*ta mē kathēkonta*], since they were already filled [*peplēromenous*] with all unrighteousness, evil, greed [*pleonexia*], badness; full of envy, murder, strife, deceit, craftiness; gossips, slanderers, God-haters, proud, arrogant, boasters, contrivers of evils, disobeyers of parents, unintelligent, unfaithful, unloving, unmerciful—people who, though knowing God's judgment that those who do such things deserve death, not only do them but also offer approval to those who do. (Rom. 1:28–32)

These verses offer us a list of sins that Paul treats as characteristic of Gentiles. Interestingly, the list does not include anything of a sexual nature, but concentrates on the sins of social disruption that concern Paul so often elsewhere. The Gentiles "were already filled" with these vices[40] and gave them their approval[41] even before God "surrendered" them to same-gender sexual acts—acts referred to in these verses not as sins, but as "things that are not proper."

Conventional reading of these verses has tended to lump the list of vices after *peplēromenous* with *ta mē kathēkonta*.[42] This is careless, at best. The Greek *peplēromenous* is not an adjective ("full") but a perfect passive participle, a form that specifically designates a state of being already in existence at the time of the main verb. The main verb, in this case, is "surrendered" (*paredoken*, an aorist form functioning as a simple past tense). The perfect passive participle *peplēromenous* implies that the people were already guilty of the following list of offenses when God "surrendered" them to the punishment of same-gender desires and acts. The deeds that make people "deserve death" are not, then, the "improper" acts of same-gender sexual intercourse, but the vices in the list itself, beginning with "unrighteousness."[43] Paul's point is that the filthiness of Gentile culture was a very mild punishment, given what the ancestral Gentiles actually deserved, for they had piled all these other offenses on top of their "original sin" of idolatry.

A close reading of Romans 1:18-32, then, does not support the conventional interpretation of the passage. While Paul wrote of same-gender sexual acts as being unclean, dishonorable, improper, and "over against nature," he did not apply his extensive vocabulary for sin to them. Instead, he treated homosexual behavior as an integral if filthy aspect of Gentile culture. It was not in itself sinful, but had been visited upon the Gentiles as recompense for sins—first and foremost the sin of idolatry but also those additional sins of social disruption listed in verses 29-31. This reading of the passage not only respects the text itself, but also brings it into reasonable accord with what we have seen of Paul's attitude to purity elsewhere.[44] Paul did not deny the existence of a distinction between clean and unclean and even assumed that Jewish Christians would continue to observe the purity code. He refrained, however, from identifying physical impurity with sin or demanding that Gentiles adhere to that code.

Malakoi *and* arsenokoitai

But if Paul did not mean to characterize such acts as sinful, why does he open Romans with such a sharp attack on Gentiles—the very people whom he normally supported, insisting that they had a place in the church without becoming Jews? We shall return to this question shortly. But first we should look at one other passage where some claim that Paul unambig-uously characterizes homosexual persons as sinners. The passage in ques-tion is a list: "Neither those given to harlotry nor idolaters nor adulterers nor *malakoi* nor *arsenokoitai* nor thieves nor the greedy [*pleonektai*]—not the drunken or the abusive or the rapacious will inherit God's reign" (1 Cor. 6:9–10). The interpretation of the two terms I have left untranslated here is the crux of the matter and has long proven troublesome. *Malakoi* basi-cally means "soft," and the King James Version translated it "effeminate."[45] *Arsenokoitai* is of uncertain meaning. It contains basic elements referring to male gender and to sexual intercourse, and the King James transla-tors, presumably relying on the guidance of etymology, used the peculiar phrase "abusers of themselves with mankind." The original edition of the

Revised Standard Version combined the two terms and translated them "homosexuals." The second edition substituted "sexual perverts."

The great problem with analyzing this vocabulary is that *arsenokoitai* never appears in a context that can give us a clear sense of exactly what the term meant to Paul or to Paul's audience or even for some centuries thereafter. There is no certain instance of it prior to the New Testament writings, and it occurs only one other time in the New Testament itself— again in a list and this time without *malakoi* (1 Tim. 1:10, a post-Pauline writing). Its etymology could suggest some such meaning as "a man who has intercourse with another man," but etymology is a notoriously bad guide to the actual, live meanings of words. In American English, for example, "outbuilding" and "outhouse" are synonymous in terms of etymology, but quite different in usage, the one meaning any outlying building on a farm, the other meaning a latrine. Usage, not etymology, determines meaning.

The next point in this regard is that the term *homosexual* and the concept behind it are modern coinages. Ancient Greeks and Romans seem to have assumed that most human beings are attracted sexually both to their own and the opposite sex. They could even debate the relative merits of the two types of love.[46] While they acknowledged that some individuals were exclusively attracted to members of the same sex, they do not appear to have had any terminology to set such a group apart. They lacked even a behavior-based category for people who showed a fixed preference for partners of the same sex. Accordingly, we cannot expect a text written in ancient Greek to address the modern concept of homosexuality in so many words.[47]

The terms and concepts available in ancient Greek were all more limited in meaning; in any case, the modern pattern of two adult men or two adult women experiencing mutual desire does not seem to have been usual. We know less about female-female partnerships than about male, though we know more than was formerly supposed.[48] The classic form of male-male partnership was pederastic, the love of an adult male (*erastēs*, lover) for a youth (*eromenos*, beloved). The older partner was expected to be the penetrator of the younger—never the reverse. This reflected the pattern of marriage, where the bride was usually much younger than the groom. In classical Greece, the youth was typically freeborn and the relationship could be open, approved, and honorable, although it must end as the youth reached young manhood. In the Roman era, the beloved was more commonly a slave, entirely at his master's bidding. There were also male prostitutes who serviced both sexes. It was degrading for an adult male to be penetrated in intercourse, although this does not, of course, mean that it did not happen.[49]

There have been two major suggestions about the meaning of Paul's terms. One, put forward by Robin Scroggs, proposes that *malakoi* and *arsenokoitai* functioned together as Greek equivalents to technical terminology in rabbinic Hebrew that designated, respectively, the penetrated and penetrative partners in anal intercourse. The terms, on this interpretation, would have been closely tied to the purity law of Leviticus and its interpretation in the scribal tradition.[50] The other suggestion, made by John Boswell, holds that there was no intrinsic connection between *malakoi* and *arsenokoitai*, that the former word, if it had anything at all do with sexual activity, meant "masturbators," and that the latter was probably a vulgar expression meaning "male prostitutes." If this is correct, it would be unclear whether Paul's use of the term was meant to condemn them for same-gender sexual acts or for acts of prostitution or both.[51]

Scroggs's argument implies that the two terms *malakoi* and *arsenokoitai* should form an invariable pair because neither would have the same import without the other. Yet in its one other occurrence in the New Testament, *arsenokoitai* appears without *malakoi* and is associated rather with "those given to harlotry" and "kidnappers" (1 Tim. 1:10). Furthermore, if Paul was indeed employing technical terminology used in the synagogue and reaffirming it in the context of the church, we should expect knowledge of this usage to continue, but the later record is at best mixed, with little evidence for *arsenokoites* as meaning anything like "homosexual."[52] Then, too, Scroggs's hypothesis is complex, requiring us to understand the vocabulary in terms of a double linguistic and cultural tradition, whereas Boswell's hypothesis stays entirely within the bounds of the Greek-speaking world. This does not prove that Scroggs is mistaken, but, other considerations being at least equal, the simpler hypothesis is preferable.[53] More recently, Dale B. Martin has presented strong arguments against the linking of the two words and has demonstrated once again that we simply do not have any adequate evidence to tell us what *arsenokoites* meant.[54]

Paul's Gentile mission and the rhetorical structure of Romans

Because the reference to *arsenokoitai* in 1 Corinthians is not helpful to us in the present discussion, whatever we are going to learn of Paul's attitude toward same-gender sexual behavior we must glean from the first chapter of Romans. There, as we have seen, Paul spoke of it as unclean but did not explicitly label it as sinful. Indeed, it is difficult to see how he could have done otherwise, for his whole mission was predicated on the principle that Gentiles did not have to become Jews to be Christians. This was not merely a question of whether males must be circumcised, but also included differences with regard to Sabbath observance (Rom. 14:5–6) and purity. Even in the matter of eating food sacrificed to idols, with the implied danger of participation in alien cults, it was impossible for Paul to prohibit the behavior of the Strong simply on the grounds of impurity. Instead, as we have seen, he merely discouraged the eating of such foods on grounds of consideration for the Weak.

Given this interpretation of Romans 1, one must ask why Paul wrote the passage at all. Why begin his longest letter by attacking one particular aspect of Gentile culture in a way characteristic of Hellenistic-Jewish polemic against Gentiles—but, at the same time, restrict his attack to the language of purity and shame, omitting any reference to sin? The answer requires an appreciation of the rhetorical shape and purpose of the letter to Romans, a topic that would require more space than this volume, with its broader focus, can afford. Because I have discussed it at greater length elsewhere, I will summarize my argument here.[55]

The rhetorical purpose of Romans was to address the Christian community at Rome, a church that Paul did not found and had never visited, in such a way as to gain its goodwill so that Paul could be welcomed there and ask its assistance in mounting a mission to Spain.[56] This was not an easy goal, given Paul's reputation as a troublemaker. To gain this end, Paul had to show the Roman Christians, a mixed community of Gentiles and Jews, that a visit from him would not be disruptive for them—indeed, that it could even be beneficial. He did this by presenting his understanding of the Gospel in a way that suggested a solution to a central problem in the life of the Christian community at Rome—the issue of food purity. He did not move directly to making his recommendations because, given his lack of authority there, such a move would have invited resistance on the part of those who were suspicious of him. Instead, he constructed a complex argument, shaped in terms of two parallel entrapments, the first aimed at Jewish Christians, the second at Gentile Christians.

Paul begins his letter by attacking Gentiles (the group with whom he is presumed to sympathize!) in terms familiar from Jewish polemic—the passage we have just interpreted.[57] It quickly emerges, however, that his real target is the sort of Jewish Christian who had an easy sense of superiority to Gentiles and who will have uttered a very hearty "Amen" to Paul's attack. Having lured this person's sense of satisfaction out into the open, Paul then focuses on showing that this person is not without fault, either. He goes on to argue that the Torah by itself does not guarantee the superiority of the Jewish people. Then, beginning in chapter 9, Paul reverses the process by attacking Jews for not believing the Christian message—an attack on his own ethnicity that shortly turns out to have been a temptation to Gentile Christians to think of themselves as superior. They get a reproof from Paul roughly parallel to the one given the Jewish Christian after the denunciation of Gentiles.

Given the complexity of this structure, it is a mistake to read Romans 1:18–32 as an essay on same-gender sexuality.[58] Paul is writing not to work out an ethical stance on this topic but to use a familiar kind of polemic to entrap another group of hearers. In exactly the same way, it is a mistake to treat Romans 9–11 as a simple, straightforward statement of Paul's attitude toward ongoing Judaism. It is not a dissertation on that topic, but an entrapment of Gentile Christians. This in itself should be enough to caution the careful reader against employing Romans 1:18–32 to decide the question of the sinfulness of same-gender sexual acts. And, in fact, Paul has been careful, despite the apparently heated character of his rhetoric, to avoid calling such acts sinful. He says they are filthy and shameful. Although the intensity of the passage must have taken his Gentile hearers aback, it was not inconsistent with his position elsewhere regarding food. Gentile culture was indeed filthy, from a Jewish perspective. Paul was only saying that this did not prevent Gentiles from being part of the Christian community.

Later readers have often begun by assuming that Paul could not possibly have taken less than a completely hostile attitude toward same-gender sexual relationships.[59] This assumption, however, has less to do with Paul than with the times in which the readers have lived. I began with that assumption myself—and without any expectation of questioning it. On reflection, however, I came to realize that Paul's situation was radically different from that of his later Christian readers. He was poised precisely on the boundary line between Jewish and Gentile cultures, endeavoring to include both within the new Christian community. He could not ignore any of the classic points that separated the two groups. These were not limited to circumcision and food purity, but also included the keeping of Sabbath and the Jewish condemnation of same-gender sexuality. The real question is why modern readers have so easily assumed that he would be willing to seek accommodations on circumcision, food purity, and Sabbath observance, but not on the matter of same-gender sexual relationships. For the most part, this assumption has been completely unconscious. Its defenders have appealed to a small number of late Stoic philosophers who disapproved of same-gender sexual intercourse because it was not procreative. The argument has been that "the best" of Greco-Roman culture shared the Jewish disapprobation of such acts and that Paul would inevitably accept this and combine it with Jewish purity law.

There are several problems with this approach. One is that Paul's knowledge of Stoicism was spotty and he had no particular commitment to the tradition. Another is that Stoic rejection of same-gender sexual acts had a different basis from the Jewish. Such Jewish writers as Philo might justify the Torah's purity rule with the help of Stoic arguments, but the Torah prohibition was explicitly framed in terms of purity, not procreation. To judge by the citation from Marcus Aurelius above, a practicing Stoic need not in fact make a sharp distinction between sex with the opposite gender and sex with the same gender: both were wrong insofar as they were intended only to satisfy desire. From the perspective of Torah, however, the two sexual objects were incommensurable. There is no reason to think that most Gentiles, even those of Stoic propensities, would admire the Jewish perspective.

The second problem is that the philosophically minded constituted only a small segment even of the elite of the Roman world. Among their elite counterparts who, for example, wrote poetry, one encounters a good deal of sneering at men who allowed themselves to be penetrated sexually, but no blanket hostility toward same-gender sexuality as such. Given that Gentile converts to early Christianity mostly did not come from the elite of the Roman world, in any case, it is unclear how far Stoic severity influenced them. The first-century Roman world was pervaded by sexuality in a way that even modern Americans might find astonishing. It was not uncommon for home furnishings, cups, plates, floor mosaics, and wall paintings to carry representations of sexual intercourse, whether same-gender or opposite-gender.[60] Nor was it uncommon for a person who owned slaves to treat one or more of them, whether of the same or the opposite gender, as a sexual partner.[61] Paul was in Gentile houses. He was scarcely ignorant of the differences in mores. He will certainly have had to come to grips with this most obvious of differences—the place of same-gender sexual relationships.

And he will probably not have been able to shrug the matter off by saying that this was one area where Gentiles had to become Jews. He found support from within Gentile culture to discourage acts of excess or license. He had support against the man at Corinth who had his father's wife. But in the particular area where the conflict of the two cultures had been so plainly stated in Jewish polemic for so long, he will scarcely have been able to ignore the question of whether here, too, a Gentile might remain a Gentile and still be a Christian. Gentiles will have been familiar with the revulsion many Jews felt toward same-gender sexual acts; given their own relative lack of interest in purity, they will have regarded this reaction as a Jewish peculiarity.

Surprising as it may seem, then, the text (Rom. 1:18–32) that currently seems to figure most prominently in Christian debates about same-gender sexual relationships probably bears witness to a situation exactly opposite that envisioned by the modern religious right. Instead of demonstrating Paul's retention of Torah purity law in this respect, it makes rhetorical sense only on the presupposition that Paul kept, in the realm of sex as well as that of food, a consistent distinction between impurity and sin: physical impurity becomes sin only when one violates one's own consciousness of what is pure. Paul's argument, in a nutshell, is this: "We all know Gentiles have sinned. Only look at the dirtiness into which God plunged them as a consequence. But what of the Jew who criticizes them? Are you claiming to be sinless?"

CONCLUSIONS

Paul's assessment of purity in relation to the Christian message is distinguished from that of Matthew, Mark, Luke, or John by greater subtlety and fuller articulation. Where the evangelists simply know a distinction between physical purity and that of the heart, Paul also recognizes that purity of the heart may require physical purity in the case of the Weak— that is, those who cannot successfully distinguish between the two. And where the evangelists give a somewhat miscellaneous account of what constitutes impurity of the heart, Paul moves toward a particular stress on socially defined greed (*pleonexia*) and other wrongs that create social discord. Also, Paul clarifies the status of the purity code in the specific area of sex both by the directness of his general principles ("nothing is unclean in and of itself") and by the careful distinction he observed in Romans 1 between the impurity of homosexual acts and the sins of idolatry and social disruption for which God imposed such impurity as "recompense."

Paul did not place sexuality outside the realm of ethics. He simply rejected Torah purity as a foundation for Christian sexual ethics; to have retained it would have been to retain the demand that Gentile Christians become Jews. To some degree, Paul did try to create a new kind of Christian purity code for sexuality, dictating that it be ensconced in long-term relationships contracted within the Christian community, but with an exception for those that predated a person's conversion. Although this initiative had some continuing influence, it was soon superseded by the development of a Christian purity code focused on virginity, for which even marriage was ethically suspect.

Modern interest in Paul's purity ethics has focused almost entirely on efforts to shore up a collapsing insistence that Christianity is fundamentally and inalterably opposed to all same-gender sexual relationships. Because many advocates of this position have recognized that neither the Sodom narrative nor the prohibitions in Leviticus are decisive in condemning such relationships, they have little to fall back on other than Paul. Unfortunately for this project, the Paul who describes same-gender sexual acts as unclean is also the Paul who insists that "nothing is unclean in and of itself."

CHAPTER 7

THE NEW TESTAMENT AND SEXUAL PURITY

We have seen that the evangelists and Paul rejected physical purity as a prerequisite of salvation or of membership in the Christian community. They did not deny its reality: dirt, as they understood it, was still dirt. They asserted, however, that the gospel transcended or even transformed it. Insofar as purity continued to be an important category for them, it now took the form of the metaphorical "purity of the heart." For them, real dirt consisted not of specific foods or sexual acts or of leprosy or corpses, but of arrogance, greed, and other sins of social oppression or disruption. If certain sexual acts, such as adultery, were still "unclean" in this new sense, it was for reasons quite different from the purity ethics in Leviticus. Greed, not physical contamination, rendered them so.

One could argue that the agreement of the evangelists and Paul in this matter constitutes a kind of theological presumption that this is the central New Testament teaching on the issue of purity. The diversity of the New Testament, however, is one of its essential characteristics. Some other writers, to be sure, have little to add. The three letters of John, for instance, scarcely use purity language; only their close relationship with the Gospel of John enables us to interpret what little they do say. On the other hand, some of the late New Testament documents show us the repudiation of the purity ethic being adapted to new circumstances, while a couple of them may give us glimpses of a search for new purity codes distinctive to the various churches. After examining these texts, we shall be in a position to sum up the ethics of purity as they are dealt with in the New Testament writings.

THE PASTORAL EPISTLES AND I PETER

Among the latest New Testament books are the three letters addressed, in Paul's name, to Timothy and Titus (called, as a group, the "Pastoral Epistles"). They were probably written decades after Paul's death, perhaps as late as the early second century. Their author wished to claim Paul's authority for one particular way of developing and adapting the Pauline teaching to a later time, and the letters show a substantial shift of perspective from Paul's undoubted writings. Their characteristic concerns are to stabilize the church's internal organization, to exclude false teaching, and to encourage behavior that would make the church seem respectable in the eyes of outsiders. The author wants the church, for example, to accept the leadership of established male householders whose sobriety and administrative talent are proven and who enjoy a good reputation with the larger public (1 Tim. 3:1–13; Titus 1:5–9). He also wants to exclude certain Christian teachers with whom he disagrees and to ensure that Christians look and act according to the standards of the general culture, partly at least to deflect hostility and potential persecution. In pursuing the goal of respectability, he is prepared to sacrifice some of the freedom characteristic of Paul's own time, particularly the prominent role that women played in Paul's original foundations.

It would not be surprising if such an author returned to the use of purity rules because respectability in itself often implies a purity code or is hedged about with purity restrictions. Yet the author stands by the Pauline tradition in this respect and even gives us one of its most emphatic formulations: "All things are pure for the pure; for the polluted and faithless, however, nothing is pure, but both their minds and their consciences are polluted" (Titus 1:15). The "faithless" in question are described as insubordinate teachers "from the circumcision," who disrupt congregations with teachings that involve "Jewish myths" and "human commandments"—and perhaps also "genealogies and conflicts and battles about the law" (1:10–14; 3:9). All this suggests that they are introducing some variant of Torah purity to largely Gentile Christian groups. With an authentically Pauline twist, our author condemns the advocates of physical purity as themselves impure by reason of their lack of faith.

The virtues appropriate to the faithful pastor—the opposite of these disruptive teachers—are "a pure heart and a good conscience and a faith without pretense," all of which combine to produce love (1 Tim. 1:5). Such a pastor, strengthened by purity of the heart, will reject the impositions of the heretical teachers, who even go beyond the purity code of Israel, "forbidding people to marry" as well as "telling them to abstain from foods" (4:3a). "These things," says our author, "God created for those who are faithful and know the truth to receive with thanksgiving, because everything God has created is good and nothing is to be rejected when received with thanksgiving, for it is hallowed through God's word and through prayer" (4:3b–5). The author even requires, perhaps in opposition to the opponents' asceticism, that bishops and deacons be married, albeit only once (1 Tim. 3:2, 12; Titus 1:6).

Two elements in the Pastorals might at first seem to suggest a tendency to institute a purity law specific to these post-Pauline communities. One is the author's use of *hagnos* and related terms, which English translations tend to render with such words as "pure" and "chaste" (e.g., in the RSV, "set the believers an example . . . in purity," 1 Tim. 4:12; "train the young women . . . to be . . . chaste," Titus 2:4–5). There may be no more exact choice of vocabulary in English; in biblical Greek, however, there is a significant distinction between *hagnos* and *katharos* (the more common term for "pure"). *Katharos*, which is used, for example, in the declaration, "All things are pure for the pure" (Titus 1:15), emphasizes separation from what is impure. It defines boundaries. *Hagnos* characterizes dedication to some serious, often religious purpose. It might better be translated "dedicated," "devoted," or "consecrated."[1]

The author wants the Christian leadership to be dedicated to the peace of the community. Thus, he directs Timothy to treat each element within the community appropriately, without displaying partiality (1 Tim. 5:1–21). He sums up his directions with reference to ordination by saying, "Do not lay hands on anyone rashly and do not share in another's sins. Keep yourself *hagnos*" (5:22). In contemporary terms, one might translate "centered" or "focused." The object of concern in this passage is not physical purity, but the welfare of the community. If Timothy were to ordain people who then introduce factions into the church, he would become a participant in their sins. He will avoid this mistake if he remains focused (*hagnos*) on his ministry, which is to preserve the unity of the church and its teaching. The same issue is at stake elsewhere, when the author warns him to "Flee the passions of youth" (2 Tim. 2:22). While the modern reader may assume that such "youthful passions" are sexual in nature, the following verses, which encourage peace, gentleness, and the avoidance of fights, make it clear that the author is concerned rather about the tendency of young males to be proud, hasty, and quarrelsome.

The second element in the Pastorals that may suggest an interest in purity is the inclusion of the term *arsenokoitai* (which the RSV here translates "sodomites") in a list of transgressors (1 Tim. 1:8–11). We have already seen that it is impossible to define this term with confidence (see p. 116), but we may at least be able to recover some sense of what it meant for the author of the Pastorals by an analysis of the list in question. The passage begins with a received truth: "We know that the law is good if anyone uses it lawfully, knowing this—that law does not apply to a righteous person but to lawless and insubordinate people." (vv. 8–9a). None of this would be new in the context of the Pauline tradition. Paul himself invoked the Law as a guide for Christian behavior, provided it was not understood in ways that counteracted the teaching of grace.[2]

The righteous, to whom the Law does not apply, are those "made righteous [or, justified] by his grace" (Titus 3:7); the insubordinate, for the author of the Pastorals, would at least include the teachers of purity (1:10–16). In the immediate context, then, the "lawless and insubordinate" are most easily understood as a general heading for the list that follows. This list gives an accounting of people who are without internal law and do not subject themselves to God's will and who therefore need some external authority to tell them when they are in the wrong. The specific items of the list begin with two pairs, "irreverent and sinners, unholy and profane." This language refers specifically to people who commit offenses against the worship of God. The next pair is "patricides and matricides." A pattern thus emerges, following the Ten Commandments: first, offenses against the worship of God, then offenses against parents. If this is the controlling model of the whole list, we should now expect references to murder, adultery, and theft. What we find is "killers of men, people given to harlotry, *arsenokoitai*, stealers of men." The list then concludes with "liars, perjurers, and whatever else is opposed to sound teaching." The reference to liars and perjurers corresponds to the commandment against false witness, and the author completes the list with a general statement, which both involves the audience silently in its completion and avoids giving the impression that the list provides an exhaustive catalogue of wrongdoers.

Where, in terms of the pattern drawn from the Ten Commandments, do the *arsenokoitai* belong? There are two possibilities, falling as the word does between "people given to harlotry" (*pornoi*) and "stealers of men." In other lists, we have seen references to *porneia* as a synonym for idolatry; here, given its position, it more likely stands in for adultery. *Pornoi* may have a generalized sense of "sexual wrongdoers"; or, if it retains some of its literal sense of "men who visit prostitutes," it could represent the Christian redefinition of adultery as including all sexual acts by married persons with outsiders. The "stealers of men" (probably kidnappers for the slave trade), on the other hand, appear here in relation to the prohibition against theft. If we take the *arsenokoitai* more closely with the *pornoi*, we shall need to understand them specifically in relation to adultery—that is, violation of the marriage bond. Because use of the word *pornoi* implies at least the metaphor of prostitution, Boswell's hypothesis that they were male prostitutes becomes particularly apropos (see p. 118). Even more to the point, such men were accused in antiquity of cultivating the elderly for the purpose of obtaining legacies.[3] From the family's point of view, such a legacy represented a theft of its goods; this links the *arsenokoitai* to the category of theft as well as that of adultery, exactly the intermediate position they hold in the list itself. Although we shall probably never have any real assurance as to the meaning of the term, this use of it (one of its earlier occurrences) suggests that it refers to legacy hunters who used their sexual services as bait. Our author is actively opposed to the reinstatement of Torah purity law, so it is unlikely that he took it as a reference to the prohibition of male-male anal sex in Leviticus.

The author of the Pastorals certainly had a sexual ethic, but it was a property, not a purity, ethic. He was anxious about the church's public reputation and wanted Christians to present a more orderly and respectable face to the larger world. He knew of Christian teachers who urged the adoption of purity codes. They may have begun from the Torah as a foundation, but moved in the direction of rejecting all sexual intercourse as unclean. In this respect at least, his letters still represent continuity with the principles enunciated by Paul. Physical purity is irrelevant to salvation or to church membership; "all things are pure to the pure." What is absolutely necessary is purity of the heart, which restrains a Christian teacher from initiating divisive quarrels and struggles for power.

Of the other New Testament letters, 1 Peter stands close to the Pastorals in this matter. It is difficult to date, but it shares the Pastorals' concern that Christians appear respectable in their neighbors' eyes. There is no clear reference to rules of physical purity. A "pure heart," however, is held up as the source of love within the community (1:22). Christians are to avoid "fleshly passions" as part of a campaign to maintain a good reputation among their Gentile neighbors (2:11–12).[4] The time for wild and idolatrous banqueting is long past (4:1–6); they are to replace it with moderation, sobriety, love, and hospitality (4:7–11). As in the Pastorals, purity is thought of not as a physical state, but as a dedication to humble and loving behavior.

HEBREWS

On purity, as on almost every topic, Hebrews occupies a distinctive position. The date and authorship of this work have been much debated, but because its theological stance is quite distinctive in the New Testament, it does not much matter, for our purposes, who wrote it or when. Purity is very important to this author, in a way otherwise almost unexampled in the New Testament. Like the Qumran community, he believes that all sin is in some sense impurity and therefore requires rites of purification. This is the significance of Christ's work: he has "accomplished purification of the sins" (1:3).[5] By this, the author means to explain what Christ has accomplished by using the analogy of the sacrificial cultus required in the Torah. This cultus, however, he treats as no more than a foreshadowing of the real sacrifice that Jesus alone could perform; only the work of Jesus effects a decisive deliverance from the impurity of sin.

One way the author explains the superiority of Jesus' priestly work is to say that the cultus of the Tabernacle (and, by extension, the Jerusalem Temple, though he does not use the term) had to do only with external, physical purity. "[B]oth gifts and sacrifices are being offered that cannot perfect the worshipper with respect to conscience, but only with reference to foods and beverages and various washings. [These sacrifices are] ordinances of flesh, in force until a time of correction" (9:9–10). Christ's sacrifice is correspondingly superior: "For if the blood of goats and bulls and a heifer's ashes, sprinkling the defiled, sanctify for the purification of the flesh, how much more will the blood of Christ, who through eternal Spirit offered himself up without blemish to God, purify our consciences from dead works to worship a living God?" (9:13–14).

The uniqueness of Christ's sacrifice is a sign of its finality. The sacrifices of the Tabernacle were repeated again and again—evidence, for our author, that they were ineffectual (10:1–4). Christ's sacrifice was made once for all time, with the consequent danger that anyone who sinned after having received its benefits would be beyond help: "For if we sin voluntarily after receiving the knowledge of truth [probably a reference to baptism], no further sacrifice for sins is left, but a certain fearsome expectation of judgment and a jealous flame that is going to devour the opposition" (10:26–27). There is no hope for the person "who has trodden the son of God underfoot and deemed the blood of the covenant, by which he was sanctified, profane and insulted the Spirit of grace" (10:29). In sum, all sins, not just violations of the purity code, require purification; only the sacrifice of Jesus can achieve this.

In practical terms, Hebrews agrees with the other New Testament writings we have studied in holding that purity of foods is of no ultimate importance among Christians: "It is a good thing for the heart to be strengthened by grace, not by foods; those who frame their conduct by them have not benefited" (13:9). In terms of sex, "Marriage is to be honored among all and the bed undefiled"; these instructions are grounded on the belief that "God will judge those given to harlotry [*pornoi*] and adulterers" (13:4). Defilement of the bed, then, consists in violations of the property ethic through prostitution and adultery. In fact, the author moves on easily to other property issues: "Let your manner of life not be money-grubbing; be content with what you have" (13:5). Although this seems a major leap in subject matter to the modern reader, it was not so in antiquity. The same point is also confirmed by the author's picture of the archetypal "*pornos* and profane person," who turns out to be not a noted libertine, but Esau in the act of selling his birthright (12:16).

The passage about Esau actually begins with an exhortation to "Pursue peace with all people and sanctification, without which no one will see the Lord, watching out lest anyone falling short of God's grace—lest any root of bitterness springing up—cause trouble and, through it, many be polluted" (12:14–15). For Hebrews as for the Pauline school, bitterness and discord in the community are at the root of pollution; true purity means pursuing peace with all. In Hebrews, then, even given its distinctive emphasis on the "purification" of sins, we find a basic attitude toward purity, physical and metaphorical, that is coherent with that of the evangelists and Paul. Purity of the heart is determinative; physical purity does not "benefit" anyone.

JAMES

The epistle of James is heavily influenced by the traditions of moral exhortation developed in Greek-speaking Judaism—so much so that some later Christian thinkers, such as Luther, felt that it had little to do with Christianity. It offers an interesting test case, then, of the picture we have gained thus far of New Testament attitudes toward purity. Here, if anywhere, we might expect to find expressed the attitude of those early Jewish Christians who insisted on the retention of the full purity code (Acts 15:1).[6] Indeed, the document is attributed to the very James whom Paul blamed for the troubles at Antioch (Gal. 2:12), although it is difficult to say who actually wrote it or when. The letter gives clear evidence, however, of sharing the broader New Testament perspective we have already become familiar with. The work's famous definition of religion is a good place to begin: "Pure and unpolluted [*katharos kai amiantos*] religion with [our] God and Father is this: to look after orphans and widows in their trouble, to keep oneself unspotted [*aspilon*] from the world" (1:27).[7] The first element of this definition, the care of the needy, is an expression of love, of the purity of the heart. What about the second part—keeping oneself "unspotted"?

The author does not give a direct answer, but there are clues as to his meaning. A little earlier, for example, he told his reader to discard all "filth" (*rhyparia*), and there he did explain what this cleansing entailed: "Let every person be quick to listen, slow to talk, slow at anger, for a man's anger does not accomplish God's righteousness. Therefore, putting aside with gentleness all filth and excess of evil, accept the implanted word that can save your souls" (1:19–21). Here, *rhyparia* stands for the efforts of angry people to assume leadership in the community while ignoring the thoughts and contributions of others; purity is what delivers from this kind of dirt, so purity stands for gentleness.

In another passage, our author writes of the tongue as a source of pollution. "The tongue is fire. The tongue constitutes the world [*or* ornament] of unrighteousness among your members, polluting [*spilousa*] the whole body and setting on fire the wheel of becoming—and is set on fire by hell" (3:6).[8] The tongue is thus the shaping factor in human sin, but in what specific sense? The following verses suggest that discord in the community is still the key issue: with the tongue one blesses God and curses "human beings made in God's likeness" (3:9–10). The truly wise person will demonstrate that he acts "with the meekness of wisdom";

but those who "have jealousy and selfish ambition" at heart, will boast and lie "against the truth." Such are the sources of social disruption (3:13–18). Here, then, as in chapter 1, James identifies pollution with whatever induces people to create discord in the community, especially by claiming unique knowledge or understanding.

The author does say that one is obligated to keep the whole law (2:10), a formula that leaves room for him to insist on the purity code. Yet the examples he gives are never simple issues of purity, but rather the commandments against adultery and murder (2:11). He tells sinners to cleanse their hands—but also to consecrate their hearts (4:8); after telling them to mourn and repent, his practical direction about behavior is that they not slander one another (4:11). If the author had any particular concern about physical purity, it does not come to the fore in this work. Indeed, as with Matthew (1:5) and the author of Hebrews (11:31), he takes Rahab the harlot as one of his positive examples, saying that she was justified by her works when she received the spies and sent them safely on their way (2:25). For James, as for our other authors, the essential purity is the purity of the heart, which sends people out to care for the needy and keeps them unblemished by worldly desires for power and domination. Such desires, wreaking havoc within the community of faith, are the only real pollution.[9]

JUDE AND 2 PETER

The epistle of Jude, short and undatable as it is—and totally absorbed in fierce denunciation of sectarian teachers—might seem unlikely to contribute anything to the present discussion. It does, however, confirm some of what we have already seen. It identifies the rival teachers as people who, following their desires (*epithymia*), are willing to divide the church for the sake of personal gain (16–19). "Desire," here, clearly has more to do with greed than with "lust" as it is now commonly understood. Also, by a clever pun, the letter indicates that its author regards fomenters of discord as the true blemishes on the church. In a long and sometimes chaotic metaphor drawn from a storm at sea, he calls them "the *spilades* in your love-feasts," *spilades* meaning both "submerged rocks" and "spots, blemishes" (12).

Jude does, however, give evidence of one concern about sexual issues unique to this letter within the New Testament and possibly belonging to the realm of purity law—sexual intercourse between human beings and angels. In asserting the reality of God's judgment, Jude lists three specific groups divinely punished in ancient times: the members of the exodus generation who did not believe, the angels who came down to earth and had children by human females (Gen. 6:1–4),[10] and the cities of the plain (Gen. 19). He links the latter two cases closely with each other: "The angels who did not keep their own place in the hierarchy, but left their proper dwelling he has kept under darkness in eternal chains for the judgment of the great day, just as Sodom and Gomorrah and the surrounding cities, having committed the same kind of harlotry as these did and having gone off after other flesh, provide an example by undergoing a judgment of agelong fire" (6–7).

The passage is difficult for the modern reader because of our presuppositions about angels. From at least the fourth century onward, Christians have usually thought of angels as pure spirits with no interest in sex. Jude, on the other hand, still thinks of them in terms drawn from Genesis 6 and *1 Enoch*, which he regarded as scripture. The angelic "Sons of God" or "Watchers," according to these sources, had sexual intercourse with human women and actually produced children with them.[11] Jude then interprets the story of Sodom and Gomorrah as parallel ("having committed the same kind of harlotry as these did") and describes the offense specifically as "going off after other flesh." This phrase makes no sense at all on the usual reading of the Sodom story as having to do with same-gender rape. It makes sense only when we remember that the "men" that Lot received into his house in Sodom were, according to Genesis, really angels.[12]

Thus, Jude's understanding of the Sodom story is that the men there wished to have sexual intercourse with angels.[13] Jude may have introduced this subject in response to his opponents, for he continues the parallelism in the following verse, where he says that these people, too, "in the same way both pollute the flesh in their dreams and negate dominion and blaspheme glories" (8). "Dominion" and "glories" here are probably names for grades or orders of angelic beings, and Jude's language suggests that certain sectarian teachers were claiming to have sexual intercourse with them.[14] All this is quite beyond the scope of the purity code of Leviticus. Even Genesis, if it disapproves at all of what the Watchers did, does so only on the grounds that humanity must not be immortal (6:3). If it is really a violation of purity for Jude, it would be on the analogy of the prohibitions of bestiality, hybridization, the sowing of a field with two kinds of seed, or the weaving of fabric from multiple kinds of fiber. Jude's primary objection to the teachers, however, is that they fail to respect the angels. The offense for him is against hierarchy rather than purity.[15]

The author of 2 Peter, probably the latest of all New Testament writings, seems to agree with Jude that some early Christian teachers practiced sexual rites. Because this author reused virtually the whole of Jude in his letter, it is difficult to be certain how far the material reflects his own concerns and how much of it merely repeats his source. Still, 2 Peter sometimes edits Jude in ways that bring it closer to the New Testament mainstream, and this suggests that what the author kept he kept deliberately. There is no hint here (2:6–8) of Jude's unusual explanation of the sin of Sodom; 2 Peter substitutes general language about "unlawful acts" and "license." One cannot be certain exactly what ethical concerns lie behind these vague terms. He threatens judgment, however, against unrighteous people "who go after flesh with a desire for pollution and despise dominion" (2:10; cf. Jude 8).

According to 2 Peter, the behavior of sectarian teachers blended license, adultery, and greed (*pleonexia*) (2:1–3, 12–14). The letter's omission of any clear reference to intercourse with angels may mean either that it was unknown to the author or that it was irrelevant to his purposes. What remains is a description of the predatory behavior of some early Christian prophets. We find parallel concerns in the *Didache*, or *Teachings of the Twelve Apostles*, a work that probably antedates 2 Peter by some decades, though it was not finally included in the New Testament canon. *Didache* 11 warns against prophets who, while seeming to speak in the Spirit, order up fine meals for themselves or command that money be given them or perform a "mystery of the church." Although the reference to a "mystery of the church" is vague, one recalls that Paul described himself as having betrothed the Corinthian congregation to Christ (2 Cor. 11:2), Ephesians describes the relationship of Christ and the church in terms of the conjugal pair (5:25–28), and early Christians, like their Jewish contemporaries, read the Song of Songs as an allegory of God's relationship with God's chosen people. Those who would profit from meals or gifts the *Didache* brands at once as false prophets; those who perform a mystery of the church, however, it tolerates as long as they do not teach others to do the same.

REVELATION

The Revelation of John was written at a time of great stress for Christians, perhaps in the last decade of the first century. The circumstances were exactly the sort in which a threatened community might want to raise barriers of purity to distinguish itself from the hostile world around it. The book uses the language of purity with some frequency, but, given its highly imagistic nature, it is often difficult to know how the author might have applied the language in practical situations. Thus, he speaks often of the "abominations," "uncleanness," and "harlotry" of Babylon (emblematic, it seems, of Rome) (14:8; 16:19; and often in chapters 17–18). The New Jerusalem, by contrast, is clothed in clean, shining linen, which is the righteous deeds of the saints (19:8); and this city will be forbidden to anyone who commits abomination or lies (21:27). But what are the "abominations" in question?

We get some help from materials at the beginning and end of the book that help us to connect the apocalyptic imagery with the particularities of the author's immediate milieu. Near the beginning of the book, for example, we encounter two groups of people accused of committing harlotry. One is a group in the church at Pergamum who followed "the teaching of Balaam, which he taught Balak to put a stumbling-block in front of the children of Israel—to eat things sacrificed to idols and commit harlotry" (2:14). The other is the congregation at Thyatira, which tolerated "the woman Jezebel, who calls herself a prophetess and teaches and misleads my slaves to commit harlotry and eat things sacrificed to idols" (2:20). He also described certain people as "committing adultery with her" (2:22).

In view of what we have read in Jude, 2 Peter, and the *Didache*, one would not wish to be hasty in ruling out an actual sexual component in these charges. Indeed, the reference to Balak may confirm it, as the narrative in Numbers suggests that his Moabite women used sexual enticements in luring the men of Israel to participate in idolatrous worship (Num. 25:1–2). On the other hand, "harlotry" can designate idolatrous practices of any kind, and "Jezebel's" historical prototype was known for her devotion to Baal, not for licentiousness (1 Kings 18:4, 19; 19:1–3). In the end, we cannot know whether the author objected to specific sexual practices at Pergamum and Thyatira. What we can be sure of is his antagonism toward Christian participation in idolatrous rites because this is a dominant theme throughout this work.

At the end of Revelation, we find two closely related lists of sinners who will be, in the one case, consigned to the second death (21:8) or, in the other, excluded from the New Jerusalem (22:15). The first list is the longer one and includes: cowards, unfaithful people, those who have become abominable, murderers, those given to harlotry, sorcerers, idolaters, and "all lying people." The common association of harlotry, sorcery, and idolatry points to the importance of the alien cult in this list; and what we know of the persecution of Christians under the early Roman Empire explains why this was of great concern for the author of this work. The authorities sought to persuade those accused as Christians to commit apostasy by performing an act of worship before the images of the gods.[16] Because those who did so were typically released without further ado, the offering of a pinch of incense or tasting of a single morsel of the sacrifice will have seemed a small price for one's life. Many gave way at once. The practice of the courts in this matter—and its evident success—explains why the list begins with the cowardly, unfaithful, and polluted—in other words, Christians who apostatized through participating in pagan sacrifices. Murderers make sense in this same context; they are the informers who gave the names of other Christians to the authorities. All these people can be summed up as "liars" who, having claimed to be servants of Christ, finally betrayed that commitment.

The shorter list, in chapter 22, is not significantly different except for its opening insult: "Outside are the dogs and the sorcerers and those given to harlotry and the murderers and the idolaters and everyone that loves and practices a lie" (22:15). This list covers the same groups of people: apostates and informers. The stress on the "lie" makes it clear that these have committed impurity of the heart and not just incurred simple physical contamination through idolatry. The author of Revelation, then, links impurity with idolatrous worship because of its connection with the persecution of Christians and with apostasy. This, in turn, explains why he also connected it to sectarian teaching in local churches. The "teaching of Balaam" and that of Jezebel must have justified Christians who saved their lives by participating in sacrifices. Accordingly, our author sees these teachers as polluted in the same way as the apostates.

Some have seen in the "dogs" at the beginning of this list a reference to Deuteronomy 23:18, where the term may refer to male cult prostitutes.[17] Although the connection may not be absolutely impossible, it is dubious at best. "Dog" was a general term of abuse in Jewish culture. One thinks, for example, of Jesus' dismissal of Gentiles in general as "dogs" in his conversation with the Canaanite or Syro-Phoenician woman (Matt. 15:21–28; Mark 7:24–30). Because the rest of the list is clearly accounted for in terms of apostates and informers, the claim that "dogs" refers to male-male sexual partners seems a particularly gratuitous example of eisegesis based on the presuppositions of the reader.[18]

Apart from this, one other reference to purity appears in a single passage of Revelation—difficult to interpret because of its isolation within this book and also in the New Testament as a whole. In chapter 14, the seer beholds the Lamb, standing on Mt. Zion and, with him, 144,000 men who have the Lamb's name and that of his Father engraved on their foreheads and who sing a new song that only they may learn. They are not angels, but human beings "purchased from the earth." The seer tells us, "These are they who have not polluted themselves with women, for they are virgins; these are they who follow the Lamb wherever it goes; these have been purchased from among human beings as first-fruits for God and the Lamb and in their mouth has been found no lie. They are blameless [*or* unblemished]" (14:4–5).

Nowhere else in the New Testament is there a comparable evaluation of virginity, much less of specifically male virginity.[19] One can find related materials outside the New Testament canon in works like the second-century *Acts of Paul*, which preached the doctrine of "encratism"—that only the sexually continent can be saved. Encratites seem to have been equally interested in both male and female virginity. Given his powerful image of the woman clothed with the sun who brings forth a male child (12:1–6), it is unlikely that the author of Revelation wished to exclude women altogether from the company of the elect. It is possible, then, to imagine that he accepted encratite principles and regarded all sexual acts as contrary to Christian teaching. Yet there is no straightforward statement to that effect in the book. At most, we might see it as an early witness to the new Christian ideal of purity, centered on virginity, that emerged in the second century. One is left without a final answer; for the rest of Revelation, as I have shown, knows no purity concern other than that connected with apostates and informers.[20]

CONCLUSION

Close study of passages dealing with sexual and other forms of purity reveals a high level of agreement on this subject among the New Testament authors. With the possible exception of Revelation, those documents that deal with physical purity at all agree in rejecting it as an authoritative ethic for Christians. Gentile Christians, in particular, were understood to be free of its requirements, and this alone made possible the inclusion of Gentiles in the church without male circumcision being necessary. Most Jewish Christians probably still maintained purity as an expression of their Jewish identity; even in their case, however, it cannot have been a requirement for church membership because that would have made salvation conditional on something in addition to "the grace of Christ" (Acts 15:11). Even Revelation does not return to the purity code of the Torah. Though we see evidence in Paul and Revelation that Christianity had the capacity to begin generating its own codes of purity, we do not see more than the beginnings of a process that grew much more important in the second century.

Many modern Christians presuppose that first-century Christians would have made a sharp distinction between purity rules about foods and those about sex, rejecting the former and retaining the latter. There is no justification for this position in the New Testament itself, which reveals that physical purity was—and had to be—rejected entirely as a defining note of Christian identity. The dirty Gentile was as welcome to the church in all respects as the pure Jew. Given the awareness, by both Jews and Gentiles, of distinctive Jewish concerns about purity, it would have been difficult to finesse the matter. New Testament writers did indeed distinguish between the ethics of food and those of sex, but the distinction was not between one kind of purity and another, for Torah purity was of a single piece. The distinction lay rather in the fact that with sex, unlike food, other kinds of ethical principles remained valid.

Once the purity ethic was set aside, there was no ethic left to distinguish permissible from impermissible foods. To enable Christians to eat together, the Jerusalem council sought a purely practical accommodation, by which Gentiles would avoid foods tainted by idolatry and blood, while Jews waived other purity demands. Paul counseled the Strong to respect the Weak without surrendering their convictions and the Weak to respect their own consciences without being critical of the Strong. In neither case was the Torah's purity code being imposed on anyone. The gradual disappearance of a strong Jewish constituency from the church meant that both the council's and Paul's recommendations became, in due course, irrelevant. The author of Revelation expressed an absolute opposition to foods sacrificed to idols; this was not simply a rule of physical purity, but rather the result of an insistence on avoiding apostasy. With sex, on the other hand, the abolition of purity rules still left in place a whole realm of ethics based on property considerations. Accordingly, the New Testament writers still considered sex to be an area subject to ethical demands, whereas food had practically ceased to be so.

The early Christians did not immediately cease to be conscious of a distinction between clean and unclean. What they abolished was the link between physical cleanness and divine favor. "Clean" and "dirty" certainly continued, particularly for Jewish Christians, as a socially defined reality and carried with them at least the degree of attraction and repulsion that clean and dirty do for the modern Gentile reader. The power of purity considerations thus remained a familiar phenomenon, and New Testament writers applied that power freely to other purposes: some by calling upon all Christians to keep the metaphorical purity of the heart, others (mainly the Johannine school) by rejoicing in the power of "unclean" rites to convey salvation.

From the New Testament onward, Christian ethics had to explain themselves in terms of purity of the heart, defined above all as willingness to respect the neighbor and contribute to the peace of the community. The war waged in the epistolary literature on the sins of social competition and disruption is perhaps the New Testament's most significant contribution to the explication of this purity of the heart. In part, this was a reaction to the centrifugal qualities of church life in the earliest decades.[21] The preaching of the gospel and the formation of new communities around it unleashed a flood of theological creativity and a sometimes fierce struggle over who would determine the shape of the new society and on what principles. Still, the rejection of social competition by Paul and others was also a basic Christian ethical insight dependent upon the cross itself. The cross represents God's willingness to be least and weakest and creates thereby a demand for all Christian behavior to be characterized by love and humility. It is to this insight that the language of purity, when used positively by New Testament authors, most often refers.

Some early Christians did hear the repeal of the purity code as signifying an abolition of all sexual morality and its replacement by unrestricted libertinism. To them, Paul and his successors reaffirmed the existence of another kind of sexual ethic, which was still authoritative. At the other extreme, some Christians supposed that their new faith demanded complete rejection of all sexual activity. The Christian demand for purity of heart may have been heard, by the casually instructed, as a command to avoid all physical dirtiness, including such as followed on ejaculation. The principal impulse behind this ascetic movement, however, must surely have lain in the widespread and still poorly understood revulsion that many sorts of people in late antiquity were beginning to feel toward all sexuality. In other words, the more extreme suspicions of sex that Paul combated at Corinth (1 Cor. 7:1–2) or the author of Revelation perhaps accepted in his vision of the 144,000 male virgins—these originated more in the spirit of the age than in that of the gospel.[22] On the whole, the New Testament writers were neither merely negative nor naïvely approving toward sex. Their rejection of the code of physical purity originated not in a program to revise sexual ethics as such, but in their effort to break down the barriers that purity rules erected between human communities and against the marginal people in a given society. Jesus' own inclusion of the unclean, confirmed by the later decision to admit uncircumcised Gentiles to the church, demanded such bracketing of purity rules, and the church quickly came to understand this as a fundamental expression of the triumph of God's grace in the cross.

The results that I have just set out are difficult for some modern readers to accept. One problem lies in the New Testament writings themselves. Their authors shift freely and without warning between two different uses of purity language: the literal, in which it denotes what I have called "physical purity," and the metaphorical, in which it points to various applications of the Christian "purity of the heart." When the New Testament writers insist on purity as a standard of Christian conduct, they intend this latter, metaphorical sense. Their original readers or hearers will have received their writings in the context of an oral culture that made this somewhat clearer. We have to tease it out by close reading of the texts. Our greater difficulty, however, arises from the presuppositions we ourselves bring to the text, presuppositions shaped by later Christianity. There is a human tendency to assume that the world of our grandparents was not radically different from the world of any prior historical epoch. And because the Christianity of the mid-twentieth century was almost universally obsessed with sex and, on the whole, repressive of it, we assume that the New Testament writers must have been the same.

Sex was not, in fact, a primary concern in the New Testament writings—far less so than among many modern Christians. Nor was physical purity a significant principle for them. To those who read the New Testament in modern terms this will always be difficult to comprehend or accept. From the second century onward, most Christian piety regarded virginity as the only truly devout use of sexuality. There was some movement in the high Middle Ages and the Protestant Reformation to retrieve the sanctity of marriage. But the exaltation of virginity still means that most Christians view all sexuality as primarily bad; at most, it may be reclaimed within the confines of lifelong heterosexual matrimony. As someone once said, the standard Christian sexual ethic came to be: Sex is dirty, nasty, and disgusting; save it for someone you love.

The history of major changes in sexual ethics among Christians is a subject worthy of study and calls for full and careful investigation in its own right.[23] I mention it here only as an aspect of the intellectual and spiritual presuppositions of the modern reader. The serious student of scripture must be prepared to set aside such preconceptions, however treasured, at least for the time required to give the New Testament a careful reading on its own terms. The historical, cultural, and ecclesiastical distance between the world of the New Testament and that of today is vast, and one must resist the temptation to read the ancient texts only in terms drawn from one's immediate experience and the tradition that has shaped it.

At no point is the distance more evident or more critical than in the area discussed in the preceding chapters. The Jesus who regularly preferred the company of the impure to that of the religious authorities of his day or who predicted that tax collectors and prostitutes would more readily gain entrance into the reign of God than the devout would not have been a popular figure in the church itself in most of the succeeding Christian centuries. He would have been seen as undermining public morality; insofar as the church itself adopted a purity ethic from the fourth century onward, that accusation would have been apt. The church, after all, became the defender of public mores from at least the time of Constantine onward—the same role that, in Jesus' world, belonged to a different set of religious authorities. Faithful reading of the New Testament demands of the modern Christian at least a temporary distancing of oneself from this role so that one does not forbid scripture to speak things unheard of in our narrow experience. One thing it announces is the end of the ethic of physical purity.

PART II

GREED

CHAPTER 8

WOMEN AND CHILDREN AS PROPERTY IN THE ANCIENT MEDITERRANEAN WORLD

Because the purity ethic focuses on bodily boundaries, people often, in a casual way, reduce all issues of sexual ethics to that of purity. On reading that "all things are pure for the pure" (Titus 1:15), some might conclude that, for the New Testament writers, sexual ethics have simply ceased to exist. But this is far from the case. Early Christian authors turn, instead, to another ethical principle deeply rooted in their world—one on which Jews and Gentiles were broadly agreed: the principle of respect for sexual property, rooted in the institution of the household or family.[1]

"Property" denotes something understood as an extension of the self so that a violation of my property is a violation of my personhood. It is a difficult concept, as both ancient and modern thinkers have recognized; pushed to extremes, it can license self-aggrandizement at the expense of the welfare of the larger human community. Early Christians were at least attracted to the idea of a fully communal existence and even claimed to have practiced it on occasion (e.g., Acts 3:43–45).[2] Yet Christian thinkers of the more orthodox sort, at least, did not include in this claim the idea of sexual communism. Tertullian, in the late second or early third century, wrote, "All things are without distinction [of ownership] among us except wives."[3] Some ancient thinkers did suggest sexual communism, including one youthful Gnostic Christian teacher, Epiphanes, son of the better known Carpocrates. On the whole, however, Christians held firmly to the notion of private sexual property and made this the foundation for constructing their sexual ethic. If impurity or dirtiness no longer served to define sexual sin, greed, the desire to have more than one's own proper share of goods, did.[4]

Greed, in this sense, is not simply desire, but a kind of grasping behavior that enhances one's own property at the expense of another or delights in possessing more than another. Because we have already seen that Paul and other New Testament writers set great store by unity and peace in the community, even characterizing the virtues contributing thereto as essential to "purity of the heart," we shall not be surprised to find them opposing acts of greed, which by definition disrupt the community. The way in which sex figures here, however, will be difficult to follow unless we first gain some insight into what sexual property meant in the ancient world. The following discussion will focus on Israel, but with reference to variations in the Greco-Roman world of the first century as well.[5]

THE PATRIARCH AND HIS HOUSEHOLD

If the purity concerns of ancient Israel are strange to the average modern reader, the other side of its sexual ethics is likely to be no less so—at least to those readers who are part of the more individually based culture of the West. The distance between us and the biblical writers becomes clearest in passages that are unintelligible or profoundly offensive when read in the context of modern family life. Take, for example, the attitude toward wife and children manifest in the book of Job. At one point in the book (chap. 31), Job invokes on himself a series of curses in conditional form: if I have committed such-and-such sin, may some appropriate punishment befall me. It is a way of asserting his innocence in the strongest possible way; the passage is, in fact, the peroration of his self-defense. Among the sins listed are deceit in business, inhumanity toward servants, indifference to the poor, trust in riches, idolatry, taking pleasure in the ruin of an enemy, concealment of crime, misappropriation of land, and adultery. Here is how he speaks about adultery: "If my heart has been enticed by a woman [*ishshah*] and I have lain in wait at my neighbor's door, let my wife [*ishshah*] grind[6] for another and other men kneel over her" (31:9–10 NRSV).

In the modern West, if one asks, "What is the wrong of adultery?" one is likely to be told that it is betrayal of trust, of the mutuality of marriage. On the basis of such an understanding, Job ought to invoke some punishment on himself for such an offense. In a similar vein, he says that if he has ignored the needs of the poor or been cruel to them, he should suffer the loss of the arm that committed the sin (31:16–23). Yet in the case of adultery, he suggests that an appropriate punishment would be for his wife to become another man's household servant and be used sexually, like a prostitute, by a number of men. This curse becomes intelligible only when we note that it is parallel to others in the chapter that deal with property offenses: if Job has practiced deceit, let his own crops be rooted out (31:5–8); if he has taken another's land, let his own grow weeds instead of good crops (31:38–40). If he has taken another's wife, let another take his. The wife was a form of property; adultery was violation of the property of another and should therefore be punished with violation of one's own.

What was true of the wife was true also of the children. At the beginning of the story, Job has seven sons and three daughters (1:2), all of whom are killed by Satan, acting with God's authorization (1:6–19). At the end of the story, after God has, in some sense, vindicated him (42:7–9), Job acquires greater riches than he had to begin with (42:10–12). In addition, he sires a new family, identical to the old in numbers and distribution between the sexes, and he lives on to see his great-grandchildren (42:13–17). From the perspective of the modern reader, this is not likely to seem very satisfactory. It is one thing to have fourteen thousand sheep in place of seven thousand, one sheep being much like another, but surely ten new children, however loved in themselves, do not really replace the ten lost. We are inclined to think of each child as a unique and irreplaceable individual. Yet the conclusion of Job makes sense only if we understand that, in its author's day, children, like wives, were first and foremost possessions.[7] The new ten would serve as well as the old to perform the basic function of such possessions, which was to reproduce and carry on the family. There is no further reason for Job to complain in the matter.[8]

The offense that the modern reader finds in this resolution of the story arises not from individual callousness on the part of the author of Job, but from the cultural distance between antiquity and our own day. Mediterranean antiquity, whether Jewish or Gentile, did not take the individual as its basic building block. The value of each individual—so fundamental to modern democracy—was inconceivable in that context. In its place stood the value of the family, which was the basic social unit. The eunuch and the bastard, who were truly individuals, incapable of being related to a family, were permanently excluded from the assembly of Israel (Deut. 23:1–2); they had no place in a society where the family was the fundamental unit.[9]

Job himself is no individual—not in the modern sense. He has meaning and significance in his world as the embodiment of his "father's house"—its patriarch, its male head who ruled it within and represented it in its dealings with outsiders. The patriarch was the family's vital link to the larger world. Widows and orphans, lacking any connection with a patriarch, were accordingly marginal people whose interests could easily be trampled on. The patriarch's task was to maintain the household's wealth and public standing in the community—even, if possible, to enhance it. He was not a free agent, but the caretaker of that larger, ongoing unit, which he embodied only for his own lifetime. Other members of the household were agents and tools for the patriarch, sharply subordinated to him in the pursuit of their common lifelong task. One of them, the eldest surviving son, would also be his successor (Deut. 21:15–17).

If the patriarch was not an individual, those below him in the hierarchy of the family were even less so. Children existed for the sake of the family—practically speaking, for the sake of their parents, as the Torah shows by its stress on reverence for parents (Exod. 20:12). The striking of a parent (Exod. 21:15) or even habitual rebelliousness against them (Deut. 21:18–21) was grounds for the death sentence. The wife was brought in from another family to preserve and sustain that of her husband through the bearing of children and the wise administration of the household. The portrait of the ideal wife in Proverbs 31, though attributed to the mother of a Gentile king, is in harmony with expectations that were equally fundamental in Israel: she is her husband's confidante, a hard worker, an intelligent businesswoman, a charitable almsgiver, a good household administrator, and a fine seamstress; her children rise up to call her blessed. She is perhaps not beautiful (31:30), for her good qualities minister not so much to the husband's personal gratification as to the building up of his ongoing family line.

THE PLACE OF WOMEN

Biblical Hebrew and ancient Greek felt no need, it seems, to make the distinction that English makes between "woman" and "wife." (In

Hebrew, the word *ishshah* does duty for both; in Greek, *gynē*.) There was little occasion to make such a distinction, for it was the ideal if not invariable destiny of an adult female to be some man's wife.[10] In childhood, a woman was a member of her father's household and she might become so again in the event of divorce or widowhood—particularly if she were childless. Normally, she was transferred to the household of a husband at about the time of puberty, and from this time onward, she lived in a kind of familial limbo, being a full member of neither household. Marriage was not equivalent to a blood relationship, though it did alienate a woman to some degree from her own blood kin. The Torah illustrates the ambiguity involved in the restrictions it imposes upon priests in the matter of mourning. A priest was allowed to mourn only for members of his immediate family, and this included neither his wife nor his married sister (Lev. 21:1–4).

A woman never became truly a member of her husband's family because she could be separated from it through divorce. The Torah gave the right of divorce only to the husband, preserving a unique power to him in the relationship (Deut. 24:1–4). To be deprived of the right of divorce was a serious punishment. If a man forcibly violated an unbetrothed virgin, he had to pay the bridal price to her father and marry her without possibility of divorce (Deut. 22:28–29). Or if a man accused his lawful wife of not having been a virgin bride and the accusation proved false, then he lost the right ever to divorce her (Deut. 22:13–19). As we shall see later, this dominance of the husband did not go unchallenged in ancient Israel. The law of divorce in Deuteronomy, however, seems to have expressed the normal practice.

The power of the father and then of the husband meant that a woman could enjoy, at most, only a secondary role in whatever household she belonged to—a status pointedly underlined by the right that the Torah gave to her father (before her marriage) or her husband to annul even her vows to God (Num. 30:3–15).[11] In fact, a woman's position could be worse than just secondary. Many found themselves in various grades of slavery, while even those who had achieved the status of wife might lose it through divorce or widowhood. The slave woman was subject not only to the patriarch, but also to a whole internal family hierarchy, including the patriarch's wife. The consequences could be devastating, as one sees in the case of Hagar, Abraham and Sarah's Egyptian slave woman. The patriarch was not ill disposed toward her; but jealousy and internal family politics resulted in Hagar's being degraded and expelled into the desert (Gen. 16:1–16; 21:9–21). Yet even Sarah's power over Hagar in this story was less her own than a result of her place as wife within the hierarchy of the family.[12]

In a culture where wives, children, and slaves were all property of male heads of household, hierarchy within the family group was the principal expression of these property relations.[13] Not all property was governed by the same rules; human property could not be disposed of in exactly the same ways as animals or land. The Torah prescribed that slaves, for example, were not to be treated in the same way as cattle: one might deal with one's cattle as one wished, but one must not deliberately kill one's slave (Exod. 21:20–21). On the other hand, the punishment of a master who kills a slave is left unspecified, whereas the Torah is clear in demanding the death penalty for one who kills a free man (21:12–14). The household was thus highly stratified and complex in its hierarchy, particularly because, before the spread of monogamy under Greek influence, it was usual for men who could afford it to have more than one wife.

One can glean from the pages of Torah some indications of the various grades of sexual property.[14] The lowest grade was the slave woman taken captive in war. Deuteronomy specifically prohibits Israelites from taking male enemies alive—or any female captives from Canaan, though such might be brought from further away (20:10–18). (One text limits this to women who have never had sexual relations; Num. 31:17.) Restrictions of this sort were related to the question of which foreign women could be accepted as wives for Israelite men: they should be virgins, to ensure that they are not bearing foreign children, and they must be from a distance so that they will not involve their husbands in Canaanite cults. Israelite men might marry such women, but the woman's status, even as wife, remained poor. A law on the subject (Deut. 21:10–14) provides that the captive must be given time to mourn her parents before the consummation of the marriage and that her master cannot afterward sell her for money, but he may send her out on her own if he comes to be displeased with her. Because she had no family to return to, this would be disastrous. Such a woman, with no native country left and without any natal family to protect her interests, was just one step removed from any other sort of slave. The gesture of constituting her as a "wife" can only have been in the interest of procuring legitimate heirs, as when Sarah gave Hagar to Abraham for the same purpose (Gen. 16:1–3).

The Gentile slave was a true chattel according to the Torah (Lev. 25:44–46). Hebrew slaves, however, enjoyed certain advantages. Males were, for example, to be released in the jubilee, celebrated every forty-nine years (Lev. 25:40), or even in the seventh year of their slavery (Exod. 21:2; Deut. 15:12). The male Hebrew slave may have entered slavery along with his family or may have been given a wife by his master. In either case, a certain difficulty arose because the relation of husband to wife was analogous to that of master and slave woman. Who, then, owned the wife of the slave? Exodus settled the issue by discerning which ownership had precedence in time. If marriage preceded the man's entry into slavery, the wife was primarily his and went with him when he returned to freedom; if slavery came first and the wife was a gift of the master, then both she and her children belonged to the master (Exod. 21:3–6).[15]

The state of the female Hebrew slave was less clear. Deuteronomy assured her of freedom after six years (15:17). Exodus, however, makes the assumption that she was originally purchased to serve as wife for either her master or his son. Accordingly, it did not provide for them to release her, but it did place certain restrictions on their control of her. Her master could not sell her to foreigners. If she was to be his daughter-in-law, he must also behave toward her in the place of her own father. After all, she would have no family to defend her interests. If she was to be his own wife, he might not discard her or slight her in favor of a better match later on. If he violated any of these rules, she automatically gained the right to her freedom—although in her case, as in that of the captive woman, this may have been a dubious advantage (Exod. 21:7–11).

A man might also take a free woman as concubine. The Torah does not define the status of concubine, but it must have been something less than that of full wife—even where the wife was of slave origin. One may guess that concubinage was a way for a younger man to acquire a first sexual partner without committing himself to treating her children as his heirs. Under some circumstances, it might be more profitable for him to postpone marriage until he was better established and could attract the attention of richer and more powerful future in-laws. The benefit to the concubine's family would come from not having to provide a dowry. That such arrangements could be mutually satisfactory to the men involved is evident from the story of the Levite's concubine (Judg. 19:3–9). The social insignificance of the concubine is equally evident in that narrative: the woman is never named nor consulted as to her wishes, and finally her master brutally sacrifices her to the mob to save himself (19:22–30).[16]

The status of full wife was, generally speaking, the best position to which a woman could aspire in ancient Israel. The woman's father would arrange the marriage in a process that intimately concerned his own prestige. The ability to attract a favorable match depended not only on the young woman's personal qualities, but also on her family's wealth, power, and civic repute. Her well-being in the marriage might also depend on these because she would always remain, to some extent, a stranger in her husband's family. If he chose to take another wife or otherwise came to lose interest in her, she had little protection except his unwillingness to offend her family.

Although the wife did not, properly speaking, become a member of her husband's family, she did become his property;[17] Deuteronomy routinely equates the acquisition of house, vineyard, and wife (20:5–7; 28:30).[18] As with these other major possessions, the wife became the property not merely of her husband, but of his family—hence the law of levirate marriage (marriage with the deceased husband's brother). A family took a wife for a son to ensure an heir. If the son died without producing one and he had surviving brothers, it was the duty of the next brother to take the widow himself. The first child of this union, however, was considered the child of the deceased brother, not of the brother who had participated in its conception. It was a disgrace for a man to refuse this duty; he would be setting his private interests ahead of those of the family (Deut. 25:5–10). The woman does not appear to have had a choice; on the whole, however, the arrangement will have been in the widow's interest as preserving her existing social position.

In general, women had little authority of their own in the society envisioned by the Torah. A partial exception lay with the woman who was an heir in her own right. Job, a Gentile, is presented as making his daughters heirs alongside his sons (Job 42:15). But the Torah recognized female heirs only when there were no sons, as in the case of the daughters of Zelophehad (Num. 27:1–11). Perhaps we meet such a person in the Shunammite who hosted Elisha (2 Kgs. 4:8–37). She is described as an "important woman" (4:8); she dwells among her own people (4:13), not those of her husband; and she, not her husband, is the principal initiator of action in the story (4:9–10, 22–27).[19] Such women created anomalies, however, in the system of inheritance, for in the usual course of events, their property would pass to their sons, who would be members not of their own, but of their husbands' families. Accordingly, the Torah required them to marry among their father's kin (Num. 36:1–12).

The picture that the Torah offers of the place of women in the family seems to have been generally stable over a very long time, into and past the New Testament era.[20] There were changes, of course, in detail. Jews in Jesus' lifetime, for example, had little occasion to concern themselves with the law about a woman captured in war. Polygamy, moreover, had largely faded away, perhaps in adaptation to Greco-Roman culture, which was monogamous. The *Temple Scroll* from Qumran actually forbade polygamy altogether for the king (56.18–19). Marriage contracts sometimes gave the bride the right to divorce her husband.[21] In the centuries before and after Jesus, women were occasionally accepted as something like religious equals: the prophet Joel predicted the revival of prophecy among both men and women (2:28–29); the contemplatives called "Therapeutae" accepted women into membership;[22] and some women held responsible positions in Greek-speaking synagogues.[23] Wives, however, continued to be a particular class of property, whose function was to produce heirs and help administer the husband's household.

OFFENSES AGAINST SEXUAL PROPERTY
Adultery

The preceding discussion helps explain why adultery was a crime against sexual property. The continuity of the family was entirely dependent on its acquiring of legitimate heirs. While other ancient cultures, notably the Romans, were willing to achieve this end through adoption as well as through conception, this seems not to have been a common alternative in ancient Israel.[24] Hence, there was a very strong concern for the legitimacy of heirs and the purity of the family line. For the same reason that an Israelite man was reluctant to marry a woman who was not a virgin, he was also anxious that his wife not have sexual intercourse with any other man.[25] If an outsider did have intercourse with a married woman, this constituted a theft of her husband's right to legitimate offspring. As with any loss of property to another, this also shamed the husband and reduced the family's status in the community.[26]

If a husband suspected his wife of adultery without any evidence, he could take her to the sanctuary and compel her to undergo the rite of the water of bitterness (Num. 5:11–31). This provided a kind of ordeal for the woman, either confirming the husband's suspicions or exonerating her. If she were guilty of the offense, it would cause some major physical problem, probably the abortion of the fetus and future childlessness. The rite offers confirmation of the concerns behind it—above all that the man should not end up including in his household a child not his own. Abortion seemed preferable to this. In one sense, the ordeal offered some protection for the woman unjustly accused. On the other hand, it graphically illustrates her subordinate status, for the assumption of the text is that the man initiates it, never the woman.[27]

It is no surprise to find that in the Ten Commandments, the prohibition of adultery is in proximity to that of theft (Exod. 20:14–15) or that one is forbidden, shortly after, to covet the neighbor's house or wife or servant or ox or ass or other property (20:17). Even the intervening commandment against bearing false witness is not unrelated because bearing false witness was another way to improve the status of one's own household at the expense of the neighbor's (20:16). It is also no surprise that adultery, in this context, referred purely and simply to a man's having intercourse with a married woman. The man's own marital status was irrelevant, for it was not a matter of violating his own vows or implicit commitments of sexual fidelity, as in a modern marriage, but rather of usurping some other man's property rights in his wife.

Adultery was different, to be sure, from other property violations in one significant way, for it involved the consent of the property. Accordingly, the Torah required that both parties to adultery, if caught in the act, should be punished (Deut. 22:22). The fact that the prescribed punishment was death is reminiscent of the concern of the Holiness Code to purge certain types of uncleanness from the people; in fact, that Code did treat adultery as a violation of purity (Lev. 20:10). On the whole, however, the Torah saw in adultery a property violation. The death penalty for the woman was a kind of limited (and back-handed) recognition of her humanity, that is, of her ability to make decisions for herself—and perhaps also a recognition that, having once received another man's semen, she was no longer of any use to her husband in the matter of legitimate offspring.

A woman became her husband's property even before entering his household, at the time of betrothal. From then on, as far as the Torah was concerned, any violation of her was a form of adultery. If the woman had entered voluntarily into the adulterous liaison, both parties were to be put to death, but not if the man had forced her. Accordingly, the Torah distinguished between an incident occurring in the city, where the woman, had she resisted, would have been heard and rescued, and one that took place in the country, where the man might have used force but no one would have heard the woman's cry for help. In true cases of adultery, both man and woman were to be executed; in cases of forcible violation, only the man (Deut. 22:23–27).[28]

Because a woman, before she became the property of her husband, was the property of her father, adultery could also become an issue, by analogy, even before she was married. Daughters were less valuable to a family than sons; Job's seven sons and three daughters were no doubt considered the perfect sort of blessing where posterity was concerned. Daughters, after all, did not continue their father's family, but those of their husbands. Still, daughters provided the wherewithal to form marital alliances, thus affording their natal families influence and political security. The virginity of a daughter was essential to this purpose, for if she were not a virgin, she was not suitable for marriage.[29]

The man who took an unbetrothed daughter's virginity without having acquired it properly through marriage negotiations and the consent of her father was, like the adulterer, a thief. There was no death penalty in such a case, but the Torah provided that the perpetrator must pay her father the bride price and, if the father consented, marry her—with no right to divorce her later (Deut. 22:28). She was unlikely, after all, to find another husband. Even if the father refused to accept the marriage, the man still had to pay him the equivalent of the bride price because the daughter was of no further value in the marriage "market" (Exod. 22:16–17). Similarly, as we saw above (pp. 29–30), in a case of adultery with a woman who belonged to two men at once (as slave to one and betrothed to the other), no one was executed, but a penalty had to be paid (Lev. 19:20–21).

The understanding of adultery, both in the Torah and in the New Testament era, thus proves to have been quite different from that current in the contemporary Western world. Among us, sexual activity outside the marriage on the part of either partner is understood as adultery; in antiquity, only such activity on the part of the wife (or the betrothed woman) qualified. The husband could commit adultery only by having intercourse with the wife (or betrothed) of another man; if he had sexual relations with a slave, a prostitute, a concubine, or a divorced or widowed woman, this did not constitute adultery against his own marriage. Again, our own explanations of what is wrong in adultery usually focus on the betrayal of trust and of formal commitments between spouses, whereas the ancient understanding of adultery assumes rather that it is a violation of another man's property. What for us is a kind of betrayal was for them a species of theft. The treatment of adultery in the New Testament documents will be unintelligible if we do not keep these distinctions in mind.

Incest

We have already seen that the definitions of incest in ancient Israel were different from ours. Where we define it primarily in terms of shared genetic endowment, the Torah defined it as violation of the intra-family hierarchy (p. 27). This hierarchy was an expression of property relations, a way of exercising ownership over human property, which could not merely be manipulated like real estate or domestic animals. Where both owner and owned were human beings, their relationship had to find some expression other than the simple right of the master to dispose of the property when and as he pleased. The solution was found in the interactions of dominance and deference that characterize hierarchical relationships. In the matter of incest, the outstanding concern of the Torah was that younger male members of a household should not usurp the rights of males who were their seniors or their siblings.

The details of Israel's laws of incest are often difficult to follow, and we need to look closely at them to comprehend how different they are from our own and what concerns animated them. The reader may be helped if I set out my conclusions in simple form at the start. The incest code can be summarized comprehensively in three general principles, all dependent on matters of hierarchy. First, a man must not infringe on the sexual property of other males who rank above him or on the same level as he in the family hierarchy. Second, a man must not interfere with the sexual property of his sons and daughters (i.e., their wives and daughters) because any affront to the honor of other members of his household would reflect on his own honor. Third, a man must not put two women in a position that would force them to violate the hierarchy prevailing among female relatives.

For a modern Western reader to make sense of the laws about incest, one must recall that, for ancient Israel, husband and wife were not next-of-kin to one another. The husband remained a member of the "father's house" in which he was born. The wife remained, in some sense, a part of her family and would return to them if she were divorced or left widowed and childless (e.g., Lev. 22:13).[30] Generally speaking, men were kin to their mothers and to both the men and the women of their father's house while women were kin only to their sons and their immediate female relatives—at least, for purposes of the law of incest.[31] These realities were reflected in the precise language of the laws against incest, to which we must give close attention.

The most serious form of incest was a son's violation of his father's wife, whether it was his own mother or another wife;[32] this was "uncovering the father's nakedness"—which was a violation of the son's subordination to his father (Lev. 18:7–8; cf. Deut. 23:1, ET 22:30).[33] Thus, Absalom had intercourse with his father David's concubines to usurp his father's place and make the break between him and his father irreparable (2 Sam. 16:20–22). In the same way, incest with the wife of one's father's brother was "uncovering the nakedness" of the uncle (Lev. 18:14); with the wife of a brother it was "uncovering the brother's nakedness" (18:16). In each case, the language makes clear that the incest was an offense not so much against the woman violated as against her husband.

The respect owed the father also extended to his immediate female kin. The Torah specifies that the father's sisters and daughters were placed off limits by reason of their relationship to him rather than to the son (18:9,11–12). There is at least a suggestion, however, that the father's link with his female relatives was weaker than with the males. In the case of a half-sister who shared only the same father, the son had to be reminded that "she is your sister," as if it might not be obvious (18:11). Indeed, in great houses with several wives, it may not have been, for the children of each wife will have tended to form a distinct sub-household. The callousness of Amnon after raping his half-sister Tamar may have arisen from a common social perception that she was not truly a close relative as well as from his own lack of moral feeling (2 Sam. 13:1–19). No equivalent reminder was given in regard to those who were half-sisters sharing only the same mother; but this type of incest will have been rare. Because children remained with the father's family after divorce or the father's death, such half-siblings will rarely have been together in the same household.

A man was not obliged to pay any particular respect to the younger members of his household. Nephews and nieces, on the whole, did not enter into the reckoning of incest. The one exception is that the nephew must avoid his father's brother's wife. There was no comparable law, however, prohibiting the uncle from having his niece or his nephew's wife. A man was, to some extent, forbidden to have sex with his children and grandchildren, but the justification for this hinged on his own paternal honor, for he could not be warned off on grounds of owing deference to his son. This reasoning was made explicit in the prohibition of incest with grandchildren: "You shall not uncover the nakedness of your son's daughter or of your daughter's daughter, for their nakedness is your own nakedness" (18:10 RSV). In other words, incest with his granddaughter (who would then no longer be a marriageable virgin) would shame his whole family, for which he was ultimately responsible. Similarly, a man was not to have sexual relations with his daughter-in-law because it would dishonor his son (18:15) and implicit in any dishonoring of his son was a dishonoring of his own house. Intercourse with a man's daughter, however, was not explicitly prohibited as such, perhaps because a patriarch had to be recognized as owning the female members of his immediate household, so that in some sense this would be an exercise of his rights.[34]

The male was also obligated to respect his mother, although her honor could never be distinguished from that of his father. Hence, the Israelite was told: "You shall not uncover your father's nakedness and your mother's nakedness; she is your mother; you shall not uncover her nakedness" (18:7). Incest with the mother was a violation of both parents at once. The son's kinship with his mother also extended a prohibition to her sister and daughter, that is, her closest female relatives (18:9, 13). This did not, however, extend to her male relatives because although the mother's brother might seem to be as closely related to a man as the father's brother, his wife was not in fact forbidden under the incest code.

There was a similar phenomenon in the case of siblings. A man's sisters were all prohibited, whether full sisters or half-sisters—the latter whether he shared a common mother with them or a common father. The Holiness Code further specified that this was true whether they were born in the same household or not (18:9).[35] Because the unmarried woman was reckoned to her father's household, a marriage could be contracted between two half-siblings who shared the same mother but belonged to different paternal households, and the code guards against this. No similar stipulation was made, however, in the case of half-brothers who belonged to different households; it is thus possible that the protection of a brother's wife extended only to those brothers who shared the same father.

Finally, within the purely female sphere, certain relationships were inconsistent with women acting as co-wives. A woman could not be co-wife with her mother or grandmother (18:17).[36] This provision would effectively prevent a man from marrying his own daughter, but that does not appear to have been its purpose. The point rather was to prohibit marriage with his mother-in-law, as the phrasing of the law elsewhere shows (Lev. 20:14; Deut. 27:23). Such a marriage would create grave problems of hierarchy, for the daughter, as first wife, would have precedence over her mother, but would still owe her, as daughter, a respect inconsistent with that position. For similar reasons, two sisters could not be co-wives (Lev. 18:18).[37]

We can form some impression of how gravely the Torah regarded the various kinds of incest from the punishments it prescribed. Leviticus imposed the death penalty for three kinds of incest: with the father's wife, with the son's wife, with a woman and her mother (Lev. 20:11, 12, 14). Of these, it required death by fire for the last, suggesting that the most aggravated form of incest was for a man to marry his mother-in-law. A less grave level of incest consisted of intercourse with one's sister or half-sister (20:17) and was to be punished by "cutting off" (20:18). A third level, which God would punish with childlessness, consisted of intercourse with a brother's wife or father's brother's wife (20:20–21). Intercourse with the father's or mother's sister was condemned, but no penalty was named (20:19). The remaining offenses from the list in Leviticus 18 (wife's sister; grandchildren) receive no notice in chapter 20. A slightly different listing of worst offenses appears in Deuteronomy, which curses just three kinds of incest: with a man's father's wife, his sister or half-sister, and his mother-in-law (27:20–23).

While the Holiness Code in Leviticus and the curses of Deuteronomy 27 both treated incest as a violation of purity, purity considerations alone are not sufficient to explain the exact specifications. These were purity rules in that they governed sexual boundaries and evoked the intense emotional engagement characteristic of purity rules, but the definition of what constituted incest was framed in terms of social roles. They were expressions of a sense of property framed as hierarchy—one vastly different from the familial presuppositions of the modern West.[38]

Prostitution

The Torah had little to say on the subject of secular prostitution. We have seen that it prohibited parents from dedicating their children as sacred prostitutes, but there is nothing to tell us whether its authors would have objected equally to the idea of a master's making his slave woman a secular prostitute or even a father's doing so with his daughter. Only two references to secular prostitution offer any details about how it was regarded. In both cases an unmarried woman is understood to have chosen this course of action on her own and thereby brought disgrace on her father. In one passage, a priest's daughter who "plays the harlot" is condemned to be burned for having "profaned" her father (Lev. 21:9). One may guess that she is part of her father's household, either as not yet married or as divorced or widowed. Her activity threatens the state of purity vital to the household because its food comes largely from the altar of the Temple.

In the other passage, a man charges that his wife was found not to be a virgin on her wedding night. If this is true, she is to be stoned for having "played the harlot in her father's house" (Deut. 22:13–21). In other words, she has engaged in sexual intercourse when she ought to have been guarding her virginity carefully to be a suitable bride. In the process, she has exposed her father to the shame of having misrepresented her state in negotiating her marriage. It is not clear from the passage that she has actually received payment for her services; the point seems to be, rather, that she has deprived her father and prospective husband of their rights in her. What was wrong with prostitution, from the perspective of ancient Israel, was not so much the giving or receiving of payment for sexual intercourse as it was the removal of sexual intercourse from the framework of property and hierarchy that normally contained it and ensured that it was placed at the service of the family.

Such an interpretation is made explicit in a more extensive critique of prostitution found in Proverbs. After warning the (male) reader against the wiles of the loose woman, the author contrasts the positive ideal of possessing a wife with the negative prospect of wasting one's resources on a courtesan:

> Drink water from your own cistern,
>   flowing water from your own well.
> Should your springs be scattered abroad,

streams of water in the streets?
Let them be for yourself alone,
and not for strangers with you.
Let your fountain be blessed,
and rejoice in the wife of your youth,
a lovely hind, a graceful doe.
Let her affection fill you at all times with delight,
be infatuated always with her love.
Why should you be infatuated, my son, with a loose woman
and embrace the bosom of an adventuress?
For a man's ways are before the eyes of the Lord,
and he watches all his paths.
The iniquities of the wicked ensnare him,
and he is caught in the toils of his sin.
He dies for lack of discipline,
and because of his great folly he is lost.
[Prov. 5:15–23 RSV]

One might sum up the sage's message by saying that, in matters sexual, one should buy, not rent.[39]

We cannot, of course, treat wisdom literature as if it were the same genre as legislation, and it is clear that Proverbs agrees with the Torah in understanding prostitution as a violation of God's will, not merely as something to be avoided for prudential reasons. Still, the justification offered for the prohibition is instructive as to the ethical framework in which the prohibition itself belonged. Prostitution was wrong because it stood outside the normal patriarchal system in which the male head of household owned one or more women as sexual partners. As such, it threatened the interests of the family. The man might feel that he had gotten full value for his expense, but the family gained nothing at all from his patronizing of the prostitute. His action, therefore, was a betrayal of his responsibilities; he existed not to gratify his own desires but to maintain and enhance the fortunes of his "father's house."

What the Torah and Proverbs agree upon, then, is the condemnation of those who place personal gratification ahead of family duty. The Torah condemns the unmarried woman who prefers sexual pleasure above her obligations as a good daughter of the household; she ought rather to have preserved her marriageability—which is, indeed, the family's investment in her. Proverbs condemns the man who spends family resources on private pleasure that benefits the family not at all. He must marry and content himself with his wife, who not only gives him sexual pleasure but also provides legitimate heirs and additional labor for the household.

We do not find here any condemnation for the woman who, whether as an obedient slave or as a free woman thrown onto her own resources, has become a professional courtesan. Proverbs was concerned to make the prostitute sound as unscrupulous and unattractive as possible, but its reproof was not for her, but for the man who would visit her. The Torah was speaking to the woman who was trying to behave as an unattached individual in the pursuit of pleasure while still remaining under the protection of her father. Either way, the heart of the problem lay in the tension between private inclinations and family responsibilities.[40] The modern moralism that attacks the independent female prostitute and says little against those who patronize her is a world removed from the scriptures of Israel, which do not treat the prostitute herself as the offender.[41]

CRITICAL VOICES

The patriarchal assumptions of ancient Mediterranean family life did not go entirely unchallenged in ancient Israel. Historical traditions preserved knowledge of a time when the system was less tightly observed and women might function as prophets (e.g., Deborah, Judg. 4–5), perform deeds of military daring (the wife of Heber the Kenite, Judg. 4:1–22), and lead prayer (Miriam, Exod. 15:20–21). The two creation stories basically omit patriarchy. The first treats humanity as having included both male and female from the beginning and implies no difference in status (Gen. 1:27). The second shows God as creating woman from Adam's side, thus implying their equality (Gen. 2:21). Only in the narrative of the fall is woman subordinated to man (Gen. 3:16).[42] At a later date, Malachi objected to the prevalence of divorce (2:13–16). The Essenes objected to polygamy.[43] And among the Pharisees of the first century, the School of Shammai allowed divorce only on the grounds of sexual wrongdoing by the wife.

Perhaps most important of all, the Song of Solomon (or Song of Songs) brought into the scriptural canon a collection of erotic poetry that is not focused on marriage and that treats both the male and female speakers throughout as equals. Although this work has been marginal in most modern readings of the Bible, it was immensely significant from antiquity through the seventeenth century, despite the fact that it might easily be read as undermining marriage. Only here (and perhaps in Genesis 2) does one find a scriptural understanding of sexuality that is clearly based on voluntary relationship, not ownership (cf. chap. 12).

On the Greco-Roman side, the theory of marriage was also undergoing a shift in Late Antiquity. Philosophically inclined writers increasingly treated the husband-wife relationship in terms of "friendship." We do not know how far popular perspectives actually shifted, but Roman women enjoyed somewhat greater freedom than had been characteristic among either Greeks or Jews. And there is good evidence that an ideal of marriage as a mutually supportive companionship had strong roots in Roman culture.[44]

SUMMARY

The ethics of sexual property in ancient Israel included both an ideal picture of what was to be desired and a set of prohibitions indicating what was to be avoided. The ideal defined the household, the fundamental building block of society, as consisting of a male head who possessed one or more women as wives or concubines and children who would either carry on the family (sons) or be used to make alliances with other families (daughters).[45] There were no "individuals" in the modern sense, unless eunuchs and bastards might fit that category. Those persons, such as widows and orphans, who had no connection with a patriarch were necessarily marginal to the society and highly vulnerable.

This property ethic gave rise to certain prohibitions deemed necessary to protect it. Adultery was wrong because it was theft of a neighbor's property. Incest was wrong because, being defined primarily as a revolt of the young against the old, it upset the internal hierarchy of the family. Prostitution, though a less serious concern, was wrong insofar as it represented the triumph of individual gratification over against the principle of subordination to the household.

There is little evidence of significant development in this ethic between the writing of the Torah and the time of Jesus. Apart from the waning of polygamy and an occasional protest against the abuse of divorce, the Torah's definition of sexual property and the ethic relative to it was the one that Jesus and Paul found current in their own time.[46] In contrast to their treatment of the purity ethic, the early Christians took over much of this property ethic. Yet, as we shall see, they also modified it drastically by redefining the ownership of sexuality, by undermining the autonomy of the household, and by subordinating all human goods to the Reign of God.

HOUSEHOLD AND SEXUAL PROPERTY IN THE GOSPELS

If we wish to understand the ethics of sexual property in the Gospels, the first step is to see what they have to say about the family or household. One of the striking features of Jesus' teaching, as preserved in these works, is the way in which he distanced himself from family and household. For the religion, as for the social structure, of Israel, family was a given and a central necessity. Because membership in the chosen people was primarily through descent, family was crucial for the continuation and definition of Israel. Descent also defined the priesthood and the expected Davidic messiah. Moreover, the whole contemporary world knew virtually no social imperative more compelling than the one that required the male head of household to devote himself to the maintenance and the improvement of his family's well-being and all other members of the household to subordinate themselves to this same task. The peace of the local community was of recognized importance; national loyalty could become an issue in times of oppression or open war. Yet one's basic loyalty was to the "father's house"; only extraordinary circumstances, such as would threaten the welfare of all households, caused other loyalties to take precedence.

The Gospels, on the other hand, tend to dismiss family or downgrade it in significant ways. They express this not only in direct references to family as such, but also in their treatment of women and of divorce and adultery. Each of the evangelists presents a distinctive portrait of Jesus and his teachings on this subject. All, however, suggest a far-reaching revision of contemporary attitudes on all these subjects.

MATTHEW

Family and Household

Given the inherent centrality of the family in antiquity, Jesus' negative judgment on it must have seemed startling and even outrageous. Matthew, in fact, presents him as expressing himself in deliberately outrageous ways. For example, when a would-be disciple asked leave to go and perform the final filial duty of burying his father, Jesus rejected his request by saying: "Follow me and leave the dead to bury their own dead" (Matt. 8:22; cf. Luke 9:60). The words have never ceased to trouble interpreters, who have sometimes invented fanciful explanations to avoid acknowledging their negative import. Their meaning, however, is not far to seek. Commitment to one's family, even the respect for parents mandated in the Ten Commandments, was of no significance in comparison with the claim of discipleship. Or, as Matthew's Jesus says elsewhere, "The person who loves father or mother more than me is not worthy of me, and the person who loves son or daughter more than me is not worthy of me" (Matt. 10:37; cf. the more extreme version in Luke 14:26).[1]

In practice, this seems to have meant that Jesus' disciples had to sever their family ties to follow him. He took James and John away from their father, depriving him of their labor in his fishing business (Matt. 4:21–22). He promised that "everyone who has left houses or brothers or sisters or father or mother or children or fields for the sake of my name will receive a hundred-fold and inherit eternal life" (19:29). Jesus told at least one would-be disciple not to turn his abandoned property over to other members of his family, as the prevailing culture expected and as the Jewish contemplatives called "Therapeutae" are known to have done.[2] Instead, he was to give it to the poor (19:21), an action sure to arouse enormous antagonism on the part of other family members. It was not surprising, then, when Jesus predicted that the Twelve, during their ministry, would meet with the utmost opposition from their family members, including even betrayal and murder (10:21). What was surprising was his claim that this was in fact one of the goals of his work: "Do not suppose that I have come to cast peace on the earth. I have not come to cast peace, but a sword. For I have come to set a person in opposition against his father and a daughter against her mother and a bride against her mother-in-law; and one's enemies will be the members of one's own household" (10:34–36).

Jesus' own behavior reflected this same distancing of family. He left home and spent his ministry as a wanderer with "no place to lay his head" (8:19–20). He publicly replaced his mother, brothers, and sister with his followers, making them his true family (12:46–50). He said that the people of his own town and household were uniquely incapable of recognizing and honoring him as prophet (13:53–58). And though the crowds at Jerusalem greeted him as "Son of David" (21:9), he told his opponents there a riddle suggesting that, even if he were so, it was not the key to understanding his real significance. If he was David's son, he was also, and more importantly, his own ancestor's lord (22:41–46)—a concept that turned normal household hierarchy on its head.

This may have been the significance, for Matthew, of the virgin birth. Matthew carefully placed Jesus in the Davidic royal line by means of the genealogy with which his Gospel begins, tracing this ancestry through Joseph (1:16). Yet Joseph, according to Matthew, was not in fact Jesus' father (1:18). Accordingly, Jesus' identity as "Son of David" had to be understood as something other than a relationship of physical descent. The virginity of Mary was important to Matthew not because of a relationship between virginity and purity (a connection important to later Christians, but not found in Matthew), but rather because it broke the physical connection of Jesus with his own "father's house." Jesus' own birth was thus a paradigm of the separation from family that he would subsequently require of his followers. Matthew actually underlines this aspect of Jesus' birth when he tells the story of the annunciation to Joseph (1:18–25); only an angelic visitation could override Joseph's unwillingness to continue with the marriage. To participate in God's work, Joseph must sacrifice the ordinary expectations of a male head of household.

The Reign of the Heavens,[3] which was central to the gospel Jesus proclaimed (4:17), demanded not only separation from one's family, but also a drastic reorientation of one's perspective on the world. Already in the present age, the hierarchical organization that characterized the family ceased to be acceptable in Jesus' ministry; in the age to come, the family as a focus of human life was expected to disappear altogether. Jesus' treatment of children is the clearest example of his overturning of the family hierarchy. When people brought children to him for his blessing, his disciples tried to keep them away, probably because they thought them too insignificant to deserve his attention. Jesus stopped them with the words, "Of such is the Reign of the Heavens" (19:13–15).[4]

The meaning of this statement is elucidated by another episode. The disciples asked Jesus who would be greatest in the Reign of the Heavens, and he placed a child before them and said, "Unless you turn and become like the children, you will never enter the Reign of the Heavens. So, whoever will lower himself [to be] like this child, that person is the greatest in the Reign of the Heavens" (18:1–4). Interpreters have differed as to what characteristic of children was being praised here, but the language of the passage, in fact, leaves little doubt. It was the low station of children in the hierarchy of the family—and of society in general. One enters the Reign of the Heavens by "lowering oneself," giving up all claim to social status, security, and respect. When the mother of the sons of Zebedee asked Jesus to grant them the two foremost places in his reign, he answered that, among his disciples, leaders must not seek to lord it over the rest, the way Gentile rulers did, but must accept the position of slave (20:20–28). The same principle stands behind Jesus' admonition to his followers not to accept such titles as "rabbi" or "teacher." "You are all brothers," he said; "and do not call anyone 'father' on earth, for you have one father—the one in the heavens" (23:8–12). In the new "family" of Jesus' followers, there are only children, no patriarchs. The household of this age is completely overturned.[5]

This was more than a transitional arrangement while the disciples waited for the full unveiling of the Reign of the Heavens. It was to be understood as a feature of the heavenly life itself, which, according to Jesus, knows nothing of marriage. This is the point made in his controversy with the Sadducees and, indeed, explains why this story was preserved in the oral tradition of Jesus' teachings even after 70 C.E., when the Sadducees disappeared as a religious and political force (22:23–33). The Sadducees, who rejected belief in the resurrection, raised a difficult question about it based on the institution of levirate marriage. Suppose that, in a family of seven brothers, the first married a woman and died childless; the second, as was his duty, married the widow, but also died childless— and so on through all seven. In the resurrection, all eight persons would be alive at one time, and what the law of levirate marriage commanded in the present world would create an inevitable violation of other laws in the world to come. Because ancient Israel did not accept the marriage of one woman to several men at the same time, she must be either the wife of the first brother or of a later one. If one of the later husbands kept the woman, he would be violating the law that defines intercourse with the living brother's wife as incest (Lev. 18:16). On the other hand, if the first husband took her back, this would violate the law forbidding the remarriage of a couple after the woman had been married to another man (Deut. 24:1–4). Therefore the idea of a general resurrection was actually inconsistent with the Torah. Jesus answered this argument by denying that the institution of marriage had any place at all in the life of the resurrection. The family and its internal hierarchy would, of course, fall along with the institution of marriage, leaving no more reason for the levirate law than for the problems it threatened to create.

The teaching about the family in Matthew is not entirely negative. Jesus upheld the honor ascribed to parents in the written Torah against exceptions made to it in "the tradition of the elders"—that is, the oral Torah. The tradition allowed dedications to the Temple (*qorban*) to take precedence over duty to parents, and Jesus rejected this (15:3–9). Again, when the rich young man asked him about the way into life, Jesus included the honor due to parents among the commandments of which he reminded him. Respect for parents is the only point of contemporary family hierarchy Matthew treated in this positive way. The few occurrences of it form a rather minor counter-theme in his Gospel as a whole, but it is worth asking what they are doing there in the context of so much anti-family teaching. One possibility is that they were introduced into the tradition of Jesus' teaching as the result of increasing social conservatism in the early churches. Such a development can be documented elsewhere (see pp. 218–26). This conclusion is not necessary, however, for another explanation lies ready to hand, which can accommodate the apparent conflict within the limits of Jesus' own ministry.

Jesus had followers at more than one level of commitment. Those nearest to him, the male disciples and the women who accompanied him on his travels, had surrendered the safety of their households to take up that peripatetic existence. (Not everyone who was invited to join their circle was willing to make the sacrifice, e.g., the rich young man, 19:16–22.) On the other hand, the great majority of those who took Jesus' message seriously, who welcomed his disciples and came to hear him preach when he was nearby, must have continued to live much as before, in families that seemed but little changed.[6] In that context, it was right to honor parents and to preserve the stability of the household. Accordingly, the oral tradition of Jesus' teaching contained at least a moderate endorsement of respect for parents. Yet even for these followers in the wider circle, the teaching of Jesus and the ongoing example of the inner circle that had abandoned family to be with him showed that, for his followers, family was no longer a central and unquestioned value. One must be prepared to sacrifice it to enter the Reign of the Heavens.

Divorce

Even for this wider circle of followers, Jesus altered marriage and family life in a highly significant way through his prohibition of divorce. This issue is important in modern conflicts about Christianity and family life. And it has long been a point of disagreement between the Western Christian tradition, which, historically, enforced the prohibition of divorce and remarriage as law, and the Eastern tradition, which took it rather as expressing an ideal. These later debates, however, have little if anything to do with the reasons for Jesus' original prohibition or what it may have meant to his original audience. We must try to separate ourselves from them for the moment to appreciate what the sayings of Jesus were getting at. Fortunately, Matthew provides, alongside the prohibition itself, some material that indicates what its contemporary significance may have been.

The account opens (19:3) with the Pharisees asking Jesus for an interpretation of the Torah: "Is a man permitted to divorce his wife for any reason at all?" This was, in fact, a difficult legal point and a subject of conflict between the two principal divisions of the Pharisees in Jesus' time, the Schools of Shammai and Hillel. The Torah did not legislate directly on the matter of divorce, but simply alluded to it in passing as something a man might do if he found in his wife "anything improper" (Deut. 24:1). The phrase could refer to sexual impropriety, for one of the Hebrew terms in it refers primarily to the female genitals. So the School of Shammai took it, limiting divorce to cases of sexual wrongdoing. On the other hand, it could be understood more broadly, as the Septuagint translators apparently did in rendering it as *aschemon pragma*, "an unseemly thing." This was the position of the School of Hillel, allowing divorce for a wider variety of causes. Jesus was being asked to engage this debate between the schools.[7]

Jesus' response, however, is to dismiss the whole question by reference to another passage of the Torah, the creation narratives at the beginning of Genesis. His argument, which thus took the form of an interpretation of scripture, is that a prior revelation of the will of God (in this case, in creation) cannot be annulled by a later provision (in this case, something that Jesus credits not to God, in any case, but to Moses).[8] Relying on the first creation account in Genesis (1:27), Jesus first argues that the female is as human as the male: "from the beginning He made them male and female." Male and female, therefore, participate equally in the image of God. Then, relying on the second creation narrative (Gen. 2:24), he held that the man and woman (*or* husband and wife) become "one flesh" in marriage. By "one flesh," it seems that Jesus understands not sexual intercourse, as Paul did (see p. 103), but full kinship. The simple fact of sexual intercourse would not prohibit divorce; the only way to ground such a prohibition in the language of Genesis 2 is to understand "one flesh" as equivalent to "the same flesh and blood."[9]

As we have seen, the family structure of ancient Israel (or the Mediterranean world at large) did not acknowledge either equality between male and female or full kinship between married persons. The wife, although in some ways an extension of her husband and an important part of his household, was not truly and fully a member of his family and was certainly not his equal. His right to divorce her was the ultimate expression of both these realities; he could dismiss her in a way analogous to his dismissal of a slave, although, as befitted her higher status, he must allege a reason—that is, must find in her "something improper." This right of the husband to divorce the wife conflicted, in Jesus' understanding, with both the "one flesh" God created in marriage and the equality of "male and female" as God originally created them in the divine image. Divorce, then, could not be seen as part of God's original creation, but only as Moses' concession to male hardheartedness (19:8). In this way, Jesus abolishes one part of scripture, the divorce law, on authority of another, the creation accounts.[10]

This abolition of divorce was of immediate and far-reaching consequence, particularly since Jesus combined with it a broadening of the definition of adultery: "I tell you that anyone who divorces his wife except for *porneia* and marries another is committing adultery" (19:9). This exemption for *porneia* (harlotry) may well refer to the provision in the Torah that allowed a man to reject a wife who had not shown proof of virginity on her wedding night (Deut. 22:13–21). Such a bride was said to have "played the harlot" (*ekporneuo* in the Septuagint) in her father's house.[11] Because the consummation of such a marriage showed that the bride was not a virgin, it was no marriage at all from the ancient point of view and Jesus allowed the man to terminate it. Divorce for any other reason, however, if followed by remarriage, was now to be understood as adultery. Jesus completely redefines adultery here. Under the provisions of the Torah, it was impossible for a man to commit adultery against his own married state. In a single phrase, Jesus created such a possibility and thus made the wife equal in this regard, as well. He not only forbade the man to divorce his wife, but also gave her a permanent and indissoluble claim on him as *her* sexual property. Henceforth, his sexual freedom was to be no greater than hers.[12]

The same notion of marriage as constituting a unity of flesh—that is, a permanent and indissoluble claim—lay behind the other Matthean pronouncement on divorce, found in the Sermon on the Mount. This saying, however, is less far reaching because it implies only that the husband retains a permanent claim on the wife. In contrast to the law of divorce in the Torah, Jesus says, "I say to you that everyone who divorces his wife except for reason of *porneia* makes her commit adultery and whoever marries a divorced woman is committing adultery" (5:32). Here again, *porneia* rendered the original marriage invalid. Divorce for any other reason, however, rendered adultery, in this new sense, more or less inevitable, since the rejected woman would normally have to marry again if possible. This passage is thus related to the more extended one in chapter 19, but is less comprehensive and less threatening to the social order because it does not explicitly render the husband property of the wife.[13]

Just how threatening the pronouncement of chapter 19 was and in what way becomes evident from the discussion between the disciples and Jesus that follows it. The disciples objected, "If this is the man's legal situation with his wife, it is not advantageous to get married" (19:10). The man, after all, has lost both his sexual freedom and his ultimate authority within the household. Jesus replied, "Not all receive the saying, but those to whom it has been granted. For there are eunuchs who were born so from the mother's womb, and there are eunuchs who have been made eunuchs by human beings, and there are eunuchs who have made themselves eunuchs on account of the Reign of the Heavens. Let whoever can receive it receive it" (19:11–12). The eunuch, as we have seen, was one of the few "individuals" in the ancient world—a man with no intrinsic relation to a family. Jesus was acknowledging, then, that his prohibition of divorce effectively dissolved the family, as then constituted, and made eunuchs of all men, since it deprived them of the authority requisite to maintain their patriarchal position and keep their households in subjection. What may appear to be a pronouncement about one or two elements of sexual ethics (divorce and remarriage) actually threatened the end of the entire hierarchical institution of the household. The prohibition of divorce and redefinition of adultery, which may appear, from a modern perspective, to protect the family, were actually undermining it in its ancient form.

Adultery

Jesus, as we have seen, redefined adultery as part of his prohibition of divorce. Henceforward, marriage was, really for the first time, to constitute an indissoluble kinship and to recognize the equality of the sexes in the image of God. As a result, even the most legal of divorces and remarriages must constitute a case of adultery. This might appear to be a form of physical purity code reasserting itself, as if to say that a spouse automatically became henceforward sexually impure to all others during the lifetime of the partner. In fact, however, Jesus recognized, here as elsewhere, the necessity of conscious and intentional participation in any act that was to be defined as sin. In saying that his pronouncement could be "received" only by those to whom it was granted, he indicated that the general public could not be categorized as guilty according to these new definitions. To accept these new principles at all was in itself a gift from God. This was not, in other words, an automatic form of pollution that operated of itself wherever the new set of rules was violated. It was a new conception of marriage to be received voluntarily and as an act of renunciation by Jesus' followers. The key here, as with all of Jesus' ethics, was intention.[14]

This emerges, too, in Jesus' other major statement on adultery: "You have heard that it was said, 'You shall not commit adultery.' But I tell you that every man who looks at a woman to desire [or covet, *epithymesai*] her has already committed adultery with her in his heart" (5:27–28). The statement is ambiguous as to exactly what the man has done. Has he simply desired[15] the woman, in a way that is more or less involuntary and prior to conscious control? In that case, Jesus was saying that all sexual desire is implicitly adulterous because it takes no account of the marital status of either the desirer or the object of desire. This, in turn, would imply that adultery is an inescapable sin. While such a statement is outrageous, it is not therefore impossible. The Jesus who could say, "You shall be perfect as your heavenly father is perfect" (5:48), was capable of making other outrageous demands, too. Immediately following the statement about desire, we find, "If your right eye makes you stumble, pluck it out and throw it away; it is better for you to lose one of your members and not have your whole body thrown into Gehenna" (5:29). Later interpreters seem to be agreed in understanding this last verse as an instance of outrageous hyperbole designed to bring one to a recognition of the gravity of one's situation. The identification of all sexual desire as implicitly adulterous could serve the similar function of revealing how deep-seated is the human indifference to the rights of others.

Another possible interpretation would note that the Greek verb here, usually translated "desire," is the one used in the Septuagint's translation of the Tenth Commandment ("Thou shalt not covet . . ."). In this case, Matthew has Jesus saying that covetousness, the desire to deprive another of his property, is the essence of adultery. Jesus was then reaffirming a traditional understanding of what is wrong in adultery. In this case, however, Jesus was asserting that adultery does not consist only in the physical union of two people at least one of whom is "one flesh" with another person; it consists rather in the intention, accomplished or not, to take what belongs to another. Matthew gives us no clue as to which meaning of the Greek verb should predominate here. Perhaps there is no need, in fact, to decide between them. Both interpretations are consistent with the teaching of Jesus as presented in this Gospel. No human being is free of sin, but the nature of sin lies in impurity of the heart even more conclusively than in the physical act by itself.[16]

Incest and prostitution

The other basic offenses against sexual property receive little notice in Matthew's Gospel. The only reference to incest has to do with the arrest of John the Baptist, who had admonished Herod Antipas, tetrarch of Galilee, for taking his brother's wife, Herodias (14:3–4). The other Synoptic evangelists report the same information (Mark 6:17; Luke 3:19–20). One may guess that Matthew and the others agreed with John's position, but they give us no indication of their reasons. Under the Torah, Herod had committed incest in compelling his brother to divorce his wife in order to marry her himself. By Jesus' definition, this was adultery as well.

The matter of prostitution receives slightly more attention, appearing in a significant pronouncement of Jesus. The tax collectors and the prostitutes, he says, were entering the Reign of the Heavens ahead of respectable religious leaders (the chief priests and elders) because they believed the preaching of John the Baptist (21:23–32). Because John preached repentance (3:2), we tend to assume that the prostitutes ceased to be such when they came to believe his message. It proves difficult, however, to be certain. The tax collectors presumably did not cease to be tax collectors. (In Luke 19:1–10, the tax collector Zacchaeus, upon his conversion, gave half of his property to the poor and made amends to those he had defrauded; there is no suggestion that he ceased to be a tax collector.) A prostitute would have found it far more difficult to change her low place in the community than a tax collector. We know little about them in the Jewish world of the time. In the contemporary Gentile world, however, most of them were slaves, who could not legally abandon their status. Even free prostitutes, if poor, would have had only the most limited of options because they would not have been acceptable as wives. Our own presuppositions, then, may perhaps dictate whether we think of these women as giving up prostitution or not; there is nothing in Matthew's Gospel to settle the question.[17] What is significant is that Jesus held them up to the religious leadership as a model of repentance for them to imitate, thus implying that the respectable are not unlike despised prostitutes in respect to sin.

MARK

Mark's Gospel, though closely related to that of Matthew, is much shorter and contains less of Jesus' teaching. In light of this, it is remarkable how much Mark and Matthew share on the subject of the family. Most of the relevant material found in Matthew is also in Mark, where it forms a larger proportion of the whole work than in Matthew. What is more, Mark often underlines the material more strongly than Matthew. Matthew, for example, shows us James and John in the boat with their father Zebedee and then has Jesus call them away as his disciples, so that they "leave the boat and their father" (Matt. 4:21–22); this makes it clear enough that they are abandoning their parent. Mark, however, includes a detail to suggest that they were Zebedee's only sons and that their departure left him without anyone to carry on his family: "At once [Jesus] called them; and, leaving their father Zebedee in the boat *with the hired hands*, they went off after him" (Mark 1:20). Again, both Matthew and Mark recount the story of how Jesus replaced his mother and siblings with his followers as his true family. Mark alone precedes the story with the statement that Jesus' relatives had come looking for him out of a conviction that he was out of his mind (3:21). When they arrived, they could not reach him for the crowd. The people told Jesus they were asking for him, but he said, "Who are my mother and brothers?" And looking round at the crowd, he announced, "Look! My mother and my brothers. Whoever does God's will, this person is my brother and sister and mother" (3:31–35).[18]

Mark reports Jesus' prohibition of divorce in a form almost identical to that of Matthew, but the redefinition of adultery that goes with it is somewhat different. Matthew's version contemplates only the husband's divorcing of the wife and its consequences. It is, after all, a discussion of the correct interpretation of the Torah, and the Torah provided for no other possibility. Mark, however, is less interested in legal exactitude and gives a more comprehensive version of the saying that would cover more of the eventualities of contemporary life: "Whoever divorces his wife and marries another commits adultery against her; and if she divorces her husband and marries another, she is committing adultery" (10:11–12).[19]

The fundamental principles behind Mark's version are the same as those implied by Matthew's: marriage establishes a unity of flesh, that is, a familial relationship, between two persons who are equals in terms of their sexual ownership of one another. Their equality of ownership means that each can commit adultery against the other. Their unity of flesh means that neither husband nor wife is free to dispose of the other as a possession. Mark's version differs, however, in that it places the whole question of adultery on the partner who initiated divorce and remarriage and says nothing to prohibit the remarriage of one who has been the object of divorce.

Because most scholars believe that Mark's Gospel was the first such work to be written, it is worth noting the context in which he chose to place this material about divorce and remarriage. He created a distinct geographical unit in his narrative, beginning with Jesus' entry into "the territory of Judea across the Jordan" (10:1) and concluding with his moving, by way of Jericho, up to Jerusalem (10:46–52). The contents of this unit, however, seem miscellaneous. They include: prohibition of divorce;

reception of the children; the rich man's question; a discussion about possessions and salvation; Jesus' third prediction of his passion, death, and resurrection; a competition over precedence among the disciples; and the healing of blind Bartimaeus. Our observation that wives and children were a kind of property, however, and that hierarchy in the family was an expression of property relationships makes the continuity in Mark's arrangement easier to see, for all the units gathered together here are really dealing with property ethics.

The prohibition of divorce and redefinition of adultery took the wife out of the realm of disposable property and made her equal to her husband. So, too, Jesus' welcoming of the children takes them from the bottom of the family hierarchy and makes them persons in their own right (10:13–16). When Jesus invites the rich man to become a disciple, he demands that he separate himself from property and family (10:21). The man fails, and Jesus says to his disciples that it would be easier to put a camel through the eye of a needle than for a rich man to be saved. The disciples, assuming that riches are a sign of divine favor and also, through almsgiving, a means to it, are shocked (10:23–27). Peter notes that the disciples have left all, both family and other possessions, to follow Jesus, and Jesus assures them that they will be rewarded, "but many who are first will be last and the last first" (10:28–31). James and John (rather than their mother, as in Matthew) ignore both this saying and Jesus' reminder that he is on his way to his own death (10:32–34) and ask for the positions of highest honor in Jesus' reign; Jesus tells them that honor, among his disciples, must be sought through service (10:35–45). Finally, as Jesus leaves Jericho on the road to Jerusalem, a blind beggar— an utterly marginal and unimportant person—calls for him. The title he uses is a royal one, "Son of David," emphasizing Jesus' place at the peak of the same hierarchy that relegates the beggar to its lowest stratum. As in the earlier episode of the children, those around Jesus try to keep the lowly person away, but Jesus summons the man and places himself at his service in illustration of his own teaching (10:46–52).

The entire chapter thus forms a unified treatment of household and related issues of property and hierarchy. Its message is that full disciples must give them all up: wealth, family, and their dominant place in the hierarchy. Even the more distant follower who retains spouse and family must give up the rights of ownership and domination over them. The household is stripped of its unquestioned centrality in the culture and in the lives of its members, while the adult males who follow Jesus are deprived of the status they had enjoyed as heads of family. All this is done "for my sake and the sake of the gospel" (10:29).[20]

LUKE-ACTS

Luke confirms the picture we have found in Matthew and Mark, although he sometimes does it in a more pointed way. For instance, where Matthew has Jesus say that "he who loves father or mother more than me is not worthy of me" (Matt. 10:37), Luke has this version: "If anyone comes to me and does not hate his own father and mother and wife and children and brothers and sisters—yes, and even his own life, he cannot be my disciple" (Luke 14:26). In this case, Luke's version is likely to be closer to Jesus' own words, for it is easier to understand how such provocative language could have been softened in the tradition than how it could have been newly introduced. Similarly, where Matthew has Jesus tell a would-be disciple that he must leave "the dead to bury their own dead" (8:22), Luke adds a further saying: "Yet another person said to him, 'I will follow you, sir, but first give me leave to say farewell to the people at home.' But Jesus said, 'No one who has once put hand to plow and then looks back is fit for God's Reign'" (9:61–62). Jesus himself left his family to begin his wandering ministry as teacher and healer; even before that, Luke tells us, as a child of twelve, he once renounced his parents' authority to pursue his true father's business in the Temple (2:41–52).

Luke's treatment of the dispute with the Sadducees about levirate marriage, an episode he shares with both Matthew and Mark, is also distinctive. All three Synoptic evangelists agree that there is to be no marrying or giving in marriage[21] in the life of the resurrection. The other two explain this simply as a result of the fact that the resurrected will be "like the angels in heaven" (Matt. 22:30; Mark 12:25). Later Christian interpreters shared with Neoplatonic philosophy the presupposition that angels (or their Greek equivalent, the *daimones*) were purely spiritual beings without any sexual component in their nature. To be like the angels, then, was to be nonsexual, with the consequent understanding that, whatever the precise language of the passage might say, Jesus really meant that there would be no sex in heaven. This, however, is in potential conflict with the scriptural tradition about angels. As we have seen, both Genesis and Jude (and also *1 Enoch*, which Jude regarded as scriptural) regarded some angels, at least, as sexual beings capable of having intercourse with human women and even of begetting children with them.[22] What Jesus may have thought about the presence or absence of sexual activity in the life of the resurrection must remain unknown; there is no clue in the saying itself. The presumed asexuality of angelic beings, however, is unlikely to be the point of his comparison, for there is no reason to suppose that he or his audience knew of it.

Luke is more specific in his version of Jesus' saying, enabling us to say precisely what he, at least, understood to be the point of comparison. Angels are immortal beings and therefore have no need for legitimate offspring to carry the life and wealth of a family across the generations. The disappearance of marriage at the resurrection is therefore simply a result of the disappearance of death and, with it, of the whole family structure characteristic of earthly society. "The children of this age," says Jesus, "marry and are given in marriage, but those found worthy to attain to that age and the resurrection of the dead neither marry nor are given in marriage. For they are no longer capable of dying, for they are equal to angels and are children [*or* sons][23] of God inasmuch as they are children of the resurrection" (20:34–36).

Luke's most extreme break with the family and its normative hierarchy appears in a tradition unique to his Gospel, the parable of the Prodigal Son (15:11–32). The behavior of the Prodigal is a complete betrayal of his family. What belonged to him only as an offshoot of his "father's house" (the elder brother, of course, would continue the direct line) he wasted on private pleasures. Having come to no good, he acknowledged what anyone in Jesus' world would surely have agreed to: that he was no longer worthy of the title *son.* He returned to his father only to beg for the position of a hired hand. Even this perhaps stretched the claims of family loyalty, but his present state was so wretched that he had nothing to lose. The truly outrageous element in the parable, however, is the father's behavior. Having seen his failed son approaching, he ran to meet him, rather than waiting with patriarchal dignity to receive him as a suppliant. He embraced and kissed him without waiting for explanation or repentance, and he received him back with the kind of rejoicing that marked him as the long-lost child returned, quite without reference to the way he had failed his household. He reaffirmed the elder son's right of succession, yet treated this as a reason for him to rejoice at his brother's return instead of punishing him. This, says the Jesus of Luke's Gospel, in a stunning reversal of the normal household hierarchies, is the way God acts.

Luke stood, then, in the same tradition as Matthew and Mark on the issue of the family—though he was perhaps willing to press that tradition a bit more vigorously at certain points. A curious and unique feature of his Gospel, however, is the way in which he leads his readers from their existing presuppositions about family, embedded as they were in the religion of Israel, to the radically new situation envisioned by Jesus' teaching. Luke's Gospel begins in an atmosphere redolent of the world of ancient Israel, the era of patriarchs, judges, and kings. An elderly priest and his wife are childless. Through an angel, the priest learns that his wife will conceive, though she is barren and past the age of childbearing. The prophecy proves true, and she rejoices that God has removed the reproach of her barrenness (1:5–25). The son born to them is John the Baptist. Reminiscences of the stories of Abraham and Sarah, of Jacob and Rachel, and of Hannah and Elkanah identify this as the narrative of yet another household in Israel that has received the Lord's blessing of fertility and offered the fruit of that blessing to God in faith and service.

Near the end of his Gospel, however, Luke has Jesus say to the women of Jerusalem: "Behold, days are coming when they will say, 'Blessed are the barren and the wombs that have not given birth and breasts that have not nursed'" (23:29). In time to come, blessing and curse will be reversed. The family will be a hindrance, and those who are free of it will be counted fortunate. The shift from the old era of family to the new and changed world comes to a focus in John the Baptist, as a series of sayings in Luke 16 shows. At first sight, they seem miscellaneous and even chaotic. Jesus insists that, like the unrighteous steward, one must sacrifice one's household for one's own well-being. Everyone must make a choice between God and Mammon—a category that covers not only property and money, but also the household that is their possessor. One cannot serve both, and the wise person will make use of the goods of this world to secure a place in the world to come (16:1–13). The Pharisees (whom Luke characterizes here as "fond of money") object, and Jesus responds, "What is exalted among human beings is an abomination before God" (16:14–15). In what at first seems a *non sequitur*, he continues, "The Law and the Prophets as far as John! From then on, the Reign of God is being proclaimed as good news and everyone is forcing a way into it. And it is easier for heaven and earth to pass away than for a single serif to drop from the Law. Everyone who divorces his wife and marries another is committing adultery, and the one who marries a woman divorced from her husband is committing adultery" (16:16–18). Then comes the parable of the Rich Man and Lazarus, which teaches that one's fortune in the world to come will be a reversal of what one enjoyed in this (16:19-31).

The theme that holds these seemingly disparate materials together is the change of worlds and the sacrifice of family and household that it demands. It is easier to change worlds than to drop even the smallest stroke from a letter of the Law. Yet Jesus has changed the Law. What the Law permitted, under the heading of divorce, he treats as sin. The life of prosperity and ease in one's family, which the Law exalted, the Pharisees esteemed, and the rich man of the parable enjoyed, Jesus undermines. The distance between these worlds is "a great gulf fixed." John, the joy of his parents' old age, was the culmination and the conclusion of the former era; in the new era, the patriarchal family, however sanctified by the Law and the Prophets, ceases to be. This is not, for Luke, a repudiation of the Law in its own place and time, but it is a decisive step beyond it into another world altogether.

Luke's second volume, Acts of the Apostles, has less to say about the household than the first. This is as one would expect in light of the treatment of the subject in his Gospel. The family was surely still tolerated, since Luke tells us enthusiastically of the conversion of whole households (e.g., that of Cornelius, 10:44–48, or Lydia, 16:15) and makes a good deal of the role of Priscilla and Aquila, who were wife and husband (18:2–3, 18, 24–26). Yet the first story he tells of an individual as distinct from a mass conversion concerns a eunuch (8:26–39). And one would never know, from the stories he tells, that Christians continued to marry and set up new family units. He presents the Jerusalem church, in its early days, as taking its meals together and sharing all its possessions freely (4:32–27), implying that it regarded itself as a single household and had obliterated the boundaries of the traditional family within its own ranks. Luke also shows the church treating women as fully responsible human beings—with negative consequences in the case of Ananias and Sapphira (5:1–11). And he stresses the importance of women such as the daughters of Philip, who prophesied (21:9); Priscilla, whose importance as a teacher appears to have outshone that of her husband (her name usually precedes his, as in 18:26); and Lydia, who was the first European convert (16:14–15).

Luke's account, then, implies that the earliest Christians, following the principles of Jesus, had allowed the family's importance to decline among them. Women, as a result, were free to participate in the life of the community in an active way. The leadership of the churches, however, seems to have remained mainly in the hands of men. Luke says nothing, for example, about women as traveling missionaries in the manner of Paul, even though they appear as prophets, teachers, and patrons of local churches. In this way, we can see in Acts the foundations of future problems and uncertainties. The early Christians wished to honor Jesus' teaching with regard to the family, yet they were not prepared, as a whole, to implement the far-reaching changes in traditional social life that it implied. Perhaps Luke's own emphasis on the importance of women was in part an effort to correct this reluctance.[24]

JOHN

The subject of family and sexual property is not prominent in the Gospel of John—certainly not to the extent that we can glean from it a "position" on the subject. The most one can say is that John is not at odds with what we have read in the three Synoptic Gospels. Jesus is closer to his mother in this Gospel than in the others. She even appears in the role of exemplary believer in the story of the wedding at Cana where she appeals to Jesus with regard to the lack of wine and perseveres in faith that he can and will act (2:1–11).[25] Even here, however, he rebuffs her in a way that seems disrespectful. In the long run, Jesus makes the church the true family of every believer by giving Mary and the Beloved Disciple to each other as mother and son at the cross (19:25–27). The essential thing about believers is that they are children of God (1:12–13), having been born from above (or again) of water and spirit (3:1–13).[26]

John's Jesus feels no difficulty about talking with a lone Samaritan woman, though both the woman and Jesus' disciples find the situation socially awkward (4:9, 27).[27] When Jesus asks her to call her husband, it turns out that the woman has had repeated marriages and is now living with a man to whom she is not married. Jesus, however, shows no evidence of concern (4:16–18), and she becomes a missionary to the people of her city (4:28–30, 39–42). Another apparently unmarried woman, Mary of Magdala, holds a particularly important place in this Gospel, being one of the few followers who stood by the cross (19:25) and the first witness both of the empty tomb and of the Risen Lord (20:1-18). Finally, Jesus has a close association with two unmarried sisters, Mary and Martha of Bethany, who actually seem to be more important and better known to the Johannine community than their brother Lazarus, whom Jesus raised from the dead (11:1–2).

John's Jesus, like the Jesus of the Synoptics, also reverses hierarchy as a key to his ministry. At the Last Supper, he strips and assumes the role of a slave by washing his disciples' feet (13:1–10). This is despite the fact that he is not only their teacher and master, but actually, as John has told his readers from the very beginning, the creative power of God, the eternal Logos from whom all creation comes (1:1–18). He then tells his disciples that they are to follow this example of humility in their relationship with one another (13:12–17): "If you know these things, blessed are you—if you do them!"

Finally, we may note Jesus' encounter with a woman about to be stoned for adultery (7:53–8:11). This is not, properly speaking, a part of John's Gospel at all; but most of the manuscripts that preserve it place it there.[28] It is undoubtedly an old tradition. In this story, Jesus does not question the existing definition of adultery or overtly alter the hierarchy of the family. Yet what he does is as devastating to the status quo as any of the teachings preserved in the Synoptics. By inviting whoever was sinless to cast the first stone, he forces the crowd to reevaluate the cheap sense of virtue that we get from committing violence in the name of familiar social institutions. The eldest, which is to say the wisest, leave first. When all have gone and Jesus is left alone with the woman, he, too, refuses to condemn her and sends her away. He says to her, "Sin no more." Adultery has not, then, ceased to be a sin, but Jesus has made the death sentence against it unenforceable, once again drastically undermining the existing social institution of the household.

SUMMARY

Although the Gospel of John is less interested in the question of household and sexual property than the three Synoptics, there is nonetheless a broad agreement manifest in all four New Testament Gospels with regard to Jesus' teaching on these issues. I shall attempt to summarize it here.

Jesus was not friendly toward the household as an institution. Although he was not understood to have abolished it entirely or among all his followers, he came close to doing so among his closest disciples. Of them, he demanded a drastic separation from family. His other followers, too, must cease to treat it as central to their world. The demands of the Reign of God are supreme, and no obligation of this world may compete with them for the allegiance of those who are already being drawn into the life of the world to come. One cannot serve God and Mammon—any kind of Mammon, even the family or household.[29]

More specifically, Jesus demanded that the wife no longer be regarded as disposable (i.e., divorceable) property. Instead, husband and wife were to be understood as human equals who now constitute one flesh—a unit of kinship. This deprived the patriarch of one important sanction for his control of the household. Jesus' rejection of the death penalty for adultery deprived him of another. It is not surprising, then, that the early Christian movement was marked by the active and independent involvement in it of women, both married and single. In addition to changing the status of the wife, Jesus also altered that of children. By making the child and not the father the model for entry into the Reign of God, Jesus again negated the household structures of the society and reversed the hierarchical assumptions that governed all of life.[30]

In regard to specific offenses against sexual property, as defined in the scriptures of Israel, Jesus retained the prohibition against adultery, although not its punishment. He redefined adultery, however, so that the principal form of it now came to be the divorcing of one spouse and marrying of another—a perfectly respectable and legal undertaking by most other contemporary standards. The result was that adultery was no longer the exceptional behavior of the vicious few, but the normal behavior of society at large. At the same time that he reshaped the formal definition of adulterous acts, Jesus also redirected attention from the act itself to the intention involved in committing it. The essence of adultery was seen to lie either in the indiscriminate character of the sexual desire itself, which ignores the marital status of the desired, or else in covetousness, that is, in the intent to possess what belongs to another, something we have learned to see as the sin of *pleonexia*.

The Gospels have little to say about incest, although they seem to affirm John the Baptist's denunciation of Herod Antipas. With regard to prostitution, too, the Gospels have little to say. Because Jesus, however, does not seem to have been anxious about unattached women and because he even held up contemporary prostitutes as a religious example at one point, we may guess that, insofar as he took prostitution to be ethically wrong, he followed the example of Proverbs in apportioning blame to the man who visited the prostitute more than to the prostitute herself. Jesus still allowed a marriage to be annulled on grounds of *porneia*, but this, as we have seen, was probably limited to the situation where a bride who was claimed to be a virgin turned out not to be.

In short, the sexual ethic based on property was maintained—but in a way that threatened the household more than it supported it. Jesus saw in the family a rival claimant for the commitment and loyalty of his followers, so it is not surprising that he should undermine it. What demands explanation is rather why he should have wished to retain any ethic of sexual property at all. The answer lies with his emphasis on purity of the heart, which prohibited one from robbing or defrauding others (Mark 7:21–22). While Jesus had little interest in the goals of the household—the bearing of legitimate heirs or the acquisition, accumulation, and passing on of wealth—he saw sexual access in itself as a basic human good, rooted in creation. Because sexual access is an important possession, he forbade his followers to rob others.

In the existing state of affairs, however, sexual access belonged only to males. To restore the created equality of women, Jesus had to arrange for it to belong equally to them—hence, the abolition of divorce and, with it, the collapse of intra-family hierarchy. This situation, in turn, called for a new explanation of how a household, or any community, was to live. The old way had been for one person to enjoy the status of patriarch and be obeyed by others. Jesus' new way was for all to assume the position of children or slaves. In the absence of competition among those advancing themselves for leadership, those who were last would become first. Even God, he taught, has given up standing on his dignity as Father of the Universe and is running out to greet returning prodigals.

CHAPTER 10

PAUL AND SEXUAL PROPERTY

According to the traditions preserved in the Synoptic Gospels, Jesus insisted on the subordination of the family to the Reign of God. In the apocalyptic teaching current in Jesus' day, the Reign of God could come into full command of the creation only through the end (*eschaton* in Greek) of the world as we know it; this is what is technically called a "future eschatology." The tradition depicts Jesus as having spoken in just this way, using the imagery of cosmic catastrophe (e.g., Mark 13). At the same time, he also speaks as though the Reign of God were already present and available in his own ministry and that of his disciples—what is technically called a "realized eschatology." In some sense, this made his ministry the true end of the familiar world, regardless of whether the actual date of the eschaton were near or distant. Because Jesus himself embodied God's Reign, he could legitimately call disciples away from their parents, spouses, and children. Yet Christians continued to expect the Reign of God in its fullness only in the future.

Paul's teaching about family and sexual ethics involves a similar insistence on both the priority of God's Reign and the dual character of its manifestation, present and future. The language he uses to convey this teaching, however, is not always the same as that of the Synoptic Gospels. (The phrase "Reign of God," for example, is not particularly common in his writings.) But he gets at the same fundamental ideas with different terms. Paul addresses the present reality of God's Reign (realized eschatology) in terms of belonging to Christ and its expected fulfillment (future eschatology) in terms of awaiting his return. We shall need to explore each of these motifs to understand how Paul used them in relation to sexual ethics. He was not, after all, a philosopher who spoke about property, sexual or other, in an organized and abstract way. His interest in it was determined rather by the lived relationship between the Gospel he preached and the ongoing life of faith.

BELONGING TO CHRIST AND WAITING ON HIS RETURN

In modern Western society, the image of "belonging to Christ" is essentially a dead metaphor because human beings no longer own other human beings in the sense that was normal in antiquity. Such metaphors can become spiritually and intellectually dangerous; once they are cut loose from their anchorage in familiar reality, we can make them mean anything we like. As a result, they may cease to teach us anything and become mere code words for whatever notions happen already to be precious to us. Thus, "belonging to Christ," in our contemporary milieu, may mean anything from "feeling a strong commitment to the Christian faith" to "feeling assured that Jesus will take care of me" to "feeling confident of my superiority over others." In a world immediately familiar with the phenomenon of slavery, Paul's own usage was more concrete and focused.

Paul, in fact, was willing to describe himself as Christ's slave, servant, or agent (*apostolos*), some variant of these expressions being found in the salutation of virtually every letter in the Pauline corpus.[1] Belonging to Christ, however, was not something unique to apostles. As Paul was "Christ Jesus' slave, a called *apostolos*," his addressees, too, were "Jesus Christ's called ones" (Rom. 1:1, 6). Again, defending the doctrine of the general resurrection against its detractors at Corinth, he explained that Jesus' resurrection implied the resurrection of all believers at the appropriate time: "Christ the firstfruits, then, at his coming, those who belong to Christ, then the end . . . " (1 Cor. 15:23–24).

This could be partly the language of partisanship. At Corinth, Paul knew of parties whose members claimed, "I belong to Paul"—or to Apollos or to Cephas or to Christ (1 Cor. 1:12). Even though he had founded the congregation himself, he may have had to defend his authority there against the pretensions of a "Christ Party," for in a subsequent letter he wrote, "If anyone is personally confident that he belongs to Christ, let him do the reckoning over again on himself, because just as he belongs to Christ, so, too, do we" (2 Cor. 10:7). Partisanship, however, by no means exhausts the significance of what Paul means by "belonging to Christ."

To the Galatians, he wrote of Christ's ownership as originating in a kind of purchase. The purpose of this letter was both to defend Paul's own teaching and to dissuade the Galatian Christians from adopting a fuller observance of the Torah, including circumcision of Gentile males. Paul asserted the incompatibility of the Gospel with such a use of the Torah and found the metaphor of ownership useful in making his point. He turned specifically to the normal ancient practice of enslaving prisoners of war—not only captured soldiers, but also the civilian populations of conquered cities. In some cases, such prisoners could be ransomed—either by payment of money or by substitution of another person of equal value. The Law, he argued, takes us prisoner by placing us under a curse when we do not fulfill it completely, but "Christ has ransomed us from the curse of the Law by becoming a curse on our behalf (because it is written, 'Cursed be everyone that hangs on a tree'), so that the blessing of Abraham might be extended to the Gentiles in Christ Jesus, so that we might receive the promise of the Spirit through faith" (Gal. 3:13-14, citing Deut. 21:23). Before Christ, according to Paul's metaphor, the Jewish people were, so to speak, property of the Law, while the Gentiles were excluded from God's elect. Jesus, by substituting himself for those imprisoned under the curse, liberated Jewish believers and, at the same time, freed God's promise from its association with the Law, thus allowing the Gentiles new access to God. "You are all one in Christ Jesus. And if you belong to Christ, then you are seed of Abraham" (3:28–29).

The ransoming of prisoners, however, did not simply restore the ransomed to their previous station. They may not have become slaves of their ransomer, but they remained, at the very least, heavily indebted and were never again free to act apart from or against their benefactor. Thus, Paul could hail the Gospel as both granting freedom and placing limits on it: "You have been called for freedom, brothers and sisters—only not freedom as an opportunity for the flesh. Rather, act as slaves to one another through love" (5:13). (Note that the duty one owes the divine ransomer is understood as abolishing intra-human hierarchies.) After offering a list of vices to be avoided and virtues that are the "fruit of the Spirit," Paul continues, "Those who belong to Christ have crucified the flesh with its passions and desires. If we are living by Spirit, let us also conduct ourselves according to Spirit" (5:24–25). The crucifixion by which Christ took our place and ransomed us has made a decisive division between the old part of our lives when we lived according to the principle of selfishness and the new part when we are to live by a principle that accords with our benefactor's death and life.[2]

When Paul speaks of the Christian as Christ's slave, he is using a household illustration to show what it means to belong to the Reign of God. Inevitably, the illustration introduces the whole question of hierarchy, whether in terms of owner to slave or parent to child. If the church is a household, who is father or master? Who is mother? Who is slave—or child? Paul refers to himself, under God, as the father of the Corinthian church and its members as his children: "It is not to shame you that I am writing these things, but to instruct you as my beloved children. Even if you have many tutors in Christ, you do not have many fathers, for in Christ Jesus through the gospel, I begot you" (1 Cor. 4:14–15).[3] This language assumes—what all of Paul's correspondence assumes—that he had a certain right to define the gospel and give authoritative rulings in churches he had founded, much like a patriarch in his own family. While Paul did not seek to impose his will on every detail of church life, neither was he shy about intervening where he thought something of importance was at stake.

At the same time, Paul recognized that the distance between the faithful as owned and the ransomer as the owner relativized most distinctions within the church to some degree or other. In the same letter where he asserted his paternal status in relation to the Corinthians, he also discouraged them from forming parties around their teachers: "Let no one boast of human beings; for all things belong to you, whether Paul or Apollos or Cephas, whether the world or life or death, whether things present or things to come—all belong to you and you to Christ and Christ to God" (1 Cor. 3:21–23). While this does not obliterate the hierarchy within the church (Paul still expected to be heard and obeyed), it does relativize it sharply by acknowledging that, as Jesus had said, "The one who wants to be first among you must be servant of all." The Christians, then, are God's slaves and God's children—and only in some lesser sense the children of Paul or of any other apostle.

Paul could also speak of the believers as Christ's bride, another way of expressing the same kind of subordination: "I am jealous of you with a jealousy on God's behalf. For I had betrothed you to a single husband, to bring you as a chaste virgin to Christ, but I am afraid that somehow, just as the snake deceived Eve with its craftiness, your minds might be corrupted from their simplicity and dedication to Christ" (2 Cor. 11:2–3).

Paul spoke here in the persona, once again, of the church's father, anxious that his daughter should not prove to be less than he has claimed. As the betrothed virgin must not let herself be seduced by other lovers, the church must resist teachers and spirits and "gospels" at variance with what Paul taught them (11:4). One of Paul's followers, the author of the epistle to the Ephesians, later elaborated the image of church as bride of Christ and reapplied it to ordinary marriage with an effect that we must consider later in this chapter.

The images of the Christian as God's slave and the church as God's bride were not the only means Paul had of directing attention to the uniqueness of life according to the gospel. In a way somewhat reminiscent of the Qumran sect, he also spoke of the Christian community as God's temple, with the rest of the world, Jewish and Gentile alike, lying outside the sacred precincts. Baptism was the transition into this sacred status and the fact that one could receive it only once meant that, unlike other sacral washings, it was an irreversible as well as an unrepeatable act. The threshold of this temple could be crossed only in one direction. Those who transgressed after baptism, even though they must expect some kind of suffering as punishment for it, would not finally be abandoned by God (1 Cor. 3:10–15)—although Paul made an apparent exception to this rule for those whose ambitions and jealousies disrupted the peace of the community (3:16–17).

Yet another image important to Paul was that of the body of Christ, with the Christians as various limbs and organs of the body. He could use this, when he wished to emphasize the equality of believers, to suggest that Christ is to the church what the whole is to its parts (1 Cor. 12:12–27). Again, when he wished to emphasize Christ's dominion over the church and to exclude that of angels or "elements" of the cosmos, he (or an early follower) treated Christ as the "head"—that is, the first principle and ruling part, which alone gives the church its unity (Col. 1:15–20; 2:8–10,16–19). Plato, many centuries before, had taken the head to be the original, essential, and dominant portion of the human body;[4] Paul was speaking out of the same kind of cultural background, which typically treated the head as the most honored part of the body and the feet as the least. Thus, the image conveyed a strong sense of hierarchy.

Yet another way Paul had of speaking about the Christian's relationship with Christ was his distinctive use of the phrase "in Christ," in which he incorporated a rich and complex set of meanings that remains difficult to interpret and impossible to exhaust. There is no need here to attempt listing the possible interpretations.[5] It will be enough to note the substantial overlap between "being in Christ" and "belonging to Christ." Those who are in Christ are free of condemnation (Rom. 8:1); those who have fallen asleep in Christ have a hope of resurrection with him (1 Cor. 15:17–22); for them, the old things have passed away and become new (2 Cor. 5:17); all are one in Christ (Gal. 3:28). One could cite more examples, but these should suffice to show that the phrase could be used synonymously with "belonging to Christ." Christians, for Paul, are sharply distinguished from the world at large by their unique relationship to God through Jesus.

This relationship is certain in the present world, but not complete. It will reach fulfillment only in the life of the world to come, and Paul considered the inbreaking of that world to be close at hand. He expected, at least in the earlier part of his ministry, that it would come before he himself died (1 Thess. 4:17; 1 Cor. 15:51–52). Thus, it was not a part of some remote or incalculable future, but an imminent reality that one must take into account in the present. One great object of Christian behavior was to conduct oneself "in a way worthy of the God who *is calling* you into his own reign and glory" (1 Thess. 2:12), for this great transition was at most a few years distant—something to be spoken of in present, not future tense. Thus, the Christian who belonged to Christ already, who was a member of Christ's body, a building block of God's temple, who lived "in Christ"—this person must frame the conduct of day-to-day life here and now in the understanding that one is already a citizen of this future world with its utterly different demands. Under the circumstances, one must avoid crediting the life of this world, through one's actions, with a permanency that it cannot possibly enjoy. One must live instead by the values of the world to come—most of all by the love that, alone of this world's goods, continues into it unchanged (1 Cor. 13). These are the ways in which the Reign of God makes itself felt here and now. Paul, like Jesus, insisted that every aspect of human life, including sex and the family, must yield to them.

SEX AT CORINTH (1 CORINTHIANS 5–7)

The only sustained discussion of sexual ethics in Paul's writings (or, indeed, in the whole of the New Testament) is found in 1 Corinthians. It owes its existence not, it seems, to Paul's own interest in the subject, but to that of the Corinthian Christians. They produced highly divergent interpretations of what the Gospel demanded in the way of sexual ethics, ranging from libertinism to a complete rejection of both marriage and sexual intercourse. Perhaps these divergences resulted from a failure on Paul's part to address the issue specifically when he was founding the congregation. Some Corinthians, having absorbed Paul's conviction that the Gospel supersedes the Law, may have separated this principle from its context and supposed that it meant the end of all moral constraints. Others observed that he was on friendly terms with relatively traditional households, like that of Stephanas, whom he describes as the "firstfruits of the province of Achaia" (1 Cor. 1:16; 16:15); they assumed that Christians were to continue that kind of family life. Still others, noting Paul's own celibate state and his negative use of the term *flesh*, concluded that the Gospel demanded (or at least encouraged) a complete separation from sexuality.

These differences within the congregation came to Paul's attention while he was in Ephesus. Some in the congregation informally reported to him about the activities of the libertines, and the congregation sent him an official enquiry about the teachings of the ascetics. The difference of these two modes of enquiry suggests that the congregation as a whole was less perturbed by the libertines than by the ascetics. Their basic assumption, in other words, was that sexual ethics was not a matter of high importance in the Christian community. Paul's understanding of purity, as outlined above in chapter 6, could easily convey that impression, especially when it was combined with hostile language about "the Law."

We have already seen (pp. 119–20) that Paul had to remind his Thessalonian converts that adultery was inconsistent with Christian behavior and that he based that judgment on a familiar property ethic. At Corinth, where his original mission may have lasted longer (a year and a half, according to Acts 18:11), he had time to lay out his own particular understanding of the gospel in more detail and he also communicated traditions about Jesus' life and teaching. In discussing the Lord's Supper or the resurrection of the dead, he could remind the Corinthians of traditions that he himself had imparted to them (1 Cor. 11:23–25; 15:1–8). In his discussion of divorce, too, he cites a tradition of Jesus (7:10–11) but does not claim to have handed it on previously. This might mean that the Corinthians had never heard it; at the very least, it suggests that it formed no major part of Paul's oral teaching. In writing 1 Corinthians, it seems, Paul could not simply "remind" the congregation of what he had already told them, but had to begin at the beginning to instruct them about sexual ethics.[6]

Incest

He began with a reported case of incest: "It is actually reported that there is harlotry among you—a kind of harlotry not [found][7] even among the Gentiles, namely that someone has his father's wife" (5:1). The verb "has" suggests something more than casual intercourse, perhaps marriage. The woman in question could be the man's mother, but there seems no reason for Paul to have avoided saying so if that were true. More likely, she was a subsequent wife, now either divorced or widowed. According to Leviticus, this would be incest just as much as intercourse with his own mother; in specifying punishments for incest, the Holiness Code made no distinction as to whether the father's wife were the son's own mother or not (20:11).

Since this was basically an offense against the patriarch's majesty, it is not surprising to find that Greco-Roman law, working with a very similar family structure, agreed with that of Israel in forbidding it.[8] This is the significance of Paul's exclamation about "a kind of harlotry not [found] even among the Gentiles." There is at least a hint of Jewish condescension to dirty Gentiles in the wording of Paul's exclamation, but there is a serious argument here, too—namely, that one cannot excuse this case of incest on the grounds that, where Jewish and Gentile laws differed, Gentiles were not compelled to abide by Jewish practices. The abolition of purity requirements, from Paul's point of view, was not an end in itself, but a necessary means to the end of including Gentiles within the Christian community. Even if this were solely a matter of purity, there would have been no need for the church to terminate a practice that was equally at home in both Jewish and Gentile society—which did not, in other words, serve to divide the two.

Yet, Paul's language shows that he thinks of the offense primarily in terms of family hierarchy, not purity.[9] He did not use purity language from Leviticus by speaking of "lying with" the father's wife or "uncovering the father's nakedness." He wrote rather of "having" the father's wife—of possessing one who properly belonged to another. We do not know, to be sure, whether the man's father was still alive. Even if the father were dead, however, the subordination of the individual to the family in ancient society meant that such a union, by setting the son on a par with his father, constituted an act of disrespect for the family that had given the son his identity and place in the world. Whether a living father was being insulted was not germane.

Many Christians at Corinth seem to have accepted this relationship as permissible under the gospel. Some may even have seen it as a laudable example of the abrogation of the Torah purity code, for Paul continued, "You people are puffed up and have not turned instead to mourning, so that the man who has committed this act might be removed from among you!" (5:2) It seems unlikely that the whole congregation was proud of the man. We know that "Strong" and "Weak" at Corinth were deeply divided over the question of eating foods sacrificed to idols. There were, then, people in the congregation who believed that some purity rules still held. It is possible, however, that even the "Weak" took this case of incest less seriously. It did not, after all, affect the community in its assembling together for meals, for the Torah does not treat the uncleanness of incest as something transferable to foods.

In the community as a whole, then, some may have been proud of the incest while others ignored the problem, regarding it as insignificant and priding themselves on their devotion to the gospel. Paul wrote, with regard to them, "Your boasting is not good. Do you not know that a little leaven leavens the whole batch of dough? Clear out the old leaven so that you may be a new batch of dough—as, indeed, you are unleavened. For, in fact, our Passover offering, Christ, has been sacrificed. Let us, then, observe the festival not with old leaven or with leaven of wickedness and evil, but with unleavened loaves of sincerity and truth" (5:6–8). Some may read this passage as a return to purity language, on the assumption that leaven was unclean. Paul's vocabulary, however, is not consistent with such a reading.[10]

The reference to the Passover here is rather a way of speaking about the new and strange "end-time" in which the Christians stood. The Messiah has come first as sacrifice and will shortly return to reign. In the meantime, Christians are living in a festival of liberation, like that which celebrated the deliverance from Egypt. As people who live permanently in the Passover festival, feeding on the flesh of the Passover offering, they must forswear things that might be overlooked during ordinary time. The leaven must be cleared out, not because it is impure, but because it is inappropriate to the new and sacred time. Violation of the honor of one's father, even if deceased, was a kind of theft, depriving him of his legitimate property. The Corinthian church, in its self-confidence, was mishandling the problem as if it were of little importance. Yet, living as it was on the verge of the world to come and even belonging already to that world by virtue of its relationship to Christ, the church must not tolerate behavior unsuited to the new time.

Paul, then, considered the case of incest to be a serious offense. This was not because of the purity element involved in incest, but because of the property/hierarchical element. He reinforced his argument by appealing to an eschatological theme—the advent of the time of liberation, here symbolized by the special qualities of the Passover festival—rather than purity. It was not a new, specifically eschatological ethic, however, that he sought to enforce through this appeal; rather, it was the familiar ethic of the existing household structure, committed to keeping the son in subordination to the father. Paul did not argue for the retention of that structure or its accompanying ethic; he simply assumed it. The distinctive time in which Christians lived simply reinforced the necessity of regarding every ethical issue as serious.

Paul issued instructions for separating the offender: "As for me, absent in body but present in spirit, I have already judged as though present the man who has so acted: with all of you gathered together in the name of the Lord Jesus and with my spirit [present] with the power of our Lord Jesus, to hand such a person over to Satan for destruction of the flesh, so that the spirit may be saved in the day of the Lord" (5:3–5). The exact nature of the scene that Paul envisaged or the punishment that would ensue is not clear. The effect, however, seems to be one of putting the offender temporarily back outside the pale of the church. It was not a final doom, but an interim action that would lead, through destruction of all that is resistant to God (the "flesh"), to eventual salvation.

Along with it went a kind of shunning, a deliberate avoidance of the offender by the rest of the congregation. Paul had suggested shunning, in general terms, in an earlier letter and now applied it specifically:

> I wrote you in the letter not to mingle with people given
> to harlotry, not at all [meaning] those of this world—or its
> greedy folk [*pleonektes*] and graspers or idolaters, since you
> would then have to leave the world. But as things are, I

> wrote you not to mingle if anyone called a brother is given
> to harlotry or greedy or an idolater or slanderer or drunkard
> or grasper—not even to eat with such a person. (5:9–110)

This passage is particularly revealing as to the nature of the sin, according to Paul. There is no purity language here, but a good deal to do with *grasping* what properly belongs to another. Even the habitually drunken person takes from the family and gives nothing back, and "idolatry" here (as in Colossians 3:5) is a synonym for greed. Paul saw the case of incest at Corinth as belonging to the same class of offenses as theft.[11]

This helps to explain why the following verses, which seem out of place to the modern reader, seemed to Paul to belong in this location. He was not finished with the topic of sexual ethics, yet he launched into an excursus on Christians and the public courts (5:12–6:11). The gist of this passage is that, since the saints will eventually, along with God, judge the universe, they should certainly be able to handle their own internal disciplinary needs. Even the least distinguished of them should be capable enough for worldly cases (6:4). This includes cases like that of the man who committed incest (5:12–13), but it also includes every kind of civil dispute among Christians: "It is already a loss to you that you have suits against one another. Why do you not rather suffer injustice? Why do you not rather suffer deprivation? But you are actually committing injustice and depriving others—and brothers and sisters at that" (6:7–8). What seems to the modern reader to be an abrupt shift of subject matter will not have seemed so to Paul or his audience. The case of incest was part of a larger picture in which Christians were overreaching one another in a variety of property matters.

Paul had not forgotten that sexual ethics was his principal topic here, for he returned to them at once, deliberately placing them in the context of a broader property ethic. This passage is framed in his "indicative-imperative" style: this is who you are, and therefore this is how you must (or, in this case, must not) behave.[12]

> Or do you not know that unjust people will not inherit God's
> Reign? Do not be deceived. Neither those given to harlotry
> nor idolaters nor adulterers nor *malakoi* nor *arsenokoitai* nor
> thieves nor greedy people [*pleonektes*]—not drunkards, not
> slanderers, not snatchers—will inherit God's Reign. And

these things some of you were; but you have been washed, but you have been hallowed, but you have been set right by the name of the Lord Jesus Christ and by the Spirit of our God. (6:9–11)

This list combines the terminology Paul applied to the case of incest (*porneia*) (5:1) with the other categories of people he directed the church to shun (5:9–11) and a few new ones as well: adulterers, thieves, and the difficult *malakoi* and *arsenokoitai* whom we discussed above (pp. 116–18). Because this list reinforces Paul's admonition to suffer injustice and deprivation rather than make use of the public courts, the passage can only make sense if all the sexual offenders listed in it are to be understood as offenders against property, whether that of their own family or that of others.[13]

What was not acceptable was sexual activity that was entirely self-regarding or preyed on the sexual property of others. Given this context, one might easily understand *malakos*, as in widespread early Christian usage, as meaning "masturbator."[14] It need not define every act of masturbation as sinful; that would be more in the character of a purity rule. As with the colloquial English "jerk-off," however, it could define the person so devoted to the pursuit of private pleasure as to be devoid of responsibility. *Arsenokoites*, as suggested above (p. 128), could refer to the male, slave or free, who used his sexual attractiveness to ingratiate himself with a rich and elderly lover in the hope of displacing the legitimate heirs. These suggestions about the meaning of the two terms are, I fear, as speculative as others, but they have the merit of making sense in the present context.

Prostitution

The next topic in 1 Corinthians is the case of men in the Christian community who use prostitutes. We have seen that Proverbs condemned this practice as a waste of family resources. Paul's approach to the subject was related, but more complex. The libertine party at Corinth may have adopted some slogans of the Cynic moralists such as "All things are permitted" and "Food is for the belly and the belly for food" (with the additional implication that sexual intercourse is as uncomplicated an expression of natural desires as eating).[15] Paul recognized that these slogans bore a certain resemblance, on the surface, to his own teaching, which held that, before God, the Torah no longer governed human existence and that there was nothing intrinsically wrong with eating food sacrificed to idols. This may, indeed, have encouraged the Corinthian libertines to adopt them.

Paul could not, however, accept them in an unqualified way, and he began his discussion by first quoting and then modifying them:

> "All things are permitted me"—but not all are profitable. "All things are permitted me"—but I for one will not have any of them make free with me. "Foods are for the belly and the belly for foods"—and God will destroy both the one and the others. The body, however, is not for harlotry but for the Lord, and the Lord for the body; and God has raised the Lord and will raise us, too, through his power. (6:12–14)

At first sight, it might appear that "body" here is a euphemism for "genitals," since it is in opposition to "belly"; but that cannot be so. Not only would it be quite different from Paul's usual use of the term *body*, but there is also no reason for him to contrast one part of the body (the stomach) with another in terms of destruction and resurrection. The whole of the existing body will die and, in that sense, be destroyed; and the resurrection body, as Paul will say later on in this letter (15:35–44), is in some sense radically different from the body that goes into the grave.

The term *body*, for Paul, normally refers to the unity and wholeness of the human being.[16] The distinction here, then, must be between foods as something relatively peripheral to the person as a whole—something that does not involve one's full humanity—and sex as being more central. What belongs to Christ now and what God will raise from death is the whole person:

> Do you not know that your bodies are members of Christ? So then, am I to take Christ's members and make them members of a harlot? May it not happen! Do you not know that the person who cleaves to a harlot is one body [with her]? "For the two," it says, "will become one flesh." But the person who cleaves to the Lord is one spirit [with him]. (6:15–17)

The Christian's body already belongs to Christ, whether this is symbolized as the unity of Christ's body or as a kind of marital union with Christ. All sexual expression, then, must take Christ's ownership into account.

Sex with a prostitute might seem to establish no relationship at all beyond the brief one required for the satisfaction of desire. Paul, however, in a daring interpretation of Genesis 2:24, claimed that every sexual act between a man and woman established a union of flesh like that of marriage, although not, apparently, indissoluble. In other words, the prostitute and the man who has used her actually belong to each other for the duration of their sexual intercourse, although not beyond. The man who rented the prostitute no doubt thought of this "ownership" as being entirely on his side. Not so, according to Paul; he also becomes her property and makes his body part of hers. In Paul's own terminology, the relationship thus established is "one body", but in the terminology of Genesis, it is a relationship of "one flesh." For Paul, "flesh" referred not to the whole person but to what in us resists God, so he could also argue that the union created by an isolated sexual act is animated by "flesh" and therefore pulls one away from God. The believer's bodily union with Christ, on the other hand, is not "one flesh," but "one spirit." That is to say, it is animated by the principle that draws one toward God.[17]

Paul was insisting that the man who had intercourse with a prostitute was not unchanged by that act. While the act was not strictly unlawful (at least, for the man), it was destructive of one's spirit, that is, one's relation to Christ and to God:

> Flee from harlotry. Every sin that a person commits is outside the body, but the man who uses harlots is sinning against his own body. Or do you not know that your body is temple of the Holy Spirit that is in you, which you have from God, and you do not belong to yourselves? For you were bought at a price; so glorify God with your body. (6:18–20)

Where Proverbs discouraged a man from using prostitutes because he belonged to his family, Paul discouraged it because he belongs to God. The body, the person as a whole, is the Spirit's temple, into which other forms of worship must not be introduced. One might well ask, then, whether this line of reasoning forbids sexual intercourse altogether.

Some later encratite Christians may have read Paul in that way. Paul's own answer, as we shall see, was more complicated than that.

Marriage

There were people in the Corinthian church who would have preferred a complete rejection of sexual intercourse—who, indeed, were advocating it already, though we do not know on what grounds. The church had sent Paul a letter with enquiries about several matters of outstanding concern, this matter being the first of them, it seems. Paul began his answer by agreeing with abstinence in principle,[18] but discouraging most people from putting it into practice:

> Now, concerning the things about which you wrote—it is a good thing for a man not to touch a woman, but on account of the harlotries let each man have his own wife and each woman have her own husband. Let the husband give to the wife what is due, and in the same way the wife to the husband. The wife does not have authority over her own body, but the husband; in the same way, too, the husband does not have authority over his own body, but the wife. Do not deprive each other, unless perhaps by agreement for a fixed time, to have leisure for prayer—and then come back together so that Satan will not put you to the test on account of your lack of self-control. I am saying this by way of permission, not command. I want all people to be as I am myself, but each person has his own gift [*charisma*] from God, one this and another that. (7:1–7)

Paul will make his reasons for prizing celibacy explicit later. For the moment, the important point was that there was nothing intrinsically wrong with sexual intercourse. Although Paul regarded celibacy as in some sense preferable, he also regarded it as a *charisma* (gift) from God, given only to certain individuals. Paul taught that such gifts were given the individual for the benefit of the church, not as a sign of one's own moral superiority (1 Cor. 12). If a person's sexual drive, then, is too strong to permit celibacy, that only means that his or her gifts lie elsewhere.[19]

For those who had not received the gift of celibacy, Paul had to specify circumstances for sexual intercourse that would not be in conflict with

Christ's ownership of the Christian's body. He found them in Christian marriage. The distinctively Christian thing in Paul's description of marriage was his careful balancing of the husband's sexual ownership of the wife with an equivalent ownership of the husband by the wife. Paul's standards are related to those set by Jesus when he prohibited divorce and expanded the definition of adultery, but they differ in emphasizing the sexual element in marriage. Sexual desire, according to Paul, is a fact of human life that must be reckoned with intelligently and faithfully; it is not to be ignored or rejected categorically. Marriage exists for the sake of mutual sexual satisfaction; neither partner can pursue a sexual course that does not involve the other, whether celibacy or the use of prostitutes, since each is property of the other.[20]

Having set forth this conception of marriage, Paul proceeds to apply it to three distinct groups: those without any marital attachments, those already married, and those who are betrothed. Paul begins, then, by encouraging the unmarried and widowed to remain as he himself is; "but," he says, "if they do not possess self-control, let them marry, for it is better to marry than to be on fire" (7:9). While this may seem a poor recommendation of marriage, it is significant that Paul recognized the satisfaction of sexual desire as a legitimate and sufficient reason for entering into it.[21] The reason for such a position is not immediately clear, but we shall see that it had to do with Paul's convictions about the nearness of the *eschaton*. Continuation of one's family could no longer be the prime reason for marriage, and he was actually constructing a new justification for it in terms of sexual desire and the Reign of God.

The second group Paul addressed was the married. To them, his advice was basically, "Stay as you are." He enunciated the general principle behind this advice at the end of the section he devoted to them:

> Only let each person proceed just as the Lord has apportioned, as the Lord called. And this is how I arrange things in all the churches. Was someone circumcised when called? Let him not be surgically altered to restore a foreskin. Was someone called in the uncircumcised state? Let him not get circumcised. Circumcision is nothing and uncircumcision is nothing—but keeping God's commandments [is what is important]. Let every person stay in the calling in which he or she was called. Were you a slave when called? Let it be

no concern to you; but even if you can become free, rather make use. For the slave called in the Lord is the Lord's freed-person; likewise, the free person called is Christ's slave. You were bought at a price; do not become slaves of human beings. Let each person stay by God, brothers and sisters, in the state in which he or she was called. (7:17-24)

That there is no overt reference to marital status in this passage occasions no difficulty, for the analogy between slaves and other family members was familiar. Paul is emphasizing that sexual and other property matters should be left as much as possible exactly as they were at the point when one became a Christian.

Paul's point—apparently an important one for him because it is how he arranges matters in all the churches—is that, even though one status may be "better" than another, either in terms of the Torah or in social terms or even (like celibacy) in his own reckoning, one cannot recommend oneself to God by changing one's status. Just as the change from uncircumcision to circumcision implied a doubt of the sufficiency of grace (see pp. 95–97), so any change in manner of life, such as a change from marriage to celibacy, could be an unnecessary and unfaithful attempt to make oneself more acceptable in God's sight. We might object that the slave was probably seeking only a more dignified and secure future; Paul assumed that there was no real future this side of the eschaton, only a brief, transitional present.[22]

It is possible that Paul allowed exceptions to this principle in cases where they might serve the good of the church or the proclamation of the gospel. He suggested in his letter to Philemon that he would like him to forgive his runaway slave Onesimus, now a convert of Paul's, and send him back to help Paul in his work; it has long been argued that he was actually hinting that Philemon should emancipate Onesimus for this purpose.[23] Again, Luke tells us that Paul circumcised Timothy, whose mother was Jewish, to make him a more acceptable member of his entourage, working in Jewish communities (Acts 16:1–3). Paul may have been willing, then, to override the principle of "staying the same" for the sake of missionary needs, but, otherwise, it held. Given that the initial subject of 1 Corinthians 7 was sexual abstinence, Paul was asserting this principle of stability to undercut any idea that married believers might "do better," either spiritually or socially, by separating from their spouses.

For Christians married to other Christians, the tradition of Jesus' teaching was decisive for Paul: "For those who are married, I direct—not I, but the Lord—that a wife not be separated from her husband (and even if she is, let her remain unmarried or be reconciled to the husband) and that husband not divorce wife" (7:10–11). Although Paul did not cite the exact words of the tradition here, we can see that he knew its substance in a form closely related to the one in the Sermon on the Mount: "Every man who divorces his wife except for reason of *porneia* makes her commit adultery, and whoever marries a divorced woman is committing adultery" (Matt. 5:32).[24] This version of Jesus' dictum says that remarriage on the part of the divorced woman constitutes adultery, but, like Paul, says nothing about remarriage on the part of the man who has divorced her. Paul probably alluded with some precision to the formula as he knew it, for elsewhere in this discussion, he himself observed an exact balance between the rights of husband and wife. Accordingly, the imbalance here is unlikely to be of his own creating. Paul's interest in the tradition, however, was somewhat different from that of the Synoptic evangelists. They used it to assert the inherent indissolubility of marriage and so deprived the husband of full property rights over the wife. Paul used it rather to discourage all changes of status after conversion. What is at issue for him is not so much the institution of marriage itself as how one ought to live in the last days.

In Paul's churches, however, a good many of his converts were married to non-Christians, who would scarcely have acknowledged a saying of Jesus as authoritative. What is more, Paul himself had drawn a sufficiently trenchant distinction between those inside the church and those outside that his converts might be tempted to think that they had a duty to withdraw from intimate association with outsiders. In this case, too, however, Paul was convinced that people should remain, if possible, as they were:

> And to the others say I, not the Lord: if any brother has a non-believing wife and she consents to live with him, let him not divorce her; and if any woman has a non-believing husband and he consents to live with her, let her not divorce her husband. For the non-believing husband is hallowed in the wife and the non-believing wife in the brother—since otherwise your children would be unclean, but as it is they are holy. If, however, the non-believer separates, so be it.

> The brother or sister is not enslaved in such cases, but God
> has called you in peace. For how do you know, wife, whether
> you will save your husband? Or how do you know, husband,
> whether you will save your wife? (7:12-16)

Paul's principal concern was that the Christian partner in such a relationship should not directly terminate it. While admitting that Jesus' own prohibition of divorce and remarriage could not apply in so unequal a situation, Paul argued that there was a benefit to the children and to the nonbelieving spouse that made the marriage worth preserving.

The nature of the benefit Paul had in mind is not immediately obvious. He describes it, in part, in purity terms. The children of a mixed marriage are "holy," but in the event of a divorce they would become "unclean." It is impossible to give any meaning to this statement in terms of the Torah purity codes because the Christian spouse might as easily be Gentile as Jewish and, in that case, unclean herself or himself.[25] The language, as noted above (pp. 103–04), suggests the creation of a new purity realm defined by baptism. Paul seems to presume that the children were not themselves Christians and would remain with the nonbelieving parent after a divorce. Because the church at Corinth was still only a few years old at this time, one may guess that the marriages in question were not recent matches between Christian and non-Christian partners, but existing marriages in which only one spouse had been converted. The nonbelieving partner, then, would have reason to claim that the other's conversion had supervened upon their prior contract for a normal Jewish or Gentile marriage. But what would be missing for the children after a divorce? Some edifying influence the Christian parent might be presumed to have on them? Perhaps. A more concrete explanation, however, is available by comparison with what Paul said about prostitution.

Paul objected to Christian males visiting prostitutes because the body that belonged to the Lord could not also belong to a prostitute. That objection might seem to be equally valid as against mixed marriages; Paul did, in fact, say later that widows might remarry "only in the Lord" (7:39). (Consistency would demand that he also forbid the contracting of mixed marriages for the young, but the subject is never mentioned.) The existing marriage, however, which became a mixed marriage only by conversion of one spouse, was another matter. The Christian spouse "belonged" both to Christ and to a nonbeliever. This created an impossible tension, which Paul apparently resolved by declaring that, actually, in these cases, Christ's ownership extended through the believing partner to the whole family. Thus, the children are "holy," because they are, at one remove, part of that community that is the Spirit's temple (6:19). Paul even applied the same principle, though more hesitantly, to the nonbelieving spouse: "How do you know whether you will save your husband or wife?"[26]

If the Christian allegiance of the believer, however, became intolerable for the nonbelieving spouse, that was another matter. The Christian was not "enslaved" and could accept a divorce initiated by the other party. Paul was not explicit as to whether the Christian was then free to remarry, but that is probably what he intended. After all, if the other partner were determined on a divorce, the Christian probably could not refuse it. If there was any point in saying that the believer was not "enslaved," it has to have meant that such a one was free both to consent to the divorce and to continue a normal life after it. While this may seem to fly in the face of the demands of Jesus cited earlier, it was in tune with the emphasis found in the Gospels that laws exist to enhance a faithful human life, not to place burdens on it: "The Sabbath was made for humanity, not humanity for the Sabbath."

For Paul, then, the unmarried were free to marry, although he advocated celibacy, and the married were not to seek any change in their status. There remained, however, an uncomfortable middle zone between these two groups—the betrothed. These will have been younger people whose families had contracted marriages for them, but who were just reaching the age when it would be normal for the marriage to be consummated. Although they were not married, they were obligated to one another—and to one another's families—in a way that was only just short of marriage. Were they, like the unmarried, to be encouraged to remain celibate? Or were they, like the married, to be admonished to stick by their existing obligations? Either way, they must inevitably make some change, since betrothal was never intended to be a permanent status.

Paul seems to have found this a thoroughly awkward situation and sought to resolve it by discouraging further betrothals and by permitting those already betrothed either to proceed with the marriage or to prolong the betrothal indefinitely:

Now, concerning the virgins, I have no command of the Lord, but I give a considered opinion as one who has received mercy from the Lord to be trustworthy. I consider, then, that what really is good in light of the imminent distress—that it is good for one to be as one is. Are you bound to a wife? Do not seek dissolution of the relationship. Are you unattached? Do not seek a wife. But even if you do marry, you have not sinned, and if the virgin marries, she has not sinned. But such will have tribulation for the flesh, and I [am trying to] spare you. . . .

But if anyone considers that he is behaving in a disgraceful way toward his virgin, if he is a person of strong passions and this is how it needs to be, let him do what he wishes; he is not sinning; let them get married. The man who has taken a firm stand in his heart, however, being under no compulsion, and has authority over his own will and has come in his own heart to a determination to keep his virgin, he will do well. Thus, the man who marries his virgin does well and the one who does not will do better. (7:25–28, 36–38)

Throughout this long and awkward passage, Paul assumes that the man alone will make the final decision to proceed with the marriage or not—a breech of his usual insistence on mutuality, but consistent with existing social realities. He offers the man the option of "keeping his virgin," apparently meaning that he would continue the betrothal indefinitely. One may guess this would mean taking on a husband's responsibilities in most respects, for the bride's family might not smile on the prospect of her living a cloistered existence under their wing for the rest of her life.[27] The other choice is to proceed with the marriage. Paul expects the man to decide on the basis of his own sexual needs.[28] If he is in an unforced control of his sexual desires, he can do what Paul most approved—remain celibate. If not, Paul is at pains to insist that sexual intercourse is not sinful and that marriage is its appropriate context.

Because Paul is abrogating existing agreements when he allows an indefinitely continued betrothal, he has to state very clearly why he thinks celibacy a good thing. He does not base his positive evaluation of it on a rejection of sexual desire or sexual intercourse as such, but on the nearness of the Reign of God, whose advent he expects will be preceded by a time of tribulation for the righteous. Celibacy will give those who practice it a kind of single-mindedness that will make this period easier to get through:

> [The married] will have tribulation for the flesh, and I [am trying to] spare you. This is what I mean, brothers: the allotted time is limited from now on, so that even those who have wives are to be as if they did not and those who mourn as if they did not and those who rejoice as if they did not and those who buy as if they did not take possession and those who use the world as if they did not use it up. For the form of this world is passing away. And I want you to be free from care. The unmarried man cares about the Lord's business, how to please the Lord; but the married man cares about the world's business, how to please his wife—and he is divided. And the unmarried woman and the virgin cares [sic; unclear whether there are one or two categories] about the Lord's business, to be holy both in body and in spirit; but the married woman cares about the world's business, how to please her husband. I am saying this for your own good, not to throw a noose over you, but with a view to [your being] presentable and constant toward the Lord without distraction. (7:28–35)

For Paul, the value of celibacy is directly related to the chaotic and troubling times that have already begun and will lead shortly to the end of this world and the inbreaking of the Reign of God. Those who are divided, being still entangled in the world's business, will have much trouble. The ideal is to be able to wait on the Lord without further distraction.[29] Paul does not therefore advocate abandonment of existing marriages or of one's livelihood, yet, even in these, one must be alert not to treat them as of ultimate importance. Hence, Paul is reluctant to see believers change their existing state, whether in terms of marriage or free/slave status or ethnic identity because such changes imply too great a concern for the world's business. The one exception is for those whose sexual desires are too strong to permit a choice of celibacy. Given his position that resorting to prostitutes is not consistent with Christ's ownership of the believer,

Paul encourages these people to marry and affirms that to do so, although not the best choice in a perilous time, is entirely innocent.[30]

Summary

1 Corinthians 5–7 shows Paul working out the implications of a few basic principles related to sexual property. Paul begins with the existing sense of sexual property. He takes the existing definitions of incest (at least, where Jewish and Gentile definitions agreed) for granted. He freely uses the language of property in speaking about the relation of husband and wife. He condemns adultery as a property offense, and he strongly opposes resorting to prostitutes. In all this, his version of the property ethic is not materially different from that of the ancient Israelite tradition. Still, what is centrally important for Paul is not that tradition, but another kind of property relationship that takes precedence over it.

All Christians belong to Christ and all other forms of ownership must be made to accommodate this overarching reality. This theme is not entirely new with Paul. His habit of speaking about women as the equals of men in the matter of sexual property is comparable to the tradition of Jesus' teaching as found in the Synoptic Gospels; his insistence on the priority of "the Lord's business" is comparable to the demands Jesus made in terms of discipleship. Still, Paul presents these ideas in terms of his own coherent framework, beginning with the principle that Christ owns the believer and insisting that sexual life acknowledge this. Sex with prostitutes cannot do so, but sex with a believing spouse does and is therefore a good thing. Even if the spouse is unconverted, the stability of the married relationship means that Christ's ownership can be thought of as extending, at one remove, to the nonbelievers in the family. New marriages, however, are to be contracted only "in the Lord." Finally, belonging to Christ means that the Christian will soon be passing through a period of trials that will conclude the time span of this world and usher in the Reign of God. Insofar as marriage means attachment to household and therefore to the values of this world, it is, like circumcision, social status, or business, a distraction from the Christian's true loyalties. Accordingly, Paul reckons it inferior to celibacy, not as being sinful, but as representing a danger to single-mindedness in the eschaton.

WOMEN AND FAMILY LIFE

Despite all that has been said, Paul, in some ways, was conservative—perhaps uncritically so—in his appraisal and acceptance of contemporary family life, particularly as regards the status of slaves and women. When he is speaking most deliberately, he asserts the equality of women, as we have seen. In 1 Corinthians 7, we have found him balancing virtually every statement of the husband's authority over the wife with an equivalent acknowledgment of the wife's authority over the husband. This had its foundation not only in the tradition of Jesus' sayings about divorce, but also in the early Christian conviction that women were capable of praying and learning as well as men. Thus, Paul allows a married couple to refrain from sexual intercourse temporarily because it will allow *both* of them leisure for prayer (7:5).

Paul refers to baptism as establishing the fundamental principle: "All of you that have been baptized into Christ have put on Christ. There is neither Jew nor Greek; there is neither slave nor free person; there is no male and female. For you are all one person in Christ Jesus; and if you belong to Christ, then you are seed of Abraham, heirs by promise" (Gal. 3:27–29).[31] When Paul uses this formula elsewhere, however, he omits the reference to "male and female" (1 Cor. 12:12–13; Col. 3:11), and his attitude toward women in the church is not always so egalitarian as in the matter of marriage. Later in 1 Corinthians—if the passage is in fact genuine—he forbids women to speak in the church gathering, "for they are not permitted to speak, but let them be subordinate, just as the Law also says. And if they want to learn something, let them ask their own husbands at home, for it is shameful for a woman to speak in an assembly" (14:34–35).[32]

Paul makes an exception for women who are "praying and prophesying" (1 Cor. 11:3–16). Yet he insists that, in doing so, they must wear a veil (or perhaps wear their hair in a certain way) as sign of their subordinate status. On behalf of this rule, he uses arguments that are in sharp contrast to the Galatian formula and even to his treatment of marriage. For example, in the opening words of the passage, he says: "I want you to know that every man's head is Christ, but a woman's head is the man, and Christ's head is God" (11:3). Or again: "It is not man from woman, but woman from man; for in fact man was not created for woman's sake, but woman for man's sake" (11:8–9). Paul must have sensed that this argument was in conflict with what he held elsewhere, for, having advanced it, he at once pulls back: "Except that there is no woman without man nor man without woman in the Lord; for just as the woman is from the man, so also the man is through the woman—and all things are from God" (11:11–12). The operative principle perhaps comes to expression only in Paul's concluding statement: "If anyone chooses to be quarrelsome, we have no such custom, nor do the assemblies of God" (11:16). Paul finds Corinthian practice peculiar and wants to bring it into line with churches elsewhere.[33]

The freedom that the women of the Corinthian church enjoyed was unexampled in Paul's experience, however much it might seem to be implicit in his own teaching. He could not very well forbid them to prophesy. That would seem to be resisting the Spirit, forbidden by Paul elsewhere (1 Thess. 5:19–20). In any case, prophesying by women had a venerable history in Israel and, according to Luke, had been a part of Christian practice from the beginning (Acts 2:1–21). Paul was convinced, however, that women in the church were still, as it were, metaphysically dependent on men. He could therefore forbid them to function in their own right in the assemblies and could demand that, when the Spirit chose a woman to prophesy, she do so in garb that expressed her subordinate status.

I have suggested elsewhere that this inconsistency reflects the sacral nature of equality in the early Christian church.[34] Women and men were fully equal as participants in the central rites of baptism and the Lord's Supper, but not always outside that context. Paul's "no male and female" was part of a formula that defined the meaning of baptism; the presence of women at the assemblies in Corinth shows that they were participating in the Lord's Supper, which took place there (11:18). In prophesying, women were exercising a gift of the Spirit that could not be denied. Yet, as Paul argued in another context, prophetic spirits were subject to the prophets (14:32–33), and this allowed the churches to specify when, where, and in what garments women might prophesy. Thus, even in the matter of prophecy, Paul was able to justify treating women as less than fully equal.

Why, then, was Paul so careful to formulate his teaching on marriage in a way that emphasized the equal and inviolable ownership of both spouses? We must note that he did so only in the case of believers who were already married to one another. In the case of mixed marriages, Christ's ownership of the believing spouse reached out through her or him to the rest of the household, but not in a permanent way because divorce could take place. In the case of Christians who were betrothed, Paul acknowledged no rights on the part of the female; the male alone was to make the decision about whether to proceed with the marriage—and he was to make it on the basis of his own sexual needs. It appears that, for Paul, equality in marriage was rather narrowly circumscribed, referring only to sexual rights in the most limited sense in marriages already consummated between believers. One begins to suspect that even this much egalitarianism, outside the strictly sacral sphere of the sacraments, was actually foreign to Paul's personal outlook. It may have owed its presence in his teaching entirely to existing practice and the tradition of Jesus' words about divorce. To be sure, Paul refers to the latter (1 Cor. 7:10–11) only in their least egalitarian form, but, even in that form, the prohibition of divorce was sufficient to bring the man's unique ownership of his wife to an end.

Paul does defend the areas of equality, marital and sacral, and insist that the goals of the household must yield to the imminence of God's Reign. He does not, however, draw the conclusion that the household itself has to be reshaped. Perhaps his conviction that the *eschaton* was very close made projects of social reform seem pointless, or perhaps his own celibacy, in response to the eschaton, meant that household structures had no existential importance for him. Whatever the reason, he says little or nothing about them in his undoubted letters. He broke this silence only in Colossians, which, if it is truly his own and not the product of one of his followers, is unusual in several respects. For one thing, it is addressed to a church that Paul himself had neither founded nor visited personally, although it emerged from his mission through the work of Epaphras. For another, its language and theology are full of an atypical cosmic concern that may reflect the interests of other teachers who were at work at Colossae—teachers the author opposed.

These Colossian teachers were probably ascetics. They told people, "Do not handle, do not taste, do not touch all the things that perish with use" (Col. 2:21–22).[35] The author grants that such rigorism has "a rationale of wisdom in the form of will-worship and humility—severity toward the body," but he also insists that it is "of no value in relation to gratification of the flesh" (2:23). "Will-worship," apparently a term here for asceticism, might even serve to gratify the "flesh," in Paul's sense of the word; for the flesh, being what in us resists God, can actually seek refuge from grace in the cultivation of a righteousness of works. Paul rejects not only the works righteousness implicit in such asceticism, but also its negative assessment of the material world—"all the things that perish with use." He considered foods, in and of themselves, to be irrelevant to salvation, and he regarded sexual desire, if it were insistent, as something to be satisfied in an appropriate way.

In responding to this asceticism, Paul seeks to lead the Colossian congregation back toward an ethic more consistent with his own teaching. As a good rhetorician, he starts with language that appeals to their existing ascetical concerns, warning them against "harlotry, impurity, passion, lust [literally, evil desire]," but he concludes the list, "and greed [pleonexia], which is idolatry," thus pulling it into the orbit of "purity of the heart" (Col. 3:5). He follows this with another list of vices, this time of a more social nature ("anger, fury, wickedness, blasphemy, shameful speech"), and then concludes, "Do not lie to one another" (3:8–9). Finally, he introduces a list of contrary virtues to be cultivated: "compassionate feelings, goodness, humility, gentleness, long-suffering," forbearance, forgiveness, "and, above all, love" (3:12–14).

This effort to lead the congregation away from asceticism and toward a more social understanding of virtue forms the context for the treatment of family life. Asceticism threatened to undercut the family even more completely than the teaching of Jesus and Paul, insofar as it wanted not just to subordinate sex to the Reign of God but also to reject it as intrinsically evil. The author responded by reaffirming traditional Greco-Roman household mores:[36]

> Wives, be subject to your husbands, as is appropriate in the Lord.

> Husbands, love your wives and do not grow bitter toward them.

> Children, obey your parents in all respects, for this is well-pleasing in the Lord.

> Parents, do not goad your children, so that they will not grow dispirited.

Slaves, obey in all respects your lords according to flesh, not in outward appearance as if you were pleasing human beings, but fearing the Lord in simplicity of heart. Whatever you do, work from the heart as for the Lord and not for human beings, knowing that from the Lord you will receive the inheritance as your reward. Be slaves of the Lord Christ, for the unjust person will get back the injustice committed and there is no favoritism.

Lords, practice justice and equity toward your slaves, knowing that you, too, have a Lord in heaven. [Col. 3:18–4:1]

Nothing in this passage will have seemed new or unusual, except perhaps for the reassurance offered slaves of an eventual righting of the imbalance. (Note that nothing comparable is offered to wives.)

The great question is why Paul, if he is the author, should have bothered to say it at all, since he did not think it necessary to do so in other letters. The principal answer suggested by the letter itself is the one already noted: reaffirming the traditional household serves to combat anti-material asceticism. There may have been another reason as well. Having urged the Colossians to pray for themselves and for him, Paul continues: "Conduct yourselves with wisdom toward the outsiders, buying up what time there is. Let your speech always be gracious, seasoned with salt, so that you will know how you must answer each person individually" (Col. 4:5–6). This concern for public opinion will not have been without cause. Ascetic teaching that prohibited sexual intercourse could create, by its disruption of family life, serious public antagonisms like those that occasioned the near-fatal misadventures of Thecla in the rousing second-century Christian romance called *Acts of Paul*. Reinforcement of traditional household mores and a concern for prudence in relationships with outsiders are parallel ways of protecting a community that was emerging into unwelcome notoriety.

The associate of Paul who drafted Ephesians appears to have used Colossians as a model. Because Ephesians is of a more general character (perhaps originally a circular letter, not addressed to any single church), it does not speak to the specific problems of asceticism and public opinion that were so prominent at Colossae. Partly for this reason, it has the effect of making the conservatism of its borrowed family ethic seem more a matter of principle and less one of temporary needs. The author enlarges on the relatively brief formulas of Colossians. In the matter of the wife's subordination to the husband, he added a theological justification related to those Paul used in 1 Corinthians 11 to justify his insistence that women wear veils when prophesying: "The husband is the wife's head, as Christ in turn is the church's head, being savior of the body" (Eph. 5:23). This is a doctrine of "one flesh," but without any egalitarian implications. The author also adapts Paul's image of the church as Christ's bride to provide a model for relations between spouses, returning to the "one flesh" pronouncement in Genesis to support this interpretation. He treats the Genesis passage, however, not as a direct statement about human marriage, but as a "mystery" to be understood allegorically of Christ's relationship to the church and only thence as a model for human marriages. The point of this exercise is not, as in Jesus' teaching, to affirm the indissolubility of marriage or the equality of the wife, but to construct a hierarchical analogy: as Christ is to church, husband is to wife. In the process, it would seem that even the degree of equality that Paul had defended in 1 Corinthians 7 has been lost.

CONCLUSIONS

Paul regarded sexual desire as a natural appetite, although one too central to human identity to be treated as casually as hunger. Christians were to restrict the satisfaction of this appetite to forms consistent with the fact that they are the property of Christ. This demanded a respect for the property of others, and Paul retained major features of Mediterranean culture's existing property code for sexuality. Adultery continued to be a serious ethical violation, and Paul was capable of becoming quite angry about a case of incest. He strongly opposed the use of prostitutes, although his condemnation is less stringent than with adultery or incest. His objection to *arsenokoitai*, whoever they were, also seems to have had a basis in respect for property. More positively, he regarded marriage "in the Lord" as normal for those Christians who did not have the gift or *charisma* of celibacy, but he tolerated existing mixed marriages and even found some value in them. He believed that, because of the imminence of the *eschaton*, celibacy was a better choice for Christians than marriage, but he was careful to avoid any implication that marriage and sexual intercourse were at all wrong in themselves.

Paul regarded women as equal to men in the receiving of baptism and the Lord's Supper and also, in a somewhat more limited sense, in terms of sexual ownership. He was careful to assert that, with regard to sexual intercourse, the wife owned the husband in the same way as the husband owned the wife. He also adhered to the tradition of Jesus that prohibited divorce, although he adapted it somewhat in dealing with betrothals and mixed marriages. Outside these rather narrow confines, he believed that women must show subordination to men, even in their exercise of the gifts of the Spirit. He manifested a continuing acceptance, on the whole, of the family mores common to both Jews and Gentiles of the time.

Paul's tendency to leave things as they were took on the character of a principle insofar as the imminence of the *eschaton* implied that working for major change, either in society or in the status of individuals, was only misplaced effort. In his earlier letters, however, he did not much trouble himself to reinforce the traditional family ethic; only in Colossians, if it is indeed his, did he explicitly confirm the validity of the patriarchal household. The ascetic nature of the heresy at Colossae—its negation of the material world as such—provided the occasion for this shift in emphasis. Paul wanted to reassert the value of the material world and also to distinguish those who adhered to his teaching from those who would disrupt households for ascetic reasons. By confirming dominant Greco-Roman household mores, he accomplished both purposes at once. The disciple of Paul who wrote Ephesians, however, converted this teaching, with the help of other Pauline motifs, into something like a principled acceptance of the very household structures that Jesus had undercut so sharply in his ministry and that the earlier Paul had apparently regarded as peripheral.

CHAPTER 11

THE NEW TESTAMENT ON SEXUAL PROPERTY

Compared with the Gospels and the core works of the Pauline corpus, the remaining books of the New Testament have less to say about sexual ethics. As regards specific issues, they share, at most, a general opposition to adultery. These works are important, however, for their ways of dealing with the household and the hierarchies implicit in it. In this area, they reveal tensions like those we have seen in the writings of Paul and his associates—tensions between the tradition of Jesus' egalitarianism and rejection of the household and the developing Christian acceptance of and adaptation to existing household structures. Some fall nearer to one pole of these tensions, some to the other.

THE CHURCH AS REPLACING THE HOUSEHOLD
1–3 John

The three letters that bear the name of John never refer unambiguously to family life, yet they are full of language expressing family relationships: fathers, brothers, and children, all of whom are "beloved." By itself, this language might not seem significant, but in a context that entirely ignores the literal family structure from which the language was borrowed, it suggests that, at least in theory, the church had replaced the family in this tradition. This shift could occasionally give rise to a peculiar way of speaking. The author, for example, wrote to Gaius: "Beloved, you are performing a faithful act in whatever you do for the brothers—and strangers at that!—who have testified to your love in the presence of the church" (3 John 5–6). The church now constituted the Christian's family, with the odd result that complete strangers might be able to claim the most intimate relationship.

The masculine gender of much of this language is notable, but it need not signify any retreat from the equality of women. Because the masculine was also the common gender in Hellenistic Greek, particularly in the plural, "fathers" could serve as the equivalent of "parents" and "brothers" would be the normal way of saying "brothers and sisters." For "children," the author used terms of neuter gender (*teknon*, *teknion*). He also addressed one of his letters to "the elect lady and her children" (2 John 1). One cannot be sure whether he was addressing an individual Christian woman and her dependents (perhaps the church that met in her home) or whether he was personifying a church in the feminine.[1] In either case, however, he did not treat the feminine gender as intrinsically less worthy than the masculine.

James

The epistle of James implies a similar set of attitudes. Like the Johannine letters, it uses the expression "brothers" to a degree that is out of proportion to its length in comparison with other New Testament writings. Its author insists on a lively and practical standard of mutual concern within the community (2:15–16) and particularly insists on the care of the "unfamilied" as a central expression of religion: "Pure and unpolluted religion with [our] God and Father is this: to look after orphans and widows in their trouble, to keep oneself unspotted from the world" (1:27). As we have seen (pp. 131–32), "to keep oneself unspotted" in this context probably meant to refrain from participating in angry contests for church leadership. The contrast, then, is between the struggle to achieve dominance in the Christian community and a willingness to devote oneself instead to the benefit of those without influence or authority—and quite without any claim on one's energies.[2]

In the teaching of Jesus, we found that this kind of negation of family was associated with a positive view of women. That the same is true for James is evident in his habit of using female imagery or language alongside male. Even in referring to the individual Christian, where "brother" by itself would have been sufficient in Greek to refer to either sex, James on one occasion specifies "brother or sister" (2:15). He also balances male with female imagery in referring to God: "Every good giving and every complete [*or* perfect] gift is from above, coming down from the Father of the [heavenly] lights, with whom there is no variation or shadow of cast by turning. He has freely given birth[3] to us by a word of truth so that we would become the firstfruits of his creatures" (1:17–18). Again, in arguing for the necessary complementarity of works and faith, James employs both a male example (Abraham's sacrifice of Isaac) and a female one: "And in the same way, too, was not Rahab the harlot justified by works when she received the messengers and hurried them off by another route?" (2:25). Such deliberate balancing of male and female is unusual in the New Testament.

James reaffirms the commandment against adultery. In the specific context, however, he seems less interested in the commandment for its own sake than for its rhetorical usefulness. He assumes that his audience will not have committed adultery, but observes that keeping one commandment is not the same as keeping the whole Law: "For the one who said, 'Do not commit adultery,' also said, 'Do not kill.' If you do not commit adultery but you do kill, you have become a transgressor of the Law" (2:11). In the immediate context of the passage, this serves to underline James's point that showing partiality to the rich is as grave an offense as any other (2:1–10). In the larger scheme of the work, it prepares for the moment when James will call his (presumptively male) audience "adulteresses" because of the strife they perpetrate within the church (4:1–12). In due course, he will even intimate that they are, in some sense, murderers, by associating them with the rich who killed Jesus (5:1–6). Thus, for James, adultery and murder, partiality toward the rich in the church, and the crucifixion of Jesus are all on a single continuum of transgression, so that the person who is guilty of one is, by extension, guilty of all. This need not mean that James regarded them all as equally grave offenses; we do not know his teaching on that aspect of the matter. It does mean that he regarded them all equally as offenses and indications of grave deficiencies in the character of their perpetrators. James, accordingly, defends the rights of sexual property, but otherwise undermines the foundations of the ancient household by the attention he pays to the poor, the widow and orphan, and women generally.[4]

THE CHURCH AS INCORPORATING THE FAMILY

1 Peter

If the letters of John and James represent the anti-family end of the spectrum, 1 Peter and the Pastorals stand at the pro-family end—and do so largely without benefit of the nuances we found in Paul's writings. The author of 1 Peter strongly affirms hierarchy in society at large and in the household.[5] Christians are to obey the imperial government strictly, even though they might in some sense claim to be free of it by virtue of their relationship with the one God (2:13–17). As an extension or application of this general social duty, Christian servants are to obey their owners (2:18–25). If this involves unfair hardships at the hands of a harsh master, they can take comfort in the fact that, like them, Jesus too suffered unjustly. "In the same way," the author continues, wives are to be subject to their husbands. Even men who are not believers may yet be converted by their wives' modest, plain, and unassuming behavior, and the women will have the benefit of knowing that they were imitating "the holy women" of old, specifically Sarah, who called Abraham her "lord" (3:1–6, referring to Gen. 18:12). Both slaves and wives, then, are to accept their subordinate roles in the household without complaint.

Unlike Colossians and Ephesians, 1 Peter has no directions about the behavior of the Christian slave-owner. This could indicate either that the author's presumed audience did not include such or that he trusts them to behave properly without special directions. He does give directions to Christian husbands. These are less demanding than those in Colossians and Ephesians but do remind them that their wives are members of the Christian community in their own right: "You husbands in the same way—live together with the female sex according to knowledge, as with a weaker vessel, apportioning honor as to those who are also co-heirs of life's grace, so as not to impede your prayers" (3:7). The "knowledge" that is to govern the husband's dealings with his wife is twofold: knowledge of her intrinsic weakness and knowledge of her status in the grace that gives life. The wife, consequently, is to be understood as having a kind of mixed status, partly inferior to the husband and partly equal. Under the circumstances, he is to remain in charge, dealing with her variously as her composite character demands.[6] The goal of all his dealings with her is to keep prayer unhindered—but whose prayers? His or those of the married couple? The language does not permit an assured answer; one cannot be sure to what extent the Christian woman was still an active participant in the church's prayer and to what extent she was now only a passive recipient of salvation.

The conservatism of these family ethics is not incidental to 1 Peter, but it serves a part in the larger purpose of rendering the Christian communities as conventional and respectable as possible. "Keep your conduct good among the Gentiles, so that when they slander you as evildoers, they may see some of your good works and glorify God on the day of visitation" (1:12). Perhaps the author is partly concerned with paving the way for conversions (as in the case of Christian women with nonbelieving husbands), but he is also aiming to moderate the kind of public hostility toward Christians that was threatening to break out into serious persecution (4:12–19). The first line of defense is to make it hard for outsiders to find a complaint against Christians: "And who will do you harm if you have become zealous for what is good?" (3:13). A conservative family life is one essential bulwark of respectability.[7]

The Pastoral Epistles

First Peter is not entirely without a sense of the church as replacing the family. "Love of the brothers" was still an important virtue (3:8). Yet the main concern was to approximate the public virtues of the environing society. The Pastoral Epistles take up a somewhat more central position in the overall spectrum. Their author is still aware of the importance of women in the church's early development. He notes that Timothy first learned his faith from his mother and grandmother (2 Tim. 1:5), and he still names Prisca (or Priscilla) before her husband (2 Tim. 4:19). He retains enough sense of the church as family to admonish Timothy that he should treat the older members as if they were his parents and the younger ones like brothers and sisters. In practical terms, however, the church functions as family mostly for those who have no alternative, especially childless widows.

The author of 1 Timothy wishes to regulate and restrict the status of "widow," which must have carried a certain prestige in the church. Officially registered widows, it seems, pledged not to remarry (5:11–12). Paul had not regarded celibacy as a virtue in and of itself, but only as a means of leaving oneself free for the Lord's business. In this later Pauline tradition, then, it seems likely that the widows will have served some special role in the church's life, and this, in turn, may have attracted to their order women of influence within the community, regardless of their need for financial support. It is even possible that unmarried women were being enrolled as "widows" in this sense. The author's anxiety about the misbehavior of the younger women, who he fears will become lazy gadabouts and busybodies (5:13), suggests that the widows were, in effect, the church's principal pastors to and among women. The author aims at reducing their numbers and converting them from an order of ministers into a class of indigents within the church.

On the whole, one must reckon this author as unfriendly to equality between the sexes. It is not surprising, then, that he is also an advocate of the traditional household within the church. Although he does not provide a detailed listing of obligations, such as those in Colossians, Ephesians, and 1 Peter, he urges the same kind of household morality. Slaves are to be obedient to their owners (Titus 2:9–10), particularly if the owners are Christians (1 Tim. 6:1–2). The older women of the church[8] are to teach the younger ones to be domestic and submissive to their husbands (Titus 2:6–8). The author says nothing at all to slave owners or to husbands about their obligations to their subordinates. Because both categories are clearly represented within the communities he is addressing, his silence probably reflects a certain identification with them and an assumption that the other groups were the "problems." He sees husbands and masters as stable, moral, respectable folk, while slaves and women tend to be unruly elements.

In the case of women, at least, the author demands their subordination not only in the household, but also in the life of the church as a whole, and he justifies this demand theologically. It is the business of the men of the congregation to pray, of the women to be modest and to adorn themselves with good works (1 Tim. 2:8–10). "Let a woman learn in silence in all submission; and I do not permit a woman to teach or to have authority over a man, but to be in silence. For Adam was made first, then Eve; and Adam was not tricked, but the woman was tricked and wound up in transgression. She will be saved, however, through childbearing—if they remain in faith and hope and sanctification with moderation. This is a reliable saying" (1 Tim. 2:11–3:1). It is difficult in the extreme to coordinate this "reliable saying" with another from the same author that insists God has saved us "not as a result of works of righteousness which we ourselves have done, but according to his own mercy through a washing of rebirth and renewal of Holy Spirit" (Titus 3:4–8). One may wonder whether he regards Paul's doctrine of justification by grace through faith alone as applying only to males, while females are to be saved through bearing children with faith, hope, sanctification, and moderation. However this may be, our author has brought us a long way from Paul—not in his demand for some degree of subordination or in his reading of the order of creation in Genesis 2, both of which are found in Paul, but in this astonishing and unprecedented theology of childbearing.[9]

The emphasis in the Pastoral Epistles on hierarchy is not confined to the household or to relationships between the sexes. On a world level, the author emphasizes the duty of Christians to pray for the emperors and others in power (1 Tim. 2:1–4) and to be obedient to them (Titus 3:1–3). Within the church itself, there is also a clear chain of authority descending from above. Speaking in Paul's persona, the author writes, "For God is one, and one also the mediator between God and human beings, the human being Christ Jesus, who has given himself as a ransom for many, the testimony for our own times, for which reason I have been appointed herald and apostle—I am telling the truth, I am not lying—teacher of Gentiles in faith and truth" (1 Tim. 2:5–7). Thus, God's sovereignty is manifest in the rule of the emperor and his subordinates (2:1–3), in the work of Christ and the ministry of his agent Paul (2:4–7), in the priority of men over women in the church (2:8–15)—and not least in the ordering or reordering of the church's formal structure that the author of the Pastorals aims to achieve (3:1–13).

Without question, one of the major desiderata of the author of these letters is the establishment of a regularized local ministry based on holders of office (*episkopoi, presbyteroi, diakonoi*) as opposed to charismatic figures such as apostles, prophets, and teachers. To that end, the author writes in the person of Paul himself, addressing associates of Paul whom he represents as the apostle's delegates, responsible for the regularization of ministry in specific provinces (Timothy in Asia, Titus in Crete). Qualifications for the offices in question, if summed up, amount to a description of the prosperous male householder who is respected both in the larger community and in the church and who can be counted on to administer the church's hospitality appropriately and not to misappropriate the church's funds for his own use or pleasure (1 Tim. 3:1–13; Titus 1:5–9). The job of such an officer is to keep order within the church, particularly by correcting or silencing false teachers (1 Tim. 4:1–7; Titus 1:10–11). It is possible that women as well as men are admitted to the diaconate (1 Tim. 3:11).

(It is unclear whether *gynaikas* refers to female deacons or to the wives of men in that office.) Even if they are, however, men clearly dominate the author's scheme for the reordering of the church.

The emphasis in the Pastorals on traditional Mediterranean family life represents the author's thoroughgoing identification with the typical male householder and, indeed, the hierarchical principle as such, whether applied to household, empire, or church. Under these circumstances, of course, it would also be necessary for the author to insist on the inviolability of sexual property, and we have already seen that he does so (pp. 127–28). In this regard, he is consistent with the earlier Pauline tradition. On the whole, however, his development of the sexual property ethic contrasts significantly with that of Paul. His subordination of women, while anticipated to a degree in 1 Corinthians 11 and 14, lacks the balancing influence of an acknowledgment of their religious equality, as in 1 Corinthians 7. What is more, the radical subordination of the household to the Reign of God essentially disappears from this author's thought.[10]

Hebrews

The epistle to Hebrews evinces very little interest in sexual ethics. In relation to the family, however, it expresses an interesting ambivalence that is integral to its author's overall theological stance. On the one hand, the author of this work values what one can only call, using Platonic terminology, the world of "being" over that of "becoming." He praises the priesthood and sacrifice of Christ because, unlike those of the Israelite cultus, they were once-for-all, singular, and eternal. In comparison, the family signifies all that is temporary—subject to decay and incapable of any final achievement. It is sufficient evidence of its insufficiency that the Aaronide priesthood had to be passed down from father to son to circumvent the reality of death (7:23–24). The true model of authentic priesthood is Melchizedek, who was "without father, without mother, without genealogy, having neither beginning of days nor end of life" (7:3). Such arguments suggest a low view of the family as an institution of this passing age, already hastening to its end (1:2).

At the same time, the phenomena of this world may afford shadowy hints of the realities of the world above, which is also the age to come. Thus, the author distinguishes Moses from Christ by the household analogy of servant and son (3:5–6). He explains persecution as a disciplinary beating, analogous to the way a father would train his sons—indeed as proof of the Christians' legitimacy, since even an earthly father would not waste a beating on bastards (12:5–11). And he treats Esau, the *pornos* who sold his birthright, as an image of the failed Christian (12:16). It is not surprising, then, that he advocates continued respect for marriage: "Let marriage be held in honor among all of you and the marriage bed be undefiled, for God will judge *pornoi* and adulterers" (13:4). *Pornoi,* here, may mean men who use prostitutes—the literal sense of the term. On the other hand, the term may be a general one for anyone who holds family property in contempt—the sense in which the author used it in reference to Esau (12:16). The following verse is certainly focused on attitudes toward property: "Let your manner of life not be addicted to money; be satisfied with what you have" (13:5). The author's emphasis on the imminence of the eschaton (e.g., 3:1–4:13) seems to have contributed, like that of Paul, to a sense that one ought to leave the institutions of this world more or less untouched.

Such a tendency may have contributed to the relatively low importance of women in this epistle. In his recital of the heroes of the faith, the author mentions Sarah, but only in passing; one translation of the verse in question is "By faith, even though Sarah was barren, he [Abraham] received power for depositing seed even at [his] time of life" (11:11).[11] In the same list, Rahab the harlot appears, but, unlike James, this author treats her as a passive recipient of rescue rather than an active participant in salvation history (11:31). He also notes that there were women who "received their dead by resurrection" (13:35). The reference is probably to the widow of Zarephath (1 Kings 17:17–24) and the Shunammite woman (2 Kings 4:18–37), but again the language treats them purely as recipients—consumers, as it were—of miracles, without acknowledging their active roles in occasioning them. The epistle to Hebrews, then, while it is not entirely averse to the prominence of women in the Christian community nor entirely committed to family, remains more traditional in this respect than any other New Testament writings except for 1 Peter and the Pastorals.

LICENSE AND SELF-CONTROL (2 PETER)

We noted above (p. 151) that the author of 2 Peter regards licentiousness as a particularly serious issue in his time and as characteristic of the false prophets and false teachers that he attacks. He predicts that "many people will follow them in their licentious acts, on account of whom the way of truth will be blasphemed; and with greed they will make you a source of profit for themselves by means of fabricated sayings" (2:2–3). Accordingly, self-control, as the opposite of license, is a fundamental Christian practice—founded upon faith, virtue, and knowledge, and leading to patience, piety, brotherly affection, and love (1:5–7). The placement of self-control in this list suggests that the author thinks of it less as an end in its own right and more as a means by which one moves from one's basic commitment to the gospel and knowledge of it toward the quasi-familial life of affection and concord in the church. Completely unbridled behavior was bound to be destructive in the church as in any other community.

While the author of 2 Peter draws this motif from Jude (2 Pet. 2:2–3 being based on Jude 4), he expands and underlines it in a way that suggests it was of particular importance to him. He not only includes self-control in his list of Christian virtues; he also interprets the sin of Sodom as license (2:7) and uses the concept of license effectively in a summary indictment of his opponents: "Uttering words of empty bombast, they lure with the desires of the flesh, with acts of license, those who have barely escaped, who are still living in error, promising them freedom, though they themselves are slaves of decay; for whatever one is worsted by, to that one is a slave" (2:18–19). Because he also describes these teachers as "having eyes full of adultery and indefatigable at sin, enticing unstable souls, having a heart practiced at greed [*pleonexia*]" (2:14) and claims that they were shamelessly sybaritic (2:13), it is safe to say that he regarded a complete rejection of limitations on their personal conduct as one of their characteristics. What he called "license," they, as he acknowledged, called "freedom."

The author of 2 Peter, as his conventional linking of adultery and greed shows, assumes that a property ethic should govern sexual acts, but he does not choose to explore that ethic in any detail. His is probably the last of the New Testament books to be written, so the mainstream of Gentile Christianity was probably fairly clear about its definition of sexual morality and he could assume that his hearers know that definition. Teachers who taught otherwise were being excluded on both doctrinal and ethical grounds and categorized as "gnostics."[12] The challenge, then, for this author is no longer one of defining a Christian sexual ethic but of insisting that Christians practice it—insisting, in other words, on the need to accept limitations on the fulfillment of one's desires to make life in an ongoing community possible.

THE REVELATION TO JOHN

The final work in the New Testament canon stands apart from the others in its treatment of the family and sexual property. It is easier, however, to say that its position is distinctive than to say exactly what that position is. There is little reference to or interest in family or household. The sense of extreme urgency about the nearness of the *eschaton* perhaps made it irrelevant. Celebrating the fall of "Babylon," the seer writes, "The voice of bridegroom and bride will never be heard in you again" (18:23). This seems to be the only reference to literal family life in the book. In addition, there is a condemnation of the adultery and *porneia* associated with "Jezebel" (2:20–24), but we have already seen that it is difficult to know exactly how to interpret these (see p. 153). By way of contrast, John's celebration of the 144,000 male virgins suggests a highly negative attitude toward family life (14:4), which, in turn, may help to explain this author's comparative reluctance to use family metaphors in dealing with God and Christ. In this work, Jesus is called "Son of God" only once (2:18),[13] and his Davidic descent is alluded to only twice (5:5; 22:16). God has the title *Father* and John refers to Christians as "brothers" only five times each.

Sexual language is very important for John, however, as a way to speak metaphorically about larger realities. All that is most deeply wrong in the present age is summed up in the figure of the "great harlot, seated beside many waters," clothed in purple and scarlet and riding on the scarlet beast. She is "Babylon," that is, Rome, the persecutor of God's saints (17:1–6). By contrast, the powers of the age to come first descend to earth in the figure of another woman, pregnant, "garbed with the sun, the moon under her feet, and a wreath of twelve stars on her head" (12:1–2). She gives birth to a male child "who is going to shepherd the Gentiles with an iron rod" (12:5)—and also to all the faithful (12:17). This same new age is consummated with the arrival of the New Jerusalem, the Bride of the Lamb (21:9–22:5). Finally, it is the Spirit and the Bride who invite the reader into the new world (22:17).

In the Revelation, sexual and family motifs have a positive value only insofar as they are connected with the world to come. The most appropriate way for the Christian to live in the present may well be virginity. The bridegrooms and brides of this age are doomed to end in sterility in any case. Only the new age can be portrayed as a fertile woman, giving birth to the Messiah and his witnesses. Only the new age affords a fit time and place for the celebration of a marriage feast. While he was never explicit enough for us to be sure, one suspects that John the Seer regarded all sexual activity in this age as inappropriate, if not necessarily sinful, for Christians.

THE NEW TESTAMENT ON SEXUAL PROPERTY

Jesus' teaching, as recounted in the Gospels, sharply diminishes the role, importance, and internal stability of the family. By treating women as equals in sexual ownership and by taking children as symbols of citizenship in the Reign of God, Jesus undercuts the rule of the patriarch, which was the organizing principle of household life among both Jews and Gentiles in his time. Also, by setting the call to discipleship in opposition to the family and its obligations, he radically subordinates family as such to the Reign of God. He does not do so out of some kind of sexual asceticism such as one encounters, later on, in Encratism or Gnosticism. Although he was himself apparently unmarried, there is no suggestion of an antisexual bent in the Gospels themselves. Even in his discussion with the Sadducees, it is marriage that he rules out of the world to come, not sexuality. Jesus does not reject the whole concept of sexual property, but he changes the content of it by making husbands the property of their wives as well as wives of their husbands. Perhaps the most immediate consequence of this shift is to broaden the definition of adultery to include sexual intercourse outside marriage on the part of husband as well as of wife. Matthew, however, depicts the disciples' awareness that this shift effectively destroys the family as they have known it.

As Christianity spread out into the larger Mediterranean world, most converts did not abandon their families, but if one person in a family were converted, this certainly disrupted family expectations about religious observance. With Paul, if not before, a process of adapting Jesus' radical teaching to existing household patterns begins. Although

Paul is careful to acknowledge the wife's ownership of the husband in matters strictly internal to their personal relationship, he demands that in most other respects the usual subordination of wife to husband be retained. He limits women's leadership in the assembly. Though he cannot refuse inspired women the right to prophesy, he prescribes clothing that expresses their subordination. In the household, if he is indeed the author of Colossians, he reasserts a conventional morality for women, children, and slaves.[14]

This does not mean that Paul is reestablishing the primacy of the family. He takes celibacy, in fact, as the form of life most appropriate to the eschatological crisis in which Christians found themselves. (In this, the author of Revelation may have joined him.) His conservatism in matters of the family is rather an expression of his conviction that this was not the time for Christians to make sweeping changes in the life of this world— the same conviction that led him to advise all Christians to remain in the state of life in which they had first been called by God. He recognizes, however, that the charisma of celibacy is not given to all. He discourages married people from denying each other's conjugal rights. And since many single Christians, if he refuses them permission to marry, would resort to forms of sexual expression of which he disapproves on other grounds, he approves of marriage as a way to satisfy male sexual needs. In the process, he becomes the only New Testament author to acknowledge sexual satisfaction as a legitimate and sufficient reason for marriage.

Paul maintains the prohibition of adultery. It is not surprising that, as the accidents of history in the church at Corinth have allowed us to see, he also regards the prohibition of incest, in the ancient Israelite sense, as of continuing validity—at least insofar as it coincided with Gentile definitions. Because he also believes that Christ's relationship with the Christian constitutes a kind of ownership analogous to the father's ownership of the rest of the family, he draws some further ethical conclusions from this principle. Paul's conservatism with regard to day-to-day family life, then, should be understood primarily as an incidental adaptation to the end time. In ethical theory, he is not materially less radical than Jesus.

The other New Testament books, however, show a more mixed picture. While the authors of James and the Johannine Epistles retain a sense of the church as replacing the family, and James gives expression to the equality of women in that context, most of the other authors lean more to the reaffirmation of the traditional household. This is particularly true in 1 Peter and the Pastoral Epistles, where the impetus of Jesus' and Paul's radicalism, at least on this subject, has very nearly spent its force. Their authors are dealing with threats to the church, both external and internal, which they feel require the church to present an unexceptionable face to the public and exert firmer control within its own community. In the process, they convert Paul's eschatologically based acceptance of traditional family mores into a principled insistence on them. Whatever their needs and intentions were at the time, however, this had the subsequent effect of nullifying most of the egalitarianism and the rejection of family found in Jesus' gospel. The Pastorals and 1 Peter have dominated most later Christian thought on the subjects of marriage and women.

Once this traditionalist ethic was widely agreed upon, the only remaining question was whether the average Christian would live up to it. Thus, the author of 2 Peter no longer had to define a sexual ethic, but only to stress the importance of restraint. He agrees with the other New Testament writers (with the possible exception of John the Seer) in accepting the reality and legitimacy of sexual property and an ethic based on it. This apparent agreement, however, masks for us a real gap between the radical ethic of Jesus and that of 1 and 2 Peter or the Pastorals. The ethic of the latter is barely distinguishable from that of the environing culture, Jewish or Gentile.

PART III

SEX

CHAPTER 12

ARE OTHER PRINCIPLES OF SEXUAL ETHICS AT WORK IN THE NEW TESTAMENT?

In the first edition of this work, I argued that no significant principles of sexual ethics other than those of purity and property were at work in the New Testament. In study and discussion since that time, other avenues of interpretation have been proposed. The present chapter will examine and evaluate four principal suggestions: the influence of a specifically erotic focus found most explicitly in the Song of Songs, but influencing New Testament writers in ways that were not widely recognized twenty years ago; the larger Greco-Roman cultural context of the New Testament, especially the influence of Stoic ethical perspectives; the effort, mainly on the part of evangelical scholars, to identify a single consistent and pervasive Biblical sexual ethic based in the creation narratives and reaffirmed in later texts; and, finally, the perspectives brought to biblical studies by "liberationist" interpreters, who perceive the Bible as always centrally concerned with the plight of poor and marginalized people.

EROTIC ETHICS:
THE SONG OF SONGS AND RELATED INFLUENCES

The people who first made me aware that the study of sexual ethics in the New Testament needed to take the Song of Songs seriously were students in my courses, who repeatedly asked about "relationships." Why, it was asked, did my analysis of sexual ethics say nothing about relationships as a foundation for ethical analysis? My first response was to say that this seemed to be a more modern way of looking at sexuality, rooted perhaps in the courtly love tradition of the Middle Ages. And, in any case, there *were* relationships involved in ancient sexual ethics, but they were interpreted in terms of purity and property considerations more than of personal emotions.

On the other side, of course, stood the Song of Songs with its extraordinary depiction of, yes, a "relationship" between two lovers, male and female, fully equal in passion and initiative, and united by their absorption in one another, not by marriage or any other form of ownership. The problem was in knowing what to make of this in relation to the New Testament writers. It was making its way into the canon of the scriptures of Israel during their time. But what was its precise status? And what was it understood to mean? And why did the New Testament writers seem to pay so little attention to it? There are, after all, no quotations from it in their writings.

Also, when presenting workshops on biblical sexual ethics, I began to create small groups and ask each to take on the task of presenting in discussion the perspectives found in a particular set of biblical passages. Thus, one group might have a couple of chapters out of the Holiness Code, another the first three chapters of Genesis, another some passages from Paul, another from the Synoptic Gospels, and so forth. I included some chapters of Song of Songs for one of the groups. Having given the groups a chance to assume their temporary personae, I would offer them brief cases drawn from recent events to discuss and then present to the larger group in terms of the perspective assigned them. To the surprise of everyone, it was often the group charged with representing the Song of Songs that was able to offer the most comprehensive and persuasive ethical analysis of each case. The other groups, by contrast, sometimes found themselves saying, "Well, this is what our author would say. But we think it ignores this factor or that." It at least raised the question of whether a relational ethic, founded in Song of Songs, might be the Bible's most important contribution to the modern discussions, regardless of whether it was deliberately echoed in the New Testament.

At about this same time, scholars such as Ann Windsor showed that there are in fact significant allusions to the Song of Songs in the New Testament.[1] Feminist theologians were calling for a reunderstanding of Christian doctrine in terms of eros as a way of reconstructing a theology that they felt focused on a questionable soteriology in which the Father God sacrificed his Son as a way of satisfying his own wrath against sinful humanity.[2] And the pioneering work of David Carr and others has begun to show the pervasiveness and importance of erotic elements in the scriptures as a whole.[3]

Scholars were slow to recognize this element in the New Testament in part because of an erroneous, but widely accepted truism of mid-twentieth-century theology that drew a sharp contrast between "love" in the Christian sense and "love" in the erotic sense. Taking the multiplicity of words for "love" in Greek as a base, theologians contrasted the good, selfless *agapē* of the New Testament with the evil and grasping *eros* celebrated in Greek literature.[4] What they failed to observe was that *agapē* and its cognates had already become, in the Greek of the Septuagint, simply the normal equivalent of the Hebrew term for love, which is as broad as the English. Even in the most explicitly erotic parts of the Old Greek version of Song of Songs, "love" is still *agapē*. When 1 John, then, proclaims that "God is *agapē*" (4:8, 16), it is not drawing a sharp contrast with eros. The Johannine context, to be sure, has to do with caring for others in the community of faith and is not explicitly about sexual issues. But the language of *agapē* carried a very broad array of meanings.[5]

We find other elements within the New Testament that reflect the openness of Song of Songs toward sexual desire. Paul allows sexual desire as a reason for marriage, even in the eschatological emergency in which he saw himself and his addressees as living (1 Cor. 7:8–9, 25–38). He recognizes with some distress that, like the lovers of Song of Songs, the newly married will become absorbed in each other and he would prefer that they remain single and therefore more attentive to "the things that belong to the Lord" (7:32–34). But he still allows their marriage. This is in contrast to important Greco-Roman philosophical traditions of the time, which recognized only the procreation of children as legitimating sexual intercourse and frowned on any pursuit of enjoyment or passion, sexual or other.

Paul also approximates long-married couples to the lovers of Song of Songs in describing both wife and husband as "having authority over" (*exousiazei*) the body of the other (1 Cor. 7:2–6). This is property language, to be sure, which may have been the easiest way for Paul to imagine the subject. But since they are now each other's mutual property, the concept of property itself begins to break up. It can no longer function along the clear, hierarchical lines of the ideal ancient household. Husband and wife here begin to become equal.

To some degree, Song of Songs must also lie behind the broad New Testament movement toward equality between men and women, not because equality is a particularly eroticized concept in itself, but because the erotic is the area in which this equality was taking root in the sacred tradition. Song of Songs was finding its way into the canon; by the third century, the first Christian commentary on it made its appearance. This paralleled some developments in the Greco-Roman world, in which companionship was becoming more of an acknowledged desideratum in marriage.[6] And it is in his discussion of marital sexuality that Paul gives us his own most unambiguous personal statement of gender equality, as clear as the baptismal teaching, probably taken over from his predecessors, that spoke of the abolition of the status distinction between men and women (Gal. 3:27–28).[7]

In other contexts, Paul had some difficulty adhering to this principle, whether because of his own reluctance to acknowledge his female co-workers as equals[8] or because he felt that his audience was not yet ready to go very far in this direction. On the subject of prophesying by women, for example, his argument falls rather easily into the presupposition of female inferiority: women reflect the glory of God only at a second remove, and woman was made from and for man, not man from and for woman (1 Cor. 11:7–9). Still, having gone this far, Paul reverses himself and leaves the two contrasting principles of subordination and equality standing alongside each other without resolving them.[9]

As we have seen earlier (chap. 10), if Paul wrote Colossians, he seems to have begun the process, carried further by his followers, of reasserting the hierarchical order of the ancient Mediterranean household among Christians (Col. 3:18–19). We can understand such inconsistencies as evidence of the tension between the ideal of equal lovers in the Song of Songs and the everyday cultural assumptions of the household, Jewish or Gentile, in Paul's world. It was easiest to incorporate the ideal of equality in the bedchamber itself, and therefore Paul could be clear and unambiguous on the sexual rights of spouses or the permissibility of marrying for reason of sexual desire. But he became less comfortable when the equality of genders began to extend to the social organization of the household or into the Christian assembly itself.

Whoever wrote the Pastoral Epistles was sharply limiting the roles of women. In his attack on the enrollment of younger women as official widows of the church (1 Tim. 5:11–15), he may actually be resisting the leadership of Christian women who vowed themselves to virginity. We get some glimpse of such a development in another strand of post-Pauline tradition, the fictional *Acts of Paul and Thecla*, where Thecla vows herself to perpetual virginity and rejects her fiancé, suffering near-martyrdom as a result. She eventually becomes a teacher, exactly contrary to the prohibition of the author of the Pastorals. Perhaps one factor promoting the rapidly developing Christian commitment to virginity was the extreme difficulty of maintaining equality of genders in a community shaped increasingly in terms of traditional households.[10]

In sum, the Song of Songs made a significant impression on earliest Christian sexual ethics, still discernible in some New Testament writings. But the first-century church was unable to follow its egalitarianism or its emphasis on relationship very far. Undoubtedly, the strong tradition of male hierarchy in the Mediterranean household, whether Jewish or Gentile, played a significant role here. We have also noted above (chap. 11), the effect of the Christians' increasing sense of endangerment as a small and unpopular minority. Several of the works that emphasize the subordination of women also express concern about public opinion (e.g., 1 Tim. 3:7; 1 Pet. 2:12). Ironically, there was some support within the larger Greco-Roman world for a degree of gender equality, but it came largely from elite sources and may not have affected opinion in those sectors of the populace that threatened the churches most directly.

CULTURAL CONTEXT AND SEXUAL ETHICS IN THE GRECO-ROMAN WORLD

Another major gain in recent research has been a richer sense of the Greco-Roman environment of the New Testament. We have a better grasp of the social and cultural context of earliest Christianity as it spread out into the wider Mediterranean world—including the place of sex in Greco-Roman culture. By combining material evidence with a cautious reading of ancient literature (which, coming from elite, usually male writers, frequently disapproved of the larger culture when it did not merely ignore it), investigators have begun to give us a livelier sense of sexual realities in the broader cultural context of the New Testament. After all, Christianity, though beginning in the Jewish community, soon acquired Gentile adherents, many of whom may have known little of Judaism before becoming acquainted with Christianity.

John R. Clarke, primarily using material remains, has shown that erotic representations were pervasive in Greco-Roman culture, both in elite contexts and also in less prestigious ones (which may have been imitating the elite). In houses, erotic wall-paintings were by no means confined to "private" spaces—a somewhat unclear classification, in any case. (The *cubicula* of a large house, for example, were used not only as bedchambers at night, but as places for conferring with visitors during the day.) Tableware, whether silver for the elite or Arretine pottery for people of more moderate means, was another common locus for erotic representations. Significantly, male-male sexual representations were not segregated from male-female ones or handled differently. In addition, representations of erect male genitalia were common, indoors and out, for purposes of warding off the evil eye.[11]

The Greco-Roman world, in other words, did not always keep the sexual behind a screen. The modern viewer can scarcely help being struck by the fact that wall paintings representing intercourse will some-times include additional figures in the room. But slaves were nonpersons, and their presence in the bedchamber, in the process of disrobing and retiring, was taken for granted. Ancient houses, in any case, even those of the elite, scarcely afforded the kind of privacy that became current among the bourgeoisie and upper classes of the modern West in the eighteenth and nineteenth centuries.[12] Less affluent houses were still less likely to afford much privacy, so that the sexual life of individuals was likely to have been more generally known, to slaves and other subordi-nate members of the household, than we are familiar with.[13]

This defines a context for references to sexuality in the New Tes-tament that is markedly different from modern ones. The difference is most obvious in comparison with modern middle-class propensities for screening sex from view. But the difference is equally significant if we compare it with the sometimes hyper-sexual atmosphere of twenty-first-century arts and advertising, where it is often specifically the trans-gressive character of the representations that enables them to seize the viewer's attention. The Greco-Roman world may not have been pre-cisely matter-of-fact about sexuality, but it defined the boundaries of its concern differently. What seems transgressive may not have then. Any-one reading New Testament texts as if they were framed in terms of the

Victorianized mores of, say, contemporary evangelical Christianity will inevitably misread them.

Scholars of the Greco-Roman world have also clarified the nature of that culture's general understanding of sexual ethics, which had more to do with social status than with any one other consideration. A free adult male might legitimately have sex with most other categories of persons, the principal exceptions being married women, which would constitute adultery, and most other freeborn males. In sex with other, lower-status males, the freeman must always be the penetrator, never the penetrated. Sex with his slaves, male or female, was considered his right. A free-woman, by contrast, ought to confine her sexual life to marriage.[14]

Ancient Jewish polemics against Greco-Roman culture regularly described Gentiles as sexually dissolute. Modern Christians have often treated these polemics as if they were literal ethnographic descriptions of Gentile culture, but that is no more likely than an equivalent judgment on the contemporary Gentile polemic against Jews, which described them as hostile to the rest of humanity because of their maintenance of strong boundaries around their community life.[15] Exaggeration and distortion are the life-blood of such interchanges, which are intended not to inform but to feed each group's sense of superiority to the other.[16] Greco-Roman satirists (for example, Juvenal in his first *Satire*) could be just as harsh on sexual offenders as any Jewish polemic; they presumably expected to find an audience interested in listening to their strictures. Adultery was as much disapproved among Gentiles as among Jews, even if individuals of both groups continued to commit it.

The Jewish sense of the dissoluteness of Greco-Roman culture may have been fed by the relative visibility of sexuality in that context. In much the same way, modern Muslims sometimes take the greater visibility of sexuality in the West as meaning that there are no sexual restrictions. In practice, however, the modern West is complex and varied in its attitudes toward sexuality and by no means indifferent to moral considerations. The same appears to have been true of Greco-Roman antiquity. What is beyond question, however, is that the standards of the two groups, Jewish and Gentile, were somewhat different. Nakedness, for example, was objectionable to many Jews (particularly the Essenes), much less so for Gentiles. Sexual intercourse during menstruation was prohibited for Jews, but not for Gentiles. Circumcision was required of Jewish males and regarded with some abhorrence by Gentiles. Some Jews, at least, condemned all male-male sexual intercourse; for most Gentiles, the ethical issues had to do not with the gender of the participants but with their relative social status.

Modern readers of the New Testament sometimes assume that, given the Jewish claim to superiority, Gentile converts to Christianity would automatically have accepted the Jewish code of sexual ethics. But they cannot have accepted them in full. For the modern reader, it may seem obvious which parts would be retained, While menstrual blood, for example, would be assumed not to be an ethical issue, same-gender sexual intercourse would continue to be. Yet contemporary Jews would have thought the issue of blood quite important, too. It is clear, from Paul's writings, that Gentile converts did not begin with a clear conception of a specific sexual ethic implied by their conversion. He found himself having to explain why, even though circumcision was no longer required, adultery or the use of prostitutes was wrong.

Did Paul expect his Gentile converts to cover up erotic wall paintings (those prosperous enough to have them!) or to discard dishes with sexual scenes? It would be hard to make such a case. David L. Balch has argued that Paul may actually have made use of mythological paintings and sculptures depicting suffering and death in his preaching.[17] Any purging of walls and tables, then, would have had to be highly selective. The same question necessarily arises in relation to male-male sexuality. For most Gentiles, even those not interested in engaging in it, it was a normal and uncontroversial aspect of Greco-Roman life as long as the proprieties of social status were being observed.[18]

There were, to be sure, minority voices of an elite, philosophical tenor in the Greco-Roman world that criticized some of the sexual mores of the culture. Modern students have sometimes characterized these voices as "the best" of Greco-Roman thought, which seems to mean that they came closest to the position of these modern readers. Accordingly, they have assumed that the earliest Christians would have adopted similar perspectives. In fact, two developments were moving the culture toward a more restrictive attitude toward sexuality. While the two were related, one was predominantly medical in its concerns, the other representative of late Stoic philosophy. The medical writers of the early Roman Empire were prone to see the body (defined, for most purposes, as the body of the elite adult male) as vulnerable to maladjustment. Accordingly, physicians wrote extensively in the areas of diet, exercise, and sexual practice.

Where, in the preceding era of Greek culture, sex might have been seen particularly in terms of pleasure, it was now likely to be discussed as constituting a challenge to the body and therefore something to be engaged in only sparingly and cautiously.[19]

Philosophical traditions of the period tended to reinforce this caution through their ideal that the human agent (again, generally conceived as an elite male) be a free actor. This was an intellectual transposition of what could previously have been taken for granted on the political level: that the elite adult male was a free man and therefore a person of independent standing. From an early time, Stoics and other contemporary schools of philosophy were insisting on the need for the individual to be in command of his own life. A person driven by passion could not be said to be free; therefore, one must cultivate the wisdom that would enable one to control one's passions.

Wayne A. Meeks has drawn attention to the ways in which Christian conversion followed patterns already familiar from philosophical ideas of conversion.[20] And Troels Engberg-Pedersen has made a strong and detailed case for the influence of Stoic ideas of conversion on Paul in particular. For the Stoics, it was never enough merely to be self-controlled (*autarkes*); such efforts were doomed to brittleness and failure. To live the truly free and philosophical life, one must behold the truth and be transformed by it. In much the same way, Paul understands the power of the gospel to transform the lives of converts. This closeness to Stoicism carried through even to some matters of detail, in particular the Stoic ideal of companionate marriage, in which the relationship of husband and wife is determined less by property considerations than by the development of a kind of friendship. Engberg-Pedersen goes so far as to suggest that, in this regard, Paul is most faithful to the Christian tradition precisely when he is most Stoic.[21]

Paul's knowledge of Stoicism, however, was probably drawn from its general currency in the culture; nothing suggests that he had a mastery of their philosophical tradition or even of its vocabulary.[22] At particular issue is the Stoic concept of "nature" as a fundamental source of ethical thought. "Nature," in this sense, does not mean the observable natural world as in the modern "natural sciences," but something more like an inner rationale of existence that is perceptible to philosophical reflection. This is an ultimate reality that occupies something like the position of the divine in Stoic thinking. Only what conforms with nature in this sense is ethical. In the sexual sphere, this meant, for the Stoics, that intercourse existed entirely for the sake of procreation. Accordingly, the man who conformed to nature would not enter into it either for the sake of pleasure or more frequently than was required to produce the heirs that were the central and legitimate goal of marriage. Too much sex even with one's legitimate spouse would suggest that one was enslaved to one's passions and not truly free. Paul was more prepared than the Stoics to countenance marriage for the purpose of satisfying male sexual desire (1 Cor. 7:8–9, 36–38) and does not speak of nature at all in this context.

If Paul was even aware of how Stoics used "nature," he ignored that and forged his own idiosyncratic array of meanings for the term, as we noted above (chap. 6). It marks identity: "we who are Jews by nature [*physei*]," that is, by descent as opposed to proselytes (Gal. 2:15); "you served beings that by nature [*physei*] are not gods," that is, not really gods, even though they are called that (4:8). It characterizes widespread cultural convention: "Does not nature itself teach you" that men have short hair and women long hair? (1 Cor. 11:14). It contrasts a former, presumably original condition or state with a changed one that has replaced it: God unnaturally (*para physin*) grafts wild olive branches (Gentiles) into domestic olive stock (Israel) (Rom. 11:21–24); God handed the Gentiles over to unnatural (*para physin*), that is, hitherto unknown, sexual practices as punishment for their idolatry (1:26–27). Because Paul clearly does not mean to accuse God of immoral practices in Romans 11, it is difficult to suppose that he used this as technical language for ethics in the Stoic sense even in Romans 1. It simply means that a significant change has taken place, a change affecting one's identity. In a similar vein, he writes of "Gentiles who by nature [*physei*] do not have the Law" and of "the uncircumcision by nature [*physei*] that keeps the Law" (2:14, 27). Whatever is usual is "by nature." Whatever alters usual practice is "contrary to nature" or "unnatural."[23] Paul's use of the language of "nature," however, has come to be associated with the "natural law" ethics of Roman Catholicism[24] and, more recently, with the evangelical construct of a "creation" ethic discussed in the following section, resulting in a major transformation of its meaning.

In sum, the diffuse influence of Greco-Roman ethical thought on the New Testament is particularly visible in the writings of Paul, who saw himself, after all, as apostle to the Gentiles. This does not, however, mean that he discipled the Stoics or any other existing school of thought. His fundamental, consciously acknowledged authority continued to be the faith of

Israel and its scriptures. He tends to appeal to them and to work with the principles of sexual ethics implicit in them more overtly and directly than to contemporary Gentile ethical thought. His use of Stoicism may have helped pave the way for the further incorporation of aspects of that tradition into later Christian thought. And, in any case, we certainly understand the New Testament better if we acknowledge its influence.

Over all, the influence of Greco-Roman ethics is probably most obvious in a broad concern for self-control that had become part of generalized ethical discourse in the period.[25] Hence the repeated, albeit generally brief, admonitions in New Testament texts against all kinds of excess and carousing. What Mediterranean people of all sorts could broadly agree upon in the first century was that respectability called for some degree of moderation and self-control in consumption and in sexual expression. One must not become the victim of one's passions.[26] To what degree this cultural principle was honored in people's behavior we cannot tell. Perhaps no more so than modern people honor their cultural principles. But it was a significant standard of moral judgment for Gentiles and Jews alike.

IS THERE A "CREATION" ETHIC FOR SEXUALITY IN THE BIBLE?

Another approach to the question of sexual ethics in the Bible, found primarily among conservative Protestant writers, focuses on the creation narratives of Genesis 1–2 as primary source, supplemented by other passages. This approach seems to serve as a counterpart to Roman Catholic "natural law," in which some sexual acts are deemed wrong solely because they are held to conflict with the basic definition of humanity. Thus, for official Roman Catholic teaching, any sexual act that is not open to conception is contrary to nature and therefore sinful. The concept of nature in this kind of discourse is, needless to say, not that in ordinary use today. The point is not whether contraception—or any other particular sexual practice—can be found "in nature." If the behavior of other animals were the standard, very little would be prohibited. The idea is drawn rather from Late Stoicism as sketched in the preceding section of this chapter.[27]

The argument from natural law is not always accepted by the faithful of the Roman Catholic Church—or even by all its theologians—but it remains official teaching. Conservative Protestants, by contrast, cannot use it directly as a theological criterion, because of the Reformation's insistence on the principle of *sola scriptura*—that scripture alone has fundamental authority in matters of doctrine and ethics. Nothing, then, can be required of the faithful that cannot be demonstrated out of scripture. For example, many Protestants read Genesis 2 as describing sexuality primarily in terms of mutual support and comfort and have therefore treated this element as a good of marriage in its own right. Procreation, for them, cannot be the sole justification of sexual relations, and no prohibition of birth control can be imposed.

If evangelical Protestants want to propose an argument for grounding sexual ethics in the fundamental character of humanity, it is not enough to try to define "natural" and "unnatural" in philosophical terms; they must identify a single created pattern of human behavior, understood to be revealed in Genesis 1–2 and reaffirmed in the New Testament by Jesus and Paul. The resultant creation ethic is developed in broadly comparable, though not identical, ways by different authors. For the sake of brevity, I offer the following summary, with sources duly noted:

> "The story of God's creation of humanity in Genesis 1–2 offers clues about God's intentions for humanity."[28] These include four basic principles: reproduction is good; sex is good; marriage is good; male and female are necessary counterparts.[29] The remainder of the scriptures of Israel reaffirms these insights in its emphasis on reproduction, in repeated reference to heterosexual marriage, in the prohibition of male-male sexual intercourse—and, some would argue, in the negative examples of such stories as the destruction of Sodom, the Levite's concubine, and Noah's curse on Ham.[30]
>
> The role of the creation narrative as the starting point for sexual ethics is further confirmed by Jesus' prohibition of divorce and equation of remarriage with adultery, in which he appeals to Genesis 1–2 as grounds for invalidating Deuteronomy's provision for divorce.[31] Paul, too, appeals explicitly to the same text in rejecting prostitution and implicitly in referring to same-gender sexual intercourse as "contrary to nature."[32]

This line of argument relies on a catena of texts, held to represent connections that are centrally important to scripture as a whole and, indeed, a central strand of the revelation embodied in it. Many proponents go so far as to identify this as the "unambiguous teaching" of the Bible on these topics. Given the absolute nature of this claim, advocates of the theory need to show clear and necessary links among the texts treated. It is not enough for this interpretation to be merely one possible exegesis among many. It must be shown to be the only convincing interpretation of these texts.[33]

Genesis 1–2

The argument for a creation ethic seems to have achieved its current prominence primarily because of a desire to find some credible biblical basis for excluding same-gender sexual relationships from Christian practice. In order for Genesis to serve this purpose, it was necessary to emphasize the "complementary" character of male and female, which could then be argued to exclude any possibility of a same-gender relationship being ethically equivalent to a heterosexual one.[34] This, of course, is an interpretation and expansion of the passage, which does not make any such emphasis explicit. Indeed, Adam's delight in the woman is grounded in her identity with him, not her difference: "This is now bone of my bone, and flesh of my flesh" (Gen. 2:23, AV).[35]

At an extreme, the argument treats Genesis 2:24 as a kind of condensed ethical imperative, commanding the full institution of heterosexual monogamous matrimony. One author summarizes the interpretation thus:

> "a man" (the singular indicates that marriage is an exclusive union between two individuals)

> "shall leave his father and mother" (a public social occasion is in view)

> "and cleave to his wife" (marriage is a loving, cleaving commitment or covenant, which is heterosexual and permanent)

> "and they will become one flesh" (for marriage must be consummated in sexual intercourse, which is a sign and seal of

the marriage covenant and over which no shadow of shame
or embarrassment had yet been cast)[36]

This exegesis picks up one element from Jesus' interpretation of this
passage (marriage as permanent) and another from that of Paul (exclusion of sex with others). There are a number of problems here both in
the exegesis of the Genesis text and in the use of Jesus and Paul.

To begin with, it is far from being a plain or literal reading of Genesis 2:24, which has traditionally been heard (and translated) not as a
command, but as an etiological story, serving to explain why young men
experience sexual desire as they grow up. Compare the RSV translation:
"Therefore a man leaves his father and his mother and cleaves to his
wife." It is doubtful that this is a commandment or even that it refers to
formal rites of marriage at all. (The Hebrew word here translated "wife"
also meant simply "woman.") The interpretation asks us to believe that
the use of the singular "man" is fraught with a meaning quite different
from the conceivable alternative "men leave their fathers and mothers,
etc." In the etiological context, however, the singular makes no difference; it simply thinks of individual instances of this behavior. The interpretation also takes the heterosexual characterization of the two lovers
to imply an exclusion of same-gender alternatives, presumably on the
problematic (and largely abandoned) hermeneutical principle that whatever is not commanded in scripture is actually forbidden. It then takes
the verb translated "cleave" to indicate that the union is to be permanent, though the editors who assembled the Torah did not understand it
in this way, since they included the possibility of divorce as well. Finally,
it treats the phrase "one flesh" as referring to sexual intercourse—a possible meaning and one accepted by Paul, but not, as we have seen, the
sense in which Jesus took it (p. 170).

A more judicious version of this interpretation of Genesis 1–2 treats
it not as establishing specific laws, but as "constituting the *symbolic world*
within which marriage is to be understood."[37] This still entails, however,
prohibition of same-gender sexual relationships and, at most, reluctant
acceptance of divorce and remarriage.[38] Is this somewhat less legalistic
interpretation more probable? It is less of an interpretive leap. But is
it *probable*? We have seen that the prohibition of male-male anal intercourse in Leviticus makes no specific reference to Genesis 1–2. Indeed,
its source, the Holiness Code, expresses little interest in the order of

creation, being concerned rather for the purity of the land of Canaan. At most, one might propose that the editors who assembled the Torah from a variety of sources, written and/or oral, saw some link. But, if so, they left no explicit indication of it. And if we move to the subjects of divorce and polygamy, we find even less within the scriptures of Israel to support this interpretation of Genesis 1–2. Within the Hebrew Bible, we find only two voices rejecting divorce: Hosea and Malachi (chap. 8). Nehemiah and Ezra actively demanded it to get rid of foreign wives (Ezra 10; Neh. 13). Only at the turn of the eras do we begin to find interpretations of Genesis 2:24 as actually prohibiting divorce (or perhaps polygamy)—at Qumran and in the teaching of Jesus.

It is sometimes urged that the creation narrative of Genesis is transcultural, at least in the sense that its Israelite authors understood it as referring to all of humanity, not just to Israel. This, accordingly, is said to mean that its presumed ethical imperatives transcend cultural differences and apply to all humanity alike.[39] This is a dubious argument, for the narrative is still a specifically Israelite narrative, even if it refers to humanity generally. But still more to the point, almost no one over the centuries when the scriptures of Israel were actually being written and compiled seems to have understood it as prohibiting either divorce or polygamy to anyone. For Christians, the prohibition of divorce and remarriage might take its authority simply from Jesus' use of the texts, without regard to their intrinsic meaning or earlier interpretation. But, on that basis, it would be difficult to expand the prohibition to other areas, such as same-gender sexual relations, without some kind of express authorization from the same source.

A further difficulty arises from the endeavor to treat the creation narratives as a full and detailed description of God's ideal for human existence. If one uses them in this way, one should do so consistently. If Genesis 2:24 mandates the details of heterosexual marriage, must it not also mandate such marriage as a moral obligation on all? This would be equally logical, although it would create a problem for Christians in that neither Jesus nor Paul seems to have married.[40] In addition, Genesis 1–2 describes other features of unfallen humanity that could equally well be taken as commandments. Our first state is represented as naked, vegetarian, monolingual, and at complete peace with the other animals. These are not trivial issues, nor do I raise them in a whimsical spirit. In classic Christian lives of hermit saints, a genre intended to provide a model of sanctity in Late Antiquity and the early Middle Ages, we typically read of a saintly man or woman who had lived for years in a remote desert place and is discovered by the narrator (with angelic assistance) only shortly before death. The narrator finds the saint naked, though modestly covered by long hair or beard. The saint's only food has been vegetables; the only companion is a fierce wild animal, such as a lion, which arrives at the time of death to bury the saint's body.[41] This is a deeply rooted Christian ideal of human sanctity—and one that should be brought into dialogue with modern ecological concerns. Interestingly, the authors of these tales never thought that their hermit saints had to be heterosexually married; they were committed rather to lifelong celibacy.

The "creation ethic" as an interpretation of Genesis is thus in danger of looking like special pleading. Rather than advocate a thorough and consistent application of the initial created state to Christian ethics here and now, it offers a highly selective choice of inferences, which just happen to be useful in ruling out same-gender sexual relationships. It ignores the rest. Moreover, it ascribes to one small text an extraordinary weight of importance and density of meaning. If this procedure is to be justified, it can only be by appeal to Jesus' and Paul's use of the passage, to which we now turn.

Jesus and Creation

As we observed earlier (chap. 9), Jesus appealed to the creation narrative to invalidate the Torah provision for divorce. I argued there that Jesus was acting to protect the woman against abuses of male privilege by making her, in effect, a member of her husband's family. He based this interpretation primarily on the phrase "one flesh," which he took as equivalent to "one flesh and blood"—that is, belonging to the same family. One cannot divorce a member of one's family.

Jesus did not interpret the text as commanding heterosexual marriage. Moreover, the traditions of his teaching, as we have seen, provide ample evidence that he distrusted the institution of the family and saw it as a primary rival for his disciples' commitment. He confirmed marriage by reaffirming the prohibition against adultery, but he did not treat marriage, in his debate with the Sadducees, as essential to human existence (Matt. 22:34–40 and parallels). To the contrary, it will disappear in the age to come. We have no clear indication of Jesus' attitude toward polygamy. Indeed, he may not have encountered it to any great extent because it does not seem to have been common in the Judea or Galilee of his time. Rich and powerful males like Herod Antipas, who might have had multiple wives in another era, had adopted instead the serial monogamy of Hellenistic culture, which forms the social background for Jesus' attack on divorce and remarriage. Interestingly, the various versions of the saying on divorce never declare that for a man to marry a second wife without divorcing the first is equivalent to adultery.

Given that Jesus said nothing on the topic of same-gender sexual relationships, the most one can say is that we do not know whether he would have regarded them as contrary to the created order. Some have argued that, as a Jew of the time, he would certainly have been antagonistic toward them, but this is to make an argument out of what we cannot know. In a variety of ways, Jesus is reported as having been quite alarming to some of the most rigorously religious people of his own *ethnos*. It is meaningless to argue, without any actual evidence, that he must have agreed with the generality on this particular point. [42]

There is one narrative, as we have seen, that may even point in the opposite direction—the account of the healing of the centurion's slave (Matt. 8:5–13; Luke 7:1–10). The slave is referred to in both accounts as his *pais* or "boy," a term that could denote a younger lover. [43] One should not lean too heavily on the term because it was also used of slaves and servants more generally. Abraham, for example, refers to himself, at age 99, as God's "boy" (Septuagint of Gen. 18:3). We cannot define the relationship of this master and this slave more precisely, but it is not intrinsically improbable that this was a case where the slave was the master's sexual companion. [44] If so, no one in the story raises the issue. It would, in any case, be largely irrelevant in this context because the centurion was not Jewish.

In sum, Jesus' use of Genesis 2:24 does not correspond well with most elements of the modern creation ethic. Jesus does not advocate heterosexual marriage nor does he forbid polygamy. He says nothing about same-gender sexuality; we have no conclusive evidence to establish his perspective on the subject. He accepts the institution of marriage (but for this age only, since there is no marriage in the age to come) and equates remarriage after divorce with adultery. But he is no enthusiast for "family values." He does use Genesis 2:24 in his response on divorce, but quite differently from the advocates of the creation ethic, stressing not the verb *cleave* so much as the phrase *one flesh*, to which the logic of his response gives the sense of family relationship, not sexual intercourse.

Some exponents of the creation ethic actually part company with Jesus on the one point where he is clear and emphatic in that they tend to make allowance for remarriage after divorce rather than reaffirming the older Western Christian stance of absolute prohibition. The upshot is that they claim the authority of Jesus for a greatly expanded use of Genesis 2:24, going well beyond anything the Jesus traditions support, while declining to take the one point Jesus explicitly made seriously.[45]

Paul and Creation

As we have seen, Paul also cites Genesis 2:24 explicitly to argue that male Christians are not to visit female prostitutes (1 Cor. 6:12–20). And he tells them that every act of sexual intercourse creates "one flesh." For Paul, however, "flesh" is not the kinship term it is for Jesus; in fact, it carries the negative connotations of evil and of opposition to "spirit." The true calling of the Christian is to be one spirit with Jesus. Paul treats Genesis 2:24 here not as a marriage text, but as referring to all sexual intercourse. He never suggests that the male who has used the prostitute is permanently united to her. Indeed, if every act of sexual intercourse created a permanent bond, the implications, given Greco-Roman presuppositions about male sexual privilege, would have been very confusing. But Paul does not take "one flesh" as creating a positive kinship obligation; he focuses rather on the presumed contrast between negative "flesh" and positive "spirit."[46] While he is using the same text as Jesus, there is little or nothing in common between their interpretations.

Some argue that Paul uses the creation narrative to ground his attack on same-gender sexual intercourse in Romans 1:18–32. If so, it is by implication, not by explicit reference. Paul is indeed interested in creation in this passage, but in reference to another topic: polytheism. He asserts that the unity of God has always been clear in the creation itself and that Gentiles were therefore without excuse when they left the true God and began to worship images of created beings (1:18–23). God punished Gentiles for the sin of idolatry by "handing them over" to impurity and disgrace in the form of same-gender sexual relations, which Paul characterizes as *para physin*, "contrary to nature, unnatural." Although the transition between "creation" and "nature" seems easy in modern English, it was not common in ancient Greek. As noted in the preceding section of this chapter, Paul uses *physis* to refer to any preexisting state of affairs or cultural expectation of normal behavior. The violation of *creation* in Romans 1 is polytheistic idolatry, not same-gender sexual intercourse. The theory, then, that Paul was citing the creation narrative as forbidding same-gender sexual relationships hangs by a particularly slender and dubious thread, amounting to little more, here, than one reference to creation in connection with a separate topic (monotheism) combined with the language of "nature" in reference to same-gender sexual intercourse.

Nowhere else does Paul ground his sexual ethic on the created order, with the single exception of his quite unrelated use of Genesis 2 to prohibit relations with prostitution. Even when Paul passes on the tradition about Jesus' prohibition of remarriage after divorce, he gives it only as a saying of the Lord, not as an interpretation of Genesis 2 (1 Cor. 7:10–11). And he proceeds to modify it on his own authority in the case of Christians who may be divorced by non-Christian spouses (7:12–16). This does not sound as if he regarded it as written inalterably in the stone of creation itself.

A Miscellany of Other Arguments

Some advocates of the creation-ethic theory attempt to show that it is actually spread broadly through scripture and forms a primary theme. To this end, they argue that the prohibition of the Holiness Code against male-male anal intercourse refers to Genesis 1–2 as its justification. As we have noted, this is doubtful at best. The language common to both is simply language that both required to deal with the subject at hand. It takes more than this to establish the probability of deliberate allusion.

In a similar way, the stories of Sodom and Gomorrah and of Gibeah are introduced as affirmations of the implied prohibitions claimed for Genesis 2:24. Again, there is no clear link. The most that can be argued is that the larger literary structure imposed on the materials by the editors who created the Torah out of older materials may have included a particular emphasis on fertility, with nonprocreative sexuality being seen as bad.[47] No clear or deliberate allusion to Genesis 1–2 has been or probably can be demonstrated.

Neither of these arguments succeeds in strengthening the basic catena of quotations. The claim that the Bible prescribes a complete sexual ethic in the creation narrative remains flimsy at best.

Conclusion

One classic Protestant standard for biblical theology holds that "whatsoever is not read [in scripture], nor may be proved thereby, is not to be required of any man, that it should be believed as an article of Faith, or be thought requisite or necessary to salvation."[48] An argument, to succeed by this standard, ought to show that it has deep roots and pervasive presence in scripture. It must deal consistently with related and similar texts. It must deal with language carefully and not slide over, for example, the difference between "creation" and "nature" or the contrast between Jesus' use of Genesis 2:24 and that of Paul. It must begin with the simplest possible meaning of a text. It must show specific reasons for linking up different passages widely separated in space and time, not simply throw in everything that sounds vaguely similar.

These are standards that the proposed creation ethic does not meet. Indeed, it is hard to imagine its having been created except for the purpose of shoring up an existing set of moral prescriptions that are being challenged, principally the opposition to the presence of lesbians and gay men in the church. My point is not to suggest that the advocates of the creation ethic are dishonest. My point rather is to say that the creation ethic is, without having acknowledged it, a variety of what is now called "ideological criticism." To give an overly brief definition: ideological criticism is any approach to the interpretation of the Bible that begins from a specific theory or perspective and proceeds to analyze and elucidate the text in ways that accord with that standpoint. Some forms of ideological criticism begin with a relatively settled theory that they assume represents the most fundamental access to reality we can have: so, for example, Freudian or Marxist interpretation. Others begin rather with the perspective of a particular group of people—Latin American campesinos, say, or African American women—and put to the text the questions that arise in that group's experience of life, questions that may well have been ignored by the demographic groups that have dominated biblical studies hitherto.[49]

The creation ethic belongs to the first of these two varieties and draws on two sources to define its basic ideology. One is the Puritan tradition, inherited by modern right-wing evangelicals, that regards scripture as a complete record of divine revelation, detailed and specific, answering every legitimate question, and merely awaiting systematic reorganization and exposition by theological interpreters. The other is the tradition of sexual mores forged in the nineteenth and twentieth centuries by Christian churches and long used to define and bolster middle-class respectability in the West. These sexual mores are assumed to be implicit in the scriptural "system," and any divergence is therefore a violation of scripture.[50]

There would be less reason to complain of this procedure if it were presented for what it is. The creation ethic, however, presents itself as simply the "plain sense" of scripture, as if it were derived from careful reading of the texts without external influence. This is an expression of the old Puritan ideal of a theology derived, in every detail, entirely and solely from scripture. However, no other significant Christian tradition has ever embraced this ideal, strong as it is in evangelical Christianity. And given the disagreements even among its adherents, who inhabit a broad range of denominations from Mennonites to Baptists to Presbyterians to Reformed to Pentecostals and "nondenominational" churches, it is difficult to believe that it is possible to identify a single, "plain" sense of scripture on issues as complex as these. Unfortunately, the theological tradition encourages its advocates to believe that this is in fact what they are doing. Accordingly, they present their conclusions as if they were nothing more than the obvious meaning of the text. Marxist and Freudian critics generally have a clearer grasp of their methods.

In fact, however, the creationist argument is chaotic. Its use of the creation narratives as ethical norm is inconsistent (mandatory in the case of heterosexuality; not mentioned in the case of, say, vegetarianism or ecological commitment; debated in terms of marriage after divorce). Its use of Jesus' saying on divorce to enforce mandatory heterosexuality while often ignoring its literal meaning in relation to marriage undermines its own premises. And its superficial reading of Paul barely rises above the level of proof-texting. All these factors combine to show that, whatever this position reflects, it is certainly not the "plain sense" of scripture. It begins with its conclusion and then attempts to ground it in scripture. It would compel more respect if it were more straightforward in its self-presentation.

READING FROM THE PERSPECTIVE OF LIBERATION THEOLOGIES

The other broad type of ideological perspective may have more to offer. Liberation theology, in particular, as it has developed over the last half-century, has a commitment to including people whose voices have tended to be excluded from academic theology: the poor, women, the sexually marginalized. It grounds this in scripture itself in the form of a "preferential option for the poor." God's commitment to the poor permeates the Bible both deeply and broadly, from the lives of the patriarchs as resident aliens in Canaan and the exodus of Israel out of slavery to the vindication of the persecuted faithful in Revelation. Unlike the Puritan tradition, however, liberation interpretation does not assume that the Bible contains a complete blueprint for human and Christian life. Typically, it does not regard every word of scripture as possessing equal authority and it takes the realities of the interpreter's world seriously as the context for interpretation, helping to frame the questions that must be put to the scriptures.[51]

Liberation interpretation, in its original Latin American form, laid particular emphasis on the poor as both the focus and, as far as possible, the practitioners of interpretation. The poor were originally conceived almost entirely in terms of economic poverty and social marginalization. Feminist liberation theology, in the industrialized West, took up the marginalized status of women; "womanist" theology stressed the double marginalization of African American women in particular. Marcella Althaus-Reid has argued that all these approaches must take sexual minorities seriously because they are typically focused in populations that are also impoverished and they disproportionately include women.[52] The same broad concerns animate the work of Marvin Ellison and lay behind the Presbyterian study, chaired by John Carey, that insisted no ethic of sex can be constructed without taking seriously the demands of justice.[53]

Tom Hanks has brought these issues to the exegesis of the New Testament in a sustained and orderly fashion. He demonstrates beyond question that most of the New Testament authors were not interested in maintaining the household structures of the ancient Mediterranean and that, indeed, most of the individuals presented in the New Testament documents would not have seemed to be models of "family values" either in their time or today. There are few persons clearly identified as married in contrast to a large number of people who are either unmarried or apparently living apart from their spouses. Some, such as the Bethany household of Martha, Mary, and Lazarus, conform to no fixed expectations of their age.[54] Even texts such as the "household codes" that reinstate something more like the familiar Mediterranean patriarchal household, Hanks argues, must be seen not as manifestations of fundamental Christian ethical principles, but rather as adaptations to the demands of the churches' immediate environment as that became more openly hostile to the believers.[55]

A related approach appears in the writings of Theodore W. Jennings Jr. He allows modern experience to ask new questions of the text, questions that had not been thought possible—or perhaps not thought at all—in previous times. By asking whether our culture's greater openness about homosexuality might give us the opportunity to see this as a more significant issue than had been assumed in the past, he is able to give a new reading to the Christian Bible in this respect. The result is a pair of books that may strike some readers as outrageous and others as improbable in their arguments, but which are in fact closely attentive both to the biblical texts and to their cultural contexts and are sometimes quite successful in making sense of materials that previously seemed perplexing or strangely irrelevant. The idea of a warrior homosexuality, not unlike that known to us from ancient Greece, enriches his reading of the scriptures of Israel with valuable insights for any reader willing to follow him through the experiment. And his awareness of the pervasiveness of male homosocial and homosexual bonds in the first-century Mediterranean world affords a significantly richer context for reading the New Testament.[56]

The goal of liberation interpretation is not to produce a conclusive reading of the biblical texts, but to create a way of reading that takes both the world of the text and the world of the reader seriously. As such, it can probably be relied on to produce further developments of significance in the discussion of biblical sexual ethics. This is not to say that the scriptural texts are completely indeterminate, but that they can look quite different from different angles and may give rather different answers to differently posed questions. It is still vital that such interpreters read the texts carefully and learn what one can of the environing cultures that set the scene for them. This involves asking new questions, not making the text say what later readers want it to say. That, oddly enough, turns out to be more characteristic of creation ethicists than of the liberation interpreters. The works of Hanks and Jennings, with their detailed and careful argumentation, show that excellent work is being done in this vein. However surprising their conclusions may be to casual readers (or offensive to readers protecting what they conceive as orthodoxy), they are, in fact, deeply grounded in attentive scholarly work.

CHAPTER 13

NEW TESTAMENT SEXUAL ETHICS AND TODAY'S WORLD

No study of Biblical ethics can, of itself, resolve the ethical questions of our own times, for the texts are framed in terms of questions and presuppositions belonging to their own day. This is not to say that the scriptures offer us no help in our own ethical thinking, but that they will seldom settle our problems without becoming part of a new conversation demanded by our own times, places, and cultures. The command "You shall not kill," for example, has been interpreted quite variously by different Christians in different times and places. For some it is a commandment that can be satisfied only by pacifism. This has often been the ethical standard of saints, even when they did not demand it of others. For most Christians, on the other hand, the commandment means rather, as in the Prayer Book translation, "Thou shalt do no murder." The meaning of murder then has to be fixed. For example, Christians long took capital punishment for granted as something other than murder, but there has been much questioning of that stance in the last hundred years.

Despite efforts over the ages to produce a single, perfect, and systematic account of the ethical dictates of the Bible, all thinking about ethics is inevitably influenced by its context. Some questions are more "live" in one place and time than others. For example, relatively few Christians today are distressed by the fact that the receiving of interest is contrary to biblical law. Of those above the poverty line, at least, most seem voluntary to participate in modern banking institutions and do so without any consciousness of engaging in a forbidden act. This could, of course, change in the future, and there may be good reasons for reopening the question. But it has not been a topic of widespread, vital concern over the past few centuries.

In modern Christian disputes over sexual ethics, not every topic garners the same interest. In internal disputes, pride of place has gone to a small number of specific issues: mainly homosexuality, abortion, and issues of gender equality. In the broader world, Christian ethicists have been dealing over the last century or so with a widespread suspicion, both inside and outside the church, that the Bible is fundamentally anti-sexual and that Christianity is therefore incapable of giving a positive account of sexuality at all. Our preceding chapters suggest that this is an oversimplification, produced partly by efforts to read texts from one culture in terms of another. It certainly does not take into account the more positive elements we have noted.

If we want a conversation with the Bible about killing, we must necessarily consider the whole range of scripture. At the one extreme, there are passages that speak of genocide in a war context without criticism.[1] By contrast, Jesus rejects all violence, declaring that the person who takes the sword will die by it, and accepts arrest and crucifixion rather than permit the use of violence by his disciples or call upon angelic protection (Matt. 26:51–54). In doing so, Jesus draws on another strand of scriptural tradition. Both Isaiah and Micah have a vision of the truly human future as one in which swords will be beaten into ploughshares (Isa. 2:1–5; Micah 4:3–7). And Isaiah's "Suffering Servant," one of the keys that New Testament writers use to interpret the person and work of Jesus, is distinguished by his refusal to retaliate against those who abuse him (e.g., 53:7). Thus, the Bible offers not only a basic principle ("You shall not kill") but also a variety of ways to contextualize the principle and work out its implications. For the Christian, the centrality of Jesus implies that the Bible's tolerance of genocide in other contexts is no longer a legitimate model for ethics—even if Christians have not invariably noticed this.

The issues of sexuality are equally complex. Scripture includes a great many rules about sex and also a great many stories where it is an important factor. And the tradition of Christian interpretation has incorporated these elements in an ongoing conversation that has taken more than one major turn over the past nineteen centuries. From the second century to the Reformation—and long past in much of the Christian world—Christians assumed that the truly virtuous life was celibate.[2] An active sexuality automatically identified a person as morally inferior if not necessarily outright sinful. Few married "saints" enjoy official recognition from Christian churches.[3] Even the line between marriage and extramarital sexuality was not always clear-cut. In the late second century, Clement of Alexandria argued that sex within marriage was sinful unless motivated by the desire to have children, while Hippolytus of Rome allowed a concubine to be baptized provided she was faithful to her master.[4] In later periods, churches have sometimes turned a blind eye to sexual partnerships they officially considered sinful.

All this raises important considerations when we bring the conclusions of the preceding investigation into conversation with modern issues of sexual ethics. First, we must allow the scriptures to be as diverse and mutually inconsistent as they want to be. There is no single "plain sense" of scripture, completely clear to any unbiased reader.

Second, even when we find larger principles at work—for example, purity and property, as we have proposed here—we cannot assume that these principles will have been worked out in exactly the same way everywhere in scripture. What the Torah condemns with complete seriousness (e.g., a man's returning to a woman after she has been sexually involved with another man) may be flagrantly violated by a prophet (Hosea) as an opportunity for revelation. Even where two different authorities agree on a principle (e.g., prohibition of adultery), they may disagree on how to treat it. Thus, the Torah calls for the execution of the known adulteress, but Jesus is reported to have prevented such an execution by asking which of the would-be executioners considered himself sinless (John 7:53–8:1).

Third, the historical, social, and cultural contexts in which Christians today must reason about sexual ethics are quite different from those in which the various biblical writers lived. To ignore this will only create confusion. This is not to deny that the ethical concerns of quite different cultures may overlap or parallel one another. It is simply to acknowledge that no two cultures are identical, that the different ways in which they structure human existence may give rise to different interpretations of the same practices, and that, even when interpretations are superficially the same, the underlying reasons may differ. To include the Bible in our conversations, we have to explore the differences between the worlds of the Bible and those of our times.

Fourth, Christian and biblical ethics are not simply concerned with rules or even with the principles behind rules. Our discussion has necessarily given a prominent role to such materials because they are the most compact expression of sexual norms. On the other hand, no culture simply lives out its expressed norms without nuance and exception. The narratives in the Bible often show us a more complex picture than the rules alone would.

Finally, the entire conversation about ethics, sexual or other, needs to be placed in the context of spirituality. The New Testament discourse about "fruits of the Spirit" (e.g., Gal. 5:22–23; Jas. 3:13–18) suggests that we are not simply concerned about conformity, but about how the living out of sexual ethics serves to encourage growth and maturation in the Spirit. The rules are means to this end, not ultimate truths in their own right. Overemphasis on them as opposed to life in the Spirit leads to a dry rigidity that is the very opposite of the good news of the Gospel.[5]

In all respects, our conversation about ethics needs to reflect the sort of patience and humility that come with growth in the Spirit. The whole truth is seldom, if ever, revealed at once or to one person or party; even if it were, we would scarcely be able to grasp it. Instead, we must pay attention to the complexities of the text and of our own world and our lives. We cannot assume that we know the full will of God in advance or that the Bible (or, more usually, one particular interpretation of the Bible) can settle all questions for us. Prayer, discernment, thoughtful reflection, patient inquiry—all these are essential to the task.

PURITY

Our study has argued that there are two principal themes being worked out in the sexual ethics we find in scripture: purity and property. Of these, earliest Christianity was deeply suspicious of the implications of a purity ethic. This suspicion was worked out primarily in the context of food purity, which affected the church's common table, but it also extended to other purity issues such as leprosy, corpses, and sexuality. Neither Jesus nor Paul ever suggests the abolition of purity. What they do, rather, is to bracket it—a profoundly important shift. To understand its importance, we must review briefly the nature and meaning of purity.

As we suggested earlier, every culture acknowledges some kind of purity rules, though some are more detailed and explicit than others. These rules help define the boundaries of the culture, identifying those who follow some other set of rules as aliens. The purity laws of the Torah serve exactly this function. Rarely are they applied to non-Israelites and then only if they are resident aliens within the community of Israel. Otherwise, they function to mark Gentiles as outside the Chosen People.

Purity laws can create distinctions within a community as well as between communities. In this case, the person who does not achieve the desired level of purity is not alien, but is still inferior. Since Leviticus linked purity law to the Temple at Jerusalem, to be pure was not only a condition for entering the Temple but a manifestation of one's devotion to the God of Israel. Ordinary life, of course, always entailed times of uncleanness, for example, from menstruation or ejaculation, which were not in any way sinful. They became sinful only if a person were to enter the Temple or undertake some activity requiring a high state of purity while actually being unclean. But habitual neglect of the requirements of purity would be a sign of religious indifference. The Jewish sectarians of the Hellenistic era accordingly used purity law to distinguish the devout sectarian from the casual, ordinary Israelite.

The positive side of purity law is that it offers a concrete, embodied means of shaping life religiously. The negative side is that it so easily becomes a barrier against the person categorized as alien or inferior. Jesus seems to have wanted only to override the potentially oppressive aspects. Thus, he accepted the touch of the woman with the hemorrhage as an act of faith rather than a violation of his purity; he touched lepers in healing them; he associated with the perennially unclean; he excused the food violations of his disciples; he even touched corpses. At the same time, Jesus presumably fulfilled many requirements of purity law. Indeed, much of it formed the ordinary customs of his people and was fully integrated into daily life. He was not hostile to purity as such, only to the use made of it by the pious in marginalizing others.

Paul, given his understanding of himself as Jesus' directly appointed apostle to the Gentiles, had a more difficult problem on his hands. He had to discern how to accommodate both Jews and Gentiles in a single common fellowship without requiring Gentiles to observe the full purity law of Judaism—something that many of his Gentile converts would probably have refused to do. Paul could take less for granted than Jesus, precisely because he was living in a mixed community, whose folkways did not reflect a single purity code. Accordingly, he resolved the issues by reserving purity to the sphere of the individual conscience: one must not violate one's own purity code (in most cases, probably identical to that of one's ethnic origin). But one was not free to impose it on others or to judge them if they failed to keep it. Neither was one to treat those who observed a more restrictive code with condescension. The Gentile Christian's relative freedom must not be used to tempt the Jewish Christian into violating the purity code of the Torah.

If we bring this bracketing of purity into our modern conversations about sexual ethics, it suggests several things. Christianity can accommodate more than one purity code. It does not have to abolish a culture's existing code, but neither can it merely accept it as authoritative without further question. Christians must resist the use of purity codes to separate humanity into the loved and unloved of God. When the church did begin to develop its own codes of sexual purity, focusing on virginity, it eventually broke with the example of Jesus by relegating those who were sexually active to an inferior status of holiness and favor with God. Purity codes have about them the capacity to thrust people away from God; the gospel welcomes them back.

On the other hand, the relatively minimal purity codes of the modern West are not intrinsically superior to the more restrictive ones of some other cultures—any more than the ancient Greco-Roman code was superior to the Jewish one. Americans or Europeans have no more right than other Christians to impose our purity codes. At times, even the "best" purity code may actually occasion evil, as when the travelers in Jesus' parable of the Good Samaritan refused to help the injured man, apparently because they feared he was a corpse and would infect them with corpse-uncleanness (Luke 10:29–37). In such cases, the purity code must yield. In other respects, no one is prohibited from adhering to a given purity code; one is prohibited only from imposing it on others.

In the beginning of the twenty-first century, how do these consideration intersect our ethical questions? We shall look more closely at specific issues below, but it is not inappropriate to state a few general principles at this point:

1. Membership in the Christian community cannot be defined by purity codes. When purity codes are used to exclude others, they have exceeded their permissible scope. The purity code that excludes is itself excluded by the gospel.

2. The observance of a purity code is permissible for Christians as a form of personal devotion so long as it does not violate the great com-

mandments of love for God and one's neighbor. No purity code can excuse the violation of these.

3. Purity reactions (feelings of revulsion) are not "evidence" for ethics. Their presence or absence is not decisive. If we believe that what revolts us is genuinely wrong and wish to commend this evaluation to others, we must justify that in terms of some ethical principle other than physical purity.

4. The one kind of purity that remains essential to Christians is purity of the heart—freedom from hatred, arrogance, violence, deceit, and all other passions that prompt us to violate the love of God, neighbor, and self.

5. Rejection of the ultimate authority of purity codes does not mean that there is no such thing as a sexual ethic.

PROPERTY AND RELATIONSHIP

The second great theme of sexual ethics in the Bible is that of property, and it appears in a form intimately linked with the patriarchal social structure normal in the cultures where the biblical writings were created. The same pattern was often repeated at higher levels of social organization, culminating in the emperor's role in relationship to the empire and that of the highest god in relationship to the universe.[6] Patriarchal hierarchy implied a kind of ownership, different in kind for different sorts of persons. The Roman emperor had to avoid suggesting that Roman senators were his "property," but the senators had to tread very carefully to observe the appropriate degree of respect toward the emperor without surrendering their own dignity. Similarly, in the household, a wife was by no means a slave, yet she, too, had her freedom circumscribed by the fact that the husband was the embodiment of his family and could give commands to everyone in the household. As we have seen (chap 8), the wife could be grouped with other sorts of property, even though her status was different from theirs as well as similar.

The patriarchal structure of ancient Israelite society was constitutive for the Torah, which addressed the male heads of household and only through them the subordinate members of society. Greek society was also organized patriarchally, although it differed in specific ways, for example in favoring monogamy rather than polygamy. The rise of

Rome brought about a little loosening of the subordination of wives; Roman culture had a long history of somewhat greater freedom of movement and expression for women, but it did not radically change the basic picture.

In both Jewish and Greco-Roman circles, there were voices suggesting that husbands and wives needed to cultivate some sort of personal relationship with each other. The patriarchal structure of the culture did not go entirely unquestioned. Accordingly, the steps taken by Jesus and Paul to undermine it were not totally without parallels, although their initiatives were more far reaching. Jesus' rejection of divorce and insistence that the wife is the equivalent of a flesh-and-blood relative to her husband had the potential to change the balance of power in the marriage radically. Still, Jesus' interest was less in the family (which he saw as a rival of the kingdom of God for the devotion of his followers) than in justice for women. Paul, too, bends property language in the direction of equality by giving each spouse authority over the other's body.

It demanded a major leap of the imagination to think such thoughts in a culture in which the family or household was the basic social unit and the privilege of the male head of household was enshrined in custom, religion, and law. Indeed, it is not clear whether Paul himself clearly grasped the implications of all that he wrote or how far he was prepared to follow them out. Paul's successors moved toward reinstating the gender hierarchy that they found in the world around them.[7] They did not erase the notion of women as full persons of faith, but they did inculcate a kind of household-centered morality that largely fit the expectations of conservative householders of the era. In this regard, Christians who live in a less patriarchal culture will inevitably conclude that the New Testament writers did not complete the reconstruction of family that their principles implied, just as they did not recognize that those principles were incompatible with continued slave holding by Christians.

The relative equality of genders in the modern West is not in itself the realization of the goal of Jesus or Paul. We can legitimately argue that it is superior to the available alternatives in terms of justice and the way it frees the human potential of women and minority groups. But this does not mean that it is identical to the kingdom of God. Indeed, our individuation sometimes leads us to ignore the reality that there is no human life that is not deeply interconnected with others. Sexual ethics, then, is not merely a "private" matter, but demands the larger scope of the political and spiritual.[8] If Jesus were to speak directly to our own time, he might well attack our obsession with our individuality and its prerogatives as functionally equivalent to the all-consuming claims of the patriarchal household in his own day. As he called his disciples away from their families, perhaps he calls us away from our careers.

What is different for Christians in the modern West is not that we have no temptations, problems, or challenges in the area of sexual property, but that the context in which we have to resolve them is different. Indeed, it is so different that we are uncomfortable with the word *property* when we try to deal with them. To begin with, in our world, one's sexuality is one's own property, not that of one's family. It is "property" in the etymological sense of an expression of the self. To violate a person's sexual being by violence or deceit, for example, is to violate not simply some possession, but the person's very being.

Again, if two people in a committed sexual partnership become the "property" of one another, what exactly does it mean to use this word? Is it still adequate? After long reflection, I am convinced that "relationship" is the modern term for sexual property without hierarchy. Neither partner can simply command, nor can either embrace simple obedience, whether as power or as a moral evasion. The only way to work out the meaning of the partnership is this complex interaction that we call "relationship." It is an interaction in which both lead and both follow, both are equal in desiring and in yielding, and each remains a full person while at the same time each belongs to the other.

Given the necessary transformations, however, the ancient preoccupation with sexual property may still be useful to contemporary ethical discussion. Our most intimate property is a kind of extension of the self, a guarantee of the freedom to be a self.[9] To identify one's sexuality as one's own sphere of activity both extends freedom and also makes the individual able to enter into new kinds of relationship. This transformation is already implicit in the changes made to sexual property by Jesus and by Paul, even if their successors backed away from it, reinstituting the subordination of women wherever they could. Some early Christians continued to maintain and develop the more egalitarian possibilities in the tradition. The importance of widows and vowed virgins from the second century onward owed much to the conviction that the Christian woman could be a real person of faith in her own right, not simply as a member of a husband or father's Christian household. The celibacy of such women was perhaps the only way their culture (including themselves) could make such a notion real in a patriarchally organized world. It was not the only conceivable way, but it was a further step in the reimagining of male and female begun by Jesus and Paul.[10]

In New Testament terms, however, to describe one's sexual being as personal property means that it represents a realm in which the person can act in obedience to the Reign of God. We worship or trust in sexuality to the soul's detriment, but it can be a means for discovering the love of God and neighbor and for the formation of a new community. As with other property, one is to administer and care for it with a view to sanctification, that is, to becoming a citizen of the Reign of God. Property, in other words, is the wherewithal of being human in this age—which can also become, by grace, the wherewithal of becoming a fit citizen of the age to come. The wherewithal of being human must include, at the very minimum, sustenance, space, the means to grow, the community of other humans, and some freedom of choice. Theft of sustenance or space is the most obvious violation of property, yet violations of trust, the foundation of human community, or of the freedom of choice are at least as grave.

Some principles emerge from this discussion as follows:

1. Christians must honor their own sexuality and respect the sexual property of others, both in terms of the right of persons to the free disposal of their property and in terms of the rights partners have in one another through their relationship.

2. The family is not the central category for sexual ethics, although it is not therefore negligible, either. The gospel does not automatically reject family life. But it rejects any automatic subordination of one adult to another in regard to one's relationship to God and therefore in one's essential humanity, and it objects to anything short of God and the Reign of God being treated as an ultimate human value.[11]

3. No cultural construct that automatically subordinates one gender to the other can have true authority for Christians. Even where it seems impossible to reform the construct immediately, the church has to protect the ways in which the less privileged gender can legitimately express its human and religious dignity.

4. The reconstruction of patriarchal into mutual sexual property implies a shift from a role-based understanding of marriage to a rela-

tional one, typified by the mutual and equal interaction of the lovers in Song of Songs.

5. The bias of the New Testament is always liberationist in the sense that it favors "the poor," including those marginalized sexually within a given culture.[12]

CONTEMPORARY ISSUES IN SEXUAL ETHICS

The issues that have become particularly prominent in our own times include at least the following: gender; marriage and divorce, polygamy, singlehood; birth control, abortion, and the well-being of children; rape, sexually transmitted diseases, sexual slavery, and other forms of sexual violence; prostitution and pornography; and homosexuality.

Gender

Despite Jesus' example, the modern movement toward gender equality did not spring primarily from Christian roots. Indeed, churches have long attached themselves to the practice of male dominance, and some still treat it as a matter of dogma. It is difficult, however, to see how anyone committed to the gospel of Jesus can fail to rejoice in recent developments that make the practice of Jesus' principles easier in our world.

If gender equality also creates difficulties, these lie in the narrowly defined individualism that accompanies it in modern Western culture. In its extreme form, this individualism suggests that no one has any responsibility besides that owed to oneself. Jesus would counter with the commandment to love one's neighbor as oneself. As usual with the two commandments of love, this creates, at first, more questions than answers. Given our human finitude, it cannot mean that we owe exactly the same level of commitment and attention to every human being in the world. And if we take the wording of the commandment seriously, neither can it mean that we are to love the neighbor *instead of* the self.

Instead, it must mean that we are always both individuals and in relationship and that our spiritual and ethical path lies in the dialogue between these polarities. Marriage, for example, can no longer exist purely in the form of traditional gender roles, according to which the male retains more individual freedom than the female and the female is expected to devote herself sacrificially to the needs of the family. Both have to enter into the kind of conversation that relationship implies.

The modern reevaluation of gender issues has also allowed us to see that gender differences are less obvious than we once supposed. The physical realities of sex are themselves more complex than the simple male-female dichotomy into which our culture has long forced everyone. And cultural definitions of gender, which frequently describe men and women as polar opposites instead of acknowledging the extensive overlap of their qualities and gifts, add further confusion. Gender continues to be an important human quality, but it is no longer possible to describe it as a kind of Platonic idea and then force everyone into just one of two categories.

The picture becomes still less clear when one adds in the possibility of psychological dissonance, which can sometimes mean that an individual experiences strong opposition between one's physical sex and one's inner sense of gender. Such transgendered persons have probably always existed, and some cultures have accommodated them more readily and more kindly than others. But medical developments have now made possible a much more radical approach to gender reassignment. Some regard such procedures as bizarre, others as a welcome advance. They become issues of public policy with regard to their availability and the question of whether insurance or government will pay for them.

For the most part, churches have not really wanted to know about such people in their midst. A more coherent ethical approach should be possible. The equalization of gender implicit in the gospel of Jesus at least removes one barrier to our thinking about the subject. Neither a transition from male to female nor the reverse is to be seen as a change in the value of a person. Christian communities, however, cannot expect to understand the meaning of such transitions except in respectful conversation with transsexual people in general and especially those who have been called by the Spirit into the church. The decisive questions become those of spiritual life: Is the move toward coherence between physical sex and psychological gender accompanied by the signs that we associate with spiritual growth?[13] Relaxation of a rigid two-gender system allows gender to serve humanity rather than making human beings slaves to a system. As Jesus said of another institution, "The sabbath was made for humankind and not humankind for the sabbath" (Mark 2:27 NRSV).

Marriage Issues: Marriage, Adultery, Divorce, Polygamy, Singlehood

Marriage continues, in our world, to be largely about the orderly disposition of property. Legal systems still function to regularize and define the ways in which property is shared with a life partner and passed on to heirs. In earlier eras when peasants rarely had any property to transmit, there seems to have been no great concern, either in church or in state, about regularizing their unions. Only in the eighteenth and nineteenth centuries did Western law move toward demanding the formal registration of all marriages. At the same time, marriage is about values other than property, above all the desire to find or create our own intimate communities as we move into adulthood. Even in cultures where marriages are arranged, the hope is typically that the newly married couple will come to form a strong personal bond. And much of Western culture has long assumed that people will actually choose their own partners on the basis of such a bond, usually based in erotic and romantic attraction.

Marriage is thus a kind of hybrid institution and will always embody some tensions as a result. The shift toward equality of the genders may have exacerbated some of these because we can no longer assume that the plans and desires of the male partner in a heterosexual union will prevail. Instead, both partners seek things that will benefit them. The thrill of romantic love is all the more important in the period of constructing the new relationship. We hope that it will form the basis and model for a deeper and more lasting intimacy, in which each partner will provide friendship, encouragement, counsel, solace, and a new sense of family to supplement and eventually occupy the central place originally given to the natal family. These are, of course, interior goods—goods that cannot be given without a genuine delight in and commitment to the other; in this respect, they stand in contrast to the goods principally sought in antiquity—legitimate heirs to carry on the existence of the husband's line of descent. External goods are involved in modern marriage as well: the expectation of security, financial support, and perhaps the desire for children. Yet we are inclined to look askance at those who marry for money, while childbearing and rearing are no longer absolute requirements in a heavily populated world. For us, the heart of sexual property in marriage and in other lasting sexual relationships lies in the interior goods.

This ideal of marriage reflects the example of the lovers in Song of Songs. Only a broad range of initiative on the part of each partner can make it possible to give the other the kind of interior goods under discussion. What holds the lovers together is not obedience to roles, but the intensity of their relationship. The kind of marriage called for in an age of gender equality will have to cultivate and foster a deep friendship between the partners to preserve the priority of this relationship. Indeed, such deep friendship between spouses is vital to the maintenance of a rich erotic relationship as well.[14]

When the nature of property in marriage changes in this way, the nature of theft necessarily changes as well. In antiquity, theft, as applied to sexual property, was easily defined. Adultery meant a man's taking the womb and family resources that belonged to another man and using them for the nourishment of his own seed. We continue in our society to regard adultery as wrong, but for a different reason. We usually say that it is wrong because it is a betrayal of trust—that is, theft of an interior good. Insofar as this is, in fact, the case in a given situation, it gives a good account of adultery in our modern context; but it does not go far enough.

Trust is not the only interior good essential to marriage, and the outsider is not the only possible thief. Because in ancient marriage, the man owned the woman, it was impossible for the man to steal from his wife. If he committed adultery he was stealing from another man. Jesus, however, by redefining adultery, altered this internal balance and made both spouses capable of taking from one another. This is even clearer under present circumstances, for partners can easily withhold from each other those interior goods that they have contracted, explicitly or implicitly, to provide and there is no way to gain them from an unwilling partner. An ancient wife need have no deep affection for her husband to bear his children and do her part in the running of the household. Neither partner, in the modern world, can fulfill his or her obligations in such a purely external, "objective" manner.[15]

The form of adultery most characteristic of our own society, I suspect, is not adultery with another person, but the purely self-regarding adultery that demands of the partner the full range of goods associated with sexual property but gives few or none of them in return. This is not to discard the older understanding of adultery, in which one person takes from another what belongs to the partner; this is certainly not dead. It is rather to stress the prevalence of adultery in the form of profiteering, the use of a sexual relationship for one's own physical, economic, emotional, or psychological satisfaction with minimal regard for that of the partner or while investing one's personal energies primarily in a career or other interests. In comparison, the technical act of adultery by sexual inter-course with a third person is sometimes literally a secondary matter, a consequence of a more basic, if less easily articulated kind of betrayal.

This kind of failure to share the goods of marriage may also be one principal occasion for divorce. If so, the current high divorce rate in the West may be not simply an expression of selfish individualism, as it is often assumed to be, but also an expression of the tensions involved in the refocusing of marriage from exterior to interior goods. If so, the constructive response is not to tighten rules, but to encourage a deeper conjugal spirituality. In the past, Christians have thought of celibacy as a special, spiritual vocation, but of marriage as simply the normal (albeit inferior) state of human beings. Our present shift in understanding the goods of marriage implies that marriage, too, is a specific vocation, to be entered into with care and discernment and with the understanding that it will require growth in the Spirit if we are to live it well.[16]

The move toward gender equality actually removes one principal motivation behind Jesus' prohibition of divorce. If the partners in a marriage are genuinely equal, then divorce may be the choice of either spouse or of both. This does not mean that there is never a weaker part-ner who is harmed by it. But it does mean that there is no partner preas-signed by gender to a role of less privilege. While there is a long tradition of Christians interpreting Jesus' words on divorce as legislation, there is also a long tradition of Christians interpreting them as an ideal. Mar-riage, when it achieves its full spiritual possibilities, is lifelong and can maintain its life-giving, sustaining qualities throughout. Marriages that continue purely because canonical regulation requires it are not likely to grow toward that goal. Divorce is always a recognition of loss. It is never in itself the goal. But it is sometimes the lesser evil.

The largest challenge before Christians in the matter of marriage is how to reimagine human unions in a time of gender equality so that they can have renewed power to enhance the lives of those participating in them and, through them, the life of the larger community. In this respect, heterosexual and homosexual couples are essentially seeking the same goals, and it is increasingly difficult to explain why marriage ought to be limited to heterosexual couples alone.[17] Indeed, the campaigns against extending it to homosexual couples seem to rely exclusively on alarming slogans about "protecting the family." These slogans, in turn, depend for their power largely on purity reactions against homosexual people and on the desire of some to retain the moral advantage that accrues to them simply by virtue of being heterosexual. Heterosexism, the assumption that heterosexual privilege is obvious and inevitable, is as much a claim to unearned power and authority as racism and misogyny.[18] The model of Song of Songs applies just as well to same-gender as to opposite-gender couples. One may have to change a few pronouns in the reading of the text, but this is hardly surprising. Most love poetry works perfectly well for either orientation in exactly this way.

Some of those most distressed by the prospect of legal recognition for same-gender partnerships also voice concern about the number of heterosexual couples living together without marriage rites. In part, this trend is simply a return to earlier norms of Western culture before the modern regularization of marriage by church and state. The deeper fear, perhaps, is that marriage no longer exercises as strong an attraction or holds people as strongly as it once did. If people in long-term partnerships do fear marriage, this may result partly from its being identified too exclusively in the past with its external goods and definitions—not only goods of physical property, but of respectability and status. For some, as a result, it may seem to distract the married from the more vital relational qualities that maintain the liveliness of their partnerships. The cure, in this case, may begin less with persuading more people into formal marriages than with persuading the married to take seriously the relational foundations of their legal status so that the institution itself is given new life. Inclusion of same-gender life-partnerships under the rubric of marriage can assist in this process because they have no advance entanglement with older gender distinctions.

Polygamy was not a significant issue for Christians for a long time. Apart from its modern revival in isolated groups such as the early Mormons, it has exerted no particular attraction in the Western world. It has become an issue again, however, because of the rapid spread of Christianity in areas, particularly in Africa, where it is a long-standing cultural norm. Does Christianity demand its abolition? Clearly, the scriptures nowhere forbid it, although they include voices raised against it.

Some African Christians argue that it is unjust to disrupt existing households by requiring Christian converts to dissolve polygamous unions. And, given the ability of Islam to make room for such households, it has also seemed problematic for missionary strategy. Some international Christian traditions have, in fact, approved maintenance of existing polygamous households with the proviso that the exception extended only to the generation of the converts themselves. This proviso has not always held, however, leaving open the question whether a full accommodation to polygamy might be emerging in actual practice.[19] Given the tendency of Christianity in other times and places (including the later documents of the New Testament) to accommodate to existing cultural norms, one could argue that there is precedent for such a development. But one major question mark stands against it: is it possible to have a polygamous society that does not automatically make one gender inferior to the other? Most such societies are polygynous (one husband with multiple wives), and I do not know of any in which women are not also distinctly inferior in terms of their social standing. Unless it is possible to find ways of reconciling polygyny with Jesus' teaching about the equality of the genders, the historic Christian stance in favor of monogamy should continue.[20]

In post-industrial societies, polygamy is less an issue than is the reality that most adults spend at least significant parts of their lives as single persons. In a world where the household was the basic social unity, such persons were typically at the margins: widows, spinsters, eunuchs, slaves—and few of them had volunteered for these roles. In our world, their status may as easily reflect personal choice as the death of a partner, a divorce, or simply not ever having found a suitable partner. While some single people may have the gift and vocation of celibacy, most presumably do not. And the Victorian assumption that they will not be sexually active is no longer determinative.

If one's sexuality is in fact one's own property in our society until such times as it is shared with a partner, the question is what spiritual goals sexual expression may encompass where there is no expectation of engaging in a life partnership. I do not believe we have any prefabricated answers to this question, but Paul at least would insist that sexual relations should embody something more than casual physical release. The spiritual significance of sexuality is honored only when there is engagement with and reverence for one's erotic counterpart, even if, for whatever reason, it seems impossible for that engagement to become a life partnership.

Issues of Procreation:
Birth Control, Abortion, and Children

Some churches continue to teach that every act of sexual intercourse must be open to procreation, even though their laity may have decided otherwise. The resulting absolute rejection of most means of contraception can work a significant hardship on women, especially the poor; it has the further damaging effect of outlawing the most effective defense against sexually transmitted diseases. Both of these considerations make the prohibition of birth control devices ethically questionable at best.

In practice, the conjugal sexual relationship is first for the "mutual support and comfort" of the partners and, second, sometimes for procreation. This would not have surprised Jesus or Paul. Jesus was, in fact, indifferent to procreation (though not to children); and Paul and early Christianity in general followed him in this. The increasing preference for celibacy in the second century was based, at least to some degree, on the sense that Christians did not need to make an investment in the continuity of this world because their citizenship lay already in the age to come.[21]

With the existence of reasonably reliable and efficient methods of birth control, the two basic goals of marriage are more easily separable than in the past, and there is no scriptural reason against this. If the first creation narrative commands humanity to "increase and multiply" (Gen. 1:28), this is the one biblical commandment that humanity has, if anything, over-fulfilled—to the point of endangering the whole planet. In most areas of the modern world, the use of birth control should be the norm and the conception of children should represent a deliberate and considered departure from it.[22] No existing method of preventing pregnancy is inherently unacceptable, though it is wrong to impose them in ways that violate individual responsibility and freedom. The bringing of children into the world, like marriage itself, ought to be thought of as a vocation, to be discerned with appropriate reverence, not simply as the inevitable consequence of sexual intercourse.

While the prevention of conception is now broadly accepted in the developed world, abortion is a very controversial topic. What does the Bible contribute to this discussion? As we have seen, the Torah may actively have commanded abortion in cases of suspected adultery (Num. 15). Jews of Jesus' time, however, objected to the practice for any other purpose. In times past, proscriptions of abortion seem to have been based primarily on property issues. The father, not the mother, was the owner of the progeny. Thus, the one provision for abortion in the Torah was designed to protect the father's property in the child. Abortion for other reasons was seen as the mother's selfish effort to avoid risk to herself, with consequent loss to the husband's family or the state.[23] Contemporary objections, by contrast, are framed rather in terms of murder, arguing that the fertilized ovum is already to be recognized as a human being.

There has never been any simple answer to the question of abortion. Before modern science gained the power to tell us about the stages of the intra-uterine process, gestation remained largely mysterious in any case. At what point does the ovum become the baby? There are very few definitive thresholds, perhaps just three: conception, implantation, and birth. The difference between those who allow abortion and those who prohibit it seems largely to depend on which threshold is taken as normative. At one point or another, they see a human life that must not be taken away. The question is where.

The moments of conception and implantation were not as clearly understood (or identifiable) in antiquity as today. Indeed, it was often thought that the sperm contained the whole being of the future child and that the womb provided nothing more than a place for the seed to grow. In later eras, people sometimes thought of "quickening" (first movement by the fetus) as the critical point at which the embryo became a living being. Others argue for the stage at which a premature infant first has a chance of survival or for the actual time of birth as the critical moment. Any of these can be defended. Those who take conception as the critical boundary argue that it is the most absolute of the four, but that does not in itself make it the most helpful in ethical reflection. In traditional practice, for example, Christians have not, in fact, treated the results of early spontaneous abortions as human subjects—for example, by baptizing, although this may certainly be done with the newborn perceived to be at risk and even with the stillborn. Our sense of the exact threshold of humanity has actually been somewhat vague, which does not automatically mean that it is less valid.

Given the New Testament witness to the full humanity of women, the question of achieving agreement on a single threshold of humanity is not the only point at issue. A question of at least equal importance is who is to make the decision about abortion. Some prefer that legal authorities make the decision, which always means it will be framed as a prohibition, though perhaps with exceptions for cases where the mother's health would be endangered or where the fetus was conceived as a result of rape or incest.[24] The alternative is that the pregnant woman should bear the primary responsibility for the decision. When Christians adopt this position, their stance is not, in fact, one in favor of abortion, but rather one that believes the responsibility is best left with the pregnant woman. The alternative is to deny the full moral status of women—and, at the same time, to leave them open to significant danger at the hands of both illegal abortion providers and of states willing to exercise callous and destructive power over (mostly impoverished) women.[25]

Abortion, like divorce, is never a good in its own right. It is always, at most, a lesser evil, never to be undertaken lightly. It should not be a normal means of birth control, which can be done in safer, less traumatic ways. Still, there are reasons for permitting it. While the ancient family ethic may have regarded the legitimate offspring as of greater importance than the mother in most cases, there can be no basis in the New Testament itself for such a judgment. For Jesus, the woman was no longer merely an instrument of her husband's natal family in their quest for heirs. This implies that her well-being is at least as important as that of a still uncertain offspring.

This does not imply that the pregnant woman should have to decide such matters in isolation. The strong Christian sense of community, of the need for one another as part of our need for God, means that the individual can and should have the context of a faithful community that gives her honest support in discernment and respect for her responsibility in making the decision. Such a community, of course, can only offer itself as a context for discernment; it cannot impose itself. And if it fails to respect the person whose discernment is centrally in question, it will rightly lose its credibility.

One unfortunate aspect of the contemporary battles over abortion is that the opponents of abortion often seem to care a great deal about controlling the decisions of pregnant women and very little about the fate of children once they are born. Jesus' own openness to and affection for children is a repeated motif in the Gospel accounts. This coheres with his repeated emphasis on the support of the weak and powerless, which sits in judgment on the tendency of society at large, then and now, to treat children as expendable hedges for the future of the family or the state. Love and care for children was certainly to be found in the ancient Mediterranean world as it is in ours. But the opposite is also known in both. In our own world, appalling numbers of children grow up with poverty, disease, war, ignorance, neglect—some even in conditions of slavery. Many, of course, do not reach adulthood. No Christian community has any right to claim the name of Jesus if it does not attend to the needs of children and treat them with the same reverence he accorded them.

Now as in other eras, parents conceive children for a variety of reasons, including social pressures, sentiment, the desire for some kind of genetic immortality, a sense of social responsibility, pure carelessness and the rest—perhaps a longer list than any one person can imagine. Yet, once born, the child is, in our age, a quite different matter from what he or she was in the first century. The ancient family had to have legitimate heirs to maintain its own existence. But what is the child to a society of individuals? The child may still be nothing more than an extension of the parents and insurance against their being left unattended in senility. Children can be expected to learn, however, from the larger culture that they, too, are expected to become responsible for their own lives and may refuse to cooperate with parents who sought to use them purely for their own ends. But they may merely continue the same self-defeating individualism unless something more loving can take its place.

What sort of alternative can the gospel suggest? That children should be understood as responsible persons in preparation. Their lives are, in other words, ultimately their property, not that of their parents, while the parents have the role not of owners but of educators, those who prepare the child to become the best of herself or himself. The model parent will be one who seeks to discern the child's uniqueness, both good and bad, and help the child form the self-discipline to make the best of his or her resources. This is not a prescription for "permissive" parenting, for the child is not yet a realized individual ready to be in full command; it is, rather, a loving and persistent assistance to children in becoming responsible for themselves, their choices, their relationships and community, their work, their world. Parents who understand that the child is not obligated to be exactly what they want will be better parents. Children who understand that they cannot evade their responsibilities either by habitually obeying or by habitually reacting against their parents are more likely to become stable, creative, and faithful adults.[26]

Parenting is thus a gift to the child of the child's self; it is the passing on of gifts that the parents received from their own parents and from all the others who contributed to who they are. This must of necessity be a somewhat disinterested task. The parent who wants only an athlete for a child will be an incompetent parent to a painter. The parent who wants a substitute for adult companionship and makes the child a quasi-spouse, will confuse the child into thinking that adulthood is a kind of manner-ism and thus make true adulthood, which is an inner centeredness, the more difficult to identify or to achieve. Above all, the parent or other senior family member who uses the trust which their position bestows to make the child his or her lover thereby makes demands on the child totally inconsistent with the disinterested love of one who seeks only the child's good.

Issues of Force: Incest, Rape, and Sexual Slavery

In the world of the scriptures, incest was thought of largely as an offense committed by younger male family members with the wives of older male relatives. In our own world the significant probability is quite dif-ferent: older males imposing themselves sexually on younger relatives, male or female. It is typically an act of abuse toward children or young adolescents who are easily intimidated by the older person. It violates not only our sense of too great a relational closeness—a widespread human taboo that perhaps recognizes in some inarticulate way the perils of inbreeding in relation to genetic disease—but also our respect for the well-being of children.

The inequality between adult and child (and, to a lesser degree, between older and younger child) means that, in a sexual relationship, the needs of the younger will always be subordinated to the desires of the older. The child loses, above all, the preparatory space and time when responsible adults encourage and assist children to know themselves before assuming full adult obligations. This, in turn, renders the child's growth into real adulthood extremely difficult, creating an alienation not only from the available adult models, but also from the child's very self. Adulthood comes to seem a rejection of the past instead of something that grows out of the experience of childhood.

All sexual abuse of children is a kind of generalized incest. For the child, every older person is to some extent a parent. The child's growth into individual adulthood is promoted if the child has a variety of adult models and so does not identify adulthood with the characteristics of one or two people. If, on the other hand, the child encounters adults as people whose only interest is to take advantage of the child for their own satisfaction, a disastrous model of adulthood emerges. Most abusers of children, it is said, are adult heterosexual males, frequently friends or relatives of the child's family. In their case, the disadvantage the young girl experiences may be compounded by an unexpressed wish on the man's part that all females would remain dependent. In any case, all such abuse contains in it the implied desire that the sexual object not grow up. Thus, it is akin to incest in the harm it does to children.

Sexually, the child must be considered his or her own property. As the child grows old enough to begin wanting to explore sexuality, the parent or other adult guide will contribute most effectively by teaching the child frankly about the realities of sex, including its dangers, and by holding the child to the necessity of making clear and responsible decisions. Refusing to discuss the issue or framing all discussion in the form of prohibitions denies the child's developing responsibility and status as an adult-in-becoming. As a result, it encourages repression and future sexual misery on the part of the quieter, more obedient child while failing to prevent rebellious irresponsibility on the part of the more energetic and unreflective one. Most adolescents will probably pass through a period of experimentation, although they should not be pushed into it against their wills. They should be shown how to do this as safely as possible. Certainly, no child—and probably few teenagers—is prepared to enter upon a true marriage of equal adults such as the gospel calls for.[27]

Even for young adults, the first choice of a sexual partner is not always the best, and their initial image of themselves in an ongoing sexual relationship is not likely to be fully formed. If we treat marriage as the only possible license to have sex, we can be quite sure that many will choose marriage partners for the most inadequate of reasons and with poor judgment. If the decision for marriage is not just about the first sexual experience but about life partners, it will be easier for people to make it in a realistic way. Some Christian thinkers suggested decades ago that the church should not rush to make the unions of the young permanent; we have yet to honor their suggestions with due discussion, even though much of Western culture has already decided, in practice, to separate early sexual experience from marriage.

Other forms of sexual predation are similar to the abuse of children in that they employ superior power, whether social or physical, to achieve their goal. Predation by clergy, psychotherapists, and other authority figures on their parishioners, patients, or clients is a significant evil for exactly this reason. All these involve the abuse of sacred office to facilitate the abuse of persons. One of the grave wrongdoings of churches in our time has been their failure to call offenders to account, a failure sometimes exacerbated by efforts to silence their victims. Happily, this has become less and less possible.[28]

All these forms of sexual predation also have something of the character of rape, although we generally reserve that term for cases where physical violence is used. Rape seems to have become very common in our world. It appears as an act of aggression in the wars of the last few decades and, on a more individual scale, as an expression of the free-floating hostilities of men who feel themselves failing in their manhood and ascribe the fault to women.

In antiquity, given the existing concept of family, adultery was the characteristic violation of sexual property; in our own age, rape has taken its place.[29] When committed by a stranger, it violates the victim's freedom of choice; when committed by a family member or presumed friend, it violates the most basic bonds of human community as well. The metaphorical space that surrounds each of us and that we characterize as "mine" is of the essence of our being human. It offers some protection for the freedom to develop and become what God is calling us to be, which is the principal goal of being human. When it is opened voluntarily to another, it is also a means of community. But when it is broken into by violence, the very possibility of being human is being denied to us. Because there is nothing more precious to us than our humanness, there is no sexual sin more serious than rape.

Rape, thus understood, includes not only the use of physical violence to gain sexual access to another, but also the use of social, emotional, and psychological violence. This includes sexual harassment in workplaces, sexual impositions by trusted authorities upon their clients, and manipulative pressures in intimate relationships. Stealth may also be a tool of rape, as when someone knowingly risks communicating a sexually transmitted disease to another. Contemporary culture, with its glorification of sex for commercial ends, tends to separate sexual experience from relationship and creates a climate in which this sort of violence flourishes. It offers leverage for the unscrupulous to press inexperienced or unwilling persons into acts that they have not freely chosen. Even within marriage or other established sexual relationships, physical violence and other forms of rape are by no means unknown.

There is also a variety of rape in which whole groups employ sexual attacks to deny to others their humanness. Assaults on women or gay/lesbian people, whether as individual attacks or as political and legal campaigns to deny them equality as citizens and human beings, are the most obvious case in point. This kind of communal violence may also be based on differences other than sexual, especially on racial, ethnic, and economic ones. Even here, however, sexual elements are often entangled in the violence. For example, in the United States, white men have sometimes justified their violence against black men by accusing them of having sexual designs on white women, while reserving to themselves the right to make sometimes violent use of black women. And in many parts of the world, rape has become a common weapon of civil war. What is more, violence may be done to others' freedom not only by direct assault, but also through subjecting the less powerful, making them dependent on and therefore properties of the more powerful. Both kinds of violence have long been characteristic of the relations of men with women and of rich with poor.

In recent years, newspapers have repeatedly taken notice of sexual enslavement that takes advantage of poverty to induce parents to sell their children or persuade girls and women in failing economies to leave home and commit themselves to the aegis of persons who then prostitute them. The offense in these situations is clearly not that of the prostitutes, but of the prostitutor and of the men who visit them. Children are categorically not of an age to commit themselves to such a life; all use of children by adults for sexual purposes is wrong. And societies have reason to share the churches' concern to prevent any kind of slave trade.

All these kinds of violence have deep roots. The Christian has an obligation to name them and struggle against them inwardly, in personal relationships, and in the larger society. In this respect, it is particularly evil that some Christian denominations have taken the side of violence themselves. Their condemnations of lesbian/gay people, for example, serve to justify violence against them and are accompanied, at the very best, by only the mildest of rebukes to those who attack them. Some denominations, such as the Roman Catholic and Southern Baptist, encourage denial of their legal rights. Some who call themselves "evangelical," "charismatic," or "pentecostal" also oppose equal freedom for women and call for complete subservience even on the part of battered wives. Until this changes, it is unlikely that our society will begin to treat rape of all kinds with the revulsion that it deserves, for to some extent such violence will always appear to offer a reaffirmation of the dominance of men over women, of heterosexuals over homosexuals, and, indeed, of the powerful generally over the weak.

Christians cannot justify such acts, ethically or spiritually. They violate Jesus' insistence that we are judged on our treatment of "the least of these." They also violate the model of Song of Songs in which the sacredness of love is manifested in the lovers' free engagement with one another. They violate the love of neighbor. They violate the ideal of sexual intimacy establishing the uniquely intimate kinship of "one flesh." The long list of other sexual sins fades into insignificance by comparison.

Finally, it would be wrong to leave the present topic without noting that rape and incest also carry with them, in our culture, a strong burden of impurity, which, paradoxically, falls more on the victim than on the perpetrator of the offense. Victims are often ashamed to reveal what has been done to them for fear of having to shoulder this burden. And, indeed, they may carry it with them whether they ever confide their experience to others or not. The perpetrator of incest may even use the threat of it to frighten the child into silence. We need to recognize that some of the harm done to the child in such cases arises when the revulsion with which the society at large regards incest spills over onto the child and encourages self-loathing. Christians have a responsibility to free themselves sufficiently from this kind of purity response that they can deal constructively and positively with individuals who have experienced incest and rape and also, one hopes, better instruct society at large. Hiding these topics or discussing them only in hushed tones and ambiguous language works harm.

Prostitution and Pornography

Prostitution is a perplexing topic in the scriptures. Prostitutes are despised and classified socially as the lowest of the low. They were typically women with no other means of support or, often, slaves. Because the prostitute was without alternatives, however, ethical disapproval, as with Paul, was more likely to fall on the man who uses her. Later Christians have tended to reverse this pattern and treat prostitutes as figures of great evil while frequently letting their male patrons off with no more than a wag of the finger. This is no doubt connected with the long history in Christian cultures of identifying women as the source of all sexual evil.

Partly because of this history, modern readers of the New Testament usually assume that when Jesus said to the religious leaders that the prostitutes were entering in the Reign of God ahead of them, he meant that they were, of course, giving up prostitution. But if so, how were they supporting themselves? We do not know exactly what their conversion entailed. In any case, it ill becomes followers of Jesus to heap disgrace on prostitutes who are simply trying to survive. The basic objection to prostitution, in the scriptures of Israel was that it wasted family resources (the marriageability of daughters, the honor of the family, the money spent by males on individual pleasure). In Paul, the objection is rather that sex with prostitutes is a use of one's sexuality that deprives it of any opening on the life of the Spirit and that disconnects it from our growth in God. This places the whole subject back under the rubric of spirituality and emphasizes once again that the ideal use of sexuality is one that creates a deepening sense of the value of the partner.

The subject of pornography is at least etymologically related to that of prostitution, since its Greek roots mean something like "representation of prostitution." The question is complicated in other ways, however, because it easily becomes caught up in traditional Christian hostility toward everything erotic. Often pornography is defined in ways that have to do primarily with purity codes: whatever the pious are revolted by is quickly forbidden. One result is that sex in general has been turned into a mystery that must never be mentioned, particularly not in the presence of the young—who are therefore left to find their own way with no advice more helpful than "Just say no!" It sometimes seems amazing that anything as erotic as the Song of Songs has survived in the Christian tradition.

It may be helpful to make a distinction between "erotica" and "pornography"—not that it will always be easy to decide what goes into which category. Representations of sexuality, visually or in words, are not intrinsically wrong and may be defined as "erotica" unless they have some specific quality, entirely apart from considerations of purity, that violate other ethical concerns we have been exploring. One such, raised by contemporary feminists, is that some heterosexual erotica reinforce images of the subordination of women and encourage violence against women. This would indeed place them in the category of wrongdoing. The same must be said for all child pornography, since the abuse of children is implicated in its very creation.

In one sense, the worst pornography of our world may be the constant and widely accepted use of the sexual in advertising, which strips human sexuality of its potential for the holy and reduces it to a means of inducing people to buy. Western culture has moved, over the last hundred years, from a state in which the sexual was unmentionable to a state in which it is everywhere around us, but reduced to being the slave and tool of trivial consumerism. When sex is trivialized in this way, it serves what is selfish and death dealing in us, not what is life giving. It becomes, by serving the purposes of commerce rather than of erotic relationship, the opposite of the free erotic play of the lovers in Song of Songs.

Homosexuality

This has come to be the supremely contentious issue of our times, with some Christians even insisting that this is a topic worth dividing churches over, despite the fact that scripture, as often noted, has little to say on the topic and is open to a variety of interpretations. It is very difficult, as the failure of "creation ethics" shows, to turn the prohibition of male-male anal intercourse in Leviticus into anything more than a purity regulation— one that was, in fact, limited in application to Israel and some other residents of the land of Canaan. What most anti-lesbian/gay authors do is appeal to the vestiges of purity revulsions in the modern audience. By suggesting to them that whatever disgusts them is immoral, they create a self-satisfied passion in their audience, who then tend to swallow these wriers' quite loosely constructed and even, at times, outright misleading biblical arguments.[30]

The high anxiety manifest in discussions of this topic owes more to the general sense of crisis and dislocation in our world than to its merits as a critical issue in Christian doctrine. There has never been a time when gay/lesbian people have not been present in the churches, but they have usually kept quiet about their presence, in accordance with the assumed standards of their communities. The question before Christians today is not really so much about homosexuality as about whether the churches are prepared to rethink the issue honestly and openly. This is something that right-wing Christians of all sorts are determined to prevent.

In terms of the ethic of property and relationship that we have been exploring, there is no reason why a same-gender relationship may not fall within the bounds of biblical ethics as easily as a heterosexual one. The qualities that would disqualify either one are the same: selfishness, the employment of physical violence or other forms of social power against another, failure to respect our own or one another's sexual property, failure to keep the sexual relationship open to our growth in the Spirit.[31]

Spirituality needs to be a key issue in the discussions of sexuality. The Bible alone will not settle the issue of same-gender sexuality because we are capable of reading it in too many different ways. Despite the high hopes of the Reformed tradition and its descendants, there is no single, universal "plain sense" of scripture. Christians will have to do what we have repeatedly had to do: ask about the qualities of the Spirit manifest in our co-believers. If Gentiles can produce the fruits of the Spirit, asks Peter, how can one keep them out? (Acts 10:47). If women manifest vocation for ordination and the gifts for such ministry, how, ultimately, can they be denied? If lesbians and gay men are living lives that manifest the grace of God and the love of God and neighbor, what else are other Christians waiting to see?

The account we have given here of Christian marriage, grounded as it is in the ways that Jesus and Paul both retained and transformed the property ethic of their place and time, contains nothing that is not equally applicable to both same-gender and opposite-gender couples. And none of the negative issues that we have identified in our discussion is particular to people of one or the other of these sexual orientations. Both groups, in short, have the same blessings and the same challenges. How they will live them out is still in the process of discovery. Heterosexual people are still dealing with the effects of the transition toward gender equality in the modern world. And the possibility of open discussion of gay/lesbian sexuality is still too new a phenomenon for Christians to feel that we have fully plumbed either its similarities or its differences. We have more to learn and reflect on, which is all the more reason not to close down further discussion as the opponents of lesbians and gay men would like to do. Christians have a lot of thinking and talking together yet to do, which is, after all, one purpose of the church as a community of faith, hope, and love.[32]

Gay men and lesbians, on the other hand, are rightly suspicious of churches that have been telling them for generations (and, in many cases, are still telling them) that they are evil or, at the very least, "intrinsically disordered." The situation cannot be one of a pure church offering its seal of approval to unclean outsiders. Churches need to repent of their past evil actions toward those they categorized as unclean and dismissed as unworthy of God's love. Only so can they hope to rebuild some sense of trustworthiness and, indeed, reclaim their own commitment to the gospel of Jesus.

For Christians who wish to stand in the ethical tradition of the Christian scriptures, affirmation of gay and lesbian co-believers is not a matter of condescension or even generosity. It is essential to the church's honesty and spiritual health. It is necessary to the spiritual well-being of heterosexuals as much as that of homosexual people. I do not believe that the former will be able to receive God's gift of sexuality for themselves without learning to delight in it for others as well. The Christian teaching about sex has too long taken the form "Sex is evil except under the following limited conditions (with a varying list following in different eras and communities)." It needs to learn a new language: "Sex is a good gift of God, provided that is it not despoiled by violence and lovelessness and rigid adherence to the social prerogatives of a dominant race, ethnic group, gender, or sexual orientation."

Sex is one of the rich blessings of creation, to be received with delight and thanksgiving. At the point where one's actions no longer express that truth, they become wrong. If I grab something for myself that belongs rightfully to another, whether through direct violence or through manipulation or any other means, I may be acknowledging that what I have grabbed is itself good, but I am no longer celebrating it as a part of the whole richness of creation—a richness that includes the neighbor I have robbed as much as myself. If I make satisfaction of sexual desire the overarching goal of my life, I put the part in place of the whole and thereby lose the sense of its real value. These considerations are what make libertinism wrong, for they condemn any pursuit of sexual pleasure that is based on megalomania and idolatry. What is less commonly observed is that they also make prudery, legalism, and the addiction to respectability wrong. For just as sex is not the final goal of the creation, neither is works-righteousness, fulfillment of the rules regardless of the cost to others, or the sense of comfort that comes from having met the demands of respectability. Life begins in God's free act of creation and concludes in God's free act of grace—or rather in the rejoicing to which it gives rise. Prudery, narrowness, or self-confident respectability will be no preparation for life in the age of rejoicing. It is not surprising that Jesus alienated those who practiced such "virtues."

This is not to suggest that the path to the age to come is all one of ease and pleasure. Its true difficulties, however, are not those self-induced by our rule-making proclivities. We do not need to make the Christian life difficult with the constant recitation and amplification of rules. The real challenges arise from our own selfishness and from the times and cultures in which we live. Marriage and family were not life giving enough to be final goals for the first-century Christian; neither they nor sexual enjoyment and cultivation of self can be our ultimate goals today. We live in times when great demands are being made on us in relation to justice, peace, and the survival of the world. At the same time, the gift of sexuality is one of the principal means by which God communicates to us the transforming power of love, beginning with God's own love in creating, forgiving, and reconciling us and setting us on the path of life.[33]

The good news of God's grace in Jesus and of the inbreaking of God's Reign has not yet finished transforming us—and will not this side of the grave. If we look at the great exemplars of its work, in the New Testament and thereafter, from Jesus to Martin Luther King Jr., we shall find that it does not normally act to make us more respectable—to produce conventional, predictable husbands and wives, devoted to nothing more than one another's happiness. For that matter, Jesus himself excepted, the gospel does not work to produce perfect people. The gospel works rather to express the power of God's love, which rejects our rejections and breaches our best defenses and draws us out from behind our fortifications to journey toward a goal that we can as yet barely imagine. The measure of a sexuality that accords with the New Testament is this: the degree to which it rejoices in God's gifts to the whole creation, in what is given to others as well as to each of us, while enabling us always to leave the final word to God, who is the Beginning and End of all things.

ABBREVIATIONS

Antiquities	Josephus, *Antiquities of the Jews*
ATR	*Anglican Theological Review*
CHab	Qumran *Commentary on Habakkuk* (1QpHab)
CNah	Qumran *Commentary on Nahum* (4QpNah)
CPs37	Qumran *Commentary on Psalm 37* (4QpPs 37)
CR	Qumran *Community Rule* (1QS)
DR	Qumran *Damascus Rule*
ET	English translation(s) (used when translations' numbering of chapter verses differs from MT)
H	Qumran *Hymns* (1QH)
ICC	International Critical Commentary
JBL	*Journal of Biblical Literature*
JECS	*Journal of Early Christian Studies*
JPS	Jewish Publication Society
JSNTSup	Journal for the Study of the New Testament—Supplement Series
JSOTSup	Journal for the Study of the Old Testament—Supplement Series
LXX	Septuagint (Old Greek version of the scriptures of Israel)
MA	Qumran *Messianic Anthology* (4Qtest)
MR	Qumran *Messianic Rule* (1QSa)
MT	Massoretic Text (standard Hebrew/Aramaic version of the scriptures of Israel)
NICNT	New International Commentary on the New Testament
NICOT	New International Commentary on the Old Testament
NRSV	New Revised Standard Version
NTS	*New Testament Studies*
RSR	*Religious Studies Review*
RSV	Revised Standard Version
SBL	Society of Biblical Literature
TDNT	*Theological Dictionary of the New Testament*
VC	*Vigiliae Christianae*
WR	Qumran *War Rule* (1QM)

Documents associated with Qumran are cited in accordance with the titles given them in Geza Vermes's English translation; the conventional scholarly sigla (for example, 1QpHab) appear in parentheses.

BIBLIOGRAPHY

Alter, Robert. "Sodom as Nexus: The Web of Design in Biblical Narrative." *Tikkun* 1/1 (1986): 30–38.

Althaus-Reid, Marcella. *From Feminist Theology to Indecent Theology: Readings on Poverty, Sexual Identity and God*. London: SCM Press, 2004.

Anderson, Janice Capel, and Moore, Stephen D. "Matthew and Masculinity." In *New Testament Masculinities*, ed. Stephen D. Moore and Janice Capel Anderson, 67–91. Semeia Studies 45. Atlanta: SBL, 2003.

Ariès, Philippe. "St Paul and the Flesh." In *Western Sexuality*, ed. Philippe Ariès and André Béjin and trans. Anthony Forster, 36–39. Oxford: Basil Blackwell & Mott, 1985.

Armstrong, A. H., ed. *The Cambridge History of Later Greek and Early Medieval Philosophy*. Cambridge: Cambridge University Press, 1970.

Attridge, Harold W. *The Epistle to the Hebrews*. Hermeneia. Philadelphia: Fortress Press, 1989.

Bailey, Derrick Sherwin. *Homosexuality and the Western Christian Tradition*. London: Longmans Green, 1955.

Balch, David L. "1 Cor 7:32–35 and Stoic Debates About Marriage, Anxiety, and Distraction." *JBL* 102 (1983): 429–39.

———. *Let Wives Be Submissive: The Domestic Code in 1 Peter*. SBL Monograph Series, no. 26. Chico, Calif.: Scholars Press, 1981.

———. "Paul's Portrait of Christ Crucified (Gal. 3:1) in Light of Paintings and Sculptures of Suffering and Death in Pompeiian and Roman Houses." In *Early Christian Families in Context: An Interdisciplinary Dialogue*, ed. David L. Balch and Carolyn Osiek, 84–108. Grand Rapids: Eerdmans, 2003.

Barclay, John M. G. "The Family as the Bearer of Religion in Judaism and Early Christianity." In *Constructing Early Christian Families: Family as Social Reality and Metaphor*, ed. Halvor Moxnes, 66–80. London: Routledge, 1997.

Barrett, C. K., ed. *New Testament Background: Selected Documents*. London: SPCK, 1956.

———. *The Second Epistle to the Corinthians*. New York: Harper & Row, 1973.

Barton, Stephen C. *Life Together: Family, Sexuality and Community in the New Testament and Today*. Edinburgh: T&T Clark, 2001.

Batchelor, Edward, Jr. *Homosexuality and Ethics*. New York: Pilgrim Press, 1975.

Best, Ernest. "Mark iii. 20, 21, 31-35." *NTS* 22 (1976): 309–19.

Betz, Hans Dieter. *Galatians: A Commentary on Paul's Letter to the Churches in Galatia*. Hermeneia. Philadelphia: Fortress Press, 1979.

Biale, David. *Eros and the Jews: From Biblical Israel to Contemporary America*. New York: Basic Books, 1992.

Booth, Roger P. *Jesus and the Laws of Purity: Tradition History and Legal History in Mark 7*. JSNTSup 13 (1986).

Boswell, John. *Christianity, Social Tolerance, and Homosexuality: Gay People in Western Europe from the Beginning of the Christian Era to the Fourteenth Century*. Chicago: University of Chicago Press, 1980.

Brawley, Robert L., ed. *Biblical Ethics and Homosexuality: Listening to Scripture*. Louisville, Ky.: Westminster John Knox, 1996.

Bray, Alan. *The Friend*. Chicago: University of Chicago Press, 2003.

Brock, Rita Nakashima. *Journeys by Heart: A Christology of Erotic Power*. New York: Crossroad, 1995.

Brooten, Bernadette. "Konnten Frauen im alten Judentum die Scheidung betreiben? Überlegungen zu Mk 10,11–12 und 1 Kor 7,10–11." *Evangelische Theologie* 42 (1982): 65–80.

———. *Love Between Women: Early Christian Responses to Female Homoeroticism*. Chicago: University of Chicago Press, 1996.

———. *Women Leaders in the Ancient Synagogue: Inscriptional Evidence and Background Issues*. Chico, Calif.: Scholars, 1982.

Brown, Peter. *The Body and Society: Men, Women, and Sexual Renunciation in Early Christianity*. New York: Columbia University Press, 1988.

———. "Late Antiquity." In *From Pagan Rome to Byzantium*, ed. Paul Veyne and trans. by Arthur Goldhammer, 235–311. Vol. 1 of *A History of Private Life*, ed. Philippe Ariès and Georges Duby. Cambridge, Mass.: Belknap Press, 1987.

Buckley, Jorunn Jacobson. "A Cult-Mystery in The Gospel of Philip." *JBL* 99 (1980): 569–81.

Budd, Philip J. *Leviticus*. New Century Bible Commentary. Grand Rapids, Mich.: Eerdmans, 1996.

Burkert, Walter. *Greek Religion*. Trans. John Raffan. Cambridge, Mass.: Harvard University Press, 1985.

Burrus, Virginia. *Chastity as Autonomy: Women in the Stories of the Apocryphal Acts*. Studies in Women and Religion 23. Lewiston, N.Y.: Edwin Mellen Press, 1987.

Carden, Michael. *Sodomy: A History of a Christian Biblical Myth*. London: Equinox, 2004.

Carr, David M. *The Erotic Word: Sexuality, Spirituality, and the Bible*. New York: Oxford University Press, 2003.

Catchpole, David R. "Paul, James and the Apostolic Decree." *NTS* 23 (1976–77): 428–44.

Charlesworth, James H., ed. *The Old Testament Pseudepigrapha*. 2 vols. Garden City, N.Y.: Doubleday, 1983–85.

Clarke, John R. *Looking at Lovemaking: Constructions of Sexuality in Roman Art, 100 B.C.–A.D. 250*. Berkeley: University of California Press, 1998.

Collins, Raymond F. *Divorce in the New Testament*. Collegeville, Minn.: Liturgical Press, 1992.

———. *Sexual Ethics and the New Testament: Behavior and Belief*. New York: Crossroad, 2000.

Conzelmann, Hans. *1 Corinthians: A Commentary on the First Epistle to the Corinthians*. Trans. James W. Leitch. Hermeneia. Philadelphia: Fortress Press, 1975.

Countryman, L. Wm. "The AIDS Crisis: Theological and Ethical Reflections." *ATR* 69 (1987): 125–34.

———. *Biblical Authority or Biblical Tyranny? Scripture and the Christian Pilgrimage*. Philadelphia: Fortress Press, 1981.

————. "Christian Equality and the Early Catholic Episcopate." *ATR* 63 (1981): 115–38.

————. *Interpreting the Truth: Changing the Paradigm of Biblical Studies*. Harrisburg, Pa.: Trinity Press International, 2003.

————. *Love Human and Divine: Reflections on Love, Sexuality, and Friendship*. Harrisburg, Pa.: Morehouse, 2005.

————. *The Mystical Way in the Fourth Gospel: Crossing Over Into God*. 2d ed. Harrisburg, Pa.: Trinity Press International, 1994.

————. *The Rich Christian in the Church of the Early Empire: Contradictions and Accommodations*. New York & Toronto: Edwin Mellen Press, 1980.

————. "Tertullian and the Regula Fidei." *The Second Century* 2 (1982): 208–27.

Cumont, Franz. *The Oriental Religions in Roman Paganism*. 1911. Reprint. New York: Dover, 1956.

D'Angelo, Mary Rose. "'Knowing How to Preside over His Own Household': Imperial Masculinity and Christian Asceticism in the Pastorals, *Hermas*, and Luke-Acts." In *New Testament Masculinities*, ed. Stephen D. Moore and Janice Capel Anderson, 265–95. Semeia Studies 45. Atlanta: SBL, 2003.

De Waal, Frans. "Reading Nature's Tea Leaves." *Natural History* (December 2000): 66–71.

Dixon, Suzanne. *The Roman Family*. Baltimore: Johns Hopkins University Press, 1992.

Douglas, Mary. *Purity and Danger: An Analysis of Concepts of Pollution and Taboo*. London: Routledge & Kegan Paul, 1966.

Draper, Jonathan A. "The Role of Ritual in the Alternation of Social Universe: Jewish-Christian Initiation of Gentiles in the Didache." *Listening* 32 (1997): 48–67.

Driver, S. R. *A Critical and Exegetical Commentary on Deuteronomy*. 3d ed. ICC. Edinburgh: T&T Clark, 1902.

Eilberg-Schwartz, Howard. *The Savage in Judaism: An Anthropology of Israelite Religion and Ancient Judaism*. Bloomington: Indiana University Press, 1990.

Elliott, Alison Goddard. *Roads to Paradise: Reading the Lives of the Early Saints*. Hanover, N.H.: Brown University Press, 1987.

Elliott, John H. *A Home for the Homeless: A Sociological Exegesis of 1 Peter, Its Situation and Strategy*. Philadelphia: Fortress Press, 1981.

Ellison, Marvin M. *Erotic Justice: A Liberating Ethic of Sexuality*. Louisville, Ky.: Westminster John Knox, 1996.

————. and Thorson-Smith, Sylvia, eds. *Body and Soul: Rethinking Sexuality as Justice-Love*. Cleveland: Pilgrim Press, 2003.

Engberg-Pedersen, Troels. *Paul and the Stoics*. Louisville, Ky.: Westminster John Knox, 2000.

————. ed. *Paul in His Hellenistic Context*. Minneapolis: Fortress Press, 1995.

Enslin, Morton Scott. *The Ethics of Paul*. New York: Abingdon, 1957.

Fatum, Lone. "Brotherhood in Christ." In *Constructing Early Christian Families: Family as Social Reality and Metaphor*, ed. Halvor Moxnes, 183–97. London: Routledge, 1997.

Forkman, Göran. *The Limits of Religious Community: Expulsion from the Religious Community Within the Qumran Sect, Within Rabbinic Judaism, and Within Primitive Christianity.* Lund, Sweden: CWK Gleerup, 1972.

Foucault, Michel. *The Care of the Self.* Trans. Robert Hurley. Vol. 3 of *The History of Sexuality.* New York: Pantheon, 1986.

Gagnon, Robert A. J. *The Bible and Homosexual Practice: Texts and Hermeneutics.* Nashville, Tenn.: Abingdon, 2001.

Gerstenberger, Erhard S. *Leviticus: A Commentary.* Trans. Douglas W. Stott. Old Testament Library. Louisville, Ky.: Westminster John Knox, 1996.

Gokhale, Jayashree B. "Castaways of Caste." *Natural History* (October 1986): 33–37.

Goodenough, Erwin R. *An Introduction to Philo Judaeus.* Oxford: Basil Blackwell, 1962.

Grant, Frederick C. "The Impracticability of the Gospel Ethics." In *Aux sources de la tradition chrétienne: Mélanges offerts à M. Maurice Goguel,* 86–94. Neuchâtel, Switzerland: Delachaux et Niestlé, 1950.

Grant, Robert M. *Paul in the Roman World: The Conflict at Corinth.* Louisville, Ky.: Westminster John Knox, 2001.

Grau, Marion. *Of Divine Economy: Refinancing Redemption.* New York: T&T Clark, 2004.

Green, Joel B. *The Gospel of Luke.* NICNT. Grand Rapids, Mich.: Eerdmans, 1997.

Grenz, Stanley J. *Sexual Ethics: A Biblical Perspective.* Dallas: Word, 1990.

———. *Welcoming but Not Affirming: An Evangelical Response to Homosexuality.* Louisville, Ky.: Westminster John Knox, 1998.

Gudorf, Christine E. *Body, Sex, and Pleasure: Reconstructing Christian Sexual Ethics.* Cleveland: Pilgrim Press, 1994.

Gundry-Volf, Judith M. "The Least and the Greatest: Children in the New Testament." In *The Child in Christian Thought.* ed. Marcia J. Bunge, 29–60. Grand Rapids, Mich.: Eerdmans, 2001.

Haenchen, Ernst. *The Acts of the Apostles: A Commentary.* Trans. Bernard Noble, et al. Philadelphia: Westminster, 1971.

Hanks, Thomas D. *God So Loved the Third World: The Biblical Vocabulary of Oppression.* Trans. James C. Dekker. Maryknoll, N.Y.: Orbis, 1983.

———. *The Subversive Gospel: A New Testament Commentary of Liberation.* Trans. John P. Doner. Cleveland: Pilgrim Press, 2000.

Hays, Richard B. *The Moral Vision of the New Testament: A Contemporary Introduction to New Testament Ethics.* San Francisco: HarperSanFrancisco, 1996.

———. "Relations Natural and Unnatural: A Response to John Boswell's Exegesis of Romans 1." *Journal of Religious Ethics* 14 (1986): 184–215.

Hederman, Mark Patrick. *Love Impatient, Love Unkind: Eros Human and Divine.* New York: Crossroad, 2004.

Hengel, Martin. *Judaism and Hellenism: Studies in their Encounter in Palestine During the Early Hellenistic Period.* Trans. John Bowden. 2 vols. Philadelphia: Fortress Press, 1974.

Heyward, Carter. *Touching Our Strength: The Erotic as Power and the Love of God.* San Francisco: Harper & Row, 1989.

Hitt, Jack. "Pro-Life Nation." *The New York Times Magazine* (April 9, 2006): 40–47, 62, 72, 74.

Horner, Tom. *Eros in Greece: A Sexual Inquiry*. New York: Aegean Books, 1978.

Houlden, J. L. *Ethics and the New Testament*. New York: Oxford University Press, 1977.

Houston, Walter. *Purity and Monotheism: Clean and Unclean Animals in Biblical Law*. JSOTSup 140. 1993.

Hubbard, Thomas K. *Homosexuality in Greece and Rome: A Sourcebook of Basic Documents*. Berkeley: University of California Press, 2003.

Hunt, Mary E. *Fierce Tenderness: A Feminist Theology of Friendship*. New York: Crossroad, 1994.

Jacobs, Andrew S. "A Family Affair: Marriage, Class, and Ethics in the Apocryphal Acts of the Apostles." *JECS* 7 (1999): 105–38.

Jennings, Theodore W., Jr. *Jacob's Wound: Homoerotic Narrative in the Literature of Ancient Israel*. New York: Continuum, 2005.

———. *The Man Jesus Loved: Homoerotic Narratives from the New Testament*. Cleveland: Pilgrim Press, 2003.

Johnson, Luke T. "The Use of Leviticus 19 in the Letter of James." *JBL* 101 (1982): 391–401.

Jordan, Mark D. *The Ethics of Sex*. Oxford: Blackwell, 2002.

———. *The Invention of Sodomy in Christian Theology*. Chicago: University of Chicago Press, 1997.

———. *Telling Truths in Church: Scandal, Flesh, and Christian Speech*. Boston: Beacon Press, 2003.

Jung, Patricia Beattie, and Smith, Ralph F. *Heterosexism: An Ethical Challenge*. Albany: State University of New York Press, 1993.

Kelly, J. N. D. *A Commentary on the Pastoral Epistles*. New York: Harper & Row, 1963.

Keuls, Eva C. *The Reign of the Phallus: Sexual Politics in Ancient Athens*. New York: Harper & Row, 1985.

Kittredge, Cynthia Briggs. *Community and Authority: The Rhetoric of Obedience in the Pauline Tradition*. Harrisburg, Pa.: Trinity Press International, 1998.

Klawans, Jonathan. *Impurity and Sin in Ancient Judaism*. Oxford: Oxford University Press, 2000.

———. "Ritual Purity, Moral Purity, and Sacrifice in Jacob Milgrom's *Leviticus*." *RSR* 29 (2003): 19–28.

Kraemer, Ross S. "Typical and Atypical Jewish Family Dynamics: The Cases of Babatha and Berenice." In *Early Christian Families in Context: An Interdisciplinary Dialogue*, ed. David L. Balch and Carolyn Osiek, 130–56. Grand Rapids, Mich.: Eerdmans, 2003.

Levine, Baruch A. *Leviticus*. JPS Torah Commentary. Philadelphia: JPS, 1989.

Lewis, C. S. *The Four Loves*. London: Geoffrey Bles, 1960.

Licht, Hans. *Sexual Life in Ancient Greece*. Trans. J. H. Freese. London: Routledge & Kegan Paul, 1932.

Loader, William. *Sexuality and the Jesus Tradition*. Grand Rapids, Mich.: Eerdmans, 2005.

Lohse, Eduard, ed. *Die Texte aus Qumran, hebräisch und deutsch*. Munich: Kosel, 1964.

MacDonald, Dennis Ronald. *The Legend and the Apostle: The Battle for Paul in Story and Canon*. Philadelphia: Westminster, 1983.

Maier, Johann. *The Temple Scroll: An Introduction, Translation & Commentary*. Trans. Richard T. White. JSOTSup 34. 1985.

Malherbe, Abraham J. "Paul: Hellenistic Philosopher or Christian Pastor?" *ATR* 68 (1986): 3–13.

Malina, Bruce J. *The New Testament World: Insights from Cultural Anthropology*. Atlanta: John Knox, 1981.

Martin, Dale B. "*Arsenokoites* and *Malakos*: Meanings and Consequences." In *Biblical Ethics and Homosexuality*, ed. Robert L. Brawley, 47–50. Harrisburg, Pa.: Trinity Press International, 2003.

———. *The Corinthian Body*. New Haven: Yale University Press, 1995.

———. "Paul and Passion." In *Constructing Early Christian Families: Family as Social Reality and Metaphor*, ed. Halvor Moxnes, 201–15. London: Routledge, 1997.

———. *Slavery as Salvation: The Metaphor of Slavery in Pauline Christianity*. New Haven, Conn.: Yale University Press, 1990.

Martin, Troy W. "Paul's Argument from Nature for the Veil in 1 Corinthians 11:13–15: A Testicle Instead of a Head Covering." *JBL* 123 (204): 75–84.

McCombie, F. "Jesus and the Leaven of Salvation." *New Blackfriars* 59 (1978): 450–62.

Meeks, Wayne A. *The Moral World of the First Christians*. Philadelphia: Westminster Press, 1986.

———. *The Origins of Christian Morality: The First Two Centuries*. New Haven, Conn.: Yale University Press, 1993.

———. "Understanding Early Christian Ethics." *JBL* 105 (1986): 3–11.

Metzger, Bruce M. *A Textual Commentary on the Greek New Testament*. 2d ed. N.p.: United Bible Societies, 1994.

Meyers, Eric M. "The Problems of Gendered Space in Syro-Palestinian Domestic Architecture: The Case of Roman-Period Galilee." In *Early Christian Families in Context: An Interdisciplinary Dialogue*, ed. David L. Balch and Carolyn Osiek, 44–69. Grand Rapids, Mich.: Eerdmans, 2003.

Milgrom, Jacob. *Leviticus*. Anchor Bible. 3 vols. New York: Doubleday, 1991–2000.

———. *Numbers*. JPS Torah Commentary. Philadelphia: JPS, 1990.

Mombo, Esther. "Resisting *Vumilia* Theology: The Church and Violence Against Women in Kenya." In *Anglicanism: A Global Communion*, ed. Andrew Wingate et al., 219–24. New York: Church Publishing, 1998.

Monti, Joseph. *Arguing About Sex: The Rhetoric of Christian Sexual Morality*. Albany: State University of New York Press, 1995.

Moule, H. C. G. *The Epistles to the Colossians and to Philemon*. Cambridge: Cambridge University Press, 1902.

Moxnes, Halvor, ed. *Constructing Early Christian Families: Family as Social Reality and Metaphor*. London: Routledge, 1997.

Murphy-O'Connor, Jerome. "The Divorced Woman in 1 Cor 7:10-11." *JBL* 100 (1981): 601–06.

Nelson, James B. *Body Theology.* Louisville, Ky.: Westminster John Knox, 1992.

Neusner, Jacob. "'First Cleanse the Inside.'" *NTS* 22 (1975–76): 486–95.

———. *From Politics to Piety: The Emergence of Pharisaic Judaism.* Englewood Cliffs, NJ: Prentice-Hall, 1973.

———. *A History of the Mishnaic Law of Purities.* Part XXII: *The Mishnaic System of Uncleanness: Its Context and History.* Leiden, Neth.: E. J. Brill, 1977.

———. *The Idea of Purity in Ancient Judaism.* Leiden, Neth.: E. J. Brill, 1973.

Newton, Michael. *The Concept of Purity at Qumran and in the Letters of Paul.* Cambridge: Cambridge University Press, 1985.

Neyrey, Jerome H. "Body Language in 1 Corinthians: The Use of Anthropological Models for Understanding Paul and His Opponents." *Semeia* 35 (1986): 129–70.

———. "Idea of Purity in Mark's Gospel." *Semeia* 35 (1986): 91–128.

Nissinen, Martti. *Homoeroticism in the Biblical World: A Historical Perspective.* Trans. Kirsi Stjerna. Minneapolis: Fortress Press, 1998.

Njiiri, Edith Njoki. "Polygamy in the African Church Today: A Kenyan Woman's Perspective." In *Anglicanism: A Global Communion*, ed. Andrew Wingate, et al., 246–48. New York: Church Publishing, 1998.

Noth, Martin. *Leviticus: A Commentary.* Trans. J. E. Anderson. The Old Testament Library. London: SCM, 1965.

Nygren, Anders. *Agape and Eros: A Study of the Christian Idea of Love.* Trans. A. G. Hebert. 3 vols. London: SPCK, 1938–41.

Oliver, Mary McPherson. *Conjugal Spirituality: The Primacy of Mutual Love in Christian Tradition.* Kansas City, Mo.: Sheed & Ward, 1994.

Olyan, Saul M. "'And with a Male You Shall Not Lie the Lying Down of a Woman': On the Meaning and Significance of Leviticus 18:22 and 20:13." In *Que(e)rying Religion: A Critical Anthology*, ed. Gary David Comstock and Susan E. Henking, 398–414. New York: Continuum, 1997.

Osiek, Carolyn. "Female Slaves, *Porneia*, and the Limits of Obedience." In *Early Christian Families in Context: An Interdisciplinary Dialogue*, ed. David L. Balch and Carolyn Osiek, 255–74. Grand Rapids, Mich.: Eerdmans, 2003.

Pedersen, Johs. *Israel: Its Life and Culture.* 4 vols. in 2. London: Geoffrey Cumberlege and Copenhagen: Branner og Korch, 1926–40.

Petersen, William L. "Can ΑΡΣΕΝΟΚΟΙΤΑΙ Be Translated by 'Homosexuals'? (I Cor. 6.9; I Tim. 1:10)." *VC* 40 (1986): 187–91.

Peterson, Eugene H. *Christ Plays in Ten Thousand Places: A Conversation in Spiritual Theology.* Grand Rapids, Mich.: Eerdmans, 2005.

Phipps, W. E. "Is Paul's Attitude Towards Sexual Relations Contained in I Cor. 7.1?" *NTS* 28 (1982): 125–31.

Pomeroy, Sarah B. *Goddesses, Whores, Wives, and Slaves: Women in Classical Antiquity.* New York: Schocken, 1975.

Presbyterian Church (U.S.A.). *Presbyterians and Human Sexuality.* 1991.

Riches, John. *Jesus and the Transformation of Judaism.* London: Darton, Longman & Todd, 1980.

Rist, J. M. *Stoic Philosophy*. Cambridge: Cambridge University Press, 1969.

Rivkin, Ellis. *A Hidden Revolution*. Nashville, Tenn.: Abingdon, 1978.

Robinson, John A. T. *The Body: A Study in Pauline Theology*. Studies in Biblical Theology 5. London: SCM Press, 1952.

Rogers, Eugene F., Jr. *Sexuality and the Christian Body: Their Way into the Triune God*. Oxford: Blackwell, 1999.

Ropes, James Hardy. *The Text of Acts*. Vol. 3 of *The Beginnings of Christianity*, part 1, *The Acts of the Apostles*. ed. F. J. Foakes Jackson and Kirsopp Lake. Reprint. Grand Rapids, Mich.: Baker, 1979.

Rowland, Christopher, and Corner, Mark. *Liberating Exegesis: The Challenge of Liberation Theology to Biblical Studies*. Louisville, Ky.: Westminster John Knox, 1989.

Sanday, William, and Headlam, Arthur C. *A Critical and Exegetical Commentary on the Epistle to the Romans*. 5th ed. ICC. Edinburgh: T&T Clark, 1902.

Sanders, E. P. *Paul and Palestinian Judaism: A Comparison of Patterns of Religion*. Philadelphia: Fortress Press, 1977.

————. *Paul, the Law, and the Jewish People*. Philadelphia: Fortress Press, 1983.

Sandnes, Karl Olav. "Equality Within Patriarchal Structures." In *Constructing Early Christian Families: Family as Social Reality and Metaphor*, ed. Halvor Moxnes, 150–65. London: Routledge, 1997.

Schmidt, Thomas E. *Straight and Narrow? Compassion and Clarity in the Homosexuality Debate*. Downers Grove, Ill.: InterVarsity, 1995.

Schnackenburg, Rudolf. *The Moral Teaching of the New Testament*. Trans. J. Holland-Smith and W. J. O'Hara. Freiburg, Ger.: Herder & Herder, 1965.

Schneiders, Sandra M. *Written That You May Believe: Encountering Jesus in the Fourth Gospel*. New York: Crossroad, 1999.

Schüssler Fiorenza, Elisabeth. *The Book of Revelation: Justice and Judgment*. Philadelphia: Fortress Press, 1985.

————. *In Memory of Her: A Feminist Theological Reconstruction of Christian Origins*. New York: Crossroad, 1985.

Schweitzer, Albert. *The Mysticism of Paul the Apostle*. Trans. William Montgomery. New York: Macmillan, 1960.

Schweizer, Eduard. *The Letter to the Colossians: A Commentary*. Trans. Andrew Chester. Minneapolis: Augsburg, 1982.

Scroggs, Robin. *The New Testament and Homosexuality: Contextual Background for Contemporary Debate*. Philadelphia: Fortress Press, 1983.

Segal, Alan F. *Rebecca's Children: Judaism and Christianity in the Roman World*. Cambridge, Mass.: Harvard University Press, 1986.

Selvidge, Marla J. "Mark 5:25–34 and Leviticus 15:19–20." *JBL* 103 (1984): 619–23.

Sinclair, Scott Gambrill. "The Christologies of Paul's Undisputed Epistles and the Christology of Paul." Ph.D. diss., The Graduate Theological Union, 1986.

Snyder, Graydon F. *Ante Pacem: Archaeological Evidence of Church Life Before Constantine*. Macon, Ga.: Mercer University Press, 1985.

Soards, Marion L. *Scripture and Homosexuality: Biblical Authority and the Church Today*. Louisville, Ky.: Westminster John Knox, 1995.

Soto, Jean Ponder. "Redeeming Eros: A Christian Ethical Spirituality of Sexual Intimacy." Ph.D. diss., The Graduate Theological Union, 2003.

Spohn, William C. *What Are They Saying About Scripture and Ethics?* Rev. ed. New York: Paulist Press, 1995.

Stott, John. *Our Social and Sexual Revolution: Major Issues for a New Century*. 3d ed. Grand Rapids, Mich.: Baker, 1999.

Swancutt, Diana M. "'The Disease of Effemination': The Charge of Effeminacy and the Verdict of God (Romans 1:18–2:16)." In *New Testament Masculinities*, ed. Stephen D. Moore and Janice Capel Anderson, 193–223. Semeia Studies 45. Atlanta: SBL, 2003.

Szesnat, Holger. "'Pretty Boys' in Philo's *De Vita Contemplativa*." *Studia Philonica Annual* 10 (1998): 87–107.

———. "Sexual Desire, 'Deviant Behaviour,' and Moral Discourse in the Writings of Paul and Philo: An Historical-Exegetical Study of the Moral Problematisation of Sexual Desire and Behaviour in First-Century Hellenistic Judaism and Christianity, with Special Reference to the Work of Michel Foucault." Ph.D. diss., University of Natal, 1998.

Thatcher, Adrian. *Liberating Sex: A Christian Sexual Theology*. London: SPCK, 1993.

Theissen, Gerd. *Sociology of Early Palestinian Christianity*. Trans. John Bowden. Philadelphia: Fortress Press, 1978.

Trible, Phyllis. *God and the Rhetoric of Sexuality*. Philadelphia: Fortress Press, 1978.

———. *Texts of Terror: Literary-Feminist Readings of Biblical Narratives*. Philadelphia: Fortress Press, 1984.

Trümper, Monika. "Material and Social Environment of Greco-Roman Households in the East: The Case of Hellenistic Delos." In *Early Christian Families in Context: An Interdisciplinary Dialogue*, ed. David L. Balch and Carolyn Osiek, 19–43. Grand Rapids, Mich.: Eerdmans, 2003.

Turner, Philip. *Sex, Money, & Power: An Essay in Christian Social Ethics*. Cambridge, Mass.: Cowley, 1985.

Underwood, Anne. "Clergy Sexual Misconduct: A Justice Issue." In *Body and Soul: Rethinking Sexuality as Justice-Love*, ed. Marvin M. Ellison and Sylvia Thorson-Smith, 300–315. Cleveland: Pilgrim Press, 2003.

Vasey, Michael. *Strangers and Friends: A New Exploration of Homosexuality and the Bible*. London: Hodder & Stoughton, 1995.

Verhey, Allen. *The Great Reversal: Ethics and the New Testament*. Grand Rapids, Mich.: Eerdmans, 1984.

Vermes, Geza. *The Dead Sea Scrolls in English*. Reprint with revisions. Harmondsworth, UK: Penguin, 1968.

———. *The Dead Sea Scrolls: Qumran in Perspective*. With Pamela Vermes. Cleveland: Collins World, 1978.

Veyne, Paul, ed. *A History of Private Life*. Vol. 1: *From Pagan Rome to Byzantium*. Trans. Arthur Goldhammer. Cambridge, Mass.: Belknap Press, 1987.

———. "Homosexuality in Ancient Rome." In *Western Sexuality*, ed. Philippe Ariès and André Béjin and trans. Anthony Forster, 26–35. Oxford: Basil Blackwell & Mott, 1985.

Via, Dan O., Jr. *The Ethics of Mark's Gospel—In the Middle of Time.* Philadelphia: Fortress Press, 1985.

Wallace, Catherine M. *For Fidelity: How Intimacy and Commitment Enrich Our Lives.* New York: Vintage, 1999.

Weil, Simone. *Waiting for God.* Trans. Emma Craufurd. New York: Putnam, 1951.

Wenham, Gordon J. *The Book of Leviticus.* NICOT. Grand Rapids, Mich.: Eerdmans, 1979.

———. *Numbers: An Introduction and Commentary.* Leicester, UK: InterVarsity, 1981.

Whittaker, Molly. *Jews and Christians: Graeco-Roman Views.* Cambridge: Cambridge University Press, 1984.

Windsor, Ann. *A King Is Bound in the Tresses: Allusions to the Song of Songs in the Fourth Gospel.* Studies in Biblical Literature 6. New York: Peter Lang, 1999.

Winston, David. *The Wisdom of Solomon.* Anchor Bible 43. Garden City, N.Y.: Doubleday, 1979.

Wire, Antoinette Clark. *The Corinthian Women Prophets: A Reconstruction Through Paul's Rhetoric.* Minneapolis: Fortress Press, 1990.

Witherington, Ben. "The Anti-Feminist Tendencies of the 'Western' Text in Acts." *JBL* 103 (1984): 82–84.

Wright, David F. "Homosexuals or Prostitutes? The Meaning of ARSENOKOITAI (1 Cor. 6:9, 1 Tim. 1:10)." *VC* 38 (1984): 124–53.

Yarbrough, O. Larry. *Not Like the Gentiles: Marriage Rules in the Letters of Paul.* SBL Dissertation Series 80. Atlanta: Scholars, 1985.

Zaas, Peter S. "As I Teach Everywhere, In Every Church: A Study of the Communication of Morals in Paul." Ph.D. diss., University of Chicago, 1982.

———. "Cast Out the Evil Man from Your Midst." *JBL* 103 (1984): 259–61.

———. "Catalogue and Context: The Vice-Lists of 1 Corinthians 5 and 6." *NTS* 34 (1988): 622–29.

ENDNOTES

Introduction

1. Occasionally, a female author is suggested for one or another book of the New Testament. Perhaps the likeliest candidate would be Priscilla as author of Hebrews.
2. The work of Michel Foucault has opened this topic up in very helpful ways. While I have not drawn on him for theoretical foundations, my historiography is indebted to his example of taking the specific language and concerns of ancient texts seriously.
3. Cf. the brief but lucid remarks of Houlden (*Ethics and the New Testament*, 1–24) and, at greater length, Verhey, *Great Reversal*, 153–97.
4. For a specifically historical approach to the issues of ethics in the New Testament, see Meeks, "Understanding Early Christian Ethics," 3–11, and, at greater length, his *The Moral World of the First Christians*. I see Meeks's concern for "social world" as providing essential context to the reading of scripture, as the following pages will show.
5. I owe the phrase to Prof. Howard Miller of the University of Texas at Austin.
6. This, I have suggested, is the principal importance of the authority of the Bible for Christians; see my *Biblical Authority*, 70–75.
7. Ibid., 54–58.

Chapter 1: What Is Purity?

1. Douglas, *Purity and Danger*, 2, 35. Douglas has elsewhere evolved complex and significant theories about the ways in which purity concerns relate to other cultural formations; here I refer to her only for the most basic of anthropological distinctions.
2. Ibid., 76–93.
3. I have seen canned slugs on sale in the Portland Airport, offering the consumer a choice between "whole body" and "kitchen sliced" varieties. But the point seemed to be to evoke a frisson of revulsion rather than to offer a serious culinary proposal.
4. By "reasoned" here, I mean not that they are based on health concerns, as has sometimes been claimed, but simply that they have been carefully thought through and made more consistent.
5. Douglas, *Purity and Danger*, 94–113.

Chapter 2: Israel's Basic Purity Law

1. The term *sect* here has its technical sense of a group within a larger religious group with a distinctive understanding or practice and, often, a particularly strong sense of devotion or piety. It is not pejorative.
2. Those that survive will generally be found in the collections entitled "Pseudepigrapha" or in the Dead Sea Scrolls.

3. The term *cult* (or *cultus*) here has its technical sense of a form of worship. It is not pejorative.

4. Milgrom, *Leviticus*, 48. It is generally assumed that these codes existed prior to their incorporation in the Torah, but some argue that the process was less clear-cut; Gerstenberger, *Leviticus: A Commentary*, 18.

5. The meaning of this last phrase is somewhat uncertain. It may mean that God will punish them with untimely death or that the court is to execute them or perhaps banish them—a very weighty punishment in antiquity: Wenham, *The Book of Leviticus*, 241–42. Another possible meaning is that the offenders will be left without posterity in Israel (Milgrom, *Leviticus*, 457–60). Baruch A. Levine proposes that the community was expected to enact "cutting off," perhaps by execution, but that God could be expected to act if it did not; *Leviticus*, 241–42.

6. Milgrom, *Leviticus*, 2–49.

7. This is usually understood as referring to the sacrifice of children, a practice known from ancient Canaan. The phrase itself, however, is ambiguous. Because "seed" can also mean "semen," it could refer to some specifically sexual rite.

8. Douglas, *Purity and Danger*, 129–33. Milgrom observes that the Holiness Code particularly used condemnatory purity terms when dealing with forbidden unions that were not violations of blood kinship, presumably to reinforce what might not otherwise have evoked much revulsion (*Leviticus*, 1374).

9. Cf. Neusner, *The Idea of Purity in Ancient Judaism*, 11–15.

10. The law about a woman's impurity after childbirth (Leviticus 12) may also be based on an analogy with the menstrual flow; Wenham, *The Book of Leviticus*, 188.

11. Cf. David's curse on the household of Joab—that it should never lack a man with gonorrhea, a leper, a "man who holds the spindle" (a tool used by women), or a victim of murder or starvation (2 Sam. 3:29).

12. Cf. Milgrom, *Leviticus*, 1:569. For a detailed analysis, see Olyan, "And with a Male," 398–414.

13. There is no reference to female-female sexual intercourse in the Jewish scriptures. The original prohibition may in fact have been quite narrow. Milgrom (*Leviticus*, 1:569) notes D. Stewart's argument that what is prohibited here is only intercourse with male relatives with whose widows one would also be forbidden to have intercourse.

14. The Old Greek translation uses *akatharsia* for *toebah* (Ps. 6:10; 24:9) and *anomia* often in Ezek. The normal use of *bdelygma* for both Hebrew terms suggests that they were perceived as synonymous in the Second Temple period, though perhaps not always. Cf. Budd, *Leviticus*, 260–61. *Toebah* may have had different meanings originally in different sources (Olyan, "And with a Male," 514 n.3), but our focus here is on its meaning in the Torah as a whole.

15. See below, chap. 3, p. 24. Milgrom argues that this is in fact the intention of the Holiness Code and that modern Jewish homosexual men can satisfy the concern by adopting children (*Leviticus*, 1566–68).

16. Jordan, *The Ethics of Sex*, 41. Similarly, the punishment for bestiality requires the death of the animal as well as the human (Lev. 20:15–16).

17. Jordan, *The Invention of Sodomy in Christian Theology,* 29–44; Carden, *Sodomy,* 164–93.

18. Cf. the pioneering work of Bailey, *Homosexuality and the Western Christian Tradition* and the analysis of the horrors and ironies of violence in the Gibeah narrative by Trible, *Texts of Terror,* 70–82. Robert Alter's proposal ("Sodom as Nexus," 33) that the Sodom story is serving mainly as part of a series of narratives dealing with the relationship of righteousness and fertility is ingenious, but he is forced to assume that the author wants us to connect the story with a critique of homosexual acts as necessarily sterile—something that is never mentioned in the text itself.

19. This was presumably related to the widespread ancient concern that the penetrated male would be "feminized"; cf. Nissinen, *Homoeroticism in the Biblical World,* 19–36, and Jennings, *Jacob's Wound,* 199–220.

20. Gagnon, *The Bible and Homosexual Practice,* 79–87. Gagnon's efforts to strengthen this argument only make it seem less probable because he has to acknowledge that all the *explicit* uses of "abomination" in Ezek. refer to arrogance and indifference to the poor.

21. Among later writings, *Testament of Benjamin* 9.1 takes the sin of Sodom as having to do with intercourse with women. The second-century Christian hymn that constitutes Book 6 of the *Sibylline Oracles* understands it as failure to recognize God at his visitation (21–25). Only in Philo (*Abraham,* 133–36) do we find a clear statement that the sin of Sodom included (though it was not limited to) same-gender sexual acts. Cf. Bailey, *Homosexuality,* 9–28, still basically correct in its presentation of the material.

22. Deut. 27:21, on the other hand, seems to connect bestiality with incest.

23. Driver, *A Critical and Exegetical Commentary on Deuteronomy,* 264–65. Nissinen shows that the data are difficult to interpret (*Homoeroticism,* 28–35). Ironically, despite the characterization of this behavior as Canaanite in the Holiness Code, there is no suggestion of it in surviving Canaanite materials; David Biale, *Eros and the Jews,* 24.

24. The prohibition on cross-dressing may have had a similar background; Driver, *Deuteronomy,* 250–51.

25. On the connection of the death penalty with idolatry, see Forkman, *The Limits of Religious Community,* 17.

26. Pedersen, *Israel,* vol 1–2:77–81; Milgrom, *Leviticus,* 1567–68.

27. Collins notes that in the rabbinic period it became a topic of concern; *Sexual Ethics and the New Testament,* 46–47.

28. Gagnon (*Bible and Homosexual Practice,* 63–71) argues that Ham did not merely see his father's genitals, but actually had intercourse with him in his drunken state. This interpretation, while not without ancient precedent, goes far beyond the text itself, which contrasts Ham's behavior with the care that his brothers took to avoid seeing their father's exposed body.

29. Similarly, Deut. 25:11–12 provides that if a woman, intervening in a fight between her husband and another man, takes hold of the other man's genitals, her hand is to be cut off.

30. Milgrom (*Leviticus*, 1374) observes that purity and shame language are being stretched hard in the incest prohibitions to cover elements other than physical kinship.
31. Pedersen, *Israel*, vol. 1–2:70.
32. RSV translates "an enquiry"; cf. Milgrom, *Leviticus*, 1668–71. For the translation "damages," cf. Noth, *Leviticus*, 143; Wenham, *Leviticus*, 270–71.
33. Wenham (*Leviticus*, 271), Noth (*Leviticus*, 143), Milgrom (*Leviticus*, 1666–68), and Budd (*Leviticus*, 280–82) all assume that the violator of the slave woman is a third party and must therefore question whether "damages" were to be paid to the woman's owner or to her intended. If we assume a third party, however, it is no longer apparent why the woman's slave status would protect the man from the death penalty. Only if her violator is also her master would her slave status be relevant, for it would require her to submit to his advances and would authorize him to make sexual use of her.
34. *Jubilees* 33.7 confirms the purity interpretation; Bilhah was polluted in relation to Jacob after Reuben slept with her even though, according to *Jubilees*, she did not participate voluntarily. Philo, however, explains the matter more in terms of property (*Special Laws* 3.30-31); the husband who accepts such a wife back would be suspect of pimping and procurement, i.e., of having connived in her marriage to another. Such a man, says Philo, would also stand condemned of weakness (*malakia*) and "unmanliness" (*anandria*).
35. One may even speculate about the functions of the "ministering women who ministered at the door of the tent of meeting" in the wilderness years (Exod. 38:8). The only thing told of them is that they dedicated their bronze mirrors for the making of the laver of bronze in which the priests were to wash (cf. Pedersen, *Israel*, 3–4:468–72).
36. As John Riches notes, "the sociological sense of . . . purity regulations was fully acknowledged and understood"; *Jesus and the Transformation of Judaism*, 116. Milgrom also observes that the food purity regulations were always intended to separate Israel from the nations (*Leviticus*, 1398).
37. Outside Canaan, the purity rules of the Holiness Code would not apply to non-Israelites; Milgrom, *Leviticus*, 1568, 1785–88.
38. *Jubilees* 33.15–17 gives exactly this reason to explain why Reuben could be forgiven his act of incest with Bilhah. It was not yet truly culpable before the giving of the Torah.
39. Cf. Wenham, *Leviticus*, 161–62.
40. Thus, *Joseph and Aseneth*, even though it does not speak of Gentiles as immoral in comparison with Jews, still insists on complete separation from them with regard to food and sex (7–8). Cf. Charlesworth, *The Old Testament Pseudepigrapha*, 2:194.
41. See Pedersen, *Israel*, 3–4:273–74. Deuteronomy draws a distinction between what is permitted to Israel and what is permitted to the resident alien in the matter of carrion (14:21). In this particular respect, if in no others, such aliens must have served as a kind of purity sink, into which unclean but otherwise usable resources might be diverted. Compare the function of Dalits in India in Gokhale, "Castaways of Caste," 32.

42. E.g., *Jubilees*, which speaks of circumcision as what separates Israel from both Gentiles and apostates (15.25–32), forbids inter-marriage with Gentiles (30.7–17), and holds that the evil of sexual defilement lies in the fact that it violates Israel's special relationship to God (33.18–20).

43. Whittaker, *Jews and Christians*, 63–85.

44. Sanders, *Paul and Palestinian Judaism*, 206–12, 374–75, 400–02. See also *Jubilees* 22.14–20; 30.10–14.

45. Greeks and Romans had their own interests in purity, but they were not as organized nor as pervasive as the Levitical system among Israelites. See Burkert, *Greek Religion*, 75–82; Dixon, *The Roman Family*, 134–35; Brooten, *Love Between Women*, 137; Foucault, *The Care of the Self*, 35. As a result, no specifically Greek system of purification ever became a part of Greek identity.

46. For a brief summary, see Houston, *Purity and Monotheism*, 69–78.

47. Pedersen, *Israel*, vol. 1–2:482–83; Houston argues that the pig was particularly associated with chthonic cults, which would make it especially objectionable (*Purity and Monotheism*, 161–68).

48. Cumont, *The Oriental Religions in Roman Paganism*, 117.

49. Douglas, *Purity and Danger*, 41–57; cf. appraisals by Wenham (*Leviticus*, 23–25, 169–71) and Houston (*Purity and Monotheism*, 93–114).

50. Cf. the treatment of leprosy in Lev. 13:12–13, which suggests that the person who is entirely covered with leprosy (a scale disease, not Hansen's disease) becomes clean. This seems completely counterintuitive when we think of leprosy, as we usually do, as a disease. But it suggests that the impurity of leprosy consisted not in its being seen as a disease, but in its creating a blotched skin. If the skin is entirely of one color again, it is no longer a source of impurity.

51. Wenham, *Leviticus*, 260.

52. The field is like the womb in "receiving seed"; the shuttle of the loom is analogous to the penis. Howard Eilberg-Schwartz observes that animals and plants can also have metaphorical reference to Israel in Torah; *The Savage in Judaism*, 115–40.

53. Milgrom, *Leviticus*, 766–68, 1000–04.

54. Houston, *Purity and Monotheism*, 124–258.

55. Regardless of the origins of the conflicts, Biale has shown how they give rise to a rich dialectic of rule and subversion in scripture taken as a whole; *Eros and the Jews*, 11–32.

56. Noth, *Leviticus*, 9–17; Wenham, *Leviticus*, 6–13.

57. Milgrom, *Leviticus*, 3–35, 1361–64.

58. Jennings, *Jacob's Wound*, 25–36.

59. An inscription warning Gentiles away from the Temple precincts has survived from the Greco-Roman period; Barrett, ed., *New Testament Background*, 50.

60. Nissinen, *Homoeroticism*, 37–44.

61. E.g., Wenham, *Leviticus*, 161–62, 260.

62. E.g., "Although the Law given from God by Moses, as touching Ceremonies and Rites, do not bind Christian men, nor the Civil precepts thereof ought of necessity to be received in any commonwealth; yet notwithstanding, no Christian

man whatsoever is free from the obedience of the Commandments which are called Moral," Article VII of the Anglican "Articles of Religion."

63. Not all Christians would always have agreed with these exclusions. The Canons of Theodore of Tarsus forbade menstruating women to receive communion, and the Book of Common Prayer long contained a service for the purification of women after childbirth.

64. Klawans, *Impurity and Sin in Ancient Judaism*, 21–42.

65. Klawans objects to describing "moral impurity" as a "metaphorical" usage. But it is difficult to see what else it can be. "Metaphorical," of course, does not imply that it is not taken seriously. The Holiness Code is quite serious about its metaphorical broadening of the purity code. Klawans's effort to distinguish two equal but independent uses of purity runs into not only the difficulty that there is no separate terminology in the Torah to distinguish them, but also the further problem that Klawans has no satisfactory place for the most widespread element in all of purity law, food prohibitions (Ibid., 31–32).

66. Ibid., pp. 21–42. Klawans goes on to show (43–118) that ancient readers of the texts noticed incompatibilities between the two codes, particularly in terms of punishment and to explore how they interpreted it.

67. It was a Stoic axiom that "All sins are equal." See Rist, *Stoic Philosophy*, 81–96. Although the Stoics understood the principle differently from the author of 4 Maccabees, the latter probably derived it from them.

68. Cf. the antagonism toward Gentile nudity in *Jubilees* 3.30–31.

Chapter 3: Purity in First-Century Judaism

1. Vermes, *The Dead Sea Scrolls*, 32–35.

2. Maier, *The Temple Scroll*, 118.

3. Vermes, *The Dead Sea Scrolls*, 149.

4. Ibid., 87–109.

5. Ibid., 170–72, 180–82.

6. Ibid., 95–96.

7. Newton, *The Concept of Purity*, 21–26.

8. As Eilberg-Schwartz observes, the twin emphases on priestly descent in the community and on mastery of its particular understanding of purity could produce conflicts if the available priest was not considered sufficiently knowledgeable; there was no easy way to resolve such conflicts (*Savage in Judaism*, 206–08).

9. This Essene interpretation was opposite to that of the Mishnah; Vermes, *The Dead Sea Scrolls*, 166.

10. Ibid., 106–9.

11. Forkman, *Limits of Religious Community*, 74–77.

12. Newton, *Concept of Purity*, 46–47.

13. Neusner, *Idea of Purity*, 54.

14. Klawans (*Impurity and Sin*, 67–91) argues that the Qumran sect developed its thinking on the subject to the point where impurity and sin were virtually identified, with ordinary impurity requiring atonement as well as purification and sin

requiring purification as well as atonement. While the language of some of the documents does seem to imply this, one is left with the question of how human life could proceed at all, at least among the lower rank of members, without the incurrence of some level of impurity. Because the sect's documents are not much interested in women, we can set aside the question of menstruation as far as it concerns women alone, but younger men, at least, will have been prone to incur involuntary impurity from ejaculations.

15. Vermes, *The Dead Sea Scrolls*, 150–52.
16. I follow the reconstruction assumed in Geza Vermes's translation in *Dead Sea Scrolls in English*, 245. For an alternative interpretation, with no reference to Gentiles, see Lohse, *Die Texte aus Qumran*, 272; a comparison with IV,10 suggests, however, that Vermes's restoration is correct.
17. Translation from Vermes, *Dead Sea Scrolls in English*, 170.
18. Contrast, for example, Neusner, *From Politics to Piety*, with Rivkin, *A Hidden Revolution*. Both offer descriptions and evaluations of the sources and of their own methods.
19. I have followed, in the main, the tradition of interpretation represented in Neusner, *From Politics to Piety*. It seems to me, however, that Rivkin's reconstruction of the history is not without merit. If his absolute identification of the Pharisees in their two earlier stages with the scribes (or legal experts) goes too far, it remains true that there must have been a substantial overlap between the two groups, which will have given the Pharisees much authority of an indirect kind, even in their second or sectarian phase.
20. Cf. Neusner, *A History of the Mishnaic Law of Purities*, 28, 110–36.
21. Ibid., 21, 293.
22. Sanders, *Paul and Palestinian Judaism*, p. 116.
23. Neusner notes that "while in 1QS one is unclean who violates the norms of the community, in Mishnaic law, early and late, one is unclean who is made unclean only and solely by those sources of uncleanness specified in Scripture or generated by analogy to those of Scripture" (*History*, 105; cf. 186). So, too, Klawans, who argues that the Pharisees were strict in maintaining a distinction between what he calls "ritual" and "moral" impurity (*Impurity and Sin*, 92–117).
24. Neusner, *From Politics to Piety*, 81–96.
25. On the relation between purity and the boundaries of the Pharisaic groups, see Forkman, *Limits of Religious Community*, 87–98. Cf. Klawans, *Impurity and Sin*, 108–09.
26. Neusner, *History*, 300–03. I would not wish to propose my "post-sectarian" explanation of these events as a substitute for Professor Neusner's better qualified and more profound observations, only as a supplement to them.
27. Ibid., 38, 101.
28. The distinction between Jew and Gentile, of course, did not cease to be important; see the appraisal by Riches, *Jesus and the Transformation of Judaism*, 119–27.
29. Neusner (*History*, 106) denies that the law was "made to define a sect." It may be that it was not originally intended to do so, but it can scarcely have failed to have that effect.

30. Philo observes that women were part of the group, which might indicate a certain indifference to purity, but in describing the great feast of the fiftieth day, he says that these were mostly aged women who had remained virgins of their own will (*The Contemplative Life*, 32–33, 68). Women past menopause presented less of a threat to purity.

31. Whittaker, *Jews and Christians*, 3–130.

32. See the summary discussion on dating by R. J. H. Shutt in Charlesworth, *The Old Testament Pseudepigrapha*, 2:8–9.

33. Hengel, *Judaism and Hellenism*, 1:268–70, 292–303.

34. We know these thinkers from Philo's attacks on them, e.g., *Migration of Abraham*, 89–93.

35. Greco-Roman objection to promiscuity was less than absolute. At an earlier time, for example, it had been part of banqueting practice at Athens; see Keuls, *Reign of the Phallus*, 16–80. Still, they mistrusted it as a temptation for males to squander family property. And, whatever actual practice may have been in the Hellenistic and Roman periods, there was disapproval of any behavior that seemed out of voluntary control.

36. The work dates from c. 250–150 B.C.E. and probably comes from Syria. In it, the Torah is understood as in some sense a universal law, directly related to "nature." See H. C. Kee in Charlesworth, *The Old Testament Pseudepigrapha*, 1:776–80.

37. Goodenough, *An Introduction to Philo Judaeus*, 30–45.

38. So, too, pseudo-Phocylides, 175–76.

39. The analogy goes back to Plato (*Laws* 8.838e–839a).

40. Cf. *Special Laws* 3.22-25, where Philo claims that incest was forbidden in order to promote these virtues.

41. The cultural accommodation of homosexual acts among the ancient Greeks and Romans is a very complex topic. Not all possible liaisons were acceptable, and even what was accepted was not always to be made public. On the other hand, there was, for most people, no presumption that intercourse with one's own sex was in any way morally distinct from intercourse with the other. For a good brief survey of Roman attitudes and a helpful analysis of the presuppositions behind them, see Veyne, "Homosexuality in Ancient Rome," 26–35.

42. The early Cynics and Stoics regarded sexual acts as a legitimate expression of the love that draws the wise together and had not therefore seen same-gender sexual acts as wrong; Rist, *Stoic Philosophy*, 60, 65–69, 79.

43. Philo (*Special Laws*, 3.32–33) condemned intercourse with a menstruating woman on precisely this basis as a violation of the "law of nature."

44. This is true both of the early materials (second century B.C.E.) in Book 3, which repeatedly contrast Romans and Jews on this score (175–95, 573–600, 762–66), and of later ones (late first century or early second century C.E.) in Books 4 (24–39) and 5 (162–79, 386–96). I follow the datings suggested by J. J. Collins in Charlesworth, *The Old Testament Pseudepigrapha*, 1:354–55, 381–82, 390.

45. Philo had in mind the Greek tradition whereby the beloved was typically a free-born adolescent; the Romans preferred slaves or freedmen. See Veyne,

"Homosexuality in Ancient Rome," 29. On Philo's denigration of the female, see Szesnat, "'Pretty Boys' in Philo's *De Vita Contemplativa*," 87–107.

46. Winston, *The Wisdom of Solomon*, 280.

47. *Sibylline Oracles*, 3.194–95, 741–95; 5.264–65.

Chapter 4: Purity and Christianity: A First-Century Historian's Interpretation

1. One can argue that he reported the circumstances of the apostolic decree on this subject (Acts 15) quite erroneously. E.g., Catchpole, "Paul, James and the Apostolic Decree," 428–44.

2. The allusion, ironically, suggests particular holiness and purity.

3. By Essene standards, this would have meant sexual abstinence as well as great caution about food. The Pharisees, however, seem to have allowed, contrary to the explicit words of Torah (e.g., Lev. 15:16), that a simple immersion purified one of many kinds of uncleanness, without waiting for the following sunset; if the early Christians followed their teaching in the matter, sexual intercourse would not have been a barrier.

4. Samaritans saw themselves as true Israelites, but Jews largely treated them as quasi-Gentiles. Luke did not specify whether the eunuch was Jew or Gentile, but he had apparently been on pilgrimage to Jerusalem. In any case, eunuchs were anomalous figures whose lack of family ties made them rather independent of ethnic distinctions.

5. For the significance of this account in relation to issues of Luke's time, see Segal, *Rebecca's Children*, 163–65.

6. There is some uncertainty in the manuscripts as to whether one should understand their audience as "Hellenes" or as "Hellenists." In Luke's usage, "Hellenes" refers to Greek-speaking Gentiles, while "Hellenists" means Greek-speaking Jews. While "Hellenists" is perhaps the *lectio difficilior*, it seems to me impossible to make any sense of it, for Luke plainly assumes a little later on that we know there are Gentile converts in Antioch (15:1).

7. Contra Haenchen who declares that the "yoke" was primarily circumcision, but has to add that it included the multiplicity of other laws; *The Acts of the Apostles*, 459.

8. Cf. Paul's declaration that every circumcised person "is obliged to practice the whole law" (Gal. 5:3).

9. There are substantial variations in the text of the decree among ancient manuscripts and quotations of Acts. "What has been strangled" is missing from some, "harlotry" from others. Omission of "what has been strangled" may have been an early effort to make the decree something other than a purity code; some mss., to the same end, add a negative form of the Golden Rule. For fuller discussions, see Ropes, *The Text of Acts*, 265–69, and Metzger, *A Textual Commentary on the Greek New Testament*, 379–84. There can be little doubt that the original text, whatever its exact wording, did indeed represent a minimal purity code, though

one that was never truly binding. It became progressively less and less intelligible as the church became exclusively Gentile and was therefore altered in the mss.

10. The specific term *alisgemata* ("pollutions") occurs nowhere else in scripture, even in the letter of the council (Acts 15:29), where *eidolōthuta* ("things sacrificed to idols") takes its place. In the LXX, however, the related verb occurs several times, always with reference to food that is somehow defiled (Dan. 1:8; Mal. 1:7; Sir. 40:29). It would scarcely be possible for most Gentile Christians to avoid absolutely all contact with idols; in any case, they could perhaps have pled the exemption granted to Naaman the Syrian by Elisha (2 Kgs 5:18–19).

11. See p. 65.

12. Romans 14–15; 1 Cor. 8–10.

13. In the New Testament, the RSV variously translates it "unchastity," "fornication," and "immorality."

14. *TDNT*, s.v. πόρνη κτλ.

15. Yet another possibility is that "harlotry" in this case equals "mixed marriage," something repeatedly associated with idolatry; e.g., *Jubilees* 20:1–13; Philo, *Special Laws* 3.29; pseudo-Philo, *Biblical Antiquities* 9.5, 18.13–14, 21.1, etc.

16. It is far from clear, however, that *pniktos*, "strangled," can be equivalent to "carrion."

17. Or perhaps only incest, as the rabbis apparently connected it with *porneia*; Haenchen, *The Acts of the Apostles*, 449.

18. Yarbrough notes the conspicuous absence of this motif from Paul's writings; *Not Like the Gentiles*, 28–29.

19. Some translate, "you will do right"; cf. Haenchen, *The Acts of the Apostles*, 453–54. Even so, the language falls short of establishing an ethical imperative, much less a condition of salvation. Some later Gentile Christians, at least in the West, did avoid eating blood, but we know this only incidentally and have no evidence that they attached great theological importance to it. Note the letter about the martyrdoms at Lyons, preserved in Eusebius, *Ecclesiastical History* 5.1.26; also Minucius Felix, *Octavius* 30.6; Tertullian, *Apology* 9.13–14. Jonathan Draper argues that the *Didache* required of Gentile converts only avoidance of what had been sacrificed to idols, although it held full Torah observance up as an ideal; "The Role of Ritual," 63–65. As for idolatrous rites, refusal to participate in them quickly became a test of faith and was rejected for quite new reasons, above and beyond the council's decree.

20. Catchpole ("Paul, James and the Apostolic Decree," 429–32, 438–43) argues that the council actually intended to impose on the Gentiles a modified purity code on the authority of the Torah and that it therefore stood diametrically in opposition to Paul's insistence on grace. If this is correct, Luke's use of Peter's speech is doubly interesting, for he thereby makes such an interpretation of the decree impossible within the context of his own narrative.

21. Theologically, Peter's position also implies that the purity code is not binding on Jewish Christians either, at least as far as salvation is concerned. It might perhaps be argued that it was still integral to their Jewish identity and that this was a good in itself; Luke, however, avoids the issue by making all his Jewish Christian lead-

ers irreproachably devout observers of the Torah. Neither in New Testament nor in rabbinic Judaism is membership in Israel simply equated with salvation; cf. Segal, *Rebecca's Children*, 168–69, 176–79.

22. This verse has proven very difficult to interpret (Haenchen, *The Acts of the Apostles*, 450 n.1)—I think because it has been wrongly taken as James's reason for *imposing* a purity law on Gentiles. It is in fact his reason for *not* doing so. The Christian community, he says, does not have to make purity a requisite for membership; its decision not to do so simply leaves the advocacy of purity to the same institution that had always advocated it, the synagogue.

23. I have omitted the virginal conception of Jesus from this list of purity motifs, since there is little evidence, if any, that virginity was considered especially pure in ancient Israel.

24. For the hostility that characterizes Luke's account of the interchange between Jesus and the Pharisees, see Green, *The Gospel of Luke*, 467–73.

25. Centurions were forbidden to marry, and it was not uncommon for the sexual partner of an unmarried man to be a younger male slave. Reference to the slave as *ho pais mou* is consistent with such a conclusion. Jennings, *The Man Jesus Loved*, 128–41. The relationship of the master and slave could also, to be sure, be understood in nonsexual terms; cf. Green, *The Gospel of Luke*, 286.

26. If, alternatively, one should be persuaded that *porneia*, for the council, did involve the sexual activities condemned in Lev. 18, it is still true that the council did not forbid these, but only urged their avoidance.

Chapter 5: Purity in the Gospels

1. Papias of Hierapolis, quoted in Eusebius, *Church History* 3.39.14–15.

2. Though I shall sometimes write "Jesus says" in what follows, I always understand it to be modified by "according to Matthew, Mark, etc."

3. Neusner, *Idea of Purity*, 62–63. Matthew's version of the saying (23:25–26), on the other hand, seems to take account of the position of the School of Shammai, namely that the inside and outside of a vessel contract uncleanness independently of one another; cf. Neusner, "'First Cleanse the Inside.'" *NTS* 22 (1975–76): 492–95.

4. As Luke makes explicit, this kind of "deepening" of purity requirements does not abolish them, but adds a dimension to them. A similar development had long been at work in Greek religion; see Burkert, *Greek Religion*, 77.

5. The Mishnah specifically exempts rue from tithe (*Shebiit* 9.1).

6. Cf. Forkman, *Limits of Religious Community*, 90.

7. Or perhaps "[what they bring] from the marketplace." In either case, some words have to be supplied that are not made explicit in the best Greek manuscripts.

8. Booth, *Jesus and the Laws of Purity*, 189–203.

9. Booth gives a thorough exposition of this possibility (Ibid., 206–10), ultimately rejecting it as unworkable.

10. So Matt. 15:20. Neusner, *Idea of Purity*, 61–62, rightly observes that two distinct authorities are at stake—the oral tradition of the Pharisees and the written

Torah. Mark and Matthew alike, however, treat the unity of the purity issue as overriding this distinction and have Jesus cancel the rules of both authorities.

11. Riches, *Jesus and the Transformation of Judaism*, 136–40, has argued that Jesus himself meant to reject the whole purity system, not merely the food laws.

12. Booth argues that the form of Mark 7:15 does indeed go back to the historical Jesus, but that he can have meant by it only that metaphorical purity was more important than physical purity (*Jesus and the Laws of Purity*, 96–114), in much the same way as Philo (83–90). This conclusion, however, seems to have been implicit in Booth's presuppositions; see, e.g., 69, where he already assumes this result. Booth may have been led astray by his presupposition that Jesus could adopt only two possible attitudes toward purity—affirming or rejecting it. I am suggesting a third alternative—declaring it irrelevant. What is irrelevant becomes a matter of personal choice: one is not more righteous for practicing purity nor less righteous for ignoring it, and no one may impose its observance on another.

13. "Harlotries, thefts, murders, adulteries, acts of greed." "Acts of greed" are violations of the command against covetousness. Cf. Neyrey, "Idea of Purity," 120, although his treatment of the list neglects to take order seriously as a component of its meaning.

14. The other NT usages of *aselgeia* may have a sexual connotation, but these are in Pauline writings, 1 and 2 Peter, and Jude. This is its only occurrence in Mark, and its immediate context hardly suggests a sexual reference for it here.

15. Cf. the highly general use of "foolishness" in the Wisdom literature.

16. Philo, too, could say that the really unclean person was the unjust and impious one and that this more general expression of impurity was of great importance (*Special Laws* 3.208–9); but he did not replace literal physical impurity with the metaphorical kind.

17. He does not reprove her for her violation of purity laws; cf. Selvidge, "Mark 5:25–34 and Leviticus 15:19–20." 619–23. On Jesus' apparent lack of anxiety about interacting with women, see Loader, *Sexuality and the Jesus Tradition*, 57.

18. Neyrey, "Idea of Purity in Mark's Gospel," 115–23, prefers to say that Mark's Jesus "reformed" the purity code. Neyrey can do so because he is confessedly using "purity" in two senses (92). In terms of the actual purity code observed among Jews of Jesus' time, one must speak rather of his setting it aside or replacing it with something new and different. In the last analysis, I am doubtful whether "purity of the heart" can in fact function as a true purity boundary; and Neyrey's proposal of an "inclusive" kind of purity, if applied on the literal, physical level, may be a contradiction in terms. At the deepest possible level, one can link literal and metaphorical purities, but even then they cannot both be practiced with equal seriousness; cf. the fine exposition by Via, *The Ethics of Mark's Gospel*, 88–96.

19. Matthew, unlike Luke, adds no palliative "into repentance"; cf. Luke 5:32.

20. Some of Jesus' parables, such as the Wheat and Tares (Matt. 13:24–30) and the Net (13:47–50) seem to be comments on the motley character of Jesus' following.

21. Luke would be more helpful because he gives us the example of Zacchaeus, whose repentance and conversion have to do not with purity, but strictly with matters of justice (19:8–9); of course, one cannot use Luke's Gospel in this way to explain what Matthew might have meant. I suppose that most readers of Matthew, myself included, have always assumed that the prostitutes left their trade when they followed John, but neither Matthew nor Luke specifies such a demand. It is not immediately clear how else they would have supported themselves, given the low mobility of women in ancient society.

22. On the impure among Jesus' followers, see Schüssler Fiorenza, *In Memory of Her,* 126–30.

23. She had a right to Shelah, but not to Judah himself. Leviticus 18:15 forbids a man to marry his son's wife, though it would not have been understood as being in force in the time of the patriarchs.

24. Cf. Deut. 22:22–27. The violated woman must cry for help if she is not to be punished as a willing partner.

25. Cf. Neusner, *Idea of Purity,* 62–63; Booth, *Jesus and the Laws of Purity,* 221–23.

26. Matthew's list of "evil intentions" that proceed from the heart includes adultery and harlotry. Because the order is different from Mark's, the sense of "harlotry" is probably different, too, but it is hard to give a confident interpretation of how Matthew understood it. He uses the term in only two other contexts, both of them suggesting that he saw *porneia* as an aspect of adultery or perhaps a synonym for it.

27. Countryman, *The Mystical Way,* 127–32.

28. Sandra Schneiders rightly observes that the import of her history has been exaggerated by scholars; *Written That You May Believe,* 137–44.

29. Countryman, *The Mystical Way,* 29–31.

30. Archeological remains suggest that early Christian baptism was usually administered by pouring water over the head of a person standing in a pool; see Snyder, *Ante Pacem,* 57–58. In the Mishnah, drawn water is precisely what one must not use for purification, which, except for hand washing, takes place through immersion; cf. Neusner, *History,* 83–86. One must wonder whether Christians deliberately adopted for their own purification rite a form that would seem impure to rabbinic Judaism. Compare their choice of fast days different from those in use among other Jews (*Didache* 8.1).

31. Cf. 1 John 5:6: Jesus came "not with the water only, but with the water and the blood."

32. The same kind of point, I believe, is being made in the difficult passage at John 7:37-39. A scripture (otherwise unknown) is cited with reference to the one who believes in Jesus: "Rivers of living water will flow out of his belly." Things that flow out of the belly would include urine, menstrual blood, the amniotic fluid and other fluids associated with birth, semen, other sexual fluxes, and blood from hemorrhaging. Most of these are unclean according to the Torah, yet John, relying on an otherwise unknown text, takes them as an image of the Spirit.

33. Riches (*Jesus and the Transformation of Judaism,* 128–35) has argued that Jesus' own position was very close to this.

34. Thus, Forkman (*Limits of Religious Community*, 170) concludes that the Gospels have no "explicit rules which indicate which deviations lead to expulsion" and "refrain from suggesting what kinds of behavior make it impossible for a member to remain in the community."

Chapter 6: Paul and Purity

1. The genuine letters of Paul are usually reckoned as Romans, 1 & 2 Corinthians, Galatians, Philippians, 1 Thessalonians, and Philemon. Colossians, although uncertain, I include as probably his; Ephesians is probably the work of a close associate.

2. Grant, *Paul in the Roman World*, 115–118

3. For an interpretation of Paul's view of purity that is diametrically opposite the one I am presenting, see Newton, *Concept of Purity*. Although I respond to details of Newton's arguments at appropriate places in the notes, it may be useful to sketch out my larger objections here. The first is that, as I have suggested, Newton fails to make important distinctions. He does not differentiate clearly between physical purity in the strict sense and its use to reinforce other types of ethics. He fails equally to distinguish between literal physical purity and its metaphorical use to denote "purity of the heart." The second is that, having skillfully elucidated Paul's application of the Temple image to the church, he then assumes that Paul will respond to the church-as-Temple in a way comparable to the sectarians of Qumran. He argues in the style of "Paul as a Jew would have felt thus and so" (see, e.g., his pp. 79, 82). This, however, is a treacherous line of argument. Paul was indeed a Jew, but one who behaved in ways quite different from those of Qumran and who was understood by some other Jews (including some Jewish Christians) as a renegade. At no point can we securely predict where he would have remained close to his Pharisee past and where he would have departed radically from it. Third, Newton lumps all sexual offenses together in English as "immorality" and assumes the same for Paul's use of *akatharsia* (uncleanness) and *porneia* without adequate analysis of that usage. Finally, Newton gives no attention to Paul's complex treatment of the question of foods sacrificed to idols and deals with Rom. 14:14 & 20, statements of central importance and exceptional clarity, in a decidedly offhand way.

4. The Greek noun *pistis* can mean either "faithfulness" or "faith," and the dependent genitive *Christou* here can bear either a subjective or objective quality—hence the uncertainty of translation.

5. Sanders, *Paul and Palestinian Judaism*, 496–99.

6. At one point, he connects with it the issue of *porneia*, in the sense of idolatrous practices associated with foreign women (1 Cor. 10:8, referring to Num. 25).

7. Dale B. Martin argues that the primary division, at least at Corinth, was between more elite and poorer members of the community. While this is possible, the dividing line somehow came to be the observance of Torah food purity. *The Corinthian Body*, 69–86.

8. Cf. *Ad Herennium* 3.9.16–18 and Cicero, *De oratore* 2.77.313–14. In a "proof," the strongest arguments were to be placed first and last, with the others, according to Cicero, in the middle as a kind of "herd," not a logical chain.

9. The Strong may even think it a good thing to eat sacrificial foods to demonstrate this truth (8:8).

10. Newton, *Concept of Purity*, pp. 100–101, holds that, for Paul, purity, although of no importance outside the church, is of great importance within it. Even within the church, however, Paul pleads for avoidance of sacrificial foods on the grounds of love, not purity.

11. Neusner, *Idea of Purity*, 59, describes this as "a highly rabbinic conception." If I have understood him correctly, however, it is also different from the rabbinic concept in an important way. For the rabbis, intention enters into the purity system in the way it makes items, by associating them with human use, susceptible of impurity (*Idea of Purity*, 16; *History*, 92–93). If one were to touch a corpse without understanding it as unclean or without expecting to become unclean oneself, this would not alter the outcome. Paul, however, implies that the purity system is entirely in the conscience/consciousness, so that if one ceases to regard a corpse as unclean, it ceases to be so.

12. The Greek *syneidēsis* means both "consciousness" and "conscience." In this text, the two ideas seem to be inseparable.

13. See the more extended treatment in Countryman, *Interpreting the Truth*, 201–09. Eilberg-Schwartz connects this rejection of purity with the nature of the earliest Christian church as a community where status was primarily achieved, not ascribed (*The Savage in Judaism*, 195–216).

14. Foucault notes that Greco-Roman medicine was more concerned to regulate food than sex (*Care of the Self*, 141).

15. Forkman, *Limits of Religious Community*, 150–51, speaks as if Paul regarded impurity as grounds for expulsion from the church, but this is simply a momentary carelessness in use of terms. Elsewhere, he speaks more precisely of "fornication" (pp. 141–47) and its link with "dissension" (172).

16. E.g., Martin, *The Corinthian Body*, 163–97. I disagree with Martin only to the extent that he is using a very broad understanding of "purity" that includes, for example, certain theories of the causation of disease, whereas I am assuming that Paul's concern with physical "purity" was limited to those points at which Torah purity separated Jewish and Gentile Christians.

17. See chapter 9, on Jesus' interpretation of the passage.

18. Robinson, *The Body*, 11–33. For an interpretation that sees Paul's fear of impurity as more intense, see Martin, *The Corinthian Body*, 170–74.

19. Some interpret "vessel" as referring to the wife, others as referring to the man's penis.

20. The association of *pleonexia* with sexual offenses was noted, but regarded as inexplicable, by Delling, *TDNT* s.v., 271. Yarbrough offers a detailed exegesis of the text from 1 Thess. comparable to the one offered here in his *Not Like the Gentiles*, 65–76.

21. E.g., Newton, *Concept of Purity*, 103.

22. Peter Zaas has argued that lists of vices and virtues are not fixed traditions flung haphazardly into the epistles, but are integrated with the epistles' subject matter; see his "As I Teach Everywhere" 1–59; "Catalogues and Context" 622–29. As Zaas observes, such catalogues were reminders of catechesis, where the vices had previously been defined in ways now lost to us.

23. Robinson, *Body*, 17–26.

24. Cf. Barrett, *The Second Epistle to the Corinthians*, 329–32, who observes that the two lists of offenses in verses 20 and 21 are difficult to tie together unless the latter is "violently allegorized." He proposes instead an accidental link of history, arising from the fact that some of those who were causing internal strife in the Corinthian community were also teaching sexual libertinism. This is possible, but also goes beyond the text itself.

25. Brown, *The Body and Society*, 33–102.

26. Cf., however, such English expressions as "He did me dirt" and "dirty tricks."

27. The one thing beyond question at this point is that Paul's use of purity language is less than entirely consistent or transparent. The principal alternative to the present proposal of distinguishing his literal from his metaphorical uses of the terminology is to assume that Paul dismissed literal purity with regard to food but retained it with regard to sexuality. It is significant that this position tends to be assumed rather than argued, even by an otherwise careful scholar such as Houston (*Purity and Monotheism*, 263–74). The proposal is in fact unlikely, precisely because Paul was having to deal with the question of applying a fully articulated Torah system to Gentiles, who objected to many aspects of it. We do not see in his writings the kind of dismemberment of the system that would have been necessary to separate the food elements from the sexual ones.

28. Sanday and Headlam, *A Critical and Exegetical Commentary*, 45. Cf. the teaching of 2 Macc. 6:12–17 that God waits to punish the Gentiles until they "have reached the full measure of their sins" (RSV).

29. John Boswell observed that Paul was talking about a change that he understood to have taken place as a consequence of the sin of idolatry. People who formerly experienced desire for the opposite sex now committed homosexual acts; *Christianity, Social Tolerance, and Homosexuality*, 109–10. He was mistaken, I think, only in treating this as a matter of individual experience, whereas Paul was writing about Gentile culture as a whole.

30. Paul actually begins the passage with reference to women, but males are his principal target—not surprising in a male-dominated culture.

31. For violations of the sexual code, see the LXX of Lev. 18 and 20 passim; on the genitalia, Exod. 20:26, 22:26 (27MT); on excrement, Deut. 23:13 (14MT).

32. Gagnon, *Bible and Homosexual Practice*, is particularly careless on this point.

33. Paul's language was related to that of contemporary Stoicism, as his use of *kathekonta* in verse 28 also shows. In the absence of any evidence of a direct acquaintance on Paul's part with Stoicism, however, one must assume that he drew these terms from popular contemporary usage, especially within the Hellenistic Diaspora. Schnackenburg notes that Paul's usage is not accurate in Stoic terms; *The Moral Teaching of the New Testament*, 290–92. In strict Stoic usage, acts

"over against nature" and "improper acts" (*ta mē kathēkonta*) were synonymous with "sins." More popular usage, however, was far from precise or rigorous. Cicero, despite his intellectual and educational advantages, got the whole system of distinctions badly garbled according to Rist, *Stoic Philosophy*, 97–111. Paul's contemporary Philo could even speak of "acts according to nature" as being blameworthy if indulged to excess (*Special Laws* 3.9)—something no true Stoic could have said. If Paul's usage here were equivalent to that of Philo or of pseudo-Phocylides, "natural" would mean "procreative," as applied to sexual acts, and "over against nature" would mean "nonprocreative." Paul's own normal usage, however, as I have analyzed it in the text, offers a more satisfactory interpretation, for Paul elsewhere shows no concern for begetting children in "these last days."

34. Hays has skillfully brought out the outrageous character of the usage in Rom. 11, where God, in effect, is said to perform "unnatural acts.; "Relations Natural and Unnatural," 198–99. He has not observed, however, that this passage makes any equation of "unnatural" and "sinful" in Paul's usage extremely difficult.

35. Some have argued that by contrasting the "natural use" with that "over against nature," Paul was actually making an appeal to the creation narrative—that the "natural" is whatever was a part of the created order as described in Gen. 1–2, while everything not a part of that order would be "unnatural/over against nature." E.g., Hays ("Relations Natural and Unnatural," 191). There are a number of problems with this argument, and we will look at the whole proposal more closely in chapter 12.

36. It is found a few times in Wisdom and in 3 and 4 Macc.

37. *Meditations* 1.17.7, my translation.

38. Bernadette Brooten shows that the language of *para physin* was widely applied to sexual relations between women in the Hellenistic world, perhaps because one woman was assumed to take a "male" role; *Love Between Women*, 124–41, 175–86.

39. E.g., Enslin, *The Ethics of Paul*, 147n.45. Robin Scroggs suggests that "the distortion of homosexuality" was its own punishment; *The New Testament and Homosexuality*, 115–16. This seems unsatisfactory, however, in rhetorical terms: a critic of Gentile culture would be dissatisfied with so intangible a penalty and Gentiles in general may not have thought it a punishment at all. Philo wrote of the "female disease" (effeminacy) that afflicted the younger partner and of the emotional and financial ruin of the elder in pursuit of a beloved (*Special Laws* 3.37–40; *Abraham*, 136; *The Contemplative Life*, 59–62); but these were far from inevitable accompaniments of same-gender relationships. Cf., however, Swancutt, "The Disease of Effemination," 193–223.

40. This, I think, makes impossible Scroggs's proposal that homosexual acts and the vice catalogue of verses 27–31 were, for Paul, interchangeable illustrations of human sinfulness (*New Testament and Homosexuality*, 113–14).

41. Cf. Philo's similar condemnation of both wrongdoers and those who take their part, *Special Laws* 3.19.

42. Even in Stoic thinking, *ta kathēkonta* ("the appropriate actions") represented a lower order of virtue than *ta katorthomata*, which the wise person would choose as an expression of wisdom; Engberg-Pedersen, *Paul and the Stoics*, 71–72.

43. By normal rules of syntax, the demonstrative *toiauta* ("such things") refers to the nearest possible antecedent, which would be the list of vices, not the references to homosexual acts.

44. E. P. Sanders has argued that in fact Rom. 1:18–2:29 is a synagogue sermon that Paul simply incorporated for convenience' sake; *Paul, the Law, and the Jewish People*, 123–32. In that case, one could not expect complete consistency with his own thinking as expressed in Rom. 14. But would Paul have begun an important letter with materials in conflict with a conviction expressed as strongly as Rom. 14:14?

45. *Malakos*, however, cannot simply be equated with "effeminate," for it was applicable to any male who was seen as less than upstanding or respectable. E.g., Philo applied the concept to the man who remarries his former wife, *Special Laws* 3.30 = 31.

46. E.g., Tatius, *Leucippe and Clitophon* 2.35–38.

47. See Petersen, "Can ΑΡΣΕΝΟΚΟΙΤΑΙ Be Translated," 187–91.

48. Thanks to Bernadette Brooten's groundbreaking *Love Between Women*.

49. Veyne, "Homosexuality in Ancient Rome," 26–35. Cf. the discussion of homosexual acts among adult males under similar circumstances in modern Greece by Tom Horner, *Eros in Greece*, 54–65.

50. Scroggs, *New Testament and Homosexuality*, 62–65, 83, 101–09.

51. Boswell, *Christianity, Social Tolerance, and Homosexuality*, 338–53. David F. Wright attempted to refute Boswell's position, but succeeded only in removing much of Boswell's evidence without in fact proving his hypothesis untenable or demonstrating another hypothesis in its place: "Homosexuals or Prostitutes?," 125–53. What he did demonstrate was that antagonism on the part of some Christians toward those who engage in homosexual intercourse goes back to at least the second century and almost certainly shows direct continuity with the same sentiment in Hellenistic Judaism. In relating these data to the NT, one must not forget that Paul was almost certainly more radical with regard to all such questions than his second-century successors; for he lived at a moment when institutional boundaries were being broken down, they at a time when they were being rebuilt. For a helpful corrective to Wright's work, see Petersen, "ΑΡΣΕ-ΝΟΚΟΙΤΑΙ," 187–91.

52. Boswell, *Christianity*, 346–48, argued that the term never meant simply "homosexual" as distinct from "male prostitute." Wright, "Homosexuals or Prostitutes," 125–53, argued the reverse. In both cases, the contexts on which the arguments depend are meager and make any certainty difficult.

53. I shall suggest (p. 144) that an analysis of the list in 1 Tim. supports Boswell's hypothesis with a slight modification.

54. Martin, "*Arsenokoites* and *malakos*," 47–50.

55. Countryman, *Interpreting the Truth*, 162–212.

56. In my ongoing study of the literary structure of Romans, I have begun with a debt to the work of Sinclair, "The Christologies of Paul's Undisputed Epistles

and the Christology of Paul," 25–55. He outlines Romans in the following large units:

I. 1:1-16 Introduction: The Gospel is for Jew first and also Greek

II. 1:17-15:13 Body of letter:

    A. 1:18-8:39 Jew must not boast over Greek

    B. 9:1-15:13 Greek must not despise Jew

III. 15:14-16:24 Personal Appendix: Both Strong and Weak should support Paul's ministry.

57. Scroggs showed that Paul's words about homosexual acts were entirely conventional in the context of Hellenistic Judaism; *New Testament and Homosexuality*, 85–98, 109–110. So, too, in more detail, Szesnat, "Sexual Desire."

58. Cf. Collins, *Sexual Ethics*, 132.

59. Hays ("Relations Natural and Unnatural," 194–95) assumes that both Gentile and Jewish Christians would have been united in their condemnation of homosexuality as a vice of pagan Gentiles. But this is to assume his conclusions as the basis of his argument. Moreover, it makes nonsense of the singling out of the Jewish critic in Rom. 2:17 because the critic would in fact be fully justified in his contempt.

60. See chapter 12.

61. See Osiek, "Female Slaves, *Porneia*, and the Limits of Obedience," 255–74.

Chapter 7: The New Testament and Sexual Purity

1. The same terminology is found in 1 John 3:3, which speaks of forming oneself on the pattern of a future hope, as yet dimly understood, not on a static definition of pure and impure.

2. On the complexity of Paul's treatment of the subject see Sanders, *Paul, the Law, and the Jewish People*, 93–114.

3. Cf. Juvenal, *Satires* 1.37–42, taunting a rich woman for such lovers. I am indebted for this interpretation of the *arsenokoitai* to my colleague, Dean Linda Clader.

4. Cf. 1 John 2:16, where the "desire of flesh . . . eyes . . . world" is connected with the "boasting of status in life" (*bios*, not *zoe*). The easy modern assumption that "flesh" equals "sexual desire" does not sufficiently explain NT usage. Simone Weil, I believe, caught the sense of the latter correctly in saying that "the flesh impels us to say *me*," *Waiting for God*, 54. Flesh is the prime marker of our finitude; in the moral sense of the term, it is the person's tendency to try to secure the self in the face of finitude by controlling all resources and shutting other people out.

5. One finds comparable language in 1 John 1:7, 9. On Qumran, see chapter 3.

6. James becomes still more interesting as test case if we read it as midrash on Lev. 19:12–18 with Johnson, "The Use of Leviticus 19," 391–401. James ignores surrounding purity materials in Lev. in abstracting these verses. If one accepts Johnson's comparison of James with pseudo-Phocylides, then the omission is still more remarkable because the latter author did incorporate portions of the purity code touching on sex.

7. Note that there is no conjunction between the injunction to care for the defenseless and to keep oneself unblemished. This apposition suggests that the latter is simply another way of saying the same thing as the former rather than a statement about physical purity.

8. This is a difficult passage, not least because of the strange expression "the wheel of becoming" (*ton trochon tēs geneseōs*). In Matthew and Luke, *genesis* occurs in the sense of "birth," but in James (the only other NT author who uses the term), it appears only here and in the equally curious reference to a man who "sees the face of his *genesis* in a mirror" (1:23). The easiest way to explain both instances of the word in James is to take *genesis* in a Platonic sense as referring to the turbulent and temporary world of "becoming" in contrast to the stable world of "being." The whole phrase, then, would be equivalent to the "wheel of life" in *Sibylline Oracles* 2.87, which speaks of the constant but unpredictable reality of change in this life.

9. For a more extended treatment, see Countryman, *Interpreting the Truth*, 134–57.

10. Jude seems to be drawing more on the account in *1 Enoch* here than on Genesis.

11. On the physical character of angels, see *Jubilees* 15:27, which holds that those of the highest rank were created without foreskins.

12. The King James translators must at least have perceived the problem, for they invented the odd phrase "going after strange flesh." The RSV and some other modern translations substitute the arbitrary phrases "unnatural lust" or "unnatural vice"—not a translation of the Greek at all and quite misleading in this case.

13. *Testament of Naphtali* 3.4 may have the same interpretation in mind when it makes a similar comparison between Sodom and the Watchers, but it is less clear than Jude. Cf. Bailey, *Homosexuality*, 14–18. Gagnon rejects this interpretation on the grounds that the Genesis text assumes that the men of Sodom did not recognize the "men" as angels (*Bible*, 87–88). But neither does it make such an interpretation impossible, and Jude specifically parallels the action of the men of Sodom with that of the Watchers. For a fuller exegesis, see Countryman, *Interpreting the Truth*, 45–51, 72–84, 117–26.

14. Very likely, Jude was disturbed by something like the rites and ideas intimated in the *Gospel of Philip*; cf. Buckley, "A Cult-Mystery in The Gospel of Philip," 570–75, 579–81.

15. All sexual intercourse in Mediterranean antiquity was normally conceived as establishing and/or reflecting differentials of power; Nissinen, *Homoeroticism*, 57–88.

16. Pliny the Younger, *Letters* 10.96.5.

17. Gagnon, *Bible*, 104–05.

18. Note that male-male partnerships were not considered incompatible with martyrdom in the third or fourth centuries; cf. the example of Saints Sergius and Bacchus.

19. Cf., however, 1 Cor. 7:1 and 1 Tim. 4:3, both of which suggest that there were teachers on the fringes of the Pauline communities who demanded complete sexual abstinence.

20. Schüssler Fiorenza argues that the male virgins are not to be understood literally at all; *The Book of Revelation*, 181–92. If she is correct (and her argument is a strong one), then even this exception to the NT rejection of physical purity falls.

21. The character of Greek culture and other tensions specific to the churches played a significant role, as I have suggested elsewhere with respect to wealth: Countryman, *The Rich Christian*, 149–73.

22. Cf. the account of the further development of sexual asceticism among Christians by Brown, "Late Antiquity," 263–67.

23. Cf. Jordan, *The Ethics of Sex*.

Chapter 8: Women and Children as Sexual Property in the Ancient Mediterranean World

1. Neither Latin nor Greek had a term for "family" in the modern English sense of "husband, wife, and one or more children." On the problems of definition, see Moxnes, *Constructing Early Christian Families*, 13–38.

2. Countryman, *Rich Christian*, 76–81.

3. *Apology* 39.11.

4. Because ancient cultures generally assumed a world of "limited good," not the expanding universe assumed in modern capitalism, they tended to define the fundamental offense against property as greed rather than, say, theft. Acquisition of new wealth could fall under this condemnation even when fully legal, if it were seen as gained at the expense of another.

5. See the useful survey of Greco-Roman sources by Yarbrough, *Not Like the Gentiles*, 31–63.

6. It has been suggested that one should read this verb, with different vowels, to mean "be ground" (in a sexual sense), making the two halves of verse 10 completely synonymous. But this seems unnecessary, since part of a woman's value as property lay in her contribution to the work of the household.

7. Compare the easy way in which the Torah links human children with animal offspring and even with agricultural produce; e.g., Exod. 13:2,11–16; Deut. 30:9.

8. Ancient Judaism was unlike its Greek and Roman neighbors in its rejection of abortion and infanticide. While the scriptures of Israel do not make a point of this, later Hellenistic Jewish apologetic did, e.g., *Sibylline Oracles* 2.252–82, 3.762–66, and pseudo-Phocylides 184–85. It is still true, however, that children were a form of property in Israel as much as among the Gentiles.

9. The occasional exception, such as Nehemiah, whose title can be translated (and was, in the Old Greek) as "eunuch," "proves" the rule in both the original and modern senses of that verb. That is, he both puts the rule to the test and demonstrates its general accuracy. In his own right, he would have had no standing whatever among his own people; it was only his status as servant to the Persian ruler that gave him the power he wielded in Jerusalem.

10. Kraemer, "Typical and Atypical Jewish Family Dynamics," 140–42.

11. In the Roman world, too, the wife could aptly be described as "like a grown child" from the point of view of the male head of household. Cf. Veyne, *A History of Private Life*, 39–40.

12. Trible, *Texts of Terror*, 10–13. Trible's analysis of the Hagar narratives, though primarily literary, is very helpful in clarifying the social dynamics of such a household.

13. This reality lay behind the way in which early Christian theology could treat slavery and marriage as related soteriological images; Marion, *Of Divine Economy*, 165–71.

14. These differed somewhat among Gentiles, but they, too, recognized distinctions among slave women whom their masters used sexually, concubines of various sorts, and legitimate wives. For the Hellenistic world, see Pomeroy, *Goddesses, Whores, Wives, and Slaves*, 127–30, 139–41. For the Romans, see Veyne, *History of Private Life*, 33–35, 75–79.

15. Lev. 25:41 treats the children as the slave's property, but says nothing about the wife. This stems from the logic of the jubilee year, in which every father's house in Israel was to be restored to its original allotment of land. The purpose of the jubilee was to ensure the continuation of each individual family on its land, so the freedman must be able to take his children—but does not require his wife because there are already children and he will have the means to support himself again and, in due course, either ransom his slave wife or marry another.

16. Trible, *Texts of Terror*, 76–82.

17. Classical Athenian presuppositions were broadly similar. See Keuls, *Reign of the Phallus*, 257–73.

18. Cf. the excuses of those invited to the Great Supper in Jesus' parable: one has bought a field, one has bought five yoke of oxen, one has married a wife (Luke 14:18-20).

19. Cf. the anxiety of some Greco-Roman writers about the rich wife's domination of her husband; see Yarbrough, *Not Like the Gentiles*, 44–50.

20. E.g., Philo regarded public life as the male sphere and "household management" as the female one. He wrote abusively of women who violated this division and even used it to justify the barbarous law (Deut. 25:11–12) requiring that a woman who, when intervening in a fight on her husband's behalf, touched another man's genitals should have her hand amputated (*Special Laws* 3.169–75).

21. Brooten, "*Konnte Frauen*," 65–73.

22. Philo, *The Contemplative Life*, 32–33, 68.

23. Brooten, *Women Leaders in the Ancient Synagogue*.

24. Even among the Romans, bastards could not inherit or, at least in theory, be adopted by their father as legitimate children; Veyne, *History of Private Life*, 76–79. Hence, marriage remained important for family continuity.

25. Philo, *Special Laws* 3.11, treats adultery as a threat to society at large because it defeats "hopes for children."

26. The Greeks, on the whole, seem to have held an equally dim view of adultery, although there were variations at different times and places; Pomeroy, *Goddesses*, 36–37, 86–87, 128–29; Hans Licht, *Sexual Life*, 24, 61–62. The Romans were

perhaps a little more indifferent to it, for their understanding of family continuity centered on name more than on blood kinship; Veyne, *History of Private Life*, 17–18, 38–40.

27. Wenham, *Numbers*, 84–85; Milgrom, *Numbers*, 41.

28. Strictly speaking, the passage refers to a betrothed rather than a married woman, but, as Philo observed in commenting on it, there was no practical difference (*Special Laws* 3.72).

29. See Deut. 22:13–21: the case of the man who falsely claims that his bride was not a virgin. The damage done is not only to the woman but also to her parents' reputation; cf. Philo, *Special Laws* 3.79–82.

30. So, too, among the Greeks (Pomeroy, *Goddesses*, 87) and Romans (Veyne, *History of Private Life*, 73–75).

31. The Essenes at Qumran reinterpreted the law so that degrees of affinity counted the same for both males and females (*DR* V,7–11; *Temple Scroll* 66.12–17). The Mishnah, however, maintains the old point of view; Vermes, *Dead Sea Scrolls*, 166.

32. The Greeks and Romans were monogamous, but since divorce was common and children remained with their father, it would not be unusual among them for an adolescent son to be living in the same household with a stepmother; Veyne, *History of Private Life*, 34.

33. *Jubilees* 33:8 makes it clear that when Reuben violated Bilhah, his father Jacob's concubine, it was an offense against Jacob himself.

34. Lev. 18:17 forbids intercourse with a woman and her daughter or granddaughter. This would, in effect, prohibit the patriarch from having intercourse with his own daughters—but only as part of a larger group including his stepdaughters as well. It can be argued, alternatively, that the prohibition of sex with a granddaughter implies the same prohibition of the daughter; Levine, *Leviticus*. 120.

35. The Tamar story does not appear to know this prohibition, however, because Tamar argues that David would have been willing to give her to her half-brother. Similarly, Abram and Sarai were half-siblings.

36. MT must be correct here as against LXX and RSV. The point is not that these women are the man's kinswomen, but one another's.

37. Philo offers essentially this same explanation of the commandment against marriage with two sisters: it would occasion jealousy or allow one sister to profit at the other's expense, both being violations of their sisterly relationship (*Special Laws* 3.27–28). Jacob's marriage to Leah and Rachel was, of course, in violation of this law. In another problematic case, that of Lot's daughters (Gen. 19:30–38), it is hard to say whether the reader is expected to blame the women for incest or praise their heroic devotion to the duty of preserving their father's line.

38. Ancient Greek definitions of incest appear to have been simpler. Marriage between ascendants and descendants was forbidden; there was some variation in attitudes toward brother-sister marriage, which was, however, widely tolerated. A man could at least be criticized for marrying his mother-in-law, but this also violated the norm of monogamy. See Licht, *Sexual Life*, 516–18.

39. Marriage, of course, was also less dangerous than adultery (Prov. 6:26); see Carr, *The Erotic Word*, 53–55.

40. Gentile society was more tolerant of prostitution. Prostitutes were frequently slaves and were generally allotted a low social rank, even when they were educated, witty, and influential courtesans. There was little ethical antagonism toward them, however, apart from the anxiety that young men would waste their patrimonies on youthful pleasures. See Pomeroy, *Goddesses*, pp. 88–91, 139–41; Licht, *Sexual Life*, 329–42, 354–56; Veyne, *History of Private Life*, 23, 25–27. In the late first and second centuries C.E., medical notions, backed by Stoic philosophy, began to discourage all intercourse on the part of young males (ibid., 24–25).

41. *Sibylline Oracles* 3.43-44 condemns the widow who becomes a prostitute. This is exceptional, however, and the passage is not one of the older parts of the work.

42. Trible, *God and the Rhetoric of Sexuality*, 127–28.

43. *DR* V.1–5, which excuses David's polygamy on the grounds that he had not seen the full Torah.

44. Dixon, *Roman Family*, 61–90. Dixon also notes an increasing tendency for Roman wives to remain legally a part of their natal family rather than coming into their husband's *manus* as in the older forms of marriage.

45. In the Roman era, pseudo-Phocylides advised his readers to marry with an eye to preserving their family wealth (205–06) and to guard their beautiful children closely to keep them away from seducers (213–17).

46. Cf. Veyne, *History of Private Life*, 36–49.

Chapter 9: Household and Sexual Property in the Gospels

1. On the extent of Matthew's rejection of the norm of patriarchy, see Anderson and Moore, "Matthew and Masculinity," 67–91.

2. Philo (*The Contemplative Life*, 13–17) asserts that the conduct of the Therapeutae was superior to that of Anaxagoras or Democritus, who simply abandoned their property rather than giving it to their kinsfolk.

3. This, rather than "Reign of God," is Matthew's usual phrase. "The Heavens" was a standard Jewish circumlocution at the time for the Name of God (or even the word *God*), which the pious avoided uttering to ensure that they did not violate the commandment against taking God's name in vain.

4. Judith M. Gundry-Volf notes the contrast with the Greco-Roman tradition, which could portray women as taking children in their arms but not men "The Least and the Greatest," 29–60.

5. Cf. Schüssler Fiorenza, *In Memory of Her*, 147–51.

6. Theissen, *Sociology of Early Palestinian Christianity*, 17–23.

7. Collins, *Divorce in the New Testament*, 189.

8. Paul used the same principle to argue that the promise to Abraham could not be nullified by the giving of the Torah (Gal. 3:17).

9. "Flesh" is used in this sense in the incest code of Lev. 18; Levine, *Leviticus*, 117–20. Note also Judah's reference to Joseph as "our brother and our flesh" (Gen. 37:27). Loader argues that, unlike Hebrew *basar*, the Greek *sarx* cannot readily

bear the sense of kinship (*Sexuality* 100–01), but it is actually found repeatedly in this sense in the LXX.

10. Cf. the analysis in Schüssler Fiorenza, *In Memory of Her*, 143.

11. Alternatively, one may, with a long interpretive tradition, understand the exception as sanctioning divorce in cases where the wife *commits* adultery, but one would expect the more explicit word *moicheia* in that case. Jesus' original pronouncement on the subject seems not to have given permission for divorce of an adulterous wife—in shocking contrast to the culture's insistence on it. See Riches, *Jesus and the Transformation of Judaism*, 138, and, for the opposite view, Loader, *Sexuality*, 68–73.

12. Loader (*Sexuality* 73–76, 112–20) argues that Jesus had no real interest in the equality of the wife but was concerned only with scriptural exegesis; one consequence is that, on his analysis, the wife divorced for reasons other than *porneia* was potentially in a worse position than one divorced for that reason because the latter was technically free to remarry. But this would require us to accept that Jesus was indifferent to the social impact of his teachings on the marginalized, which is difficult to square with his overall welcoming attitude toward them.

13. For the wide variety of interpretations of this exception, see Collins, *Divorce*, 199–205.

14. This passage also makes it clear that Matthew understood Jesus' prohibition of divorce as a spiritual and ethical goal, attainable only by those to whom it is granted; it is not a new law for Christians. Cf. Grant, "Impracticability of the Gospel Ethics," 90–91. Mark saw a similar tension in Jesus' ethical demands, which are both realizable and unrealizable in that they are dependent on the Reign of God, which is both present in the gospel and yet to come in the fullness of the new age; see Via, *Ethics of Mark's Gospel*, 121–24.

15. The commonly used English phrase "lusted after" is an over translation here. The Greek verb in question is not as extremely pejorative.

16. Loader (*Sexuality*, 18–20) restricts the offense to "looking with intent." But this seems to make the look more a prelude to a subsequent act than is implied by the passage, where it is parallel with anger and insult in 5:22, which do not constitute intent to murder.

17. Cf. Luke 7:36–50, where Jesus is anointed by a woman who is a public sinner. While she is not called a prostitute, that is one possible conclusion about her. Jesus accepts her attentions, contrasts them favorably with those of his host, a Pharisee, and finally says, "Her sins, many as they are, are forgiven because she has loved much" (7:47). This does not tell us what Jesus preferred prostitutes to do, but it does suggest that he did not make grace conditional on a prostitute's escaping her place in society.

18. This remains the most satisfactory interpretation of this passage; cf. Best, "Mark iii. 20, 21, 31-35," 309–19.

19. Mark may have adapted the formula for his largely Gentile Christian audience because among Gentiles the woman, too, commonly had the right to divorce her spouse. Brooten ("*Konnten Frauen*," 78–80) shows, however, that this also agreed with contemporary Jewish practice, which could give the wife the power

of divorce by means of a specific provision in the marriage contract, as distinct from the more limited provisions of the Torah.

20. For analysis of the relationship of this ethic to Mark's narrative about Jesus and his understanding of the Reign of God, see Via, *Ethics of Mark's Gospel*, 67–168.

21. Women could not "marry" in the ancient sense, but only be "given in marriage."

22. See pp. 150–51. Note also the evidence of *Testament of Reuben* 5, although it blames the whole incident on human women who seduced the Watchers and it is unclear whether the author thought that actual sexual intercourse took place. *Jubilees* tells us that the angels of the presence and of sanctification (the highest angelic ranks) were created circumcised (15:27) and that acts of fornication, impurity, and injustice committed by the Watchers brought on the Flood (7:21–25).

23. The phrase "sons of God" may be a reminder of the story of the Watchers, for that is the title given them in Gen. 6:2.

24. Alternatively, Luke may be seen as having suppressed information about a time of greater female participation and leadership in the church; cf. Fiorenza, *In Memory of Her*, 160–62. In any case, later transmitters of the text of Acts found Luke too favorable to women and revised it accordingly; see Ben Witherington, "Anti-Feminist Tendencies," 82–84.

25. Countryman, *Mystical Way*, 24–26.

26. Ibid., pp. 16–17, 29–31, 118–19.

27. Schneiders (*Written That You May Believe*, 135) points out echoes of erotically charged meetings at wells in the scriptures of Israel (Gen. 24, 29; Exod. 2).

28. For a summary of the textual questions, see Metzger, *Textual Commentary*, 187–89.

29. Moxnes, *Constructing Early Christian Families*, 132–33.

30. John Riches has drawn a connection between this tendency and Jesus' disregard of purity; both represent the deliberate breaking down of boundaries (*Jesus and the Transformation of Judaism*, 132–33).

Chapter 10: Paul and Sexual Property

1. On the background and meaning of this language, see Martin, *Slavery as Salvation*, 1–49, 136–46.

2. On "flesh" in Paul, see pp. 116–18.

3. Paul also described his behavior toward the Thessalonians as paternal (1 Thess. 2:11). On the androcentric perspective Paul adopts in 1 Thess., see Fatum, "Brotherhood in Christ," 183–94.

4. Plato, *Timaeus* 44 d–e.

5. Cf. Schweitzer, *The Mysticism of Paul the Apostle*, 101–40.

6. For a different explanation of the origins of different sexual perspectives at Corinth, see Dale Martin, *Corinthian Body*, 205–12.

7. Some manuscripts have an expressed verb in the clause (*onomazetai*), which gives the reading "is not even named among the Gentiles." This is probably an effort by a later scribe to fill in Paul's elliptical style of writing. My own "found" is a similar effort—made necessary by the narrower scope of English grammar.

8. Robert M. Grant, *Paul*, 115–22.

9. Jerome H. Neyrey has interpreted most of 1 Cor. 5–7 as an application of purity concerns; "Body Language," 138–42. I think he is mistaken, however, in assuming that all control asserted over the sexual orifices necessarily springs from purity considerations and in ignoring Paul's failure to apply the purity vocabulary available to him to the subject.

10. There are two objections to seeing this as a purity issue. One is that leaven was not forbidden as *unclean* by the purity system of Israel. Although in some sense its prohibition during Passover resembles a purity rule, it does not seem to have been perceived in that light. Cf. McCombie, "Jesus and the Leaven of Salvation," 450–62. The second objection is that the verb *ekkathairo*, though etymologically linked to the purity vocabulary, was not used as part of that set of technical terms—at least, not in the LXX, where it and the related *ekkatharizo* refer to the clearing of land (Deut. 32:43; Josh. 17:15, 18), the sorting out of soldiers (Judg. 7:4, B text), the cleaning of wounds (Isa. 4:4), and even the removal of what is holy (tithe) from one's house (Deut. 26:13). It once has the metaphorical meaning of "purging evil" (Judg. 20:13). In the NT, it appears only here and in 2 Tim. 2:21, where it refers to separating oneself from false teachers. The Passover image in 1 Cor. 5:7, then, should not be read in terms of the Torah purity code.

11. Peter Zaas has noted that Paul invokes the common excommunication formula found in Deut., but less as a technical procedure than for the sake of its traditional resonances: "Cast Out the Evil Man from Your Midst," 259–61.

12. Unless Paul meant to contradict his other assurances that those who belong to Christ cannot be lost, he presumably did not mean that the baptized person who reverted to behavior inconsistent with the Gospel would be damned. Indeed, the exclusion of the man who was committing incest looked ahead to his eventual salvation (1 Cor. 5:5; cf. 3:10–15). Paul's ethics are subtle and were open to misunderstanding already in his own time. It appears, however, that for him the ultimate sanction of ethics was not the threat of damnation, but the danger of being found incoherent with the salvation one has already been given by grace.

13. Philippe Ariès combines this list with the one in 1 Tim. 1:9–10 and produces a more complex analysis: "St. Paul and the Flesh," 36–39. For the Corinthians passage, he seems to suggest a division into four diminishing categories: sins against God (idolatry), against the flesh (harlotry, adultery, and whatever the *malakoi* and *arsenokoitai* do), and against property (theft, greed, drunkenness, "snatching"), and sins of the tongue (slander). This requires a substantial rearrangement of the list. If one wishes to analyze the exact order of terms, the Ten Commandments offer a better model. Harlotry and idolatry are sins against the commandments to have only one God and to eschew images. Paul then jumps to the area of his immediate concern, the commandments against adultery and theft, which are closely related to each other; and he concludes with two or three elements related to the commandments against false witness and covetousness.

14. Cf. Boswell, *Christianity, Social Tolerance, and Homosexuality*, 363–64. For a good summary of the ancient notion of "softness," see Veyne, *History of Private Life*, 178–79; it was compounded of indolence and a propensity toward sensuality. See also Martin, "*Arsenokoites* and *Malakos*."

15. Cf. Conzelmann, *1 Corinthians*, 108–10.

16. Cf. Robinson, *The Body*, 26–33.

17. Engberg-Pedersen, *Paul and the Stoics*, 152–53.

18. "It is a good thing for a man not to touch a woman" is so absolute a formula that it may be the teaching of the Corinthian ascetics rather than of Paul himself. Cf. Phipps, "Is Paul's Attitude," 127–29. Whatever its origin, however, he cites it as if he agreed with it before he begins his modification of it—a reasonable rhetorical approach to a volatile situation.

19. A subsidiary point in this passage is worthy of mention: the allowance for sexual abstinence is to give *leisure* for prayer, not to purify the couple for it. In other words, it is a temporary simplification of life, not a disguised purity observance.

20. For a Stoic tendency in much the same direction, see Grant, *Paul*, 127.

21. Yarbrough (*Not Like the Gentiles*, 22–23) notes that some rabbis taught that marriage was necessary because of the male passions, but even they presented it only as the alternative to impurity. Paul makes it the proper response to normal sexual need.

22. This remains the simplest reading of the passage. I suspect that the effort to interpret "rather make use" as meaning "grasp the opportunity of freedom" rather than the more obvious "remain a slave" is prompted by later Christians' embarrassment that the great apostle should have dismissed the legitimate grievances of slaves so lightly. *Mallon* ("rather"), of course, creates a contrast with something preceding it; the *ei kai* ("even if") of the immediately preceding clause underlines it so emphatically as to make almost inescapable that this is the source of the contrast.

23. E.g., Moule, *The Epistles to the Colossians and to Philemon*, 177.

24. Paul's passive verb, "be separated," implies that the husband would be the initiator of any divorce, and only remarriage of the divorced woman occasions adultery. Jerome Murphy-O'Connor has argued that Paul did not, in fact, feel bound consistently by Jesus' dictum, but applied it pastorally according to principles that Murphy-O'Connor does not make explicit; "The Divorced Woman in 1 Cor 7:10–11," 601–6. Paul may indeed have been inconsistent, but perhaps one should not move to that conclusion without exhausting alternative explanations.

25. For a similar usage, see 2 Cor. 6:14–7:1. Paul tells his audience not to be "crossyoked with non-believers"; that is, he uses the image of different species of animals being crossbred (something forbidden in Lev. 19:19, where the LXX uses the same unusual vocabulary that Paul uses here) to admonish Christians against inappropriate association with nonbelievers. Such associations could include inter-marriage; but if the passage is genuinely Pauline and is in its correct context, then it must be an exhortation to the Corinthians to withdraw from rival teachers, for it is preceded and followed by appeals to "make room for" Paul in their affections (6:11–13; 7:2). In a similar vein, Yarbrough (*Not Like the Gentiles*,

88–93) understands Paul, in 1 Cor. 5–6, to be stressing the purity of the Christian community. This would refer, however, to the distinctiveness of the new community and not to a revival of Torah purity.

26. See the similar interpretation in Gundry-Volf, "The Least and the Greatest," 48–53.

27. It is possible that we are seeing here the remote origins of one or two early Christian traditions: that of women vowed to virginity and living with their natal families and that of nonsexual marriages, where two people were vowed to live together as spouses but without sexual intercourse.

28. So my translation above. It is also possible to translate, in v. 36, "if she is getting beyond marriageable age and this is how it needs to be." No certainty seems possible, but the passage otherwise shows no particular concern for the woman's desires in the matter. Yet another possibility is that the woman's unfulfilled sexual desire is harming her health; Martin, *Corinthian Body*, 219–28.

29. Loader (*Sexuality*, 193–207, 223–25) argues that Paul also presupposes that sexuality and gender difference will disappear in the age to come.

30. Balch ("1 Cor 7:32–35," 398–435) has illuminated the Stoic background of Paul's language about marriage. Yet Paul's language still suggests that the eschatological context was the primary determinant. In seeking to maintain that Paul did not prefer celibacy to marriage, he, with others, ignores the plain sense of v. 38: "the man who does not marry will do better." The chief desideratum for Paul, however, is that one should remain as one is, whether married or not.

31. This formula was probably pre-Pauline and may actually represent a period in the Gentile mission more radical than Paul. Cf. Schüssler Fiorenza, *In Memory of Her*, 208–12.

32. These verses are located after 14:40 in some manuscripts of 1 Cor., leading some to question their authenticity. They may, indeed, be a later interpolation, which would make Paul somewhat less inconsistent with the principles of baptism that he inherited. The textual evidence for rejecting them, however, is not particularly strong.

33. For a more positive reading of this passage in relation to the equality of women, see Schüssler Fiorenza, *In Memory of Her*, 228–30. Antoinette Clark Wire, however, sees Paul as attempting to reduce the authority of the women prophets in a rhetorically effective way; *The Corinthian Women Prophets*, 98–134. Troy Martin offers a surprising, but quite possible explanation of the passage in terms of ancient understanding of sexual physiology; "Paul's Argument from Nature for the Veil," 75–84.

34. Countryman, "Christian Equality and the Early Catholic Episcopate," 116–27.

35. Although not the most common translation of the passage, this is the simplest and most literal. It is usually avoided because it appears to be nonsense; but it is fully intelligible as a deliberate exaggeration, on Paul's part, of ascetic rules designed to keep one separate from selected or representative elements of the material world. "Perishable," here, is being equated with "evil." The first prohibition of the series ("Do not handle") could refer to sexual intercourse; cf. Schweizer, *The Letter to the Colossians*, 166–67.

36. For the background of this and similar NT lists of household duties, see Balch, *Let Wives Be Submissive*, 21–62.

Chapter 11: The New Testament on Sexual Property

1. The most literal reading is that he was addressing a woman who was patron and leader of her local Christian community; Schüssler Fiorenza, *In Memory of Her*, 248–49.

2. Contrast the more conventional wisdom of *Letter of Aristeas* 228, where King Ptolemy asks a Jewish sage, "To whom should one show favor?" The sage replies, "To parents, by all means, for God has in fact established a commandment of the highest importance on the matter of honor shown to parents. And, next, he reckons the treatment shown to friends, having described the friend as 'equal to the self.' But as for you, you do well in bringing all people into friendship with yourself." It is the unique and supererogatory goodness of a king to treat all as his friends; ordinary mortals need attend only to family and friends in the usual, more restricted sense.

3. The verb *apokyeo* is used overwhelmingly of the mother's role in procreation, not the father's.

4. For a more extended exposition of James, see Countryman, *Interpreting the Truth*, 128–59.

5. He did not therefore completely reject the idea of church as household; cf. Elliott, *A Home for the Homeless*, 200–08. Despite Elliott's arguments, however, 1 Peter still seems to represent a retreat from an earlier Christian position that was less friendly to the family.

6. The tone of these directions is closely related to that of *Letter of Aristeas*, 250–51, which gives advice about women's nature (bold, but irrational and weak) and affirms that the man must always be the "pilot."

7. Balch, *Let Wives Be Submissive*, 61–109, has shown how the passage in question is responding to specific charges typically brought against eastern religious sects and minority groups at the time.

8. These may, in fact, have been female "presbyters," in the official sense, but it is impossible to be sure because the Greek expression could mean either thing. The opposition of "older" to "younger women" in the text, however, suggests a distinction purely of age because *neoteros* was not elsewhere in the NT a title of office. For the opposite interpretation, see Schüssler Fiorenza, *In Memory of Her*, 289–91.

9. On efforts to interpret the passage on childbearing, see Kelly, *A Commentary on the Pastoral Epistles*, 69–70.

10. On the thorough way these letters are "masculinized," see D'Angelo, "Knowing How to Preside over His Own Household," 271–78. The opposite perspective is preserved in some apocryphal "Acts," probably written at a time not too distant from the Pastoral Epistles; Jacobs, "A Family Affair," 105–138.

11. The verse is syntactically difficult; see Attridge, *The Epistle to the Hebrews*, 324–26.

12. E.g., see Countryman, "Tertullian and the Regula," 214–26.

13. The title "son of God" is extended to the individual martyr in 21:7.
14. Barclay, "The Family as the Bearer," 66–80; Olav Sandnes, "Equality Within Patriarchal Structures," 150–65.

Chapter 12: Are Other Principles of Sexual Ethics at Work in the New Testament?

1. Windsor, *A King Is Bound in the Tresses*.
2. Brock, *Journeys by Heart;* Heyward, *Touching Our Strength,* 87–118. On the cost to men of the suppression of the erotic, see Nelson, *Body Theology,* 93–104.
3. Carr, "Gender and the Shaping of Desire," 233–48; *The Erotic Word*. Biale, *Eros and the Jews,* 11–32. Jennings, *Jacob's Wound,* and *The Man Jesus Loved*. Ellison, *Erotic Justice,* 76–93.
4. Nygren, *Agape and Eros*. The idea was popularized by C. S. Lewis, *The Four Loves*.
5. Mark Jordan notes that the influential fourth-century mystical theologian known as pseudo-Dionysius "goes out of his way to rescue the word *eros* for Christian use"; *Telling Truths in Church,* 67.
6. Foucault, *The Care of the Self,* 72–80, 165–85.
7. Betz, *Galatians,* 181–201.
8. See Kittredge on Paul's relationship with Euodia and Syntyche; *Community and Authority,* 53–110.
9. Wire argues, successfully I believe, that Paul was rejecting the women prophets' claim to be honorable in their own right; *Corinthian Women Prophets,* 98–134.
10. Cf. MacDonald, *The Legend and the Apostle*.
11. Clarke, *Looking at Lovemaking*. Cf. Trümper, "Material and Social Environment of Greco-Roman Households," 19–43.
12. In the seventeenth century, it was still usual even for the wealthy and aristocratic to have retainers sleeping with them in their bedrooms, whether on the floor or in the same bed. See Bray, *The Friend,* 153–56.
13. On disposition of space in houses of the Eastern Mediterranean, see Meyers, "The Problems of Gendered Space," 44–69.
14. Foucault, *Care of the Self,* 34–36. We do not know how early Christians dealt with all these presuppositions; cf. Osiek, "Female Slaves, *Porneia,* and the Limits of Obedience," 255–74.
15. Whittaker, *Jews and Christians,* 63–91.
16. Cf. Yarborough, *Not Like the Gentiles,* 13: "the primary result of the claims that regarding marriage and sexual morality the Jews were morally superior to the nations—they were prohibited from intermarrying with them."
17. Balch, "Paul's Portrait of Christ Crucified," 84–108.
18. Male authors did not extend this openness to female-female sexuality, but it certainly existed. See Brooten, *Love Between Women,* 1–186.
19. Foucault, *Care of the Self,* 120–44.
20. Meeks, *The Origins of Christian Morality,* 18–36. Cf. his *Moral World,* 40–64.
21. Engberg-Pederson, *Paul and the Stoics,* 33–79. Cf. Foucault, *Care of the Self,* 72–80, 152–54.

22. Paul's language was not learned in a philosophical school, in any case. "Even though he uses a variety of Greek anthropological terms to explain aspects of human behavior in sections of his letters, he often does so on an ad hoc basis with the result that there is little overall consistency evident when these passage are compared. Paul was an eclectic" (David E. Aune, "Human Nature and Ethics in Hellenistic Philosophical Traditions and Paul: Some Issues and Problems," in Engberg-Pederson, *Paul in His Hellenistic Context*, 291.

23. The conventional translations of 11:14 take *physei* with the following verb; e.g. NRSV: "When Gentiles, who do not possess the law, do instinctively [*physei*] what the law requires." This translation is grammatically and syntactically possible, but introduces a sense of *physis* not otherwise found in Paul's writings. Despite having taken this tradition of translation for granted for many years, I am now convinced that the parallelism with v. 27 requires taking the passage in the alternative way proposed here.

24. See Jordan (*Ethics*, 76–106) on this development.

25. Foucault, *Care of the Self*, 39–68.

26. The tradition continued and was expanded by second century Christian authors, e.g., Clement of Alexandria. For a convenient summary, see Chadwick, "Philo and the Beginnings of Christian Thought," 175–76. See also Martin, "Paul and Passion," 201–15.

27. For a positive assessment of the value of natural law theory, see William C. Spohn, *What Are They Saying About Scripture and Ethics?* Rev. ed. (New York: Paulist Press, 1995), 41–45. For a contemporary scientist's take on the language of "nature," see Frans de Waal, "Reading Nature's Tea Leaves," *Natural History* (December 2000): 66–71.

28. Schmidt, *Straight and Narrow?* 39.

29. Ibid., 42–45.

30. Gagnon, *The Bible and Homosexual Practice*, 63–100; Grenz, *Welcoming but Not Affirming*, 36–40. Not all would agree with this use of the narratives listed; see Hays, *Moral Vision*, 381.

31. Hays, 347–76.

32. Gagnon, *The Bible and Homosexual Practice*, 229–70, 289–97.

33. For a rather different Evangelical approach, see Vasey, *Strangers and Friends*, especially p. 12, where he acknowledges that much Evangelical ethics seems rigid and oppressive to outsiders.

34. E.g., Karl Barth, *Church Dogmatics*, Pt. 2, Vol. 4, pp. 164–66, excerpted in Batchelor, *Homosexuality and Ethics*, 48–51; cf. the related but more nuanced view of Helmut Thielicke, also in Batchelor, 52–60.

35. I owe this observation to my colleague Professor Mary Ann Tolbert. For the opposite position, see Stott, *Our Social and Sexual Revolution*, 111–14; in fact, however, Stott offers no real exegesis in this part of his argument, finding his support instead in modern authors who emphasize the differences of the two sexes.

36. Ibid., 200.

37. Hays, *Moral Vision*, 351 (emphasis original to the text). Hays is referring to the way Jesus uses the passage in Mark's Gospel, but this does seem to correspond to his own understanding of it.
38. Hays, *Moral Vision*, 372–74, 389–94. Hays does not comment on polygamy.
39. Stott, *Our Social and Sexual Revolution*, 202–03. In a similar, but more careful way, Philip Turner argues that the creation narrative lays out a theological program opposed to modern personalist ethics; *Sex, Money, & Power*, 45–61. The difficulty in the argument is in demonstrating that the Genesis authors and editors ever thought of such a possibility; the subordination of individual to family that he notes was simply a given of their culture and, like modern personalism, could produce both good and bad results. It would be dangerous to try to turn ancient Near Eastern culture, as flawed as any other, into a revelation of the divine will.
40. On Barth's inadvertently falling afoul of this problem, see Rogers, *Sexuality and the Christian Body*, 180–91.
41. Elliott, *Roads to Paradise*.
42. Gagnon makes exactly this mistake; *Bible and Homosexual Practice*, 185–227.
43. Luke introduces the slave as *doulos* (7:2), but has the centurion himself use the term *pais* (7:7); Matthew uses *pais* throughout when referring to the individual involved. Luke further describes the slave as *entimos*, "valuable" or "highly valued" (7:2).
44. Such a relationship, with either a male or female slave, was not unusual, especially since centurions were forbidden to marry. Cf. Jennings, *The Man Jesus Loved*, 128–41.
45. Hays, *Moral Vision*, 372–74. Grenz, *Sexual Ethics*, 99–125.
46. Robinson, *The Body*; cf. Engberg-Pederson, *Paul and the Stoics*, 209–16.
47. Thus Alter, "Sodom as Nexus," 30–38.
48. Book of Common Prayer, Articles of Religion VI.
49. For the latter approach, see especially Segovia and Tolbert, *Reading from This Place*.
50. Thatcher, *Liberating Sex*, 24.
51. E.g., Hanks, *God So Loved the Third World*; Rowland and Corner, *Liberating Exegesis*.
52. Althaus-Reid, *From Feminist Theology to Indecent Theology*.
53. Ellison, *Erotic Justice*; Ellison and Thorson-Smith, *Body and Soul, Presbyterians and Human Sexuality*.
54. Hanks, *The Subversive Gospel*.
55. Ibid., 129–31, 212–23.
56. Jennings, *The Man Jesus Loved* and *Jacob's Wound*.

Chapter 13: New Testament Sexual Ethics and Today's World

1. E.g., Joshua's destruction of Ai (Josh. 8) or Gideon's destruction of Succoth and Penuel (Judg. 8). Indeed, God actively assists in the destruction of the Amalekites by Moses and Joshua and commands ongoing war against them (Exod. 17:8–16). God commands a second genocide of the Amalekites through the prophet Samuel and is angry with Saul because he does not make a complete

job of it (1 Sam. 15). God directly kills the firstborn male children of Egypt to force Pharaoh into expelling Israel (Exod. 11–12), and Revelation accepts that slaughter can be a justified element of divine agency (e.g., 19:11–21).

2. Mark Jordan, *Ethics of Sex*, 47–75.

3. Cf. the Roman Catholic list in Oliver, *Conjugal Spirituality*, 110–18.

4. Clement, *Paedagogus* 2.92.2; Hippolytus, *Apostolic Tradition* 16-23. Cf. Martin, "Paul and Passion," 206.

5. Peterson, *Christ Plays in Ten Thousand Places*, 144–47.

6. There were also modifying influences from other political traditions in the area, particularly those expressed in aristocratic, oligarchic, or democratic institutions, where power was shared among the male heads of a more or less narrowly defined group of households.

7. Paul may have begun this process, if he is indeed the author of Col. 3:18–4:1.

8. Ellison, *Erotic Justice*, 1–12; Thatcher, *Liberating Sex*, 57–58.

9. Ellison, *Erotic Justice*, 41.

10. Burrus, *Chastity as Autonomy*.

11. Stephen C. Barton argues that Christians must ground family life in the life of the Trinity as a "creative fidelity" to scripture, not an imitation of first-century family life; *Life Together*, 38, 53.

12. Ellison notes that Christian sexual ethics have traditionally become an ethic not of sex but of marriage; *Erotic Justice*, 24–28.

13. "God teaches Christian communities about moral matters in any number of ways, but perhaps especially through the holy lives of their members"; Jordan, *Ethics of Sex*, 153; cf. 163–70. See also Rogers, *Sexuality and the Christian Body*, 28–36.

14. Soto, "Redeeming Eros: A Christian Ethical Spirituality of Sexual Intimacy," 314–35. For the contribution lesbian experience offers to this goal for all, see Hunt, *Fierce Tenderness*.

15. For a powerful account of the nature of fidelity, see Wallace, *For Fidelity: How Intimacy and Commitment Enrich Our Lives*.

16. Joseph Monti argues that the churches will accomplish more of value by cultivating the integrity of marriage than by their current preoccupation with non-marital behaviors; *Arguing About Sex*, 227–47.

17. Thatcher, *Liberating Sex*, 144–57.

18. Jung and Smith, *Heterosexism: An Ethical Challenge*.

19. Njiiri, "Polygamy in the African Church Today," 246–48; cf. Esther Mombo, "Resisting *Vumilia* Theology: The Church and Violence Against Women in Kenya," 219–24.

20. Recently, in the West, the issue has been raised in another form under the term *polyamory*. The discussion of the topic has not developed far enough for me to attempt to include it here. As with any proposed change in the tradition, the first step is for its advocates to explain what they understand by it and why they feel it can contribute to or at least coexist with the ethics implied in the scriptures.

21. Brown, *Body and Society*, 5–82.

22. A significant exception must be made for those human groups that are threatened with disappearance or with diminution to numbers too small to maintain their cultural traditions.

23. Grant, *Paul in the Roman World*, 112–14.

24. It is unclear, however, why the fetus, if defined as fully a human being, should suffer any consequences for the offenses of one or both parents. On the preference for absolute rules in patriarchal Christianity, see Ellison, *Erotic Justice*, 55–62.

25. Hitt, "Pro-Life Nation."

26. Gudorf, *Body, Sex, and Pleasure*, 169.

27. For the possibility that a few Gospel texts specifically condemn sexual violation of children, see Collins, *Sexual Ethics*, 62–70. The argument is far from conclusive; but the basic stance of Jesus in relation to children is decisive in its own right.

28. Underwood, "Clergy Sexual Misconduct: A Justice Issue," 300–315.

29. The difference between the cultures in this respect is vividly apparent in Philo, who argued that the law of Moses specified no punishment for the forcible violation of a widow or divorced woman because that was, in effect, only half the crime that adultery was (*Special Laws* 3.64). So, too, in ancient Athens, rape was considered a less grave offense than seduction; Pomeroy, *Goddesses*, 86–87.

30. The focus on sex also serves to suggest that those who are denouncing others are themselves pure and, in the process, it often distracts Christians from more serious issues; Thatcher, *Liberating Sex*, 64.

31. Monti treats marriage as controlling norm rather than invariable rule for all sexual relationships, but he persists in limiting it to heterosexuals and allows only a lesser rite for lesbians and gay men; *Arguing About Sex*, 247–53. In practice, I believe all such rites will come to be indistinguishable.

32. For the difficulty and importance of the conversation, see Jordan, *Telling Truths*, 34–58; cf. Barton, *Life Together*, 68.

33. Countryman, *Love Human and Divine*; Hederman, *Love Impatient, Love Unkind*.

INDEX OF PASSAGES

INDEX OF SUBJECTS

INDEX OF MODERN AUTHORS

DATE DUE

DEC 1 2016			
DEC 2017			

Demco